NINTH EDITION （第9版）

Technical Report Writing Today

最新商务报告写作（下）

Daniel G. Riordan
University of Wisconsin-Stout

北京市版权局著作权合同登记号 图字 [01-2010-5299] 号

图书在版编目 (CIP) 数据

最新商务报告写作·下 = Technical Report Writing Today (Ninth Edition) / (美) 里奥登 (Riordan, D. G.) 著. —北京：北京大学出版社，2011.1
(商务英语写作系列丛书)
ISBN 978-7-301-17920-8

Ⅰ. 最… Ⅱ. 里… Ⅲ. 商务—英语—应用文—写作—教材 Ⅳ. H315

中国版本图书馆 CIP 数据核字（2010）第 197153 号

Technical Report Writing Today (Ninth Edition)
Daniel G. Riordan
Copyright © 2005 by Wadsworth, a part of Cengage Learning.
Original edition published by Cengage Learning. All rights reserved.
本书原版由圣智学习出版公司出版。版权所有，盗印必究。

Peking University Press is authorized by Cengage Learning to publish and distribute exclusively this edition. This edition is authorized for sale in the People's Republic of China only (excluding Hong Kong SAR, Macao SAR and Taiwan). Unauthorized export of this edition is a violation of the Copyright Act. No part of this publication may be reproduced or distributed by any means, or stored in a database or retrieval system, without the prior written permission of the publisher.
本书由圣智学习出版公司授权北京大学出版社独家出版发行。此版本仅限在中华人民共和国境内（不包括中国香港、澳门特别行政区及中国台湾）销售。未经授权的本书出口将被视为违反版权法的行为。未经出版者预先书面许可，不得以任何方式复制或发行本书的任何部分。

Cengage Learning Asia Pte. Ltd.
5 Shenton Way, # 01-01 UIC Building, Singapore 068808

本书封面贴有 Cengage Learning 防伪标签，无标签者不得销售。

书　　　名：	Technical Report Writing Today (Ninth Edition) 最新商务报告写作（第 9 版）(下)
著作责任者：	[美] Daniel G. Riordan 著
责 任 编 辑：	黄瑞明
标 准 书 号：	ISBN 978-7-301-17920-8 / H·2667
出 版 发 行：	北京大学出版社
地　　　址：	北京市海淀区成府路 205 号　100871
网　　　址：	http://www.pup.cn
电　　　话：	邮购部 62752015　发行部 62750672　编辑部 62754382　出版部 62754962
电 子 邮 箱：	zbing@pup.pku.edu.cn
印　刷　者：	河北滦县鑫华书刊印刷厂
发　行　者：	新华书店
	787 毫米 × 960 毫米　16 开本　23.5 印张　300 千字 2011 年 1 月第 1 版　2011 年 1 月第 1 次印刷
定　　　价：	48.00 元

未经许可，不得以任何方式复制或抄袭本书之部分或全部内容。

版权所有，侵权必究　举报电话：010-62752024
　　　　　　　　　　　电子邮箱：fd@pup.pku.edu.cn

专家委员会

顾问 文秋芳

主任 王立非

委员（按姓氏笔画排序）

丁言仁	于兰祖	卫乃兴	马广惠	王东风	王俊菊
文 旭	文 军	方 琰	邓鹂鸣	朱 源	刘世生
许德金	严明秦	苏 刚	杨永林	杨达复	杨鲁新
李小华	李文中	李正栓	李生禄	李炳林	李霄翔
肖德法	吴红云	汪 红	张世耘	张佐成	陈法春
陈新仁	周 平	郑 超	封一函	赵永青	胡一宁
胡 健	战 菊	俞洪亮	洪 刚	袁洪庚	晓 晴
徐 珺	郭海云	黄国文	常玉田	梁茂成	程幼强
程晓堂	程朝翔	傅似逸	蔡金亭		

总　序

　　北京大学出版社继《英语写作原版引印系列丛书》之后，2010年，又专题引进商务英语写作原版系列教材。这套教材体系完整，应用性强，商务内容丰富，十分贴近英语教学改革的需要和广大学生提升未来就业能力的需求，填补了我国商务英语写作领域内没有高质量商务英语写作教材的空白，并得到15所商务英语专业院校教学协作组和中国英语写作教学专业委员会相关专家的联合推荐。

　　随着我国对外开放的不断深入，高水平的商务英语写作人才一将难求，能用地道规范的英文起草法律合同、撰写咨询报告的专业写作人才更是凤毛麟角，部分国际咨询机构提供的一份英文公司咨询报告价格高达百万美元，如此激烈的竞争值得我们认真反思现有的写作教学。即将出台的高等学校商务英语专业本科教学要求（试行）明确指出，商务英语写作是学生的核心能力，商务英语专业应加大毕业设计的比重，鼓励学生采用商务报告（如市场调研报告、商业计划书、营销方案等）多种形式。而全面提升商务英语写作能力，按照过去传统的写作教学模式，已无法适应，必须要有新的改革思路，要改变"费时低效"的困境，就必须做到以下几个转变：(1) 从重写作技能转向技能与内容并重；(2) 从传统写作教学转向机辅写作教学模式；(3) 从开设单一写作课转向开设写作课程群；(4) 从大班课堂写作教学转向个性化写作教学中心。通过对美国普林斯顿大学、英国华威大学等世界名校的考察，我们建议，可分阶段分层次为不同水平的学生开设商务英语写作课程群（Writing Portfolio），具体可包括：基础英语写作、国际贸易写作、国际营销写作、金融英语写作、法律英语写作、学术英语写作、财经新闻写作、商务函电写作、商务报告写作、职业应用文写作等，全面提升学生的写作能力。

　　本套系列教材在国外畅销经久不衰，多次再版或重印，此次由北京大学出版社首批引进出版10本：《商务沟通：以读者为中心的方法》（上、下册）、《商务沟通与写作》（上、下册）、《最新商务报告写作》（上、下册）、《职场英语写作》（上、下册）、《成功商务英语写作》（上、下册），由对外经济贸易大学商务英语写作教学团队的教师魏明博士、冯海颖博士、杨颖莉博士、李玉霞博士、尹珏林博士分别撰写导读。

本套丛书既是职场英语写作的优质教材，又是商务写作的经典教材，教材深入浅出，语言简明，可帮助学生理解、记忆和应对多种国际商务场合下的写作需求。通过本丛书的学习和训练，学生可提高写作水平，为踏入职场做好准备。本套丛书可用作全国大专院校的商务英语学生和教师的写作课教材和参考书，还可供经管类学生学习商务英语写作之用，同时也可供爱好商务英语写作的广大社会读者和各类公司企业人员提高英语写作使用。

中国英语写作教学专业委员会主任
对外经济贸易大学英语学院院长
教授、博士生导师
王延
2010年国庆节于北京

导 读

一、本书的特色

1. 作者简介

Daniel G.Riordan 毕业于美国北卡罗来纳州 Chapel Hill 分校，获得美国文学方向博士学位，目前是美国威斯康星州立大学斯特奥特分校的教授，曾担任该校高级写作教研部主任，专业与科技写作委员会主席。他在专业与技术写作、多媒体教学、信息设计、自由写作、技术修辞等方面颇有造诣，多年来为学生开设了网页设计、自由写作与专业写作、多媒体写作、多媒体项目等多门专业课程，并担任专业写作协会顾问。他曾编撰威斯康星州立大学斯特奥特分校跨学科写作简报 *Coyote*，并多次在学术会议上做专业写作教学方面的报告。

2. 本书特色

《最新商务报告写作》是作者多年写作教学经验的凝练和总结，自首次出版以来，深受读者欢迎，已再版八次。本书集中介绍商务报告写作的方法，内容涵盖商务报告写作的基础、技巧，以及网络写作、职场写作等多个话题。学生可通过详实的例证和丰富的练习系统学习并掌握专业写作的要点。每章内容都辅以工作表（worksheet），逐步引导学生对课后练习进行构思，习作实例详细阐释了不同类型的写作风格和写作方法。本书还配以精美的图片、图表，清晰生动地介绍了商务报告写作的流程。第九版增加了电子简历写作以及全球化与电子资源的使用，为读者开阔了视野，同时了解商务报告写作领域的最新进展。

本书语言简洁流畅，教学活动新颖有趣，兼具可读性与实用性，是商务报告写作领域的一本好教材。

3. 使用对象与方法

本书适用于从英语写作初学者到专业技术写作人员的广泛读者群，也是广大英语教师和英语爱好者的良师益友。本书的教学方式灵活多样，教师在教学过程中可以选择按章节教学，也可以选择重点介绍一些章节，并辅以练习进行教学，时间以一学年为宜。本书还配有辅助教学网站，读者可以从网站获取更多学习资源。

二、本书内容

本书共有 20 章，分为三个部分。

第一部分 商务报告写作基础（第 1–10 章）

第一部分主要是让学生了解商务报告写作的基本概念和过程。

第一章 商务报告写作的定义

本章讲述了技术写作的基本定义以及特征以及落笔之前的准备工作。首先，要根据不同的读者选择相应的写作方法，包括运用小标题，选择简明清晰的语言，以及运用图表辅助文字等。同时，作者还要具有全球化的视野，掌握各民族的语言文化特征，这样才能达到跨文化交流与沟通的目的。

第二章　读者概述

本章阐述了在写作之前,作者应该如何了解目标读者群,包括考虑读者是个人还是团体,他们的知识体系,以及他们对于报告的预期。

第三章　商务报告写作过程

本章阐释了写作过程中需要考虑到的诸多因素,并描述了写作过程中做计划,拟草稿,编辑,以及与团队讨论各个环节的注意事项,并通过流程图展示了技术写作的步骤。

第四章　商务报告写作方式

本章详细讲解了技术写作的文体风格,并列举了写好技术报告的六条原则,包括使用主动语态,使用排比结构,句子长度在 12–25 个字之间,减少 "there are" 句型的使用,避免使用花园路径句(garden path sentences),以及通过选择词汇来改变语气。

第五章　研究

本章讲解了如何在写作之前做好调研,并重点详述了调研过程中的两个主要方法,一个是通过问问题来引入主体,另一个是通过输入主题词来进行信息的搜索。

第六章　页面设计

本章探讨了进行视觉布局的两个关键因素:即"标题"和"内容"。标题应简明扼要地将主要信息传达给读者,内容也应该进行合理安排以突出主题。还可以通过固定的模板来统一格式,使做出的文档更加专业。

第七章　使用视图

本章详细介绍了各种视觉辅助工具的用法,包括线型图,柱形图,圆形图等。

第八章　概述

集中探讨了概述的写法。读者往往通过浏览概述来决定是否需要阅读全文,因此概述应言简意赅地概括全文的内容。

第九章　定义

比较了两种下定义的方法。传统的下定义方式是解释此事物与其它同类事物的区别。扩展定义则是通过比较、举例、解释因果关系等方式让读者对该事物有更清晰的认识。

第十章　描述

集中讲解了对事物进行描述的方法。通过大量例证和图表阐述了如何对事物机理和过程进行描述。

第二部分　商务报告写作应用(第 11–17 章)

第二部分重点介绍了商务报告写作的应用,包括如何写备忘录以及非正式的报告,怎样制作网页,如何撰写可行性分析报告、提案、说明书等等。每一章节都配有各种案例和图片,此外,大量的学生习作、课后作业以及网上作业可以帮助学生巩固所学习的内容,单元后面的参考文献为学生提供丰富的课后自学资源。

第十一章　指令集

介绍了撰写指令集的四大要素。首先,在介绍部分要为读者解释相关术语,列出需要用到的工具。其次,要向读者详细解释每一个步骤,格式要清晰规范,最后,语气要坚决肯定。

第十二章　备忘录和非正式报告

讨论了备忘录及非正式报告的写作策略。分别介绍了备忘录和非正式报告的特征和使用范围以及写作方法。

第十三章 网站开发

网页和网络文件是信息的重要载体，制作网页包括策划、草稿和测试三个步骤。在设计网页之前，一定要考虑到浏览网页的人群，此外，还要设计一个流程图，对网页进行整体布局和设计。网页的图片也要精美生动，但不要占据太多空间。在网页设计好以后，可以通过测试初步了解网页效果并进行调整。

第十四章 正式报告

综合介绍了正式报告的撰写方法。正式的报告包括报告首页、目录、内容简介和主题介绍。

第十五章 推荐和可行性报告

推荐和可行性报告都要基于具体的数字和事实，写这两类报告时要考虑到这一点。在写报告之前，要为读者把事情发生的场景介绍清楚，再为他们提供选择标准，以帮助他们做出判断或分析。

第十六章 提案

写好提案的要点包括清晰明了地陈述问题，简明扼要地提出解决问题的方法，深入细致地分析解决方法的益处，最后全面具体地解释解决方法的实施步骤。

第十七章 使用说明书

使用说明书可以使读者了解机器的操作方法，因此在撰写说明书时要从机器设计者的角度出发，详细说明每个部件的使用功能，最好能辅以操作图来进行讲解。

第三部分 职场写作

在介绍了商务报告写作的基本概念和应用之后，本书还专门开设一部分专门介绍职场写作，为学生介绍了求职、就业，以及工作场所中所需要的各种文体。本书还以全球化为背景，着重介绍了跨文化交际中可能遇到的文化差异，以及跨文化交际过程中的礼仪与习俗等话题。为了给学生提供职场写作的最新信息，本书还增加了电子简历的制作部分。

第十八章 口头陈述

口头陈述的形式和长度多种多样。做好口头陈述首先要做好计划，确定听众，制作好幻灯片，清晰准确地传达报告内容。其次，陈述语速要适中。最后，在着装上也要注意细节，举止要大方得体。

第十九章 信函

着重介绍了职场信函的体例和要求，并提供了多个信函范例供学生参考。

第二十章 求职材料

求职信和简历是求职的两块敲门砖，也是给潜在雇主留下的第一印象。本章对求职信和简历的基本要点一一加以介绍，并介绍了面试的技巧。

三、推荐相关参考书

1. 秦荻辉，2001，《实用科技英语写作技巧》，上海外语教育出版社。
2. 王建武，李民权，曾小珊，《科技英语写作：理论·技巧·范例》，（第 3 版），西北工业大学出版社。
3. 丁西亚，2006，《英语科技论文写作：理论与实践》，西安交通大学出版社。
4. John Langan，2007，《美国大学英语写作》，（英文版），第六版，McGraw Hill 出版，外语教学与研究出版社引进。
5. Sharon J.Gerson，2004，《技术写作：过程与产品》（英文版），第四版，高等教育出版社。
6. William Sanborn Pfeiffer，2006，《科技交流实践教程》，（英文版），第六版，电子工业出版社。

7. Jean Wyrick，2008，《成功写作入门》（英文版）（第10版），北京大学出版社。
8. Bonnie L.Tensen，2008，《数字时代写作研究策略》（英文版）（第2版），北京大学出版社。
9. Steven H.Gale，2008，《公司管理写作策略》（英文版），北京大学出版社。
10. David Rosrnwasser，2008，《分析性写作》（英文版）（第5版），北京大学出版社。
11. Edward P.Bailey，2010，《实用写作》（英文版）（第9版），北京大学出版社。

对外经济贸易大学

杨颖莉

译 者 序

丹尼尔·里奥登现为美国威斯康星州立大学斯特奥特分校的教授,主要讲授商务报告写作、网页设计、专业写作以及多媒体制作等课程。他早年毕业于北卡罗来纳州立大学,获得博士学位。在多年的教学生涯中,除了从事自由创作之外,里奥登对多媒体技术、信息设计、修辞运用和教学技术等都有涉猎。里奥登创作不息,发表多篇相关学术论文,但最有影响的还要数摆在读者面前的这本《最新商务报告写作》。该书自出版以来,很受读者青睐,先后九次再版,对有志于提高商务报告写作水平的人士帮助极大。

《最新商务报告写作》一书全面涵盖了商务报告写作入门要领、写作技巧和实际应用等。通过对丰富的教学实例和练习的实际讲解,该书的读者可以掌握如何创作出一份条理明晰、内容详实、格式标准的商务报告。

全书设计新颖,重点突出。每章内容都由"本章提要(IN A NUTSHELL)"、"主要内容(CONTENTS)"、"阅读贴士(TIP)"、"相关练习(EXERCISES)"、"参考文献(WORKS CITED)"和"重点聚焦(FOCUS)"几大部分组成。这样的设计不仅让有空的读者可以细细阅读,也能方便匆忙的浏览者迅速查阅。例如:书中的"项目工作表"设计对读者整理创作思绪和准备工作任务很有帮助;"重点聚焦"栏目则用"突显"的手法展现了商务报告写作的关键信息和最新发展动态。海量的练习则可以让读者自己选择是独立进行还是协作处理在商务报告写作中的一些实际问题并找到解决方案。为了增加可读性,作者引用了一百多个学生创作实例,向读者展示了不同的写作风格和解决问题的不同途径。通过大量篇幅不一的创作文本,作者告诉人们在不同的职业情况下,处理不同专业性文本的方法是存在不同的。书中还运用了大量的表格、图形,这既符合现代工作的最新特点,又让读者对所阅读的内容一目了然。

该书既是一本介绍商务报告写作的入门读物,又是一本融合多学科的权威教材。作者运用了符号学、传播学、统计学、管理学和人类学等众多学科的内容,将商务报告写作这一原本极为严肃的活动变得生动而有趣。值得一提的是,作者每章所布置的练习,其答案都为开放性的,没有标准答案。这可能让早已习惯选出"唯一正确"答案的中国读者感到无所适从。但细心的读者会发现,恰恰是经过这样的一种"无奈、困惑"的阶段,找到"没有答案"的答案,解决问题的能力才会得到实实在在的提高。

展现在读者面前的第九版《最新商务报告写作》介绍了用计算机处理商务报告写作的最新信息,尤其强调了在该领域内特别为人们所重视的创作道德和全球视野两大问题。

安徽财经大学外国语学院
周　平

Brief Contents 简短目录

To the Instructor — xxv

Section 1 Technical Communication Basics 商务报告写作基础

- **Chapter 1** Definition of Technical Communication 商务报告写作的定义 2
- **Chapter 2** Profiling Audiences 读者概述 35
- **Chapter 3** The Technical Communication Process 商务报告写作过程 55
- **Chapter 4** Technical Communication Style 商务报告写作方式 87
- **Chapter 5** Researching 研究 112
- **Chapter 6** Designing Pages 页面设计 137
- **Chapter 7** Using Visual Aids 使用视图 164
- **Chapter 8** Summarizing 概述 194
- **Chapter 9** Defining 定义 203
- **Chapter 10** Describing 描述 216

Section 2 Technical Communication Applications 商务报告写作应用

- **Chapter 11** Sets of Instructions 指令集 250
- **Chapter 12** Memorandums and Informal Reports 备忘录和非正式报告 275
- **Chapter 13** Developing Websites 网站开发 309
- **Chapter 14** Formal Reports 正式报告 342

Chapter 15 Recommendation and Feasibility Reports　推荐和可行性报告　**369**

Chapter 16 Proposals　提　案　**403**

Chapter 17 User Manuals　使用说明书　**429**

Section 3 **Professional Communication**　职场写作

Chapter 18 Oral Presentations　口头陈述　**462**

Chapter 19 Letters　信　函　**485**

Chapter 20 Job Application Materials　求职材料　**501**

Appendix A Brief Handbook for Technical Writers　专业文档撰写简要手册　**541**

Appendix B Documenting Sources　记录来源　**561**

Contents 目 录

To the Instructor   *xxv*

Section 1   **Technical Communication Basics**   商务报告写作基础

Chapter 1   **Definition of Technical Communication**   商务报告写作的定义   2

Chapter 1 In a Nutshell 概 要 2

A General Definition of Technical Communication   商务报告写作的基本定义   3
    What Is Technical Communication?   什么是商务报告写作？   3
    What Counts as Technical Communication?   哪些算是商务报告写作？   3
    Who Creates Technical Communication?   谁创建了商务报告写作？   4
    How Important Is Technical Communication?   商务报告写作有多重要？   5

Major Traits of Technical Communication   商务报告写作的主要特点   5
    Technical Communication Is Audience Centered   商务报告写作应以读者为中心   5
    Technical Communication Is Designed   商务报告写作是设计出来的   12
    Technical Communication Is Responsible   商务报告写作是有责任的   15
    Technical Communication Is Global   商务报告写作是全球性的   20

● Globalization and Cultural Awareness   全球性和文化意识   21

Exercises • 27   Web Exercise • 31   Works Cited • 31   Focus on Codes of Ethical Conduct • 34
练习·27   网络练习·31   引用的作品·31   关注合乎伦理道德的行为规范·34

Chapter 2   **Profiling Audiences**   读者概述   35

Chapter 2 In a Nutshell 概 要 35

An Example of Technical Writing   专业文档撰写的例子   36
Who Is the Audience?   谁是读者？   38
    What Are the Audience's Demographic Characteristics?   读者的人口特点是什么？   39

Exercises • 39   练习·39

What Is the Audience's Role? 读者的角色是什么？ 39
How Does the Reader Feel About the Subject? 读者对主题的感受是什么？ 41
How Does the Reader Feel About the Sender? 读者对发送者的感受是什么？ 41
What Form Does the Reader Expect? 读者期待什么样的形式？ 42

What Is the Audience's Task? 读者的任务是什么？ 43
What Is the Audience's Knowledge Level? 读者的知识水平怎么样？ 43
Adapting to Your Audience's Knowledge Level 适应读者的知识水平 43
Finding Out What Your Audience Knows 发现你的读者了解什么 45

Exercises • 45 练习 · 45

What Factors Influence the Situation? 影响这个情况的因素是什么？ 46
What Consequences Will Occur from This Idea? 这个想法会有什么后果？ 46
What Is the History of This Idea? 这个想法的历史背景是什么？ 46
How Much Power Does the Reader Have? 读者有多少影响力？ 46
How Formal Is the Situation? 这个情景有多正式？ 47
Is There More Than One Audience? 是不是不止一群读者？ 47

Creating Audience Profiles 创建读者简介 48
Questions for an Audience Profile 读者简介的问题 48
Information-Gathering Strategies 信息收集的策略 49

Exercises • 50   Worksheet for Defining Your Audience • 51
Writing Assignments • 51   Web Exercise • 52   Works Cited • 53
Focus on Credibility • 54 练习 · 50   界定读者的工作表 · 51   写作任务 · 51
网络练习 · 52   引用的作品 · 53   关注可信度 · 54

Chapter 3   The Technical Communication Process 商务报告写作过程   55

Chapter 3 In a Nutshell 概　要   55

An Overview of the Process 写作过程概况   56
Planning Your Document 设计你的文件   56
Situate Yourself 给自己定位   58
Create an Audience Profile 创建读者简介   60
Create a Document Plan 制定文件计划   60
Design Your Information 设计你的信息   62
Design Your Template 设计你的模板   62
Create a Production Schedule 创建一个生产进度表   63

Worksheet for Planning—Short Version • 65   Worksheet for Planning—Long Version • 66   Exercises • 67 计划工作表—短期 · 65   计划工作表—长期 · 66   练习 · 67

Drafting and Finishing Your Document 起草并完成你的文件   68
Research to Discover Information 通过调研发现信息   68

Contents

    Design Your Information to Help Your Reader 设计信息来帮助你的读者 **68**
    Use Context-Setting Introductions 介绍写作背景和意图 **69**
    Place Important Material at the Top 把重要材料放在前面 **70**
    Use Preview Lists 使用预览列表 **71**
    Use Repetition and Sequencing 使用重复和排序 **71**
    Use Coordinate Structure 使用并列结构 **71**
    Testing 测试 **72**

Worksheet for Drafting • **73**   *Exercises* • **74**   草稿的工作表 · **73**   练习 · **74**

Editing 编 辑 **75**
    Producing the Document 制作文件 **77**

Worksheet for Editing • **78**   *Exercises* • **78**   *Writing Assignments* • **81**
Web Exercise • **82**   *Works Cited* • **82**   *Focus on Groups* • **84**
编辑的工作表 · **78**   练习 · **78**   写作任务 · **81**   网络练习 · **82**   引用的作品 · **82**
关注小组 · **84**

Chapter 4 Technical Communication Style 商务报告写作方式 87

Chapter 4 In a Nutshell 概 要 **87**

Write Clear Sentences for Your Reader 为你的读者写清楚的句子 **88**
    Place the Main Idea First 把主要意思放在前面 **88**
    Use Normal Word Order 使用正常的单词顺序 **89**
    Use the Active Voice 使用主动语态 **89**
    Employ Parallelism 运用平行句 **90**
    Write Sentences of 12 to 25 Words 写12–25词的句子 **91**
    Avoid "Garden Path" Sentences 避免晦涩难懂的句子 **91**
    Use *There Are* Sparingly 节约使用"There be"句型 **92**
    Avoid Nominalizations 避免名词化 **92**

Exercises • **92**   练习 · **92**

    Avoid Strings of Choppy Sentences 避免大量的不连贯句子 **94**
    Avoid Wordiness 避免冗长唠叨 **95**
    Avoid Redundant Phrases 避免重复累赘 **95**
    Avoid Noun Clusters 避免名词成群 **96**
    Use *You* Correctly 正确使用"你" **96**
    Avoid Sexist Language 避免性别歧视语言 **96**

Exercises • **92**   练习 · **92**

Write Clear Paragraphs for Your Reader 为你的读者写清楚的段落 **97**
    Put the Topic Sentence First 把主题句放在前面 **98**
    Structure Paragraphs Coherently 段落结构要连贯 **98**

● Globalization and Style 全球化和风格 100
Choose a Tone for the Reader 为读者奠定基调 102
● Ethics and Style 伦理道德和风格 103

Worksheet for Style • *105*   *Exercises* • *106*   *Writing Assignments* • *108*   *Web Exercise* • *109*   *Works Cited* • *109*
Focus on Bias in Language • *110*

风格的工作表·105   练习·106   写作任务·108   网络练习·109
引用的作品·109   关注语言歧视·110

Chapter 5   Researching 研 究 112

Chapter 5 In a Nutshell 概 要 112

The Purpose of Research 研究目的 113
Questioning—The Basic Skill of Researching 质疑——研究的基本技能 113
    How to Discover Questions 如何发现问题 113
    How to Formulate Questions 如何阐述问题 115
Collecting Information from People 向客户收集信息 115
    Interviewing 采 访 115
    Surveying 问 卷 117
    Observing and Testing 观察和测试 118
Collecting Published Information 收集发布的信息 119
    Develop a Search Strategy 制定搜索策略 119
    Search Helpful Sources 寻找有帮助的资源 121
    Record Your Findings 记录你的发现 128

Worksheet for Research Planning • *130*   *Exercises* • *130*
Writing Assignments • *131*   *Web Exercise* • *135*   *Works Cited* • *133*
Focus on Using Google • *134*

研究计划工作表·130   练习·130   写作任务·131   网络练习·133
引用的作品·133   关注谷歌搜索·134

Chapter 6   Designing Pages 页面设计 137

Chapter 6 In a Nutshell 概 要 137

Using Visual Features to Reveal Content 利用视觉特点来揭示内容 138
    White Space and Chunks 白色空间和组块 138
    Bullets 项目符号 139
    Head Systems 顶端标题 140
    Headers or Footers, Pagination, and Rules 标头或脚注，分页和标尺 141
Using Text Features to Convey Meaning 利用文本特点来传达意义 143
    Highlighters 醒目标记 143

Font, Font Size, Leading, Columns and Line Length,
and Justification 字体，字号，引导，分栏和句子长度，对齐 145
Combining Features to Orchestrate the Text for Readers
把所有特色结合起来为读者精心编写文本 148
Developing a Style Sheet and Template 制定一个风格样单和模板 151
Worksheet for a Style Sheet • 153 *Examples* • 154 *Exercises* • 156
Writing Assignments • 162 *Web Exercises* • 162 *Works Cited* • 162
风格样单工作表·153 例子·154 练习·156 写作任务·162 网络练习·162
引用的作品·162

Chapter 7 Using Visual Aids 使用视图 164

Chapter 7 In a Nutshell 概 要 164

The Uses of Visual Aids 视图的使用 165
Creating and Discussing Visual Aids 创建和讨论视图 166
How to Create Visual Aids 如何创建视图 166
How to Discuss Visual Aids 如何讨论视图 167
How to Reference Visual Aids 如何借助视图 167
Guidelines for Effective Visual Aids 有效视图指南 168
Using Tables 使用表格 168
Parts and Guidelines 组成部分和使用准则 169
When to Use a Table 何时使用表格 170
Using Line Graphs 使用直线图 171
Parts and Guidelines 组成部分和使用准则 171
When to Use a Line Graph 何时使用直线图 173
Using Bar Graphs 使用柱状图 175
Parts and Guidelines 组成部分和使用准则 176
When to Use a Bar Graph 何时使用柱状图 178
Using Pie Charts 使用饼状图 178
Parts and Guidelines 组成部分和使用准则 178

● **Ethics and Visual Effects** 使用视图的注意事项 180

When to Use a Pie Chart 何时使用饼状图 181

● **Globalization and Visual Aids** 全球化和视图 182

Using Charts 使用图表 183
Troubleshooting Tables 故障检修表 183
Flow Charts 流程表 184
Decision Charts 决策表 184
Gantt Charts 甘特表 185
Layouts 布局图 185

Using Illustrations 使用插图 186
   Guidelines 指导方针 186
   Photographs 图 片 186
   Drawings 绘 图 186

Worksheet for Visual Aids • 188   Exercises • 189   Writing Assignments • 192   Web Exercise • 193   Works Cited • 193
视图工作表·188   练习·189   写作任务·192   网络练习·193   引用的作品·193

Chapter 8 Summarizing 概 述 194

Chapter 8 In a Nutshell 概 要 194

Summarizing 概 述 195
   Definitions of Summaries and Abstracts 概述和摘要的定义 195
   Audiences for Summaries and Abstracts 概述和摘要的读者 195
   Planning Summaries 设计概述 196
   Writing Summaries 写概述 197

Worksheet for Summarizing • 200   Examples • 200   Exercises • 201   Web Exercise • 202   Works Cited • 202
概述工作表·200   例子·200   练习·201   网络练习·202   引用的作品·202

Chapter 9 Defining 定 义 203

Chapter 9 In a Nutshell 概 要 203

Creating Formal Definitions 创建正式的定义 204
   Classify the Term 术语的阐明 204
   Differentiate the Term 术语的区分 204
   Avoid Circular Definitions 避免循环定义 206

Creating Informal Definitions 创建非正式定义 206
   Operational Definitions 可操作性定义 206
   Synonyms 同义词 206

Developing Extended Definitions 提出拓展性定义 207
   Explain the Derivation 词源的解释 207
   Explicate Terms 术语的解释 207
   Use an Example 结合例子 207
   Use an Analogy 利用对比 208
   Compare and Contrast 比较和对照 208
   Explain Cause and Effect 因果解释 209
   Analyze the Term 术语分析 209

Planning Your Definition 设计你的定义 210

Worksheet for Defining Terms • 210   Examples • 210   Exercises • 213   Writing Assignments • 214   Web Exercise • 215   Works Cited • 215
术语界定工作表·210   例子·210   练习·213   写作任务·214   网络练习·215   引用的作品·215

Chapter 10 Describing 描 述 216

Chapter 10 In a Nutshell 概 要 216

Planning the Mechanism Description 设计机制描述 217
- Consider the Audience 考虑读者 217
- Select an Organizational Principle 选定一个组织原则 217
- Choose Visual Aids 选择视图 218
- Follow the Usual Form for Descriptions 按照常规的描述方式 219

Writing the Mechanism Description 机制描述的撰写 219
- Introduction 介 绍 219
- Body: Description of Mechanism 主体：机制的描述 220
- Other Patterns for Mechanism Descriptions 机制描述的其他模式 221

Planning the Process Description 设计过程描述 223
- Consider the Audience 考虑读者 223
- Select an Organizational Principle 选定一个组织原则 224
- Choose Visual Aids 选择视图 225
- Follow the Usual Form for Writing Descriptions 按照常规的描述方式 225

Writing the Process Description 过程描述的撰写 225
- Introduction 介 绍 225
- Body: Description of the Operation 主体：操作的描述 226
- Conclusion 结 论 228

Planning the Description of a Human System 设计一个人员机制的描述 228
Writing the Description of a Human System 人员机制描述的撰写 229
- Introduction 介 绍 229
- Body: Sequence of a Person's Activities 主体：一个人的行动顺序 229
- Conclusion (Optional) 结论（可选） 230

Worksheet for Planning a Description • 230   Worksheet for Evaluating a Description • 231   Examples • 233   Exercises • 241   Writing Assignments • 245   Web Exercises • 246   Works Cited • 247
设计描述工作表·230   评估描述工作表·231   例子·233   练习·241   写作任务·245   网络练习·246   引用的作品·247

Section 2 Technical Communication Applications 商务报告写作应用

Chapter 11 Sets of Instructions 指令集 250

Chapter 11 In a Nutshell 概 要 250

Planning the Sets of Instructions 指令集设计 251
- Determine Your Goal 确定你的目标 251
- Consider the Audience 考虑你的读者 251

● Globalization and Instructions 全球化和指令 252

Analyze the Sequence 顺序分析 253
Analyze the Tasks 任务分析 255
Choose Visual Aids 选择视图 255
Follow the Usual Form for Instructions 按照常规的指令方式 256
Writing the Set of Instructions 指令集的撰写 258
Write an Effective Introduction 有效介绍的撰写 258
Write an Effective Body 有效主体的撰写 258
Field-Testing Instructions 实地试验的指令 262
Worksheet for Preparing Instructions • 262   Worksheet for Evaluating Instructions • 262   Examples • 268   Exercises • 271   Writing Assignments • 274   Web Exercises • 274   Work Cited • 274
指令准备的工作表·262   评估指令的工作表·262   例子·268   练习·271   写作任务·274   网络练习·274   引用的作品·274

Chapter 12 Memorandums and Informal Reports 备忘录和非正式报告 275

Chapter 12 In a Nutshell 概 要 275

The Elements of Memos 备忘录的组成 276
Memo Headings 备忘录的抬头 276
A Sample Memo Report 备忘录样本 277

The Elements of Informal Reports 非正式报告的组成 278
Introduction 介 绍 278
Discussion 讨 论 280

Types of Informal Reports 非正式报告的类型 282
IMRD Reports IMRD 报告 282
Brief Analytical Reports 简要分析报告 285
Progress Reports 进程报告 289
Outline Reports 大纲报告 291

Worksheet for Planning a Project • 291   Worksheet for IMRD Reports • 292   Worksheet for Informal Reports • 293   Worksheet for Evaluating IMRDs • 293   Examples • 294   Exercises • 301   Writing Assignments • 302   Web Exercise • 303   Works Cited • 304   Focus on E-mail • 305
项目计划工作表·291   IMRD报告工作表·292   非正式报告工作表·293   IMRD报告评估工作表·293   例子·294   练习·301   写作任务·302   网络练习·303   引用的作品·304   关注电子邮件·305

● Ethics and E-Mail 使用电子邮件的注意事项 308

Chapter 13 Developing Websites 网站开发 309

Chapter 13 In a Nutshell 概 要 309

Basic Web Concepts 网页基本概念 310
Hierarchy 层次体系 310

Web Structure　网页结构　310
Reader Freedom　读者自由度　314
Guidelines for Working with Web Structure　网页结构工作指南　316

Planning a Website or Web Document　设计网站或网页文件　316
Decide Your Goal　确定你的目标　316
Analyze Your Audience　分析你的读者　317
Evaluate the Questions the Audience Will Ask　评估读者可能问的问题　317
Create a Flow Chart of Your Site　创建你的网站流程表　317
Create a Template　创建一个模板　318

Drafting　草案　319
Orient Your Reader　引导你的读者　321
Write in a Scannable Style　以可浏览方式撰写　321
Establish Credibility　建立可信度　322
Use Visuals Effectively　有效使用视图　323

Testing　测试　323
Basic Editing　基本编辑　325
Audience Effectiveness　读者有效性　325
Consistency　连贯性　325

● **Ethics and Websites**　使用网站的注意事项　326
Navigation　导航　327
The Electronic Environment　电子环境　327
Clarity　清晰度　328

Worksheet for Planning a Website or Document • 328　Worksheet for Evaluating a Website • 329　Examples • 330
设计网站或文件工作表・328　网站评估工作表・329　例子・330

● **Globalization/Localization and Websites**　全球化/本地化和网站

Exercises • 338　Writing Assignment • 339　Web Exercise • 339　Works Cited and Consulted • 340　Focus on HTML • 341
练习・338　写作任务・339　网络练习・339　引用或参考的作品・340　关注HTML・341

Chapter 14　Formal Reports　正式报告　343

Chapter 14 In a Nutshell　概　要　343

The Elements of a Formal Report　正式报告的组成　344
Front Material　前面的材料　345
Transmittal Correspondence　沟通函件　345
Title Page　标题页　345
Table of Contents　目　录　346

Contents

    List of Illustrations 插图列表 347
    Summary or Abstract 总结或摘要 348
    Introduction 介绍 349
    Conclusions and Recommendations/Rationale 结论和建议/基本原理 352
The Body of the Formal Report 正式报告的主体 353
    Paginating 分页 354
    Indicating Chapter Divisions 标示章节安排 354
End Material 后面的材料 354
    Glossary and List of Symbols 术语表和符号列表 354
    References 参考书目 355
    Appendix 附件 355

Worksheet for Preparing a Formal Report • 355   Examples • 356
Exercises • 366   Writing Assignments • 367   Web Exercise • 367
Works Cited • 368
准备正式报告的工作表 · 355   例子 · 356   练习 · 366   写作任务 · 367
网络练习 · 367   引用的作品 · 368

Chapter 15 Recommendation and Feasibility Reports
推荐和可行性报告 369

Chapter 15 In a Nutshell 概要 369

Planning the Recommendation Report 设计推荐报告 370
    Consider the Audience 考虑读者 370
    Choose Criteria 选择标准 370
    Use Visual Aids 利用视图 372
    Select a Format and an Organizational Principle 选择格式和组织原则 373
Drafting the Recommendation Report 起草推荐报告 374
    Introduction 介绍 374
    Conclusions 结论 376
    Recommendations/Rationale Section 推荐/基本原理部分 376
    Discussion Section 讨论部分 376
Planning the Feasibility Report 设计可行性报告 377
    Consider the Audience 考虑读者 377
    Determine the Criteria 确定准则 378
    Determine the Standards 制定标准 378
    Structure by Criteria 按标准排序 378
Writing the Feasibility Report 撰写可行性报告 378
    Choose a Format 选择一个格式 378
    Write the Introduction and Body 撰写介绍和主体 379

Contents

*Worksheet for Preparing a Recommendation/Feasibility Report • 380
Worksheet for Evaluating Your Report • 381   Worksheet for Evaluating
a Peer's Report • 382   Examples • 382   Exercises • 396   Writing
Assignments • 401   Web Exercises • 402   Works Cited • 402*
准备推荐/可行性报告的工作表·380 评估报告的工作表·381 评估同行报告的工作表·382
例子·382 练习·396 写作任务·401 网络练习·402 引用的作品·402

Chapter 16   Proposals 提 案 403

Chapter 16 In a Nutshell 概 要 403

The External Proposal 外部提案 404
Planning the External Proposal 设计外部提案 404
    Consider the Audience 考虑读者 405
    Research the Situation 情况调研 405
    Use Visual Aids 利用视图 406
Writing the External Proposal 撰写外部提案 406
    The Executive Summary 行政总结 406
    The Technical Section 技术部分 406
    The Management Section 管理部分 407
    The Financial Section 财务部分 407
The Internal Proposal 内部提案 407
Planning the Internal Proposal 设计内部提案 407
    Consider the Audience 考虑读者 407

● **Ethics and Proposals** 撰写提案的注意事项 408

    Use Visual Aids 利用视图 408
    Organize the Proposal 组织提案 409
    Design the Proposal 设计提案 413
Writing the Internal Proposal 撰写内部提案 414
    Use the Introduction to Orient the Reader 利用介绍来引导读者 414
    Use the Discussion to Convince Your Audience 利用讨论来说服读者 415

*Worksheet for Preparing a Proposal • 415   Worksheet for Evaluating
a Proposal • 417   Examples • 417   Exercises • 425   Writing
Assignments • 427   Web Exercise • 428   Work Cited • 428*
准备提案的工作表·415 评估提案的工作表·417 例子·417 练习·425
写作任务·427 网络练习·428 引用的作品·428

Chapter 17   User Manuals 使用说明书 429

Chapter 17 In a Nutshell 概 要 429

Planning the Manual 设计使用说明书 430
    Determine Your Purpose 确定你的目的 430

Contents

    Consider the Audience 考虑读者 430
    Determine a Schedule 确定一个进度表 431
    Discover Sequences 发现顺序 432
    Analyze the Steps 分析步骤 433
    Analyze the Parts 分析组成部分 433
    Select Visual Aids 选择视图 434
    Format the Pages 设置页面 435
Writing the Manual 撰写说明书 438
    Introduction 介　绍 438
    Arrange the Sections 安排内容 438
    Test the Manual 测试说明书 443

*Worksheet for Preparing a Manual • 446　Examples • 447
Exercises • 458　Writing Assignments • 459　Web Exercise • 459
Works Cited • 460*　准备说明书的工作表·446　例子·447　练习·458
写作任务·459　网络练习·459　引用的作品·460

Section 3　Professional Communication 职场写作

Chapter 18　Oral Presentations 口头陈述 462

Chapter 18 In a Nutshell 概　要 462

Planning the Presentation 设计陈述 463
    Plan for Your Audience 为读者作计划 463
    Plan for the Situation 视情况作计划 464
    Plan Your Organizational Pattern 设计安排模式 465
    Plan Your Presentation 设计你的陈述 465
Making an Effective Presentation 作有效的陈述 475
    Develop the Introduction 展开介绍 475
    Navigate the Body 主体导航 476
    Develop a Conclusion 得出结论 476
    Rehearse Your Presentation 陈述预演 477
    Deliver Your Presentation 发表陈述 478

● **Globalization and Oral Presentations** 全球化和口头陈述 479

*Worksheet for Preparing an Oral Presentation • 481　Worksheet for Evaluating an Oral Presentation • 481　Exercises • 482　Speaking Assignment • 482　Writing Assignment • 483　Web Exercises • 483
Works Cited • 484*
准备口头陈述的工作表·481　评估口头陈述的工作表·481　练习·482
演讲任务·482　写作任务·483　网络练习·483　引用的作品·484

Chapter 19   Letters 信 函   485

Chapter 19 In a Nutshell 概 要   485

Three Basic Letter Formats   信函的三种基本格式   486
- Block Format   齐头式   486
- Modified Block Format   混合式   486
- Simplified Format   简化型格式   486

Elements of a Letter   信函的组成部分   486
- Internal Elements   内部组成部分   486
- Envelopes   信 封   491

Planning Business Letters   设计商务信函   491

● **Globalization and Letters**   全球化和信函   492
- Consider Your Audience   考虑你的读者   493
- Consider Your Tone   考虑你的基调   493
- Consider Format   考虑格式   494

● **Ethics and Letters**   撰写信函的注意事项   495

Types of Business Letters   商务信函的类型   495
- Transmittal Letters   商务沟通信函   495
- General Information Letters   通用信函   495

Worksheet for Writing a Business Letter • 498   Exercises • 498   Writing Assignments • 499   Web Exercise • 500   Works Cited • 500
撰写商务信函的工作表 · 498   练习 · 498   写作任务 · 499   网络练习 · 500   引用的作品 · 500

Chapter 20   Job Application Materials 求职材料   501

Chapter 20 In a Nutshell 概 要   501

Analyzing the Situation   情况分析   502
- Understand Your Goals   明白你的目标   502
- Understand Your Audience   了解你的读者   502
- Assess Your Field   评估你的领域   503
- Assess Your Strengths   评估你的强项   504
- Assess the Needs of Employers   评估雇主的需求   505

Planning the Résumé   设计简历   505
- Information to Include in a Résumé   简历需包含的信息   505
- Résumé Organization   简历内容的安排   505

Writing the Résumé   撰写简历   508

Planning a Letter of Application 申请信的设计 511
    Analyze the Employer's Needs 分析雇主的需求 511
    Match Your Capabilities to the Employer's Needs 将你的能力和雇主需求匹配 511

● **Ethics and Résumés** 撰写简历的注意事项 512

Writing a Letter of Application 申请信的撰写 513
    Apply in the Introduction 在介绍部分申请 513
    Convince in the Body 在主体部分说服 513

● **Globalization and Job Applications** 全球化和工作申请 514
    Request an Interview 请求面试 515
    Select a Format 选择一种格式 517

Interviewing 面试 518
    Prepare Well 做好准备 518
    Use Social Tact 运用社交技巧 518
    Perform Well 好好表现 518
    Ask Questions 提出问题 519
    Understand the Offer 了解录用职位 519

Writing Follow-Up Letters 撰写跟进信函 519

Worksheet for Preparing a Résumé • 520   *Worksheet for Writing a Letter of Application* • 520   *Worksheet for Evaluating a Letter of Application* • 521   *Examples* • 521   *Exercises* • 529   *Writing Assignments* • 533   *Web Exercise* • 533   *Works Cited* • 533   *Focus on Electronic Résumés* • 535

准备简历的工作表·520   撰写申请信的工作表·520   评估申请信的工作表·521   例子·521   练习·529   写作任务·533   网络练习·533   引用的作品·533   关注电子简历·535

Appendix A   Brief Handbook for Technical Writers   专业文档撰写简要手册 539

Problems with Sentence Construction 句子结构的问题 539
    Identify and Eliminate Comma Splices 识别并删除逗号拼凑句 539

Exercises • 540   练习·540

    Identify and Eliminate Run-On Sentences 识别并删除流水句 541

Exercises • 541   练习·541

    Identify and Eliminate Sentence Fragments 识别并删除句子碎片 541

Exercises • 543   练习·543

    Place Modifiers in the Correct Position 把修饰语放在正确的位置 543

Exercises • 544   练习·544

    Use Words Ending in *-ing* Properly 正确使用以ing结尾的词 544

Exercises • 544 练习·544

  Make the Subject and Verb Agree 主谓要一致 545

Exercises • 545 练习·545

  Use Pronouns Correctly 正确使用代词 546
  Problems with Number 数字的问题 546
  Problems with Antecedents 先行词的问题 546
  Problems with *This* 使用This的问题 547

Exercises • 547 练习·547

Punctuation 标点符号 548
  Apostrophes 撇号 548
  Brackets 方括号 549
  Colons 冒号 549
  Commas 逗号 549
  Dashes 破折号 551
  Parentheses 圆括号 551
  A Note on Parentheses, Dashes, and Commas
  圆括号、破折号和逗号的使用注意事项 552
  Ellipsis Points 省略号 552
  Hyphens 连字号 552
  Quotation Marks 引号 554
  Semicolons 分号 554
  Underlining (Italics) 下划线（斜体） 555

Abbreviations, Capitalization, and Numbers 缩写、大写和数字 555
  Abbreviations 缩写 555
  Capitalization 大写 556
  Numbers 数字 557

Works Cited • 558
引用的作品·558

Appendix B Documenting Sources 记录来源 559

  How Internal Documentation Works 内部记录的运行方式 559
    APA Method APA方式 560
    MLA Method MLA方式 560
    Numbered References Method 参考文献排序方式 560
    The "Extension" Problem "外延"的问题 561
  The APA Method APA方式 561
    APA Citations APA引用 561
    APA References APA参考 563

The MLA Method　MLA方式　568
　MLA Citations　MLA引用　568
　MLA Works Cited List　MLA引用作品列表　570
Numbered References　参考文献排序　575
　Alphabetically　按字母顺序　575
　By Position of the First Reference in the Text　按文中第一个参考文献的位置　576

Exercises • 582　Writing Assignment • 583　Works Cited • 583
练习·582　写作任务·583　引用的作品·583

To the Instructor

Since the first edition of *Technical Report Writing Today* appeared on instructors' desks some three decades ago, technical writing has changed dramatically. Yet with each successive edition, this book has consistently reflected an emphasis on the last word in its title—*today*. In every aspect of its up-to-date coverage, this book focuses on the state of the field right now and the tools technical communicators need in today's workplace. Upon mastering this text's principles for effective technical communication and learning the latest approaches and standards, students using *Technical Report Writing Today* will succeed not only in today's workplace but also in the workplace of tomorrow.

New to the Ninth Edition

The ninth edition of *Technical Report Writing Today* has been revised—as with past editions—to incorporate current issues important to teachers and students of technical communication in the new millennium. Sections on globalization, ethics, and electronic presentations keep the text abreast of new communication demands in the workplace. These new features, coupled with the text's accessible style and abundance of exercises, will help students prepare for the communication demands they will face in college and on the job.

New Coverage of Globalization. The globalized world economy requires students to be able to assess how to interact with audiences across the world. No longer is the audience for memos and e-mails those people somewhere down the hall, on another floor, or at another company office within the United States. Now the audience is likely to be in India or South America. Students must learn to function effectively in this new situation. The ninth edition incorporates in Chapter 1 a lengthy section on globalization and then in many chapters provides sidebars that relate global issues to the contents of those chapters, for instance, global concerns in relation to Web design.

Expanded Coverage of Ethics. The ethical role of the communicator also becomes more important in this new communication situation. Thus the book also includes in Chapter 1 a section on ethics and provides sidebars addressing ethical concerns throughout the chapters. These sidebars discuss important concerns such as ethical handling of résumés and e-mail.

To the Instructor

Changes in Overall Structure. The structure of the book has been reduced from four sections to three: Technical Communication Basics, Technical Communication Applications, and Professional Communication. The book continues to include appendixes on style and research citations.

The "repertoire" section of the book, Technical Communication Basics, has been changed to include ten chapters. These chapters are grouped more effectively than in previous editions. The new order is Definition of Technical Communication, Profiling Audiences, The Technical Communication Process, Technical Communication Style, Researching, Designing Pages, Using Visual Aids, Summarizing, Defining, and Describing. (Summarizing has been moved to a more appropriate position with other kinds of basic writing.) Section 2, Technical Communication Applications, now includes Instructions. Section 3, Professional Communication, now includes Oral Presentations.

Updated Exercises. The exercises have all been categorized to indicate different types of goals for students—you create, you analyze, you revise, and group exercises. Many of the examples at the end of the chapters have been replaced. Many exercises have been revised.

Chapter-by-Chapter Changes. Chapters 7 (Using Visual Aids), 14 (Formal Reports), and 19 (Letters) have remained the same. All other chapters have been revised, as outlined below:

- **Chapter 1, Definition of Technical Communication.** Chapter 1 has been expanded. It now includes complete sections on ethics and globalization. Theoretical sections have been updated to include current thinking about the role of communication. New exercises and examples are included.
- **Chapter 2, Profiling Audiences.** This chapter has been revised to include current thinking about defining audiences, including an emphasis on the tasks that audiences must perform after reading and a section on creating audience profiles. Worksheets have been revised and a section on meeting "quality benchmarks" has been added.
- **Chapter 3, The Technical Communication Process.** The description of the process of creating documents has been updated to include recent thinking on information design. The key graphic in this chapter now includes questions based on information design principles.
- **Chapter 4, Technical Communication Style.** The examples throughout this chapter have been largely replaced. A brief treatment of "garden path" sentences has been included. New sample papers are included.
- **Chapter 5, Researching.** This chapter now includes a focus section on using keywords and on using Google to research items on the Web.
- **Chapter 6, Designing Pages.** Chapter 6 has been simplified to make the rather difficult process of designing pages easier for students to grasp. In particular, the number of graphics has been reduced, thus giving more prominence to effective design principles.

To the Instructor

- **Chapter 8, Summarizing.** A new article, explaining computerized ordering, is the basis for summarizing activities. New summaries and abstracts are included in the chapter and in the examples.
- **Chapter 9, Defining.** This chapter includes many new examples of definitions.
- **Chapter 10, Describing.** This chapter includes new examples.
- **Chapter 11, Sets of Instructions.** New examples have been added to this chapter.
- **Chapter 12, Memorandums and Informal Reports.** Chapter 12 now includes more emphasis on and new examples of the IMRD report ("Lab Report") genre. The chapter also includes a focus section that treats e-mail in depth.
- **Chapter 13, Developing Websites.** A new form for evaluating websites has been added.
- **Chapter 15, Recommendation and Feasibility Reports.** This chapter has two new feasibility reports; one of them was created by a small business to determine whether to market an item.
- **Chapter 16, Proposals.** This chapter includes new examples of effective proposals.
- **Chapter 17, User Manuals.** Chapter 17 includes a new student model as well as a complete usability report.
- **Chapter 18, Oral Presentations.** This chapter now focuses on PowerPoint presentations. The theory of oral reports is expanded to include recent criticisms of PowerPoint presentations and to give advice on the effective creation of PowerPoint presentations.
- **Chapter 20, Job Application Materials.** New letters of application and new résumés provide even more examples for students.
- **Appendix A, Brief Handbook for Technical Writers.** Most of the examples in this appendix are new to this edition.
- **Appendix B, Documenting Sources.** Most of the examples in this appendix are new to this edition. All sections have been updated in accord with the latest MLA and APA guidelines.

Overall Organization

The structure of the book remains a sequence from theory and skills to applications. Early chapters present current information on how to handle the repertoire of technical communication skills from audience analysis through research and design. However, the chapters are organized as modules so that you may assign chapters in the sequence that best meets the needs of your course. For instance, you could easily begin your course with a discussion of audience and design or you could start with applications such as descriptions or letters. Moreover, all of the introductory chapters have extensive exercise sections so that students can either practice the concepts covered or go right into writing memos and short reports.

The approach of this edition is the same. The book's emphasis continues to be on such skills as definition and description and on such common writing forms as memos, informal reports, proposals, and letters of application. Each chapter is self-contained, asking students to follow a process of creation that emphasizes analyzing audience, analyzing information design, and addressing problems related to creating the type of document under consideration. Each chapter contains exercises, assignments, models, planning worksheets, and evaluation worksheets designed to guide students through all phases of document creation. Exercises provide a variety of strategies to help students learn. For instance, in Chapter 20, Job Application Materials, students are encouraged to analyze or revise a letter, to create a letter, or to follow an extended process of group interaction to create and test the letter.

The basic question for a technical communication textbook is, "Will it help teachers help students understand the communication demands they will meet on the job in the near future?" The ninth edition blends instruction on traditional tools of the trade with new strategies and information to help your students develop not just their skills but also their "savvy." This book will position students as effective communicators in the early twenty-first century and will position you and teachers like you as effective mentors for those students.

Features

Technical Report Writing Today retains the features that have made it the useful and popular text it is—and adds new ones.

The following list highlights some of the features that have proven effective in previous editions of *Technical Report Writing Today* and continue to be highly praised by users of the book.

- **Clear and Concise Presentation.** The chapters in this book are designed as "read to learn to do" material. The book assumes the reader is a student with a goal. By providing short paragraphs and clear presentation, the text helps the student achieve the goal of becoming an effective technical communicator.
- **Pragmatic Organization.** The text proceeds from theory to skills to applications, but teachers may assign chapters in any sequence that fills their needs. For instance, teachers could easily begin their course with an application such as descriptions or letters. Because of the situational approach used in many chapters, students can start writing without having to read many theory chapters.
- **Helpful Chapter-Opening Features.** Each chapter opens with two features to help orient students to the material that follows. "Chapter Contents" provides an outline of the chapter's main sections. "In a Nutshell" briefly summarizes the chapter's most important concepts.
- **Focus Boxes.** The text contains numerous "focus" boxes (appearing in selected chapters), which discuss concepts that build on issues introduced in the chapter. These boxes discuss important topics such as credibility,

research using Google, e-mail, and bias in language, all of which students must master to become effective professionals.
- **Worksheets.** Every major project has a worksheet that helps students organize their thoughts and prepare for the assignment. Each genre chapter also has an evaluation worksheet so that students working in groups have a basis for making helpful critical remarks.
- **Annotated Student Examples.** This edition contains more than 100 sample student documents, illustrating different writing styles and approaches to problems.
- **Numerous Professional Examples.** Professional examples in the book illustrate contemporary ways to handle writing situations. Many students and teachers have commented on the helpfulness of the examples, which appear both within chapters and at the ends of chapters. Numbered examples at the ends of chapters provide a greater level of detail than the necessarily brief examples within chapters.
- **Exercises (including Writing Assignments and Web Exercises).** Appearing sequentially at the ends of all chapters, Exercises, Writing Assignments, and Web Exercises balance individual and group work, as well as traditional and Web work, exposing students to different kinds of technical communicating problems and solutions. Exercises appear in all chapters, even theory chapters, making it easy to get students writing. In many chapters, the exercises are actually steps in the planning and drafting process required by the writing assignments for the chapter. As students complete the exercises, they also will be developing the project required for that unit.
- **Situational Approach.** Each of the genre chapters (e.g., proposals, instructions, job application letters) is built on situational principles. The student finds in the chapters all the necessary information, ranging from the audience to the rhetoric of the situation to the organization, format, and type of visual aids that work best in the situation. For instance, Chapter 15, Recommendation and Feasibility Reports, includes a discussion of generating criteria. Chapter 16, Proposals, includes a brief discussion of Gantt charts. Chapter 17, User Manuals, includes a discussion of storyboarding and of usability reports.
- **Appendixes.** The book's two appendixes provide easily accessible material on grammar and mechanics (Appendix A, Brief Handbook for Technical Writers) and MLA and APA documentation (Appendix B, Documenting Sources).

Ancillary Materials

Instructor's Resource Manual. The *Technical Report Writing Today* Instructor's Resource Manual retains its chapter-by-chapter organization, but it offers more features to help teachers teach. Each chapter provides an abstract of a chapter in the book, teaching suggestions (including suggested schedules for sequencing an assignment), and comments on the exercises and writing assignments. Over

50 student examples responding to assignments in the text will show your students how others have solved the problems posed in this book. The goal is to provide your students with material that they can sink their teeth into. Use these examples as models or as the basis for discussions and workshops on effective or ineffective handling of the paper in the situation. You may photocopy these examples and use them as class handouts or create transparencies from them.

Technical Report Writing Today **Website.** The website has been expanded to include PowerPoint slides for each chapter and extensive lists of links to sites dealing with global and ethical materials. The PowerPoint slides provide topical coverage of each chapter and, in many places, include examples. For instance, the slides for Chapter 7, Using Visual Aids, annotate the parts of a table, a line graph, and a bar graph. In Chapter 20, Job Application Materials, the slides contain a brief annotated sample résumé. This extensive website is divided into two sections: Student Resources and Instructor Resources. The Student Resources section features chapter overviews, additional exercises, additional sample documents, links to professional technical writing organizations, and other materials that expand on the student text. The Instructor Resources section features an overview of the book, chapter outlines and abstracts, a transition guide outlining changes in the book since the previous edition, and other materials of use to instructors.

Other Houghton Mifflin Products for This Course

- *Creating Websites That Work*, **by Kathryn Summers and Michael Summers.** In this unique and inexpensive primer, Kathryn Summers, veteran technical writing instructor at the University of Baltimore, and her brother, Michael Summers, user experience specialist with Nielsen Norman Group, teach you to build a website that meets the needs of both the site owner and the site user. This easy-to-follow text provides a wealth of illustrations and examples to take you from creating a site map and considering credibility issues through designing content elements and site testing. An excellent companion website includes examples of effective work at each stage of the Web development process, summary checklists, links, exercises, and evaluation sheets.
- *A Guide to MLA Documentation*, **Sixth Edition, by Joseph Trimmer.** This concise guide to the documentation system of the Modern Language Association of America is briefer, cheaper, and easier to use than the MLA's own handbook. *A Guide to MLA Documentation* includes numerous examples, a sample research paper, an updated appendix on American Psychological Association (APA) style, and helpful hints on such topics as taking notes and avoiding plagiarism. The booklet is thin enough to slip into a notebook and inexpensive enough to serve as a supplement for a main text. A complete sample research paper on Internet chat rooms is annotated with explanations of proper MLA format.

- *Pocket Guide to APA Style*, **by Robert Perrin.** This quick reference to the APA documentation style provides an inexpensive, portable, and easy-to-use alternative to *The Publication Manual of the American Psychological Association*. In addition to a thorough overview of APA conventions, this guide features an overview of the research process, four chapters of sample APA-style citations, two sample APA-style papers, and appendixes on poster presentations, APA abbreviations for states and territories, and APA-style shortened forms of publishers' names.
- *The American Heritage Dictionary*, **Fourth Edition.** This standard reference is available in a hardcover, thumb-indexed College Edition or a briefer, less expensive, but still durable hardcover Concise Edition. Both dictionaries can be purchased at a deep discount when ordered in a shrinkwrapped package with *Technical Report Writing Today*.

Acknowledgments

I would like to thank the following technical writing teachers who offered valuable and insightful comments about the manuscript:

Harryette Brown, Eastfield College
Timothy R. Lindsley, Nicholls State University
Susan Malmo, St. Louis Community College at Meramec
Debbie Reynolds, Florida Community College at Jacksonville
Judith Szerdahelyi, Western Kentucky University
Carol Yee, New Mexico Institute of Mining and Technology

In addition, my appreciation goes to the many students who over the years have demanded clear answers and clear presentations and who have responded with quality writing. For allowing their material to be reprinted in this book, my thanks to these students:

Jill Adkins	Mark Eisner	Holly Jeske
Dan Alexander	Louise Esaian	Kris Jilk
Mark Anderson	Craig Ethier	Mike Jueneman
David Ayers	Curt Evenson	Pat Jouppi
Sandra Baker	Carol Frank	Kim KainzPoplawski
Karin Broekner	Greg Fritsch	Cindy Koller
Scott Buerkley	John Furlano	Mary Beth LaFond
Josh Buhr	Bret Gehring	Chris Lindblad
Fran Butek	John Gretzinger	Chris Lindner
Tony Bynum	Cheryl Hanson	Jerry Mackenzie
Kevin Charpentier	Rob Hoffman	Eric Madson
Nikki Currier	Tadd Hohlfelder	Matt Maertens
Susan Dalton	Jodi Hubbard	Todd Magolan
Melissa Dieckman	Kevin Jack	Richard Manor
Rodney Dukes	Rachel A. Jacobson	Julie McNallen
John Dykstra	Jim Janisse	Shannon Michaelis

(*continued*)

To the Instructor

Heather Miller	Ed Salmon	Sharon Tobin
Jim Miller	Aaron Santama	M. R. Vanderwegen
Tracy Miller	Jocelyn Scheppers	Steve Vandewalle
Keith Munson	Jim Schiltgen	Mike Vivoda
Mark Olson	Stacy Schmansky	Steve Vinz
Hilary Peterson	Brian Schmitz	Rosemarie Weber
Nicole Peterson	Julie Seeger	Michelle Welsh
Steve Prickett	Chad Seichter	Marya Wilson
Steve Rachac	Dave Seppala	John Wise
Cara Robida	Michelle Stewart	
Dana Runge	Brad Tanck	

Special thanks to Jane and Mary for their patient work with a difficult manuscript. Jane has grown up with this book and has become a clear writer in her own right. Her contributions to this edition, both textual and editorial, are significant. Her knowledge, gained from travels throughout the world, added immensely to the globalization text of this edition. I also thank Nathan for his clear contributions to sidebars on ethics; my colleague, Michael Martin, for important contributions on ethics and citations; my colleague, Scott Zimmerman, for gracious permission to use his PowerPoint material; my former student Fran Butek for in-depth research on definitions and descriptions; and my former students Amy Reid and Michelle Stewart for permission to publish the kind of résumé that makes former teachers proud.

I am especially grateful for the insightful, even-handed editing of Maggie Barbieri. For their insight and patience I would also like to thank Michael Gillespie, Bruce Cantley, and Tracy Patruno at Houghton Mifflin and Nancy Benjamin at Books By Design. Although Dean Johnson has passed away since the last edition, I especially want to acknowledge the fine guiding hand he provided to this book through its first eight editions. As is so often true, the contributions of others has enabled me to produce a revision more extensive and insightful than I had imagined.

Finally, thanks once again to an understanding family who offered encouragement and support throughout this project—Mary, Jane, Simon, Kelly, Clare, Nathan, Shana, and Mike and Tim Riordan.

D.G.R.

Section 2
Technical Communication Applications
商务报告写作应用

Chapter 11   Sets of Instructions 指令集

Chapter 12   Memorandums and Informal Reports 备忘录和非正式报告

Chapter 13   Developing Websites 网站开发

Chapter 14   Formal Reports 正式报告

Chapter 15   Recommendation and Feasibility Reports 推荐和可行性报告

Chapter 16   Proposals 提 案

Chapter 17   User Manuals 使用说明书

Chapter 11 Sets of Instructions
指 令 集

Chapter Contents
Chapter 11 In a Nutshell
Planning the Set of Instructions
Globalization and Instructions
Writing the Set of Instructions
Field-Testing Instructions

Chapter 11
In a Nutshell 概 要

The goal of a set of instructions is to enable readers to take charge of the situation and accomplish whatever it is that they need to do.

Introduction
- Tell the end goal of the instructions (or do that in the title).
- Define any terms the readers might not know; if necessary, explain the level of knowledge you expect.
- List tools they must have or conditions to be aware of.

Body Steps
- Explain one action at a time.
- Tell the readers what they need to know to do the step, including warnings, special conditions, and any "good enough" criteria that allow them to judge whether they have done the step correctly.

Format
- Use clear heads.
- Number each step.
- Provide visuals that are big enough, clear enough, and near enough (usually directly under or next to) the appropriate text.
- Use lots of white space that clearly indicates the main and the subordinate sections.
- Write the goal at the "top" of the section—so the readers can skip the rest if they already know how to do that.

Tone
- Be definite. Make each order explicit. If the monitor "must be placed on top of the CPU," don't say "should."
- Discover what readers feel is arbitrary by asking them in a field test.

Sets of instructions appear everywhere. Magazines and books explain how to canoe, how to prepare income taxes, and how to take effective photographs; consumer manuals explain how to assemble stereo systems, how to program VCRs, and how to make purchased items work. On the job you will write instructions for performing many processes and running machines. This chapter explains how to plan and write a useful set of instructions.

Planning the Set of Instructions 指令集设计

To plan your instructions, determine your goal, consider your audience, analyze the sequence, choose visual aids, and follow the usual form. In the following discussion, the subject is exposing Dylux paper in order to make a "proof" or "review copy" of a color print that many people will review for accuracy and effectiveness.

Determine Your Goal 确定你的目标

Instructions enable readers to complete a project or to learn a process. *To complete a project* means to arrive at a definite end result: The reader can complete a form or assemble a toy or make a garage door open and close on command. *To learn a process* means to become proficient enough to perform the process without the set of instructions. The reader can paddle a canoe, log on to the computer, or adjust the camera. In effect, every set of instructions should become obsolete as the reader either finishes the project or learns to perform the process without the set of instructions.

Consider the Audience 考虑你的读者

When you analyze your audience, estimate their knowledge level and any physical or emotional constraints they might have.

Estimate the Audience's Knowledge Level

The audience will be either absolute beginners who know nothing about the process or intermediates who understand the process but need a memory jog before they can function effectively.

The reader's knowledge level determines how much information you need to include. Think, for instance, about telling beginners to turn on a computer. They will not be able to do this because they will not know where to look for the power switch. For an intermediate, however, "turn it on" is sufficient.

Globalization and Instructions 全球化和指令

Knowing your international audience means knowing their cultural norms. You need to know how to present ideas to them. Martin Schell warns writers that in some countries the phrase "Turn Power On" is an essential first step for any set of instructions, whereas in other cultures this step is assumed and unnecessary, and, in some cases, it is insulting to include such an obvious step.

The same rules of clear and concise writing that you apply to other documents are especially important in writing instructions. Keep your prose simple and succinct. As much as possible, use the present tense; stay away from contractions; pare down your writing to one idea per sentence; avoid using jargon and clichés (Dehaas).

When writing the actual instructions, understand that someone will read them very literally. Use the active voice. Instead of "The lever should be positioned at the 'on' position," write "Put the lever in the 'on' position." The passive voice makes the sentence vague and unclear; the reader may not know what is expected of him or her, especially as many languages do not use passive voice. By changing the instructions to the active voice, you will make the instructions more precise (Dehaas).

Consider the word order in your sentences; each idea should build on the one before it. If you are describing the steps in a task, write them in the order in which they are performed. It will be easier for someone with limited English skills to follow short, numbered steps than to try to understand long, complex sentences (Dehaas).

Be aware of the kinds of prepositions that you use. These parts of speech are often very hard to learn. If you write a complex sentence that uses a lot of prepositions ("Open the program that is on the desktop or in the start menu under program"), the reader may miss one or more relationships and will not be able to perform the task.

For further reference:
Nancy Hoft Consulting at www.world-ready.com is a training and consulting firm that specializes in effective techniques for communicating with multilingual and multicultural audiences. Look here for advice on writing and designing for a global community and for links to other helpful sites.

Works Cited
Dehaas, David. "Say What You Mean." *Occupational Health and Safety Magazine.* 31 Jan. 2004 <www.ohscanada.com/Training/saywhatyoumean.asp>.
Schell, Martin A. "Frequently Asked Questions About Globalization and Localization." *American Services in Asia.* 31 Jan. 2004 <www.globalenglish.info/faq.htm#two>.

Identify Constraints

Emotional and physical constraints may interfere with the audience's attempts to follow instructions. Many people have a good deal of anxiety about doing something for the first time. They worry that they will make mistakes and that those mistakes will cost them their labor. If they tighten the wrench too hard, will the bolt snap off? If they hit the wrong key, will they lose the entire contents of their disk? To offset this anxiety, include tips about what should take place at each step and about what to do if something else happens. Step 5 in the example "Making a Dylux Proof," page 261, explains what it means when the overhead light turns off—nothing is wrong; the process is finished.

The physical constraints are usually the materials needed to perform the process, but they might also be special environmental considerations. A Phillips screw cannot be tightened with a regular screwdriver; a 3-pound hammer cannot be swung in a restricted space; in a darkroom, only a red light can shine. Physical constraints also include safety concerns. If touching a certain electrical connection can injure the reader, make that very clear. Step 1 in the example on page 260 tells readers that it doesn't make any difference how they lay the Dylux into the frame—either way achieves the same result.

Examples for Different Audiences

To see how the audience affects the set of instructions, compare the brief version below with "Exposing a Single Color" (pp. 260–261). The section on pages 272–273 explains the steps in detail, assuming that the beginner audience needs detailed "hand-holding" assistance. The brief example below, designed for an intermediate audience, simply lists the sequence of steps to jog the reader's memory.

Instructions for an Intermediate

1. Lay the Dylux and black film in the frame.
2. Select the channel and key it in. Enter.
3. Close and latch. Open after the light goes out.

Analyze the Sequence 顺序分析

The sequence is the chronological order of the steps involved. To analyze the sequence, determine the end goal, analyze the tasks, name and explain the tasks, and analyze any special conditions. (See the sample flow chart of an analysis in Figure 11.1, p. 254.)

Determine the End Goal

The end goal is whatever you want the reader to achieve, the "place" at which the user will arrive. This goal affects the number of steps in your sequence because different end goals will require you to provide different sets of instructions, with different sections. In the preceding example, the end goal is "The user will finish exposing a single color," and the document ends at that point. Other end goals, however, are possible. For instance, if the goal were "The user will finish exposing four colors," the sequence would obviously include more steps and sections.

Figure 11.1

Flow Chart of an Analysis

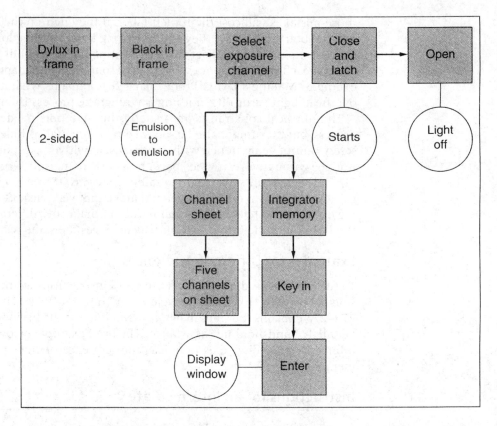

Analyze the Tasks 任务分析

You have two goals here: determine the sequence and name the steps. To determine the sequence, you either go backward from the end goal or perform the sequence yourself. If the end goal is to remove the exposed film, the question to ask is "What step must the user perform before removing the exposed film?" The answer is "Close and latch the frame." If you continue to go backward, the next question is "What does the user do before latching the frame?" As you answer that question, another will be suggested, and then another—until you are back at the beginning, walking into the room with the film. You can also do the process yourself; as you do it, record every act you take. Then perform the task a second time, following your written notes exactly. You will quickly find whether or not you have included all the steps.

Name and Explain the Tasks

Having decided on the sequence, you name each task and explain any subtask or special information that accompanies it. The Dylux example has five subtasks labeled a to d under the task "Select the exposure channel," and many of the

Planning the Set of Instructions

steps include explanations for the audience. For instance, step 3d (p. 273) tells the user that channel 1 is for the black exposure.

Analyze Conditions

You must also analyze any special conditions that the user must know about. For instance, step 2 explains that the films must be emulsion to emulsion. Safety considerations are very important, and safety warnings are an essential part of many instructions. *If it will hurt them or the machine, tell the audience.* Warn the user not to touch a hot bulb and to turn off the machine before working on it.

Example of Process Analysis.

An easy way to conduct your analysis is to make a flow chart of the process. Put the steps in boxes and any notes in circles (see Figure 11.1).

Choose Visual Aids 选择视图

Visual aids either clarify or replace the prose explanation. Figure 2 in the Dylux example (p. 273) *replaces* text; to describe the position of the Memory button in words would take far more than the seven words used to convey the instruction.

The figure below *clarifies* the text—and reassures the readers that their actions are correct—by showing what the screen will look like as the actions occur on a computer.

> At the TO: prompt type their NAME, not their real name but their e-mail user name, and then press enter. The SUBJ: prompt will appear. (See Figure 1—note that you do not have to type in all capital letters, though you

```
mail>SEND
TO: SMITHJ
SUBJ: Learning e-mail
Enter your message below
```

Figure 1
On-Campus E-Mail Address

may.) On our system, the user name is generally the last name and the first one or two letters of the first name.

Here are a few guidelines for choosing visual aids:

- Use a visual aid to orient the reader. For instance, present a drawing of a keyboard with the return key highlighted.
- Use a visual aid to show the effect of an action. For instance, show what a screen looks like *after* the user enters a command.
- Decide whether you need one or two visual aids for the entire process or one visual aid per step. Use one per step if each step is complicated. Choose a clear drawing or photograph. (To determine which one to use, see Chapter 7.)
- Place the visual aid as close as possible to the relevant discussion, usually either below the text or to the left.
- Make each visual aid large enough. Do not skimp on size.
- Clearly identify each visual aid. Beneath each one, put a caption (e.g., *Figure 1. E-Mail Address* or *Fig. 1. E-Mail Address*).
- Refer to each visual aid at the appropriate place in the text.
- Use *callouts*—letters or words to indicate key parts. Draw a line or an arrow from each callout to the part.

Follow the Usual Form for Instructions 按照常规的指令方式

The usual form for a set of instructions is an introduction followed by a step-by-step body. The introduction states the purpose of the set of instructions, and the steps present all the actions in chronological order. The models at the end of this chapter illustrate these guidelines. Make a style sheet of all your decisions.

For steps and visual aids, use these guidelines:

- Place a highlighted (underlined or boldfaced) head at the beginning of each section.
- Number each step.
- Start the second and following lines of each step under the first letter of the first word in the first line.
- Use margins to indicate "relative weight"; show substeps by indenting to the right in outline style.
- Decide where you will place the visual aids. Usually place them to the left or below the text.
- Use white space above and below each step. Do not cramp the text.

For columns, the decisions are more complex. Basically, you can choose one or two columns, but their arrangement can vary, and each will have different effects on the reader. Figure 11.2 presents several basic layouts you can choose. You can place visual aids below or to the right or left of the text. To the left and below are very common places. Generally, you place to the left (text or visuals) whatever you want to emphasize.

Planning the Set of Instructions

Figure 11.2

Different Column Arrangements for Instructions

Writing the Set of Instructions 指令集的撰写

A clear set of instructions has an introduction and a body. After you have drafted them, you will be more confident that your instructions are clear if you field-test them.

Write an Effective Introduction 有效介绍的撰写

Although short introductions are the norm, you may want to include many different bits of information, depending on your analysis of the audience's knowledge level and of the demands of the process. You should always

- State the objective of the instructions for the reader.

Depending on the audience, you may also

- Define the process.
- Define important terms.
- List any necessary tools, materials, or conditions.
- Explain who needs to use the process.
- Explain where and/or when to perform the process.
- List assumptions you make about the audience's knowledge.

A Sample Introduction to a Set of Instructions

In the following introduction, note that the writer states the objective ("These instructions enable you to make a single- or multicolored Dylux"), defines the topic, lists knowledge assumptions, and lists materials.

MAKING A DYLUX PROOF

INTRODUCTION

End goal
Background

Knowledge assumption
Materials list

These instructions enable you to make a single- or multicolored Dylux. A Dylux proof is a single-color proof that uses different shades of blue to represent each of the process colors. A Dylux is used to check for copy content, layout, and position.

These instructions assume you know how to operate the integrator. Before you start, you need regular Scotch tape and films to proof.

Write an Effective Body 有效主体的撰写

The body consists of numbered steps arranged in chronological order. Construct the steps carefully, place the information in the correct order, use imperative verbs, and do not omit articles (*a*, *an*, and *the*) or prepositions.

TIP
Two Style Tips for Instructions

1. Use imperative verbs.

    An imperative verb gives an order. Imperative verbs make clear that the step must be done. Notice below that "should" introduces a note of uncertainty about whether the act must be performed.

    Say

    Turn on the exposure frame.

    Rather than

    You should turn on the exposure frame.

2. Retain the short words.

    Use *a*, *an*, *the* in all the usual places. Eliminating these "short words" often makes the instructions harder to grasp because it blurs the distinction between verbs, nouns, and adjectives.

    No short words:

    Using register marks on Dylux film, register film with image on Dylux.

    Short words added:

    Using the register marks on the Dylux film, register the film with the image on the Dylux.

Construct Steps Carefully

To make each step clear, follow these guidelines:

- Number each step.
- State only one action per number (although the effect of the action is often included in the step).
- Explain unusual effects.
- Give important rationales.
- Refer to visual aids.
- Make suggestions for avoiding or correcting mistakes.
- Place safety cautions before the instructions.

Review the Examples on pages 265–271 to see how the writers incorporated these guidelines. An example of how to write the body follows.

Sample Body

Here is the body of the set of instructions that follows the introduction on page 258.

PREPARATION

Head for sequence

1. Turn on the exposure frame. (See Figure 1.)

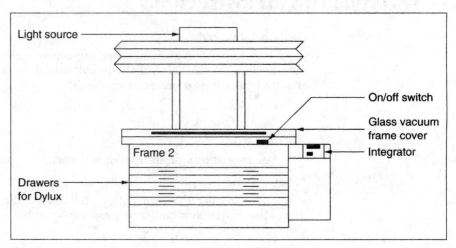

Figure 1
Exposure Frame

Instruction
Explanatory comment

Special condition

Action
Action

2. Lay your films on the work counter (emulsion down; emulsion side is the dull side) in the order in which you will proof them (first film to be exposed on top, and the last film to be exposed on the bottom—usually black, yellow, magenta, cyan).
3. Clean both sides of the glass on the vacuum frame using the glass cleaner and cheesecloth (located on a shelf to the left of frame 2).
4. Raise the glass cover on the vacuum frame.
5. Get one sheet of Dylux, large enough to hold the entire image. The Dylux paper can be found in the drawers under frame 2.

EXPOSING A SINGLE COLOR (OR THE FIRST COLOR IN A SERIES)

1. Lay the Dylux in the vacuum frame. The Dylux paper is two-sided, so it does not matter which side is up.
2. Place the film to be exposed on top of the Dylux. Black is usually the first color to be exposed. Film must be emulsion down, so Dylux and film are emulsion to emulsion.
3. Select the exposure channel for the first exposure.

Note that use of substeps keeps the number of main steps small

   a. Refer to the sheet listing the channels and what material each is set to expose. This sheet is posted above the integrator.
   b. Locate the proper channel on the sheet. There should be five channels on the Dylux: one channel for each of the four process colors (black, yellow, magenta, cyan) and one for clearing.
   c. Push the **Memory** button on the integrator. (See Figure 2.)

Writing the Set of Instructions

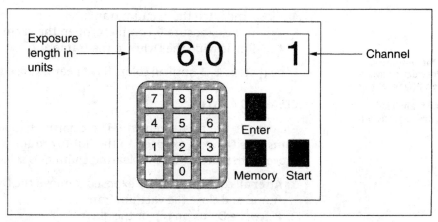

Figure 2
Integrator

      d. Key in the appropriate channel number on the number pad. (For example, channel 1 is for the black Dylux exposure.)
      e. Press the **Enter** button on the integrator. After you press **Enter,** the exposure time in units will appear in the top left display window.
4. Close and latch the vacuum frame.
   Note: The exposure starts when the frame is latched.
5. When the exposure is complete (when the overhead light goes out), open the vacuum frame and remove the film.
   Note: After this exposure there will be an image on the Dylux paper.

If You Have a Single-Color Proof

Remove the Dylux from the vacuum frame and skip to the "Clearing a Dylux" section.

If You Have a Multicolor Proof

Leave the Dylux in the frame and continue with the next section, "Exposing Additional Colors."

EXPOSING ADDITIONAL COLORS

The first exposure will image register marks onto the Dylux. From this point on, each film must be lined up (registered) to the register marks on the Dylux.

1. Place the next negative film (probably yellow) over the Dylux paper. Using the register marks on the Dylux and the film, register the film with the image on the Dylux.
2. Tape the Dylux and film together.
3. Select the proper exposure channel for the color you are exposing.

One sentence instruction avoids lengthy repetition

All main heads emphasize action

4. Close and latch the vacuum frame.
5. When the exposure is complete, open the vacuum frame and remove the film, leaving the Dylux in the frame.

Repeat steps 1–5 until all colors have been exposed.

CLEARING A DYLUX

Clearing is the final exposure. The clearing exposure is made without films. The Dylux is exposed to the light through a clearing filter, which moves into place when the clearing channel is selected.

1. After all colors have been exposed, remove the Dylux from the vacuum frame and close the vacuum frame.
2. Place the Dylux on top of the glass.
3. Select the channel for clearing a Dylux.
4. Push **Start** to clear the Dylux. (See Figure 2.)
5. Once the Dylux has been cleared, trim it according to the specifications on the job ticket.

Field-Testing Instructions 实地试验的指令

A field test is a method of direct observation by which you can check the accuracy of your instructions. To perform a field test, ask someone who is unfamiliar with the process to follow your instructions while you watch. If you have written the instructions correctly, the reader should be able to perform the entire activity without asking any questions. When you field-test instructions, keep a record of all the places where the reader hesitates or asks you a question.

Worksheet for Preparing Instructions

指令准备的工作表

☐ Assess the audience for these instructions.
  • Estimate the amount of knowledge the audience has about the process. Are they beginners or intermediates?
  • What will you tell the readers in the introduction? What will you assume about them? What do they need to know? What can they get from your instructions? How do they decide if they want to read your instructions? What will make them feel you are helpful and not just filling in lines for an assignment? How will you orient them to the situation?

☐ What is the end goal for your readers?

- ☐ Analyze the process.
  - Construct a flow chart that moves backward from the end goal.
  - Use as many boxes as you need.

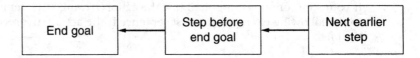

- ☐ List all the conditions that must be true for the end goal to occur. (For instance, what must be true for a document to open in a word processing program? The machine is turned on, the disk is inserted, the main menu appears, and the directory appears.)
- ☐ List all the words and terms that the audience might not know.
- ☐ List all the materials that a person must have in order to carry out the process.
- ☐ Where do the readers need a visual aid to "give them permission," or to orient them to the situation, or to show them something quickly that is easy to see but hard to describe in words?
- ☐ Draw the visual aids that will help readers grasp this process. Use visuals that illustrate the action or show the effect of the action.
- ☐ How will you arrange this material on the page so that it is easy for readers to read quickly, but also to keep their place or find it again as they read?
- ☐ Construct a style sheet. Choose your head system, margins, columns, method of treating individual steps, and style for writing captions.
- ☐ Convert the topic of each box in the flow chart into an imperative instruction. Add cautions, suggestions, and substeps. Decide whether a sequence of steps should be one step with several substeps or should be treated as individual steps.
- ☐ How will you tell them each step? How—and where—will you tell them results of a step? How—and where—will you tell them background or variations in a step?
- ☐ Why should you write them a set of instructions in the first place? Why not write them a short report or an article? A report tells the results of a project, an article informally explains the concepts related to a project, and a set of instructions tells how to do the project.

TIP
Information Order in a Step

If your step contains more than just the action, arrange the items as action-effect. In the following example, the first sentence is the action, the second sentence is the effect.

Press **Enter** on the integrator.
After you press **Enter**, the exposure time in units will appear in the top left display window.

If your step contains a caution or warning, place it first, before you tell the audience the action to perform.

1. CAUTION: DO NOT LIGHT THE MATCH DIRECTLY OVER THE BUNSEN BURNER!

Light the match and slowly bring it toward the top of the Bunsen burner.

Worksheet for Evaluating Instructions
评估指令的工作表

☐ Evaluate your work. Answer these questions:
  - Does the introduction tell what the instructions will enable the reader to do?
  - Does the introduction contain all the necessary information on special conditions, materials, and tools?
  - Is each step a single, clear action?
  - Does any step need more information—result of the action, safety warning, definitions, action hints?
  - Do the steps follow in a clear sequence?
  - Are appropriate visual aids present? Does any step either need or not need a visual aid?
  - Are the visual aids presented effectively (size, caption, position on page)?
  - Does the page layout help the reader?
  - Are all terms used consistently?

Examples 例子

The three examples that follow exemplify sets of instructions.

Example 11.1

Instructions for a Beginner

INSTRUCTIONS: HOW TO USE THE MODEL 6050 pH METER

Introduction

This set of instructions provides a step-by-step process to accurately test the pH of any given solution using the pH Meter Model 6050. The pH meter is designed primarily to measure pH or mV (millivolts) in grounded or ungrounded solutions. This set of instructions assumes that the pH meter is plugged in and that the electrode is immersed in a two-molar solution of potassium chloride.

Materials Needed

- Beaker containing 100 ml of 7.00 pH buffer solution
- Beaker containing 100 ml of 4.00 pH buffer solution
- Thermometer
- Squeeze bottle containing distilled water
- Four squares of lint-free tissue paper

How to Program the pH Meter

1. Press the button marked pH (A in Figure 1) to set the meter to pH mode.
2. Set pH sensitivity by pushing the pH sensitivity button down to .01 (B in Figure 1).
3. Gently remove the pH electrode (C in Figure 1) from the plastic bottle in which it is stored, and rinse it gently with distilled water from your squeeze bottle.
4. Carefully lower the electrode into the beaker containing the pH 7.00 buffer solution.
5. Set temperature control.
   a. Using the thermometer, take the temperature of pH 7.0 buffer solution.
   b. Turn the temperature dial (D in Figure 2) to the temperature reading on the thermometer in degrees Celsius.

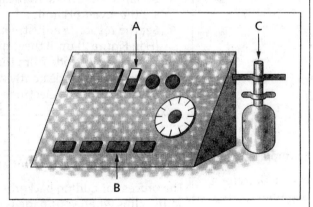

Figure 1
Sargent-Welch pH Meter Model 6050

(continued)

Example 11.1
(continued)

> 6. Set electrode asymmetry (intercept) by rotating the dial marked "intercept" (E in Figure 2) until the digital display (F in Figure 2) reads 7.00.
> 7. Raise the electrode from the 7.00 pH buffer solution, rinse gently with distilled water from your squeeze bottle, and dry tip of the electrode using lint-free tissue paper.
> 8. Lower the electrode (G in Figure 2) into the buffer solution of pH 4.00 to set the lower pH limit.
> 9. Set the response adjustment (slope) by rotating the dial marked "slope" (H in Figure 2) until the digital display reads 4.00.
> 10. Raise the electrode from the 4.00 pH buffer solution.
> 11. Rinse the electrode gently with distilled water from your squeeze bottle.
> 12. Dry the tip of the electrode using lint-free tissue paper.

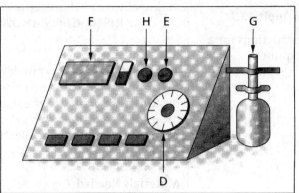

Figure 2
Sargent-Welch pH Meter Model 6050

Example 11.2
Instructions for a Beginner

> ### HOW TO ADD BACKGROUND SOUND TO A WEBPAGE
>
> The process of adding background sound to a website will allow you to hear sound clips when your page is opened in a browser. By adding background sound to your webpage, you will add excitement to your site! Consider using background sound that enhances the information on your site and is interesting and pleasing for the listeners. There are many different sound file types that you can use. Some of these file types include MIDI, RMF, RMI, WAV, and MOD. Prior to adding sound to an HTML document, you must have a sound file and an existing HTML document saved in the same directory.
>
> **To Add Background Sound to a Webpage**
>
> 1. Open Notepad by selecting **Start/Programs/Accessories/Notepad**.
> 2. Open an existing HTML file by selecting **File/Open** and then finding the HTML file to open.

3. Add the following code to the **BODY** section of the HTML file to add the music file **cheers.mid** to the background:

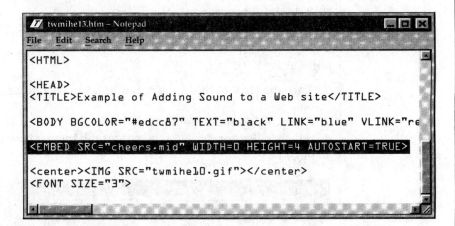

The **WIDTH** and **HEIGHT** parameters are set to small numbers so there will be no visual changes to the webpage. The **"AUTOSTART=TRUE"** statement is added so the sound will begin playing as soon as the webpage is opened in a browser.

4. Select **File/Save** to save the modified HTML document to your disk.

To View Your Modified File in Internet Explorer

1. Double-click on the **My Computer** icon on the desktop.
2. Double-click on the **3½ Floppy (A)** icon in the My Computer window.
3. Double-click on the **HTML file name** you modified to view your changes in Internet Explorer.

Example 11.3

Multiple-Section Instructions

Indentation Instructions for FrontPage

INTRODUCTION

This document is a set of instructions for using indentation in Microsoft FrontPage 2000. In order to use these instructions effectively, you must know how to start up FrontPage, create a new webpage, enter text into that webpage, and open menus such as "File," "Format," and "Help." The first instruction set, "Accessing a paragraph menu for a specific paragraph," is a required

(continued)

Example 11-3
(continued)

precursor to using the final three instruction sets. Read it first if you are not familiar with opening the paragraph menu for a specific paragraph. All italicized text is supplementary to the main instruction set and can be read at your discretion.

ACCESSING THE PARAGRAPH MENU

Method 1

1. Place the cursor within the paragraph you wish to perform indentation on.
2. Open the "Format" menu.
3. Left click "Paragraph...". (The paragraph menu shown in Figure 1 will open.)

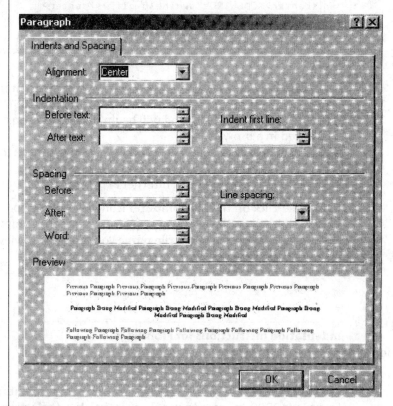

Figure 1
The FrontPage Paragraph Menu

Method 2

1. Right click within the paragraph on which you wish to perform indentation.

2. Left click "Paragraph..." from the pop-up menu. (The paragraph menu shown in Figure 1 will open.)

It is possible that the values seen in the entry boxes of your paragraph menu are different from those shown in Figure 1. This is not a problem, and quite normal.

LEFT-INDENTING THE FIRST LINE

Method

1. Access the paragraph menu for the paragraph you wish to perform indentation on. (The paragraph menu will open.)
2. In the "Indentation" subsection of the paragraph menu, locate the "Indent first line" box. (See Figure 2.)
3. Enter the size (in *points*) of the indentation into this box. (A number of points will now be shown in this box.)
4. Left-click the "OK" button on the paragraph menu. (The first line of the paragraph will be left-indented.)

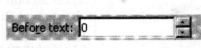

Figure 2
Indent First Line Box

When entering the value into the box, you can see an example of the effect in the "Preview" section of the paragraph menu shown in Figure 1.

LEFT-INDENTING A PARAGRAPH

Method

1. Access the paragraph menu for the paragraph you wish to perform indentation on.
2. In the "Indentation" subsection of the paragraph menu, locate the "Before text" box. (See Figure 3.)
3. Enter the size (in *points*) of the indentation into this box. (A number of points will now be shown in this box.)
4. Left-click the "OK" button on the paragraph menu. (The paragraph will be left-indented.)

Figure 3
Before Text Box

When entering the value into the box, you can see an example of the effect in the "Preview" section of the paragraph menu shown in Figure 1.

(continued)

Example 11.3

(continued)

RIGHT-INDENTING A PARAGRAPH

Method

1. Access the paragraph menu for the paragraph you wish to perform indentation on.
2. In the "Indentation" subsection of the paragraph menu, locate the "After text" box. (See Figure 4.)
3. Enter the size (in points) of the indentation into this box. (A number of points should now be in this box.)
4. Left-click the "OK" button on the paragraph menu. (The paragraph will be right-indented.)

Figure 4
After Text Box

The results of a right indent may not be apparent if your text does not extend to the right margin.

When entering the value into the box, you can see an example of the effect in the "Preview" section of the paragraph menu shown in Figure 1.

Example 11.4

Professional Instructions

Source: Elizabeth Castro, *HTML4 for the World Wide Web: Visual Quickstart Guide,* p. 38, © 1998. Republished by permission of Pearson Education, Inc. Publishing as Peachpit Press.

Understanding the HEAD and BODY

Most webpages are divided into two sections: the HEAD and the BODY. The HEAD section provides information about the URL of your webpage as well as its relationship with the other pages at your site. The only element in the HEAD section that is visible to the user is the title of the webpage (*see page 39*).

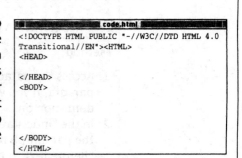

Figure 2.18
Every HTML document should be divided into a HEAD and a BODY.

To Create the HEAD Sections

1. Directly after the initial !DOCTYPE and HTML tags (*see page 37*), type **<HEAD>**.
2. Create the HEAD section, including the TITLE (*see page 39*). Add META information (*see pages 290–293*) and the BASE (*see page 113*), if desired.
3. Type **</HEAD>**.

The BODY of your HTML document contains the bulk of your webpage, including all the text, graphics, and formatting.

To Create the Body

1. After the final </HEAD> tag and before anything else, type <BODY>.
2. Create the contents of your webpage.
3. Type </BODY>.

Tip

For pages with frames, the BODY section is replaced by the FRAMESET.

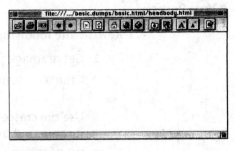

Figure 2.19
With no title and no contents, a browser has to scrape together a little substance (in the form of a title) from the file name of the HTML document.

Exercises 练 习

▶ **You Create**

1. Construct a visual aid that illustrates an action. For instance, show a jack properly positioned for changing a tire. Then write the instructions that would accompany that visual.

2. Write a set of instructions for a common activity, such as wrapping a package, tying a shoe, or programming a telephone. Choose one of the columnar formats shown in Figure 11.2 on page 257. Have a classmate try to perform the process by following your instructions. Discuss with the class the decisions you had to make to write the instructions. Consider word choice, layout, visual aids, sequence of steps, etc.

3. Make a flow chart or decision chart of a process. Choose an easy topic, such as a hobby, a campus activity, or some everyday task. In class, write the instructions that a person would need to perform the process. Depending on your instructor's preferences, you may either use your own chart or exchange charts with another student and write instructions for that student's chart.

▶ You Revise

4. Rewrite the following steps from the instructions for changing a car's oil:

    1. Get drainage pan and place it under the oil pan of the car.
    2. Grab a crescent wrench and locate the oil plug, on one side of the oil pan.
    3. Use the crescent wrench to turn the plug counterclockwise (ccw) until it comes out and oil drains out.
    4. While this is draining, grab a filter wrench and locate oil filter.
    5. Turn the oil filter counterclockwise with the filter wrench until it comes off and the oil drains into the drainage pan.

5. Rewrite the following steps from instructions for controlling text on a webpage. Draw visuals that would clarify the instructions. If you write these instructions on your computer, create screen captures that illustrate the steps.

    1. Pick the webpage that you want to do this to.
    2. Click on Table symbol, scroll down to darken in one box, and then click on that box.
    3. Double-right-click on the table anywhere and another window should pop up like the one below. On this table you want to click on Table Properties . . .

    Once you have completed step three you will see the box below.

    4. In this box you need to make the border Size 0 like I have done here and click "Apply." This will make your table look like this.
    5. Highlight your **whole** page by putting your curser at the very top and scrolling down selecting everything. This should change some of the background color and shows how much you have highlighted.
    6. Click on "Edit" and scroll down to "Copy". After you click on this put your curser into the table that you made after step four.
    7. Go back to "Edit" and this time select "Paste."

    This will place your whole webpage inside of the table and you will not be able to see the boarder of the table on the web like you can see it now.

    8. Erase your old webpage and you are done!

6. Convert the following paragraphs into a set of instructions:

    First I went to the website www.uwstout.edu/place/studentwebregistration.html to read the general instructions given by the Co-op and Placement Office to reach the new website and log in to my profile. I was directed to www.uwstout.edu/place/ and was instructed to click on the *"Students create or update your eRecruiting profile"* link to enter the log-in screen. The username is the last 5 digits of my ID number with the word *"stout"* added on the end, and the password is the last 4 digits.

I next chose to enter my personal information by clicking on the *"Edit your profile"* link. There are then options to update *"Personal Info, Academics, Future Plans,"* and *"Administration"* links to choose. In each of these, I either typed in information about myself, my education, my qualifications, and plans or chose information from drop-down lists containing possible options. As each section was completed, more information about me was saved in my profile.

After finishing entering personal information, I chose to post my résumé online. I clicked on the *"Documents"* link and read the instructions there to upload files. After clicking on *"Upload Documents"* and choosing *"Résumé,"* I was instructed to type in the name of the file containing my résumé or search for it among the folders on my computer and push *"Upload."*

7. Rewrite all of the items in Exercise 4 from the point of view of a "chatty help" columnist in a newspaper. Use paragraphs, not numbered steps.
8. Rewrite Example 11.3 as a report structured in paragraphs.

▶ Group

9. Compare Example 11.2 with Example 12.2 (pp. 297–298). In groups of three or four, discuss the differences in tone and in the presentation of the action. Report to the class which document you prefer to read and why.
10. For Writing Assignment 1 or 2, construct a flow chart of the process. Explain it to a small peer group who question you closely, causing you to explain the steps in detail. Revise the chart based on this discussion.
11. For Writing Assignment 1 or 2, create a template for your instructions, including methods for handling heads, introduction, steps, visual aids, captions, and columns. Review this template with your peer group, explaining why you have made the choices you have. Your peer group will edit the template for consistency and effectiveness.
12. For Writing Assignment 1 or 2, bring the final draft of your instructions to your peer group. Choose a person to field test. With your instructor's permission, field-test each other's instructions. Note every place where your classmate hesitates or asks a question, and revise your instructions accordingly.
13. Bring an article instruction to class. Computer and household magazines offer the best sources for these articles. In groups of three or four, analyze the models and decide why the authors decided to use the article method. Depending on your instructor, either report your analysis to the class, or as a group rewrite the instructions, either with a different tone (say, as a coach) or as a numbered set.

Writing Assignments 写作任务

1. Write a set of instructions for a process you know well. Fill out the worksheet and then write the instructions. Use visual aids and design your pages effectively, using one of the columnar formats shown on page 269. Pick a process that a beginning student in your major will have to perform or choose something that you do as a hobby or at a job, such as waxing skis, developing film, ringing up a sale, or taking inventory.
2. Divide into groups of three or four. Pick a topic that everyone knows, such as checking books out of the library, applying for financial aid, reserving a meeting room, operating an LCD projector, replacing a lost ID or driver's license, or appealing a grade. Then each team should write a set of instructions for that process. Complete the worksheet on pages 262–263. When you are finished, decide which team's set is best in terms of design, clarity of steps, and introduction.
3. Write a learning report for the writing assignment you just completed. See Chapter 5, Writing Assignment 7, page 133, for details of the assignment.

Web Exercises 网络练习

1. Give instructions to a beginner on how to create a webpage using a wizard, template, or Web-authoring tool with which you are familiar.
2. Convert the process paper that you wrote for Chapter 10, Web Exercise 3, into a set of instructions for a beginner.

Work Cited 引用的作品

Castro, Elizabeth. *HTML for the World Wide Web*. Berkeley, CA: Peachpit, 1998.

Chapter 12: Memorandums and Informal Reports
备忘录和非正式报告

Chapter Contents
- Chapter 12 In a Nutshell
- The Elements of Memos
- The Elements of Informal Reports
- Types of Informal Reports
- Focus on E-Mail
- Ethics and E-Mail

Chapter 12 In a Nutshell 概　要

Memos. A memo is any document (regardless of length) that has memo heads (Date, To, From, Subject) at the top. The subject line should relate the contents to the reader's needs.

Informal reports. Informal reports are usually short (1 to 10 pages). Their goal is to convey the message in an understandable context, from a credible person, in clear, easy-to-read text.

Informal report structure. The informal report structure is the IMRD (Introduction, Method, Results, and Discussion).

The *Introduction* explains your goal and why this situation has developed.

The *Method* outlines what you did to find out about the situation. It establishes your credibility.

The *Results* establish what you found out, the information the reader can use.

The *Discussion* describes the implications of the information. It gives the reader a new context.

Informal report strategies. Key strategies include

- Explain your purpose—what your reader will get from the report.
- Use a top-down strategy.
- Develop a clear visual logic.
- Provide the contents in an easy-to-grasp sequence and help the reader out by defining, using analogies, and explaining the significance to the person or organization.

Chapter 12 Memorandums and Informal Reports

The day-to-day operation of a company depends on memos and informal reports that circulate within and among its departments. These documents report on various problems and present information about products, methods, and equipment. The basic informal format, easy to use in nearly any situation, has been adapted to many purposes throughout industry.

This chapter explains the elements of memos, the elements of informal reports, and the types of informal reports, including analytical reports, IMRD reports, progress reports, and outline reports.

The Elements of Memos   备忘录的组成

Memos are used to report everything from results of tests to announcements of meetings. In industry you must write memos clearly and quickly. Your ability to do so tells a reader a great deal about your abilities as a problem solver and decision maker. This section explains memo headings and provides a sample memo report.

Memo Headings   备忘录的抬头

The memo format consists of specific lines placed at the top of a page: *To, From, Subject,* and *Date* lines. That's all there is to it. What follows below those lines is a memo report. Usually such a report is brief—from one or two sentences to one or two pages. Theoretically there is no limit to a memo's length, but in practice such reports are seldom longer than four or five pages.

Follow these guidelines to set up a memo or memo report:

1. If using a preprinted form, fill in the blanks; if not, follow guidelines 2–5.

2. Place the To, From, and Subject lines at the left margin.

3. Place the date either to the right, without a head, or at the top of the list with a head (Date:).

4. Follow each item with a colon and the appropriate information.

5. Choose a method of capitalization and placement of colons (see examples).

6. Name the contents or main point in the subject line.

7. Place the names of those people who are to receive copies below the name of the main recipient (usually with the head cc:).

8. Sign to the right of your typed name.

The Elements of Memos

Memo Format: Example 1

| | | February 14, 2007 |

Date on far right

Copy line
Signature

To:	E. J. Mentzer
cc:	Jane Thompson
From:	Judy Davis *Judy Davis*

Subject line—only first letters capitalized

| Subject: | Remodeling of Office Complex |

Memo Format: Example 2

Date line
Memo heads in all caps
Signature

DATE:	February 14, 2007
TO:	E. J. Mentzer
FROM:	Judy Davis *Judy Davis*

Subject line capitalized for emphasis

| SUBJECT: | REMODELING OF OFFICE COMPLEX |

Memo Format: Example 3

March 29, 2007

Memo heads aligned on colons

| To: | E. J. Mentzer |
| From: | Judy Davis *Judy Davis* |

| Subject: | Remodeling of Office Complex |

A Sample Memo Report   备忘录样本

A memo can contain any kind of information that your audience needs. The following memo is a recommendation based on criteria.

April 1, 2007

To:	Bill Foresight
From:	Carol Frank, Food Service Director
Subject:	Purchase of an open-top range

Purpose of memo
Credibility of writer

Basic conclusion first

Data to support conclusion
Four criteria: cost, energy efficiency, rating, design features

Here is a preliminary recommendation on which brand of open-top range to purchase for the Food Service Department. After comparing the specification sheets of several brands, I found that two brands satisfy our needs: Montague and Franklin, but Montague is the better choice.

    The Montague is cheaper ($499 vs. $512). It is more energy efficient; it has an overall rating of 103,000 BTU/hour, whereas the Franklin has a rating of 138,000 BTU/hour. The Montague has several design features not found on the Franklin, including a 3-position rack, a removable oven bottom, a continuous-cleaning oven, and a solid hot top. I will provide a detailed report next week.

The Elements of Informal Reports 非正式报告的组成

Informal reports are those that will not have wide distribution, will not be published, and are shorter than 10 pages (General Motors). This kind of report follows a fairly standard format that can be adapted to many situations, from presenting background to recommending and proposing. The format basically has two parts: an introduction and a discussion.

Introduction 介 绍

Introductions orient readers to the contents of the document. You can choose from several options, basing your decision on the audience's knowledge level and community attitudes. To create an introduction, you can do one of three things: provide the objective, provide context, or provide an expanded context.

Provide the Objective

The basic informal introduction is a one-sentence statement of the purpose or main point of the project or report, sometimes of both. This type of introduction is appropriate for almost all situations and readers.

Objective of the project	To evaluate whether the customer service counter should install an Iconglow personal computer system
Objective of the report	To report on investigation of the feasibility of installing an Iconglow personal computer system at the customer service counter

If this statement is enough for your readers, go right into the discussion. If not, add context sections as explained below.

Provide Context

To provide *context* for a report means to explain the situation that caused you to write the report. This type of introduction is an excellent way to begin informal reports. It is especially helpful for readers who are unfamiliar with the project. Include four pieces of information: cause, credibility, purpose, and preview. Follow these guidelines:

- Tell what caused you to write. Perhaps you are reporting on an assignment, or you may have discovered something the recipient needs to know.
- Explain why you are credible in the situation. You are credible because of either your actions or your position.
- State the report's purpose. Use one clear sentence: "This report recommends that customer service should install an Iconglow computer system."
- Preview the contents. List the main heads that will follow.

Here is a sample basic introduction.

<table>
<tr><td>Cause for writing

Source of credibility

Purpose
Preview</td><td>I am responding to your recent request that I determine whether customer service should install an Iconglow computer system. In gathering this information, I interviewed John Broderick, the Iconglow Regional Sales Representative. He reviewed records of basic personnel activities. This report recommends that customer service install an Iconglow system. I base the recommendation on cost, space, training, and customer relations.</td></tr>
</table>

Special Case: Alert the Reader to a Problem. Sometimes the easiest way to provide context is to set up a problem statement. Use one of the following methods:

- Contrast a general truth (positive) with the problem (negative).
- Contrast the problem (negative) with a proposed solution (positive).

In either case, point out the significance of the problem or the solution. If you cast the problem as a negative, show how it violates some expected norm. If you are proposing a solution, point out its positive effect. Here is a sample problem-solution introduction.

<table>
<tr><td>Negative problem and its significance

Proposed solution
Positive significance
Purpose of report</td><td>Processing customers at the service desk is a time-consuming process. The service representative fills out three different forms while the customer and those in line wait, annoyed. Some customers go elsewhere to shop. An Iconglow computer system would eliminate the waiting, cutting average service time from 10 minutes to 1 minute. This report recommends that we purchase the Iconglow system.</td></tr>
</table>

Provide an Expanded Context

To provide an expanded context, create a several-paragraph introduction. You must include a purpose or an objective, and then add other sections that you might need: a summary, a background, a conclusions/recommendation section, or a combination of them.

The *summary*—also called an "abstract" or sometimes "executive summary"—is a one-to-one miniaturization of the discussion section. If the discussion section has three parts, the summary has three statements, each giving the major point of one of the sections. After reading this section, the reader should have the gist of your report.

The *background statement* gives the reader a context by explaining the project's methodology or history. If the report has only an objective statement, this section orients the reader to the material in the report.

Writers present the *conclusions and/or recommendations* early in the report because this section contains the basic information that readers need. It can provide information that differs from the summary, but it replaces the summary.

Examples of Introductory Options

VERSION 1

Objective

Objective

To evaluate whether to install an Iconglow system at the customer service counter.

Conclusions and Recommendation

Context

1. The system will pay for itself in one year.
2. The office area contains ample space for the system.
3. The system will not interfere with attending to customers.

I recommend that we install the Iconglow System.

Background

Context

Customer service proposed installation of an Iconglow system to handle all updating functions. The system would reduce the number of employee hours required to complete these functions. The system includes two computers, a printer, programs, and cables. I reviewed personnel figures and discussed the proposal with Iconglow's sales representative.

VERSION 2

Introduction

Cause for writing

Source of credibility

Purpose
Preview

I am responding to your recent request that I determine whether customer service should install an Iconglow computer system. In gathering this information, I interviewed John Broderick, the Iconglow Regional Sales Representative. He reviewed records of basic personnel activities. This report recommends that customer service install an Iconglow system. I base the recommendation on cost, space, training, and customer relations.

Conclusions

1. The system will pay for itself in one year.
2. The office area contains ample space for the system.
3. The system will not interfere with attending to customers.

Discussion 讨 论

The discussion section contains the more detailed, full information of the report. Writers subdivide this section with heads, use visual aids, and sometimes give the discussion its own introduction and conclusion. If you write the introduction well, your reader will find no surprises, just more depth, in the introduction.

The Elements of Informal Reports

Two format concerns that arise in planning the discussion section are pagination and heads.

Pagination

Paginate informal reports either with just a page number or with header information as well. Follow these guidelines:

- If you use just page numbers, place them in the upper right corner or in the bottom center.
- If you use header information, arrange the various elements across the top of the page. Generally, the page number goes to the far right and other information (report title, report number, recipient, and/or date) appears to the left.

Iconglow Recommendation   12/24/07   2

Heads

Informal reports almost always contain heads. Usually you need only one level; the most commonly used format is the "side left." Follow these guidelines:

- Place heads at the left margin, triple-spaced above and double-spaced below. Use underline or boldface.
- Capitalize only the first letter of each main word (do not capitalize *a, an, the,* or prepositions).
- Do not punctuate after heads (unless you ask a question).
- Use a word or phrase that indicates the contents immediately following.
- At times, use a question for an effective head.

Side left, boldface
Double-space

Will the New System Save Money?

The new Iconglow system will pay for itself within 6 months. Currently, employees spend 87 hours a month updating files. The new system will reduce that figure to 27, a savings of 60 hours. These 60 hours represent a payroll savings of $435.00 a month. Because the new system costs $2450, the savings alone will pay for the system in 6 months ($435 \times 6 = 2610$). This amount of time is under the 1-year period allowed for recovery.

Triple space

Double-space

Is There Enough Space for the System?

The computers will easily fit in their allocated spaces. One computer and the printer will occupy space at the refund desk, and the other computer will sit on the customer service counter. Both areas were reorganized to accommodate the machine and allow for efficient work flow.

Will the Computers Affect Customer Relations?

The Iconglow system will allow employees to process customer complaints more quickly, reducing a 15-minute wait to seconds. This speeded-up handling of problems will eliminate customer complaints about standing in line.

Types of Informal Reports 非正式报告的类型

Writers use informal reports in many situations. This section introduces you to several variations.

IMRD Reports IMRD 报告

An IMRD (*I*ntroduction, *M*ethodology, *R*esults, *D*iscussion) report is a standard way to present information that is the result of some kind of research. This approach can present laboratory research, questionnaire results, or the results of any action whose goal is to find out about a topic and discuss the significance of what was discovered. The IMRD report causes you to tell a story about your project in a way that most readers will find satisfying. This kind of report allows you to provide new knowledge for a reader and to fit that knowledge into a bigger context. Your research project started out with some kind of question that you investigated in a certain way. You found information, and you explain that the information is important in various ways.

▸ For the *introduction*, present the question you investigated (the goal of the project) and the point of the paper. It is helpful to give a general answer to the question. Consider these questions:
  • What is the goal of this project?
  • What is the goal of this report?

▸ For the *methodology section*, write a process description of your actions and why you performed those actions. This section establishes your credibility. Explain such things as whom you talked to, and describe any actions you took and why. This description should allow a reader to replicate your actions. Consider these questions:
  • What steps or actions did you take to achieve the goal or answer the questions? (Explain all your actions. Arrange them in sequence, if necessary.)
  • Why did you perform those actions?

▸ For the *results section*, tell what you discovered, usually by presenting a table or graph of the data. If a visual aid is all you need in this section, combine it with the discussion section. If you add text, tell the readers what to focus on in the results. Honesty requires that you point out material that might contradict what you expected to discover. Consider these questions:
  • What are the results of each action or sequence?

- Can I present the results in one visual aid?
- In the *discussion section,* explain the significance of what you found out. Either interpret it by relating it to some other important concept or suggest its causes or effects. Relate the results to the problem or concerns you mentioned in the introduction. If the method affects the results, tell how and suggest changes. Often you can suggest or recommend further actions at the end of this section. Consider these questions:
  - Did you achieve your goal? (If you didn't, say so, and explain why.)
  - What are the implications of your results? for you and your goals? for other people and their goals?
  - What new questions do your results raise?

THE HISTORY OF HTML

IMRD Report

INTRODUCTION

The goal of this IMRD Report is to describe my research for my history of HTML (*HyperText Markup Language*) research report. The goal of this project is to produce an HTML document that describes the history of HTML. This report will inform the reader of the methods used to obtain the information for the report, the results of the application of the methods, and questions that arise because of the results.

Importance of HTML's History

The history of HTML is important to anyone who wants to know more about how and why the Internet works. HTML is the language per se of the Internet. Documents on the Net are written using HTML or using an editor that places the HTML into the document. Knowing why HTML was created, how it has developed, and why it has changed are all important points in understanding why the Internet has developed as it has. The functionality and limits of HTML dictate how we can illustrate our ideas on the Internet and how we view the ideas of others.

METHODS

Internet Searches

The methods used in my research consisted exclusively of Internet searches, and my goal was to collect enough information to write a document on the history of HTML. I chose to use the Internet because HTML has been related to the World Wide Web since its inception, and, hence, much of its history can be found on-line. The primary search engines I used were Google and Metacrawler. Search terms/phrases used to locate information in conjunction with both of these search engines were

"HTML History," "History of HTML," "W3C," and "CERN." Using these search terms in both search engines produced a multitude of results, of which I had to choose the most pertinent.

Drilling for Information

After using these search engines to locate pertinent sites, I had to drill down through these sites to locate more specific information. This consisted of looking for specific dates, places, and names that had to do with the development of HTML. Each time I found a page that gave me specific information that I thought would be useful, I used Internet Explorer's Favorite menu to bookmark the page for later use in writing my report.

RESULTS

The application of my methods yielded a plethora of information on the history of HTML. Specific information on how HTML originated at CERN (Conseil Européen pour la Recherche Nucléaire) and how HTML was originally proposed by Tim Berners-Lee was helpful in formulating the early history of HTML. I was also able to find two different time lines of the development of HTML on two independent sites. All of the pages that I found and used for information are listed in Figure 1. The webpage title,

Webpage	Description
The Early History of HTML	This page covers HTML history from 1990 to 1992.
HTML History	This page covers all of HTML's specifications as well as cascading style sheets.
The History of HTML	This page covers basic terminology associated with HTML and the origin of HTML at CERN.
HTML Overview	This page contains an excellent glossary of terms as well as an HTML time line and narrative on the early development of HTML. It also contains links to the different HTML specifications.
Some Early Ideas for HTML	This page contains information on hypertext systems that came before HTML and gives a description of what hypertext is. It is published by the current HTML regulatory agency, the W3C (World Wide Web Consortium).
The History of HTML	This page contains a description of each version for HTML, what changed from version to version, and why.
What Is HyperText	This page contains a description of hypertext.
Quick HTML History	This page contains a small time line of HTML's history.

Figure 1
Useful Webpages

which is also a link to that page, as well as a short description of each page, can be found there.

DISCUSSION

The results above show I have met my goal for information collection, and I am now prepared to write my HTML history. My information, while answering many of my questions, raised more. These questions need further study: Why did HTML became so popular, while other hypertext systems did not? Why did certain browsers such as Mosaic outclass other browsers to such a great degree?

Brief Analytical Reports   简要分析报告

Brief analytical reports are very common in industry. Writers review an issue with the goal of revealing important factors in the issue and of presenting relevant conclusions. The two reports below illustrate varied uses of this form.

CREDIBLE RESOURCES AVAILABLE FOR USE BY DIETITIANS

INTRODUCTION

The use of computers and the Internet has become a part of the daily life of most Americans. As dietetics professionals, being aware of the resources available on the World Wide Web is necessary. Dietitians can access nutrition education materials, current legislation information, job opportunities, government programs, disease/disorder information, and more with the click of a button.

FINDING CREDIBLE RESOURCES

When doing a simple Internet search using the search engine Google and using the keywords "dietetics" or "dietitian," several Web matches appear. When utilizing Web resources, it is important to use the CAR (Credibility, Accuracy, and Reliability) method to determine whether the information provided is appropriate for use in one's practice. The CAR method was utilized reviewing websites related to dietetics. All websites described in this report passed the CAR examination. A summary of the findings are given in Table 1.

WEB RESOURCES AVAILABLE

Government Sites

The most detailed and reliable information found on the Internet came from government resources. The website www.nutrition.gov is the official nutrition site for the United States government. This site links to all nutrition-related information, ranging from food safety and security to diabetes and disease management. The best part of this site is that it links to all federal nutrition programs. These sites give important information as well as provide the ability to download and print forms. Nutrition education, tools and resources are also available on this site. The second government site, agriculture.senate.gov, provides archived federal bills as well as current legislation regarding nutrition, forestry, and agriculture.

Professional Sites

Professional websites that provided many links and extremely reliable information include www.webdietitian.com and www.eatright.org. Both websites contain a wide variety of resources beneficial to dietitians, ranging from current nutrition issues to patient education materials.

The website dietetics.co.uk is a message board forum for dietitians across the world. It is based in the United Kingdom. Dietetics professionals can post and reply to message boards dealing with all aspects of the dietetics profession, including enteral/parenteral feedings, professional issues, nutrition assessment and screening, freelance and private practice dietetics, and more.

Dietetics.com houses links to state and national dietetic associations, antiquackery information, and other basic information to help the dietetic professional.

Dietetic Career Searches

The American Dietetic Association has a career link page that is a national database of current openings in the field of dietetics. A search can be narrowed by choosing an area of discipline or choosing by location. However, the career link is not extensive at this point and does not offer many positions.

The site Jobs in Dietetics, jobsindietetics.com, offers a nationwide career search. There is a membership charge for utilizing this Web resource. Its member-only approach makes it impossible to summarize its usability or quality.

RESULTS OF QUERY

Table 1 summarizes the above paragraphs. The websites were placed into three categories: professional, government, and career search. It was noted whether the website provided outside links. The availability of links on pages was taken into consideration in the overall rating of the quality and usefulness of the websites. Based on the CAR analysis, each site was scored with a 1 to 5 rating with 5 being the highest quality and most beneficial to dietetic practitioners.

Table 1

Summary of Dietetics Resources on the Web

Name of Site	Web Address	Category	Links Available?	Rating (5 = best)
American Dietetic Association	www.eatright.org	Professional	Yes! Many	5
Web Dietitian	webdietitian.com	Professional	Yes! Many	5
U.S. Senate Committee on Agriculture, Forestry, and Nutrition	agriculture.senate.gov	Government	Yes! Some not nutrition related.	4
Nutrition.Gov	www.nutrition.gov	Government	Yes! Many	5
American Dietetic Association Career Link	www.adacareerlink.org	Dietetic Career Search	Yes! Other medical career searches	3
Jobs in Dietetics	jobsindietetics.com	Dietetic Career Search	No	2
Dietetics.Com	dietetics.com	Professional	Yes	3
Nutrition and Dietetics Forum	dietetics.co.uk	Professional	No	3

CONCLUSION

There are many beneficial resources available to dietetic professionals on the World Wide Web. When viewing websites; it is important to keep the CAR (Credibility, Accuracy, and Reliability) method in mind. Professional, government, and dietetic career search capabilities can be found and utilized easily using the Internet. Becoming familiar with this process will enhance the dietetic professional.

Resources

American Dietetic Association. 5 Nov. 2002 <www.eatright.org> (November 5, 2002).

American Dietetic Association Career Link. 7 Nov. 2002 <www.adacareerlink.org> (November 7, 2002).

Dietetics.Com. 5 Nov. 2002 <http://dietetics.com> (November 5, 2002).

Jobs in Dietetics. 5 Nov. 2002 <http://jobsindietetics.com> (November 5, 2002).

Nutrition and Dietetics Forum. 6 Nov. 2002 <http://dietetics.co.uk> (November 6, 2002).

Nutrition.Gov. 6 Nov. 2002 <http://nutrition.gov> (November 6, 2002).

U.S. Senate Committee on Agriculture, Forestry, and Nutrition. 7 Nov. 2002 <http://agriculture.senate.gov> (November 7, 2002).

Web Dietitian. 5 Nov. 2002 <www.webdietitian.com> (November 5, 2002).

CHIPPEWAVALLEYHELPWANTED.COM VERSUS MONSTER.COM
Content Analysis

INTRODUCTION

This section deals with the content of the job search websites Chippewa ValleyHelpWanted.com and Monster.com. I researched the number of ways to apply for a job on each website, the number of available job results for several cities, and the general length of the job descriptions from these results.

WAYS TO APPLY

I found that the two websites had similar methods for applying for jobs. Monster.com has one more option, as shown in the following table, but otherwise the sites were comparable in this aspect. There is more information about some companies listed in Monster.com that isn't included in the other website that may be helpful in deciding whether a company would be a desirable place to apply and work for the future.

	Post Résumé for Free	Automatically Send Résumé to Chosen Employers	Company E-Mail Addresses/ Web Links	View All Company Job Opportunities	Learn About Company
ChippewaValley HelpWanted.com	X	X	X	X	
Monster.com	X	X	X	X	X

NUMBER OF JOBS LISTED

The following table illustrates the number of jobs that are listed for certain cities in the central Wisconsin area as well as the total number of jobs listed for the area. Monster.com had many more jobs by far, but often didn't have jobs listed in smaller cities that ChippewaValleyHelpWanted.com did include. The larger database of jobs would be beneficial for those looking for jobs in larger cities or just in the area in general, while listings for smaller cities would be helpful to those searching for a job in a specific area that may not be as populated.

	Menomonie	Eau Claire	Chippewa Falls	Madison	Total
ChippewaValley HelpWanted.com	1	19	2	1	32
Monster.com	0	74	1	>400	654

LENGTH OF JOB DESCRIPTIONS

I looked at postings for the same job on both websites and compared the information that the posting included and found that the basic information was the same, but Monster.com had more specific details, such as salary ranges, position types, and a reference code to easily distinguish the particular job from others listed by the same company. Depending on the focus of a person's job search, this information may be a key factor in deciding whether to apply for a job. Once again, if the major deciding factor in applying for a job is based on location or job type, ChippewaValley HelpWanted.com provided this information and would be an adequate resource for job searching.

CONCLUSION

I have found ChippewaValleyHelpWanted.com and Monster.com to provide much of the same information in their job search functions. Monster.com contained more information about companies and a larger listing of available jobs, but the majority of jobs were located in larger cities. ChippewaValley HelpWanted.com seemed to be targeted more for people looking for jobs specifically in this area and included job listings for smaller towns that were not included in the other website.

Sources

ChippewaValleyHelpWanted.com
Monster.com

Progress Reports 进程报告

Progress reports inform management about the status of a project. Submitted regularly throughout the life of the project, they let the readers know whether work is progressing satisfactorily—that is, within the project's budget and time limitations. To write an effective progress report, follow the usual process. Evaluate your audience's knowledge and needs. Determine how much they know, what they expect to find in your report, and how they will use the information. Select the topics you will cover. The standard sections are the following:

- Introduction
- Work Completed
- Work Scheduled
- Problems

In the Introduction, name the project, define the time period covered by the report, and state the purpose: to inform readers about the current status of the project. In the Work Completed section, specify the time period, divide the project into major tasks, and report the appropriate details. In the Work Scheduled section, explain the work that will occur on each major task in the next time period. In the Problems section, discuss any special topics that require the reader's attention.

PROGRESS REPORT

Date: March 29, 2006
To: Dan Riordan, Practicum Manager
From: Julia Seeger
Subject: Progress Report on Construction Manual

SUMMARY

I am working on developing a user manual for the Universal Test Machine, TestWorks QT, for the UW-Stout Construction Lab. Tests have been modified for the students' use, which will require a new set of instructions. The instructions will be designed to help guide the student through machine setup, starting up the TestWorks QT software program, running the test, and proper shutdown.

WORK COMPLETED

The client and I have decided that the manual will be hard copy, 5.5" × 8", bound with a plastic spiral. Each step of the process will include an illustration. The client decided that the manual would include instructions for three different types of tests: Bending, Compression, and Tensile. I have written instructions for the Compression test. Additional information will be added after the client reviews the instructions. Thursday, March 28, I met with the client in the construction lab where approximately 15 photos were taken for the Tensile, Compression, and Bending tests. All photos will use JPG format.

WORK SCHEDULED

Digital photos of the Bending, Compression, and Tensile tests will be viewed and enhanced using Photoshop. I plan to have the photos prepared and sent to the client by Wednesday to view and approve.

The next client meeting occurs on April 6. After that meeting I will develop the written instructions. The client will receive the rough draft of the instructions by April 15.

PROBLEMS

The Universal Test machine is scheduled to be used for classes during the only hours I have free to conduct usability testing in the instructions. At present no students have agreed to serve as usability testers. I will work with the lab instructor to resolve these issues.

Outline Reports 大纲报告

An expanded outline is a common type of report, set up like a résumé, with distinct headings. This form often accompanies an oral presentation. The speaker follows the outline, explaining details at the appropriate places. Procedural specifications and retail management reports often use this form. The brevity of the form allows the writer to condense material, but of course the reader must be able to comprehend the condensed information. To write this kind of report, follow these guidelines:

- Use heads to indicate sections *and* to function as introductions.
- Present information in phrases or sentences, not paragraphs.
- Indent information (as in an outline) underneath the appropriate head.

Sample Outline Report

REPLACE GYMNASIUM FLOORING?
December 10, 2007

Researcher: Aaron Santana

Side heads serve as introductions to each section

Purpose: Evaluate whether Athletic Department should install new flooring in the Memorial Gymnasium.

Method: Interview Athletic Director, Athletic Trainer, vendors. Used these criteria:

Essential material presented in phrases and lists

- Cost—not to exceed 250K
- Time—less than 3 months
- Benefits—personal health and overall usage must be impacted

Conclusions: Gym floors meet all criteria

- Cost is less than 250K allocated
- Time to install is less than 3 months
- Benefits—fewer injuries; likelihood of increased usage with greater durability.

Recommendation: Install the new floor.

Worksheet for Planning a Project 项目计划工作表

☐ Write the question you want answered.

☐ Create a research plan.
  a. List topics and keywords that might help you find information on your question

(continued)

(continued)

    b. List a method for finding out about those topics. Tell which specific acts you will undertake. E.g., "Explore Compendex and Ebscohost using X and Y as keywords." or "Talk to all employees affected by the change, using questions X and Y."

☐ Carry out your plan.

Worksheet for IMRD Reports

IMRD报告工作表

☐ Write an introduction in which you briefly describe the goal of your project and your goal in this report. Give enough information to orient a reader to your situation.

☐ Write the methods statement.
- Name the actions that you took in enough detail so that a reader could replicate the acts if necessary.
- Use terms and details at a level appropriate to the reader, but necessary for the subject.
- Explain *why* you chose this strategy or actions.

☐ Name the actual results of the actions. This section might be very short.

☐ Tell the significance of your actions.
- What do the results indicate?
- How do the results relate to the audience concerns?
- What will you do next, as a result of this project?
- Did you accomplish your goals?
- How is this important to your classmates, in this class?

☐ Develop a style sheet for your report.
- How will you handle heads?
- How will you handle chunks?
- How will you handle page numbers?
- How will you handle visual aids?
- How will you handle the title/memo heads?

☐ Develop an idea of how you will present yourself.
- Will you write in the first person?
- Will you call the reader "you"?
- Will you write short or long sentences?
- Are you an expert? How do experts sound? What will you do to make yourself sound like one?
- *Key question:* Why should I believe you? Why are you credible?

Worksheet for Informal Reports
非正式报告工作表

- ☐ Identify the audience.
  - Who will receive this report?
  - How familiar are they with the topic?
  - How will the audience use this report?
  - What type of report does your audience expect in this situation (lengthier prose? outline? lots of design? just gray?)
- ☐ Determine your schedule for completing the report.
- ☐ Determine how you will prove your credibility.
- ☐ Outline the discussion section. Will this section contain background? Divide the section into appropriate subsections.
- ☐ For IMRDs, outline each of the three body sections.
  - Clearly distinguish methods and results.
  - In the discussion, relate results to the audience's concerns.
- ☐ Prepare the visual aids you need.
  - What function will the visuals serve for the reader?
  - What type of visual aid will best convey your message?
- ☐ Prepare a style sheet for heads (one or two levels), margins, page numbers, and visual aid captions.
- ☐ Select and write the type of introduction you need
  - To give the objective of the report.
  - To provide brief context.
  - To provide expanded context.
- ☐ Select the combination of introductory elements you will use to give the gist of the report to the reader. Write each section.

Worksheet for Evaluating IMRDs
IMRD报告评估工作表

Read your report or a peer's. Then answer these questions:

- ☐ **Introduction**
  - Is the goal of this project clear?
  - What is the basic question that the writer answers?
- ☐ **Methods**
  - Does the writer tell all steps or actions that he or she followed to achieve the goal or answer the question? Often there are several sequences of them.
  - Is it clear why the writer took those steps or actions?
- ☐ **Results**
  - Does this section present all the things that the writer found out?

(continued)

(continued)

- If there is a visual aid, does it help you grasp the results quickly?

☐ **Discussion**
- Does the discussion answer the question or explain success or failure in achieving the project's goal?
- What are the implications of the results? Implications mean (1) effects on various groups of people or their goals, or (2) perceptions about the system (e.g., Web search engines, Web authoring programs) discussed in the report.
- What new questions do the results cause?

Examples 例子

Examples 12.1–12.4 show four informal reports. These reports illustrate the wide range of topics that the informal report can present. Note the varied handling of the introduction and of the format of the pages. The goal in all the reports is to make the readers confident that they have the information necessary to make a decision.

Example 12.1

IMRD Report

EVALUATION OF COLLABORATIVE SOFTWARE APPLICABILITY AT UW–STOUT BY JAMES J. JANISSE

INTRODUCTION

Technical professionals are faced with an increasing number of tools intended to help their job productivity. Technology has also changed the environment and context of their work. Traditional teamwork can now be performed in an electronic or virtual manner and with collaborative software tools purported to significantly enhance job performance. A key part of UW–Stout's continuing mission is to monitor and evaluate these industry tools.

Groove (version 1.3) is considered the leading-edge collaboration software package in the industry and was developed by Groove Networks. This privately held company was created in 1997 and its headquarters are in Beverly, Massachusetts. The founder, Ray Ozzie, is best known as the creator of Lotus Notes, the world's leading groupware product. (There are more than 75 million users worldwide.)

The purpose of this report is to evaluate the applicability and feasibility of using Groove collaboration software in selected technical areas at the University of Wisconsin–Stout (UW–Stout).

METHODOLOGY

This cursory evaluation targeted two areas of technical study at UW-Stout: the Technical Writing Practicum and development of the new, on-line

Industrial Management Case Studies Course within the College of Technology, Engineering, and Management (CTEM). The selection was based on the strong interest and support from groups and the fact they represented different parts of the technical spectrum. There was a special consideration for the CTEM evaluation of Groove. Any new software tool must provide some instructional delivery capability like the incumbent tool, BlackBoard.Com. Therefore, from a CTEM perspective, Groove was essentially evaluated against the test criteria and an existing software tool.

The evaluation of the Groove software was performed by

1. identifying a subject matter expert in each area. Professor Dan Riordan and Chairperson Donna Stewart represented Technical Writing and CTEM, respectively.
2. downloading the latest demonstration version of the Groove software from www.groove.net/downloads/ to test laptop and desktop computers.
3. developing a functional profile of the Groove software that would serve as an evaluation checklist. This technique is commonly used in software development in an activity called the Application Walk-Through. Evaluators list all major software categories and functions in a table format to establish the beginning of a simple but powerful scorecard.
4. defining typical test group project activities, scenarios, and testing media to be addressed by each item in the evaluation checklist.
5. conducting a series of tests, with each expert assessing the applicability of Groove functions against the Technical Writing Practicum and Industrial Case Studies Course evaluation checklist.
6. summarizing the evaluation findings by jointly grading the fit or feasibility of each functional area for the two target groups.

RESULTS

Evaluators assessed each criterion by determining the level of

- functional fit to test scenarios
- performance
- ease-of-use
- intangibles such as departmental considerations, software personality, etc.

The range of subjective ratings was noted as

- low (L)—limited function or no match
- medium (M)—moderate function or adequate match
- high (H)—high function or significant match
- not applicable (N/A)

Additionally, each test group designated three criteria as critical or must-have, and noted these ratings with asterisks.

(continued)

Example 12.1 (continued)

The findings of the Groove collaborative evaluation are summarized in Table 1. Nine of the fourteen criteria for Technical Writing were low, including several functions needed for dynamic and joint editing. The Industrial Case Studies ratings included six lows, two not applicable ratings, and a note about prohibitive costs.

Table 1

Ratings of Groove Functional Applicability to Test Groups

Groove Functional Area	Technical Writing Practicum	Industrial Management Case Studies Course
Shared workspaces	H	H
Collaboration—Common File Directory with version control	M	L**
Collaboration—Discussion Space	L–M**	M** No statistics of readers or number of visits to the discussion thread
Collaboration—Notepad	L**—Didn't permit the desired dynamic editing; slow to refresh	L
Collaboration—Outliner	L**—Performance didn't permit reasonable joint editing	N/A
Collaboration—Pictures	L—FYI only	L
Collaboration—Sketchpad	L—No practical use found	L
Collaboration—common Web browser	L	N/A
Productivity—calendar	L	L
Productivity—contacts	L	M
Productivity—course delivery and administration	N/A	L**
Messaging—instant text	M	L
Messaging—asynchronous audio recordings	L	M
Security and privacy	H	H
Costs	M—Might be for a small workgroup	L—Cost prohibitive for desired class size of 20+ students ($49 each)

DISCUSSION

The results of the collaborative evaluation show that Groove would have limited applicability and value to either the Technical Writing Practicum or Industrial Case Studies Course. Existing or alternative software solutions should be persued.

From a Technical Writing Practicum perspective, Groove had some interesting functions. Initial impressions anticipated dynamic editing, but testing the software in actual project scenarios proved otherwise. Groove did not provide the right functionality to permit a team to rapidly perform quality creation or editing of text. For example, evaluators had a difficult time converting a table of text into a paragraph using Groove Outliner, Notepad, and Discussion Space functions. While some other tests yielded moderate ratings, Groove did not address the most important criteria for the Technical Writing Practicum.

Similarly, Groove did not score high for the key criteria established by the Industrial Case Studies team. Neither the file directory nor collaborative functions provided the interactive discussion and analysis needed for students to perform case study work. Although there might be some potential for interaction with Groove, there were deficiencies in delivering basic course activities and addressing course administration as a standalone product.

It is worth noting that Groove should still be monitored as a tool for educational delivery. The April issue of *InfoWorld* previewed an impending release of Groove 2.0 with extensive enhancements and a total integration partnership with Microsoft.

Example 12.2

IMRD Report

IMRD: ADDING BACKGROUND SOUND TO WEBPAGES

INTRODUCTION

I set out to add background sound to a webpage. My resources included an IBM-compatible PC with Windows 98 and software that included Notepad and Internet Explorer 4.0. Computers with these resources can be found in the Main Lab of the Micheels Hall Computer Lab. Before I began, I downloaded a sound file from the Internet and had an existing HTML document to which I wanted to add the sound file. These two files were in the same directory on my disk. Some of the different sound file types that you can use include .midi, .rmf, .rmi, .wav, and .mod.

METHOD

I opened Notepad by selecting Start/Programs/Accessories/Notepad. I then opened up an existing HTML file that I wanted to add sound to by selecting File/Open and then finding the HTML file I wanted to open.

(continued)

Example 12.2
(continued)

Once the file was open, I added the following code to the body section of my HTML file to add the music file, *cheers.mid,* to the background:

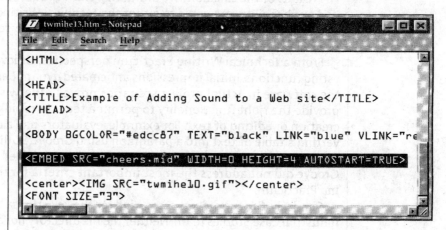

I then selected File/Save to save the modified HTML document.

Once the file was saved, I wanted to view the modified page in Internet Explorer. I did this by first double-clicking on the My Computer icon. Then I double-clicked on the 3½ Floppy (A) icon. I finally opened the file by double-clicking on the filename.

RESULT

In the HTML code that I inserted in my file, the WIDTH and HEIGHT parameters are set to small numbers so there will be no visual changes to the webpage. AUTOSTART = TRUE is used so that the sound file will start playing as soon as the page is opened.

Once I modified and saved my HTML document in Notepad, I had a current copy of the document on my disk in the same directory as the sound file.

When I double-clicked on the My Computer icon, a list of the available drives appeared in the window.

When I double-clicked on the 3½ Floppy (A) icon, a list of the files on my disk appeared in the window.

When I double-clicked on the HTML filename that I modified, Internet Explorer opened with my HTML file and the *cheers.mid* sound file playing in the background. There were no visual changes to the webpage.

DISCUSSION

My webpage was made more interesting by following this easy process of adding music to the background.

If you are working at a computer that has a sound card, but no speakers, you can still hear the audio by plugging headphones into the computer.

Example 12.3

Analytical Report

Date: April 29, 2006
To: Joseph King
From: Chris Lindblad
Subject: Purchase of a function generator for the control module tester

The module test area will be conducting the testing and troubleshooting of the SSD control module upon receiving the control module tester. The testing of this module will require the use of a function generator, which the test area does not currently have.

I have talked with numerous sales representatives and have discussed the purchase with other technicians in the test area. Basing my criteria on budget allowance, operating features, ease of operation, and future applications, I recommend the purchase of the Tektronix model AFG 5101 function generator.

Table 1
Cost of Function Generator, Options, and Accessories

Item	Tektronix AFG 5101	Philip PM 5192
Function generator	$3695	$4050
Options	350	425
Accessories	55	45
Total	4100	4520

TEKTRONIX IS WITHIN THE BUDGET

Currently the budget allows up to $6000 for the purchase of a function generator for the control module tester. As you can see from Table 1, both function generators are priced below the allowed budget. Not reflected on the total purchase price is a 10% discount the company currently receives on the purchase of electronic test equipment from Northern States Electronics Inc., the regional distributor of Tektronix Inc. With this discount included, the purchase price of the Tektronix model would drop to a total of $3690.

TEKTRONIX HAS BETTER OPERATING FEATURES

The Tektronix model AFG 5101 function generator has the ability to produce the required 10-MHz clock sine wave along with four other signal wave forms in a frequency range from .012 to 20 MHz. The Philips model PM 5192 function generator has the ability to produce the required clock signal and four other signal wave forms but only in the range of .1 to 20 MHz. The Tektronix model also has the feature of changeable pods, which can be quickly replaced if the unit should fail, whereas the Philips model would have to be returned to a service center for repair, which would result in downtime on the tester.

(continued)

Example 12.3
(continued)

TEKTRONIX HAS BETTER OPERATIONAL SUPPORT

Both function generators are relatively easy to operate and are fully programmable. Both allow for the programming of selected wave forms, eliminating the need to lead information into the function generator before each test is run. A Tektronix representative will present a one-day training session to the module test technicians and will be available by phone for any further questions. The Philips model is accompanied by a manual and a 20-minute training video.

TEKTRONIX WILL UPGRADE EASIER

With the future module designs that will be coming into the test area and the faster speeds in which they will operate, the Tektronix model AFG 5101 has a larger operating frequency range, and the changeable pod feature will allow it to be upgraded for possible future uses. The Philips model has a lower frequency range and cannot be upgraded.

If you require any further information or documentation on my recommendation, please contact me at the module test department.

Example 12.4

Memo Recommendation

Date: July 17, 2006
To: Marcus Hammerle
From: John Furlano
Subject: Recommendation of tooling schedule

This letter is a follow-up of our discussion pertaining to the Storage Cover tooling schedule, which we discussed briefly during your visit at MPD on Thursday, June 27.

There are three main options available to expedite the pilot run date from October 2 up to the week of October 14.

1. Postpone the tool chroming until after the pilot run.
2. Postpone any major tool modifications until after the pilot run.
3. Expedite the tool building.

I believe that option 1 is the best choice. There will not be any additional costs for this option, and quality parts will still be produced for the pilot run. Option 2 may not be a reliable option because we cannot judge until after sampling what modifications may be necessary. Option 3 will carry additional cost due to overtime labor.

I am also optimistic, yet concerned, about the September 9 sample date (two samples at your facility, hand drilled and bonded, no paint). My concern

> is with delays through customs for shipping parts from the tool shop in Canada to the United States for assembly and back to Canada.
>
> We are taking every step possible to stay on schedule with the Draft #3 tooling schedule, which you have a copy of. The enclosed tooling schedule (Draft #4) shows the projected pilot run date if option 1 above is employed. I welcome your comments or suggestions on any of the above issues. Thank you.
>
> enc: tooling schedule draft #4

Exercises 练 习

▶ You Create

1. Create an objective/summary introduction for the Iconglow report on pages 281–282.
2. Create a different introduction for the analytical report on purchasing a function generator on pages 299–300.
3. Write a methodology statement that explains how you recently went about solving some problem or discovered some information. When you have finished, construct a visual aid that shows the results of your actions. Compare these statements and visuals in groups of two to three.
4. Write the introduction for the material you wrote in Exercise 3.
5. Write the discussion section for the material you wrote in Exercise 3.

▶ You Analyze

6. Because introductions imply a lot about the relationship of the writer to the reader, analyze the introductions of the reports in Examples 12.1–12.3 to determine what you can about the audience-writer relationship. How is that relationship affected when you change the introduction as you did in Exercise 2?
7. Read the introduction and body of another student's paper from one of the Writing Assignments below. Does the discussion really present all the material needed to support the introduction? Are the visual aids effective? Is the format effective?

▶ Group

8. In groups of three or four, analyze the sections of the IMRD report on collaborative software on pages 294–297. How is the introduction related to the discussion? Do you feel that you know everything you need to know after reading the first few paragraphs? What does the discussion section add to the report?

9. In groups of three, read the introduction of each person's paper from one of the Writing Assignments below. Decide whether to maintain the current arrangement; if not, propose another.

10. a. In groups of two or three, decide on a question that you will find the answer to. A good example is how to use some aspect of e-mail, the library, or the Web. Before the next class, find the answer. In class, write an IMRD that presents your answer.

    I = question you wanted to answer and goal of this paper
    M = relevant actions you took to find the answer
    R = the actual answer
    D = the implications of the answer for yourself or other people with your level of knowledge and interest

    b. In groups of two or three, read each other's IMRD reports. Answer these questions:

    Do you know the question that had to be answered?
    Could you perform the actions or steps given to arrive at the answer?
    Is the answer clear?
    Is the discussion helpful or irrelevant?

11. In groups of two or three, compare the differences in Example 11.2 (pp. 266–267) and Example 12.2 (pp. 297–298). Focus on differences in tone and in presentation of the actions. Report to the class which document you prefer to read and why. What principles would affect your choice to write an IMRD or a set of instructions?

Writing Assignments 写作任务

1. Write an informal report in which you use a table or graph to explain a problem and its solution to your manager. Select a problem from your area of professional interest—for example, a problem you solved (or saw someone else solve) on a job. Consider topics such as pilferage of towels in a hotel, difficulties in manufacturing a machine part, a sales decline in a store at a mall, difficulties with a measuring device in a lab, or problems in the shipping department of a furniture company. Use at least one visual aid.

2. Write an IMRD report in which you explain a topic you have investigated. The report could be a lab report or a report of any investigation. For instance, you could compare the fastest way to reproduce a paper, by scanning or retyping, or give the results of a session in which you learned something about navigating on the Internet, or present the results of an interview you conducted about any worthwhile concern at your school or business. Your instructor may combine this assignment with Writing Assignment 3.

3. Bring a draft of the IMRD you are writing to class. In groups of two or three, evaluate these concerns:

a. Is the basic research question clear?
b. Does the method make you feel like a professional is reporting?
c. Could you replicate the actions? Could other people?
d. Does only method—and not results—appear in the method section?
e. Is the method statement written like instructions or a process description? Which is best for this situation?
f. Are the results clear? Are they a clear answer to the original question?
g. Does every topic mentioned in the discussion section have a clear basis of fact in the methods or results section?
h. Is the significance the writer points out useful?
i. Does the visual aid help you with the methods or result section? Would it help other people?
j. Is the tone all right? Or is it too dry? too chatty? too technical?
k. Does the formatting of the report make it easy to read?

4. Rewrite the IMRD from Writing Assignment 2 from a completely different framework—for instance, a coach explaining the subject to a high school team. After you complete the new IMRD, in groups of three or four, discuss the difference "author identity" makes and create questions to tell writers how to choose an identity.

5. Convert your IMRD report from Writing Assignment 2 into an article for a newsletter.

6. Convert your IMRD report from Writing Assignment 2 into a set of instructions. After you complete the instructions, in groups of three or four, construct a list of the differences between the two, especially the method statement. Alternate: In groups of three or four, construct a set of guidelines for when to use instructions and when to use IMRD. Hand this list in to your instructor.

7. Write an outline report in which you summarize a long report. Depending on your instructor's requirements, use a report you have already written or one you are writing in this class.

8. Write a learning report for the writing assignment you just completed. See Chapter 5, Writing Assignment 7, page 133, for details of the assignment.

Web Exercise 网络练习

Write an IMRD that explains a research project on the effectiveness of a search strategy on the Web. Choose any set of three words (e.g., plastic + biodegradable + packaging). Choose any major search engine (Yahoo!, AltaVista). Using the "advanced" or "custom" search mode, type in your keywords in three sequences—plastic + biodegradable + packaging, packaging + plastic + biodegradable, biodegradable + packaging + plastic. Investigate the first three sites for each search. In the IMRD, explain your method and results and discuss the effectiveness of the strategy and of the search engine for this kind of topic.

Large group alternative: Divide the class into groups of four. All members of the class agree to use the same keywords, but each group will use a different search engine. After the individual searches are completed, have each group compile a report in which they present their results to the class orally, via e-mail, or on the Web.

Works Cited　引用的作品

General Motors. *Writing Style Guide*. Rev. ed. GM1620. By Lawrence H. Freeman and Terry R. Bacon. Warren, MI: Author, 1991.

Keppler, Herbert. "SLR: Going Where No Macro Has Dared to Go Before." *Popular Photography* (August 1997).

Focus on E-Mail 关注电子邮件

E-mail has become a major way by which people communicate, sending everything from birthday greetings to intergovernmental communications. E-mail has revolutionized interpersonal communications, so much so that a problem has arisen: How do we deal with the glut of e-mail? Steve Gilbert, who has run a LISTSERV for many years, says, "I try to limit the number of messages to a few each week to avoid making even worse the e-mail glut many of my friends and colleagues are experiencing." How do you fashion your e-mail so it doesn't sit unread in your recipient's in-box or, worse, is dumped altogether?

Here are a few tips that will help you write effective, clear e-mail messages that will be read and acted upon in a timely manner.

Write a Clear Subject Line Experts who have studied e-mail find that the subject line is the most important item when trying to connect with the intended reader. Messages are often displayed in a directory that lists the sender's name, the date, and the subject. Many readers choose to read or delete messages solely on the basis of the subject line, because they can't possibly take the time to respond to so much mail. Your message will more likely be opened if the subject line connects with the reader's needs. If the reader is not engaged by the subject line, he or she will often simply delete the message unread. Here are some tips:

- Start with an information-bearing word. Say
  "Budget Request—meeting scheduled"
  rather than "budget meeting" or "meeting."
  Or
  "Hi—meet me after your class?"
  rather than "Hi."
- Keep the subject line relatively short. This tip could conflict with the previous one, so be judicious in your phrasing of the information-bearing word or phrase.
- People often open messages with RE in the subject line (so don't change the subject when you reply). In a subject line, state content—"Response to your 7-25 budget request."
- Make the subject line a short summary of your message. (Nielsen; Rhodes; "ITS")

Use the To and CC Lines Effectively The To line should contain only the names of persons who you are asking to do something. In the CC line, list people who should know about the message, or who are getting the e-mail simply for information purposes ("ITS").

Check Addresses Many e-mail addresses are remarkably similar. It is quite easy to make a typing mistake, so that the e-mail intended for jonessu goes instead to joness or jonesd. Although this is often a minor annoyance, it can be a major embarrassment if the content is sensitive or classified ("ITS").

Consider Whether to Send an Attachment Attachments take more time to download and often easily become separated from the original e-mail. In addition, many attachments can't be opened at all by the receiver, especially if they were created in another platform or by an application not owned by the receiver.

If you do send an attachment, be sure that the document contains such information as a title and the name of the person who sent it. Sometimes this information appears only in the e-mail; if the e-mail is deleted, the attachment becomes difficult to make meaningful. If the attachment is long, consider posting it on a website (if that option is easily available to you) and sending your recipients an e-mail with the RRL to that space ("ITS"). In order to avoid "losing" an attachment, or to ensure that there are no problems opening the document, paste the contents directly into the e-mail. Note, however, that this strategy makes the e-mail long, so in the introduction establish the context for the content. Be sure to give the attachment a meaningful filename. If the attachment is opened

(continued)

(continued)

directly from the e-mail, the context for it is clear. But if the e-mail is gone and the attachment resides in a directory with many other files, the filename must be meaningful. Say "jonesresume" rather than "resume," or "ABCapplicationform" rather than "ABCaf."

Keep Messages Short and to the Point Research has established that readers categorize e-mails. "To-do" messages require some action from the recipient. Often, these messages stay in in-boxes as a reminder to the recipient of work to do. "To read" messages usually are long documents that take time and effort to read. Although the content could be important, the length causes recipients to delay reading them. "Indeterminate" messages are those whose significance is not clear to the reader. Like long messages, these messages are usually not read, but left in in boxes so that when there is time enough, the reader will make the effort to read the message and determine the significance (Rhodes).

Establish the Context In the body of the e-mail, repeat questions or key phrases. Briefly explain why you are writing, then go on with your message. If a person has sent out 20 messages the day before, he or she might not easily remember exactly what was sent to you. Offer help. Remember that you are not in a dialogue in which the other person can respond instantaneously to your statements, so avoid the temptation to use one-line speeches. For instance, don't just write one word—"No"—but explain the topic you are saying "No" to. One respondent to an e-mail survey said, "X is unbelievable in that he never puts in the context of what he is replying to. He always comes up with these one-line responses, and I have no idea what it is that he's talking about" (Rhodes).

Remember to Use Paragraphs E-mail's format has a kind of hypnotic quality that encourages people to write as if they were speaking. And, of course, in speech there are no obvious paragraphs. However, remember that e-mail is text that a person reads, so chunk into manageable paragraphs. Use keywords at the beginning of units in order to establish the context of the sentence or paragraph that follows.

Signal the End Because e-mail exists in scrolling screen form, there is no obvious cue to its end, unlike a hard copy where you always know when you are on the last page. Therefore, signal the end by typing your name, with or without a closing. You may also use the words "the end" or a line of asterisks.

Avoid Mind Dumps The point of e-mail is to satisfy the reader's needs as concisely as possible. Do not ramble. Plan for a moment before you start to write. If you have "on-line fear," the same strange emotional response that often makes people give awkward, rambling messages on an answering machine, type your message first on a familiar word processing program, when you have time to gather your thoughts and get them down coherently. Edit in the word processor, then upload and send (know the capabilities of your system).

Don't Type in All Caps The lack of variation in letter size makes the message much harder to grasp and gives the impression that you're shouting.

Get Permission to Publish E-mail is the intellectual property of its creator. Do not publish an e-mail message unless the creator gives you permission.

Be Prudent Technically (and legally), the institution that provides you the e-mail service (such as your university or employer or governmental agency) owns the e-mail you are sending and receiving. As a result, any number of people can access individual e-mails if they have some reason to. Be careful about sending sensitive or personal information. In addition, remember that any e-mail is easily forwarded—and so is any attachment—

without your knowledge. Although you might think that the sensitive meeting notes that you send to the committee chair will remain only on her computer, or that the personal comments you make about another person will stay buried in an in-box, it is all too easy for these messages to be forwarded, deliberately or accidentally, to others.

Works Cited

Gilbert, Steve. "Personalizing Pedagogy with E-Mail." *Syllabus Magazine* March 2003. 13 Oct. 2003 <www.syllabus.com/mag.asp?month=3&year=2003>.

"ITS Email Tips." Email and Network Services, Yale University 17 Aug. 2002. 13 Oct. 2003 <www.yale.edu/email/emailtips.html>.

Nielsen, Jakob. "Microcontent: How to Write Headlines, Page Titles, and Subject Lines." *Useit.com* September 1998. 13 Oct. 2003 <www.useit.com/alertbox/980906.html>.

Rhodes, John S. "The Usability of Email Subject Lines." 8 Feb. 2001. *Webword.tom* 13 Oct. 2003 <http://webword.com/moving/subjectlines.html>.

Ethics and E-Mail 使用电子邮件的注意事项

E-mail is a form of written electronic communication only a little over ten years old. Being aware of the ethical guidelines for conduct when sending communications over the Internet is important in remaining professional and courteous.

Frequently, the recipient of an e-mail passes on all or part of its content to other recipients. The professional is conscientious of attributing true sources of such material, even in a medium as informal as e-mail. The following excerpt from an e-mail policy contains guidelines for being professional and sensitive to the concerns and contributions of others when forwarding material from a previous sender:

> Good practice [in the use of quotations in e-mail] includes:
> - quoting only that part of another message that is relevant
> - including enough context when quoting so that the recipient will not be misled as to the meaning or intentions of the person quoted
> - attributing quotations to the person quoted
> - not using quotations in messages to someone who was not a recipient of the original message, unless you have the permission of the original sender, or unless you can be reasonably satisfied that the original sender would not object to being quoted. (Lynmar Solutions)

Perhaps the most controversial topic concerning ethics and e-mail is the practice of "flaming"—sending angry e-mails inciting "flame wars" (Shapiro and Anderson).

The absence, in e-mail, of the facial expression, tone of voice, and feedback in face-to-face conversations, together with the speed of response that is possible with e-mail, can lead to "flaming" and "flame wars."

> To avoid these, it is good practice:
> - to avoid *ad hominem* expressions such as "you must be stupid if you don't understand that . . ." or "only an idiot would think that . . ."
> - to allow yourself a "cooling off" period, before responding to e-mail that annoys you, and to be temperate in your response; you should be particularly careful if your response will go to more than just the original sender, e.g., to an entire mailing list
> - to make sure when appropriate, for instance by the addition of conventional symbols such as ":-)", that humorous remarks cannot be taken seriously. (Lynmar Solutions)

Works Cited

Lynmar Solutions. "E-mail Ethics and Good Practice: A Sample Policy." 2004 March 1 <www.lynmarsolutions.co.uk/files/emailethics.doc>.

Shapiro, Norman Z., and Robert H. Anderson. "Toward an Ethics and Etiquette for E-mail." July 1985. *Rand*. 1 March 2004 <www.rand.org/publications/MR/R3283/#rece>.

Chapter 13 Developing Websites
网站开发

Chapter Contents
Chapter 13 In a Nutshell
Basic Web Concepts
Planning a Website or Web Document
Drafting
Testing
Ethics and Websites
Globalization/Localization and Websites
Focus on HTML

Chapter 13
In a Nutshell 概 要

Websites and Web documents are important methods of conveying information. Creating effective websites requires careful planning, drafting, and testing.

To plan effectively, you need to consider your audience. Determine who they are. Of course, on the Web they could be anyone in the world, but that's too broad. A helpful way to create a sense of your audience is to define a role for them, as if they were actors in your "Web play." Are they customers? students? curiosity surfers?

In addition to considering your audience, you need to plan a flow chart and a template. The flow chart is a device that indicates how you will link your material together. For instance, if you have four files and if you want your reader to link from any one to any other one, your flow chart would look like Figure 1. Each line is a link and each box is a webpage.

Your template is a design of your site's look. It shows how you will place various kinds of information (title, text, links, visuals) so that your reader can easily grasp the sense of your site.

Websites create special concerns for writing. Good Web text is scannable (easy to find key ideas), correct (no spelling, grammar mistakes), and consistent (all items treated in a similar fashion).

Visuals must be legible, but not so large that they take up most of the screen or take a long time to load.

Websites must be tested to make sure links work, visuals appear, and the site displays consistently in various browsers.

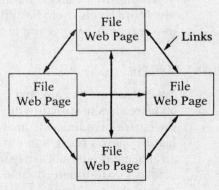

Figure 1
Sample Flow Chart

The Web is one of the primary means of communication today. Millions of people use it every day to find information, to purchase items, and to entertain themselves. Because it is so easy to use, the Web has changed the method of disseminating information. In the past, vital information (of whatever kind—from research data to sale items) was printed on paper (as a report or a catalog, for instance) and sent to intended audiences. Now the vital information is "posted," and the intended audience must search for it. Universities, corporations, organizations of all types, and private individuals all maintain large websites to make information available to viewers.

Because of this shift, technical communicators must know how to create documents that are both clear and easy to read on screen. Creating such documents requires the same general process of planning, drafting, and finishing as in creating any document, but with special considerations for the on-line situation.

This chapter covers basic Web concepts, planning, drafting, and testing Web documents. Examples show Web reports and Web instructions.

Basic Web Concepts 网页基本概念

Three basic concepts that will help you create effective websites and documents for readers are hierarchy, Web structure, and reader freedom.

Hierarchy 层次体系

Hierarchy is the structure of the contents of a document. All websites and Web documents have a hierarchy, that is, levels of information. The highest level is the *homepage*, a term that can apply either to an entire site or to a document. Lower levels are called *nodes*; the paths among the nodes are the *links*.

Figure 13.1 shows three levels in the hierarchy, each giving more detail. *Writing* is the most general category. *Technical* and *fiction* are the two subcategories of writing. *Reports* and *novels* are subdivisions, respectively, of their types of writing. More levels could be added. For instance, reports could be broken down into feasibility reports and proposals.

Web Structure 网页结构

"Web structure" means that the document contains hyperlinks (or "links") that allow readers to structure their own reading sequence. When the reader clicks the cursor on a link, the browser opens the screen indicated by the link. This feature allows readers to move to new topics quickly and in any order. This arrangement is a radical departure in organizing strategy. The author gives the readers maximum freedom to choose the order in which they will view the site or read the document.

Figure 13.1

Hierarchy

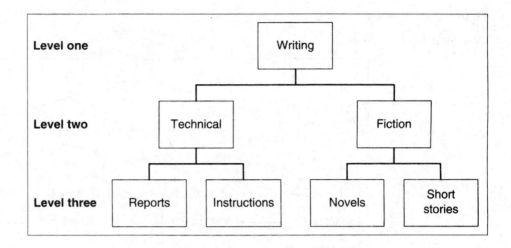

To see the difference between traditional and Web structures, consider these two examples. If a document has seven sections and a traditional (or "linear") structure, then a reader will progress through the sections as shown in Figure 13.2. But if the same seven sections have a Web structure, then they would look like Figure 13.3 (p. 312), with each line a link. Once readers arrive at the start, or home, screen, they may read the document in any order they please.

The two Web homepages in Figures 13.4 and 13.5 show two ways that authors used Web structure. Both have a lengthy report, which they want the readers to be able to read without having to scroll through various screens. Maertens (Figure 13.4, p. 312) has divided the report into five linkable sections. The homepage provides an index and brief abstract of each section. The reader can choose any section and link to it. Currier (Figure 13.5, pp. 313–314) has provided "anchor links" that move the screen to that part of the document without scrolling.

To "think Web" is a radical departure in organizing strategy. You can give readers maximum freedom to choose in what order they read your document.

Figure 13.2

Linear Structure

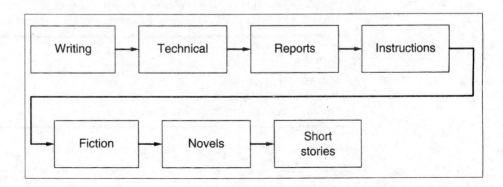

Figure 13.3

Web Structure

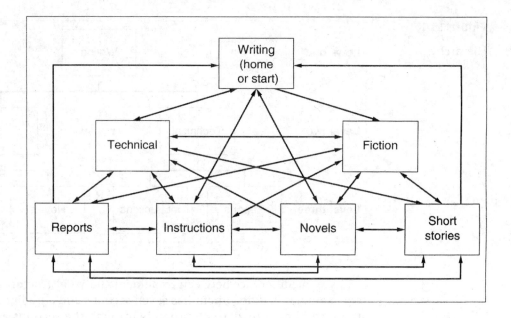

Figure 13.4

Linked Section Report

Clicking on a link causes that page to open on the screen.

Tips for Making a Good Website

The following report contains some ideas that I feel are important to consider if one is going to produce a good website. These are just some of the ideas I have learned through my Technical Writing class. Remember, you are free to do whatever you want, but the following ideas may be helpful in achieving your goal.

Go to

- <u>Planning Is Key</u> -Planning is essential in order for you to produce a good..........
- <u>Establishing a Purpose for Your Website</u> -Before you embark on this voyage..........
- <u>Implementing Links in Your Website</u> -In order to make your site easy to use..........
- <u>Handling Visuals and Text</u> -These seem to spice up your website, but..........
- <u>Interactive Websites</u> -People do not just want to see a webpage, they want to..........

Return to

- <u>Matt Maertens Homepage</u>
- <u>Technical Writing Index Page</u>
- <u>English Department Student Projects Page</u>

Let me know what you think! e-mail me <u>maertensm@uwstout.edu</u>

Figure 13.5

Anchor Link Strategy

Links to anchor. Clicking on the link causes that text to appear at the top of the screen.

Click on "Top" to jump back to the first paragraph.

Anchor

Anchor

Anchor

Anchor

How to Create a Great Webpage

HTML stands for Hypertext Markup Language. This language allows the computer to read your document and makes it appear in Web format. Once you get the hang of this computer language, the possibilities are endless. However, good quality writing and construction of your website could determine how many people will stop and stay long enough to check out your site. The following areas are important to consider in order to create a great website:

<u>Before You Begin|Here Goes|Introduction|Chunks and Heads|Graphics</u>

BEFORE YOU BEGIN
Before you start typing anything into the computer, sit down and plan out what you are going to do. Designing a website is 90% planning and 10% actual work. Figure out the purpose of your website. Things can get out of control fast, so knowing your boundaries is essential.

It is incredibly helpful to draw a map of your website. When creating links, things can get confusing. Good links enable you to get in, through, and out of the document easily. Nobody likes to get trapped in a webpage with no way out. Having a map of links in front of you can make linking your pages easier. You will save yourself a lot of time and hassle, if you work out what you are going to do before you do it. **<u>Top</u>**

HERE GOES!
Now that you know what you are going to do, it is time to acquire the things necessary to get it done. You will need a computer, a simple word processing program, a list of HTML commands and what they do, and a browser. Type your information in a simple word processor, such as Simple Text, or save it in your present word processing program as a text file. You will need knowledge of HTML commands to convert your page into a language the computer can read. A browser allows you to open up your document on the Web to see what it looks like. **<u>Top</u>**

Introduction
An introduction is an important part of the website. The introduction contains a lot of necessary information, such as the reason for the site and why it would be of interest to the viewer. In the introduction, the purpose of the website should be clearly stated. If viewers don't know what the site is about or how it will benefit them, they are not going to stick around. **<u>Top</u>**

Chunks and Heads
People like information presented in small chunks. It is easier for them to digest. It also gives you a better chance of holding their attention. People don't have the desire or patience to read through a lot of unbroken text. It is also a good idea to use heads. They are also useful in breaking up the page. Heads inform the reader about each section's content, giving them the option of whether they want to read it. **<u>Top</u>**

GRAPHICS
When incorporating graphics into your webpage, there are several things to consider. Determine how long it takes the graphic to load. If it takes too long, try to make the graphic smaller. If that doesn't help, you should cut it out. People don't like to wait very long for a graphic to

(continued)

Figure 13.5

(continued)

> load. Another thing to consider about graphics is if they will appear when the document is loading or if the viewer will have to click on a graphics icon to bring up the picture. Either one is acceptable. It is up to the designer which way to go. The Web can provide additional options for incorporating a graphic into you site.
>
> <u>**Top**</u>
>
> <u>*My Set of Instructions\How to Reply in Eudora*</u>
>
> <u>*Nikki's Index\Technical Writing Home Page*</u>

Reader Freedom 读者自由度

Reader freedom is the degree to which the reader of the website can easily select the order in which he or she will read sections of a document. Whereas hierarchy imposes control on the reader's freedom, Web structure provides freedom. The Web author must find a way to combine the two. Figures 13.6 to 13.8 demonstrate how authors can use the two concepts to affect the way readers view the document or site.

In Figure 13.6, the reader starts at the home page and can progress only to one of the two level 2 nodes, and then to one of the level 3 nodes. To arrive at *reports*, the reader must click to *technical* and then to *reports*. To get to *instructions* from *reports*, the reader must first go back to *technical*. To get to *novels* from *reports* the reader must follow the path back to *writing* and then click forward to *novels*.

Figures 13.7 and 13.8 show progressively less control by the author and more control for the reader. In the hierarchy shown in Figure 13.7, the reader can move directly from *reports* to *instructions* without clicking back to *technical*. In the hierarchy shown in Figure 13.8, the reader can move to any document from any other document. A reader could click from *reports* to *fiction* and then to *instructions*.

Figure 13.6

Little Reader Freedom

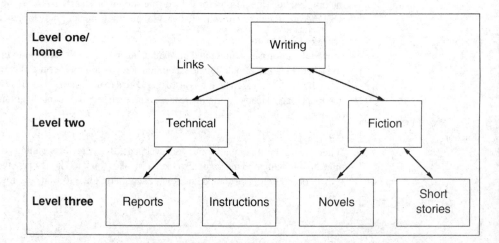

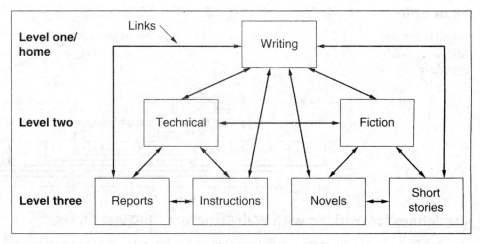

Figure 13.7

Moderate Freedom

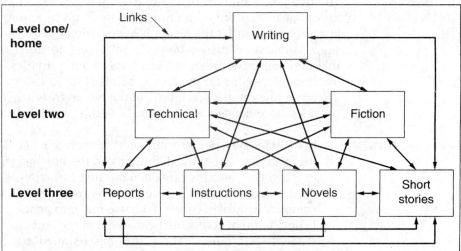

Figure 13.8

Absolute Freedom

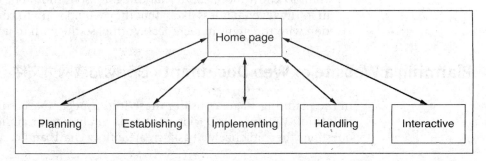

Figure 13.9

Controlled Hierarchy

The Maertens model in Figure 13.4 appears to have a tightly controlled hierarchy, as shown in Figure 13.9. But if he would supply links between each section, then the document would have a hierarchy of little control and great reader freedom, as in Figure 13.10 (p. 316).

Figure 13.10

Web Structure Allowing Reader Freedom

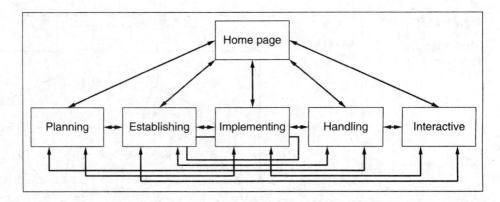

Guidelines for Working with Web Structure 网页结构工作指南

The two possibilities of rigid hierarchical organization and loose Web organization mean that the writer must choose to insert enough links to be flexible, but not so many that the reader is overwhelmed with choices. William Horton suggests that an effective strategy is to "layer" documents, "designing them so that they can serve different users for different purposes, each user getting the information needed for the task at hand" (178).

Horton suggests that each level of the hierarchy is a layer and that each layer provides more detailed information. Use this principle in these ways:

- In higher layers, put information that everyone needs. To learn about writing, everyone needs the definitions on the homepage, but only a few readers need the concepts explained on the instructions page.
- Control reader's paths. Figure 13.6, for instance, indicates that readers have complete control in either of the two major categories, technical writing and fiction, but that accessing the material in the other category will require the reader to "start over." The author has assumed that readers in fiction will want to know more about that category, so it should be easy to get around in it. However, it is less likely that they would want to compare items in fiction with the items in technical writing, so the path to it is restricted.

Planning a Website or Web Document 设计网站或网页文件

In the planning stage, consider these four aspects (based on December; Horton; Hunt; Wilkinson): Decide your goal, analyze your audience, evaluate the questions the audience will ask, create a flow chart, and create a template.

Decide Your Goal 确定你的目标

Your site or document should have a "mission statement"—for instance, "To explain the purposes and services of the campus antique auto club." Make this

Planning a Website or Web Document

statement as narrow and specific as possible. It will help you with the many other decisions that you will have to make.

Analyze Your Audience 分析你的读者

Ask the standard questions: Who is the audience? How much do they know? What is their level of expertise? (See Chapter 2 for more information on audience analysis.)

Do not answer: Anyone who comes onto the Web. Such a broad answer will not allow you to make decisions. Narrowly focus these answers—they are people who are interested in antique cars, the university in general, or clubs in particular. They know a little or a lot; they will have experience or not. A website aimed at an audience of people who have restored antique cars is quite different from a website aimed at students who have some interest in old cars and wish to join a university group.

One helpful way to think about audience is to think about the site or document as a stage (Coney and Steehouder). Your audience member is a member of a cast and thus has a "role" in the site. For instance, the audience can assume the role of "antique car experts" or "students who want to join a club." Most audience members find it easy to adopt such a role if it is clear to them. If you understand the role you want your audience members to play, you will be able to make better decisions about how to present your site or document to them.

Evaluate the Questions the Audience Will Ask 评估读者可能问的问题

Speculate on general questions: What is the purpose of the club? When does the club meet? What are the club activities? What antique cars does the club have? Can I learn about where to purchase an antique car? Can I learn how to restore an antique car? What are the bylaws of the club?

You can decide which of these questions you want to, or should, answer. Your audience decisions will help you. For instance, if you feel that only car buffs will look at the site, then there is no need to provide rudimentary information about cars.

Create a Flow Chart of Your Site 创建你的网站流程表

A flow chart indicates the site's or document's nodes, their hierarchy, and the degree of freedom that the reader will have. The flow chart gives a visual map of your site, allowing you to control the creation of the links. It shows you how much control you will allow your audience, and because it is a blueprint of the site, it gives you a method to check whether you have inserted all your links. In the flow chart in Figure 13.11, the arrows indicate a link from one file to another, and the curved lines indicate escape links back to the homepage from each of the files. Notice that this structure is much like the one shown in Figure 13.7 (p. 315). The reader has total control inside each section of the hierarchy, but must return at least to the second level in order to transfer to another category.

Follow these guidelines for degrees of control (Figure 13.11 illustrates all of these points):

- Provide a link from the homepage to all nodes.
- Provide a link from the node to all subparts of the node.
- Provide a link between nodes.
- Provide shortcut links from higher levels to key data at lower levels. Note the two lines that run from the homepage to the items marked "K."
- Provide shortcut or "escape" links from all levels back to the home page. Escape links are shown by the lighter curved lines in Figure 13.11.
- Provide enough links for multiple paths. Unless you have a compelling reason to prevent random navigation, readers should be able to read the site and the documents in it in any order. Use links to create paths that will allow this type of reader freedom.

Create a Template   创建一个模板

Your site or document must have a consistent visual logic. Select a background color, a font (but be aware that individual users can change the font that appears

Figure 13.11

Full Flow Chart of a Website

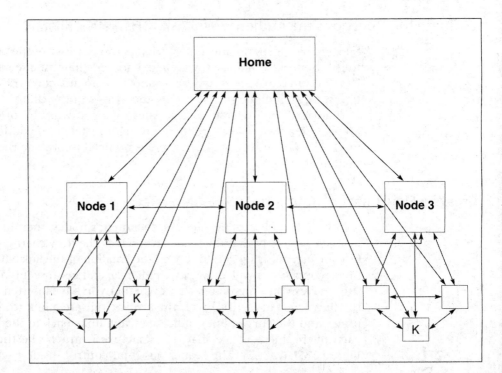

on their screen), and a consistent spot to place titles, introductions, lists, return links, and e-mail links. The information on each screen will change, but the way it is presented will remain the same.

The easiest way to create a template is to make a sample page and keep a record of each of your decisions. As you make the template, include all of these items:

- Title
- Introductory text
- List of nodes (actually a table of contents for the document or site)
- Shortcut links
- Escape links
- Color/font/size of heading
- Color/design of background
- Color/font/size of text
- Placement of blocks of similar types of text

Consider, for instance, Figures 13.12 and 13.13 (p. 320), pages from the Geology node of the Arches National Park website. Each page looks the same. Similar elements appear in the same position, color, and font. Notice all of the following:

1. Title of the section—flush left, sans serif font, rule beneath
2. Links to other nodes—left-hand column, serif font
3. Title of the page—flush left in right-hand column, sans serif font, black
4. Heads—flush left in right-hand column, serif font, color
5. Text—block paragraphs, double-space between paragraphs, serif font
6. Shortcut links—2 lines below text, serif font
7. Privacy/author information—3 lines at bottom left, serif font
8. Two-column format
9. Visually separated elements. Note that white space and color bands clearly separate the various elements of the page. Each element is said to be "grouped," a visually effective method of helping the reader grasp the information.

Drafting 草案

Creating a website or document takes several drafts. Creating clear content, effective structures for reader freedom, and accessible pages seldom happens in one draft. As you create your site or document, orient your reader, write in a scannable style, establish credibility, and use visuals effectively (Nielson; Spyridakis; Williams).

Figure 13.12

Arches National Park Geology Introduction Home Page

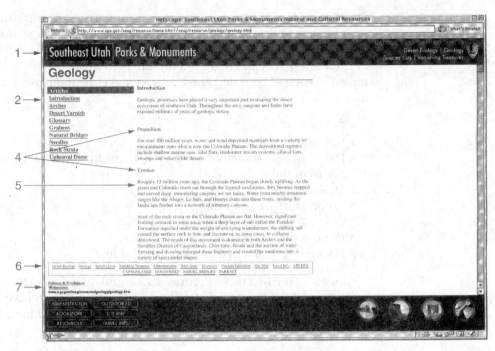

See webpage at <www.nps.gov/seug/resource/home.html>.

Figure 13.13

Arches National Park Desert Varnish Web Page

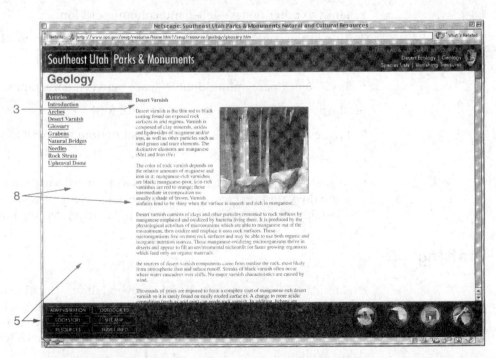

See webpage at <www.nps.gov/seug/resource/home.html>.

Orient Your Reader 引导你的读者

As readers surf through websites and documents, they lose track of where they are. This disorientation causes confusion and diminishes the ability to draw meaning from a page. Three key methods to orient the reader are shown in Figures 13.12 and 13.13:

- Provide an informative title at the top of the page.
- Provide an introductory sentence that either announces or defines the topic under discussion.
- Repeat key information at consistent spots on the page.

Write in a Scannable Style 以可浏览方式撰写

A scannable style is one that presents information by highlighting key terms and concepts and placing them first in any sequence. Because reading from a screen is a physically difficult task, a scannable style often makes text easier to read (Nielson). Several strategies will help you make the page scannable:

- Use chunks. Create smaller chunks; use more short paragraphs. Notice the short paragraphs in Figures 13.12 and 13.13.
- Use headings. Place heads throughout the text to help readers grasp the overall structure. Heads function as an "in-text" outline, which helps readers orient themselves (see Figure 13.12).
- Use bulleted lists. Notice the "Go To" list in Figure 13.4. It is much easier to read than this linear version: Go to: Planning Is Key; Establishing a Purpose for Your Website; Implementing Links in Your Website; Handling Visuals and Text; Interactive Websites.
- Add abstracts after the link. If the word in the link is not self-evident, add a brief description. For instance,

    Instructions: The steps you need to build a better telescope.

- Make a link-title connection. Use a word in the link that repeats a word in the title of the section where the reader will arrive. If the link is *Planning*, the title of the page that appears should include *Planning*.
- Use one idea per paragraph. Notice the two paragraphs under "Erosion" in Figure 13.12. Each deals with only one idea: the creation of canyons and the creation of spectacular shapes.
- Use the inverted pyramid style. The term *inverted pyramid* is a synonym for top-down. Put the key idea of the paragraph first, and then give supporting detail. Notice in the "concise" example below that the first sentence gives the main idea ("prepares students") and the rest of the paragraph supplies details on how the program actually prepares students.
- Use introductions that tell the purpose of the screen, especially if it is a node screen. See Figure 13.4 or Figure 13.12.

- Write concisely. Because it is difficult to read text on a screen, excess wording simply compounds the problem. Jakob Nielson suggests that writing can be *promotional* (overblown, to be avoided), *concise,* or *scannable*. Writers should try for the latter two.

PROMOTIONAL

This fun program leads young scholars into the exciting world of technical communication. Scholars have the unprecedented opportunity to study multimedia in all the state-of-the-art software and hardware. They can also, in a particularly innovative aspect, develop an Applied Field that will allow them to interact with specialists in other areas. And they can, as students in many majors cannot, take a course that readies them to enter the challenging world of work.

CONCISE

This program prepares students for the exciting world of Technical Communication. The program features state-of-the-art multimedia software and hardware; Applied Fields that develop expertise in a specialty; and a professional development course which facilitates beginning a career.

SCANNABLE

Three key features of the new technical communication programs are

- State-of-the-art multimedia hardware and software.
- Applied Fields to develop specialized expertise.
- Professional development to facilitate finding a job.

Establish Credibility 建立可信度

Because anyone can post anything on a website, readers look for, and are reassured by, some proof of credibility (Coney; Nielson; Spyridakis). Some features that enhance a site's credibility are

- Information about the author, including name, e-mail address, and organizational affiliation. A website on effective dieting is more credible if the author is a person with an e-mail address who is an associate professor in a dietetics department at a university.
- The date that the site was posted or updated.
- A statement about privacy. Many websites include a "Privacy" link to a file that explains their policy.
- No typos or spelling or grammar mistakes. These mistakes seem even more glaring on the Web. If all the world can see your material, shouldn't you care enough to get it correct?

Drafting

- Links to other sites. These links show that the authors know the field. Be careful of such links because they lead viewers off your site. Careful Web authors often add a statement near an "off-site" link, telling the readers that they are about to leave the site and reminding them to use their browser's Back button or Go menu to return. Check such links regularly to make sure that they work.
- High-quality graphics. The ability to present quality graphics shows that the writer knows how to use software and hardware, as well as that the writer wants to make a clear contact with the reader. The clear visual in Figure 13.13 makes the reader confident that the author has a high level of expertise.

Use Visuals Effectively   有效使用视图

Visual aids in a Web document perform all the same functions as in a paper document (see Chapter 7). Visuals summarize data, allow readers to explore data, provide a different conceptual entry point into a report, and engage expectations. Used well, visuals enhance webpages; but used poorly, the visuals are annoying. Visual aids must be sized correctly and interact with the text (Horton).

Correct size can be electronic size or physical size or both. Electronic size is the number of kilobytes (K) that the visual uses. The larger the K, the slower the image loads. A site with several large-K (above 150K) color images will take a long time to load on a 56K modem.

Follow these guidelines to control the electronic size of your visuals:

- Use fewer visuals.
- Use a software program to compress visuals to reduce their electronic size.
- Use a "thumbnail" linked to a larger version (see Figure 13.14).

Figure 13.14

Use of Thumbnails

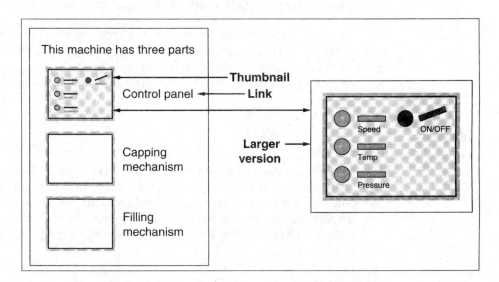

Figure 13.15

Effective Sizes of Visuals on Screen

Physical size is related to the number of pixels occupying the screen. The average screen is 15 inches with 480 × 640 pixels. If the visual aid occupies most of that pixel space, there is nothing left for text (see Figure 13.15).

Learn to manipulate image size. All programs that help you produce images (such as Photoshop) allow you to alter dimensions. Often, if you make an image smaller, you make it more illegible. If you capture the image of a screen, for instance, and then reduce it to one-fourth its original size, the text on the screen will probably be illegible. To fix this problem, Web authors *resample* the image, a process that restores legibility. Consult the help menu or manuals of programs like Photoshop or Front Page to learn how to resample.

Notice Figures 1 and 2 in "Focus on HTML" (pp. 341–342). The image of the cabin, as scanned in, originally was approximately four times as large as it is on screen. Notice in Figure 1 that the writer has sized the image by inserting *width* and *height* commands into the code.

Follow these guidelines for the best presentation of physical size:

- If the text and visual complement each other (as in a step in a set of instructions), use no more than half the screen width for the visual.
- If you reduce a visual in size, resample it.
- Use visuals on screen to clarify your message for your readers.

Testing 测 试

Your Web document must be usable. Readers must be able to navigate the site easily and access the information they need. In order to ensure easy navigation and access, you must test your document. Either perform the test yourself or have another person do it. Testing consists of checking for basic editing, audience effectiveness, consistency, navigation, the electronic environment, and clarity.

Basic Editing 基本编辑

Web documents include large amounts of text that must be presented with the same exactness as text in a paper document. If the editing details are handled effectively, the credibility of the site is increased.

Check your site for stylistic elements.

- Spelling
- Fragments, run-ons, comma splices
- Overuse of *there are, this is*
- Weak pronoun reference
- Scannable presentation, including use of the inverted pyramid style

Audience Effectiveness 读者有效性

Your site must put the audience into a role. Checking for audience role is highly subjective.

- Is it apparent what role the audience should assume, either from direct comments or from clear implications in the way the audience is addressed?
- Do all parts of the site help the audience assume that role?

Consistency 连贯性

Readers find sites easier to navigate and access if all items are handled consistently (Pearrow). The document has many text features that should be repeated consistently in order to establish visual logic. These features include font, font size, color, placement on the screen, and treatment (bold, italics, all caps). In addition, a document has many visual features that must remain consistent in order to establish the visual logic. These features include size and placement on the screen.

Check these textual items for font, font size, color, placement on the screen, and treatment:

- Titles
- Headings
- Captions for figures
- Body text
- Lists
- Links

Check these visual items for size and placement on the screen:

- Clip art
- Photographs
- Tables and graphs
- Screen captures

Ethics and Websites 使用网站的注意事项

For websites, as for all sources of information, technical communicators must act ethically. As with all documents, it is unethical to manipulate data, use deliberately misleading or ambiguous language, exaggerate claims, or conceal information that your users need in order to make good decisions (Summers and Summers 127).

However, communicators must also act ethically in regard to all the elements of websites: their design, code, graphics, and text. A major issue is plagiarism, using someone else's work without permission or acknowledgment. To state it succinctly, all aspects of websites are protected by copyright law. You are not permitted to copy anything from a website and use it on your website unless you either have permission or clearly acknowledge the source. As one expert says, "A work is copyrighted by the author at the moment of creation." A copyright notice or symbol, or "official" registration of a copyright, is not necessary—the rights automatically exist (Pfaff-Harris).

Another expert says this: "Simply put, by the time you see a webpage posted on the Web or a Usenet message posted in a newsgroup, it . . . is protected by copyright. You are not permitted to copy it, even if there is no copyright notice on the page or message" (Bunday). If you do post without permission or acknowledgment, you are not only violating the copyright law, "you are acting unethically because you are benefiting from someone else's work, without permission or due compensation. You are taking something that does not belong to you" (Murtaugh).

The best way for a communicator to ensure that she or he is using resources ethically is simply to ask the administrator of a website or the author of an e-mail message for permission to use the material and to give credit where credit is due. Often an e-mail request is all that is needed.

From another point of view, creators of websites can encourage ethical action by placing copyright notices on their sites, even though such notice is not required in order to be protected by the copyright law. Such a notice includes a copyright symbol, the years of creation and last modification, the name of the copyright holder, and the phrase "All rights reserved" (Murtaugh).

Another, somewhat different ethical strategy is to help viewers situate themselves. Summers and Summers suggest that you should include information on the creator and purpose of the site, and on the date it was last updated. This type of information will "help users evaluate the quality of the content you have provided" (Summers and Summers 130).

For a helpful overview of websites and ethical issues, see the article by Pfaff-Harris.

Works Cited

Bunday, Karl M. "Building Better Web Sites." 2000. Learn in Freedom. 24 April 2004. <http://learninfreedom.org/technical_notes.html>.

Murtaugh, Tim. "Pointing and Laughing: FAQs." 4 April 2002. New Press: Pirated-Sites.com. 24 April 2004. <www.pirated-sites.com/faqs/>.

> Pfaff-Harris, Kristina. "Copyright Issues on the Web." The Internet TESL Journal II.10 (October 1996). 24 April 2004. <http://iteslj.org/Articles/Harris-Copyright.html>.
> Summers, Kathryn, and Michael Summers. *Creating Websites That Work.* Boston: Houghton Mifflin, 2005.

Navigation   导 航

To check for navigation is to investigate whether all the links work and whether the path through the material makes the material accessible. To check whether all the links work is easy. Simply try each link. Make note of any that are "broken," that is, do not lead to any document. To determine if the path through the material makes the material accessible is more subjective. An effective way to investigate accessibility is to ask questions of yourself or your tester (Pearrow):

- Starting at the homepage, can you find information X quickly?
- From any point in the site or document, can you easily return to the homepage or top?
- Does the homepage give the reader an overview of the purpose and contents of the site or document?
- Does the title of any page repeat the wording of the link that led to it?
- At any time is the user annoyed? For instance, does a visual take a long time to open?

The Electronic Environment   电子环境

The electronic environment of your site or document is the way in which it interacts with the reader's viewing equipment—modem, computer, and browser software. The basic guideline is that all your material should appear on screen quickly and be designed as you intended.

Check these electronic aspects:

- How long does the site or document take to load? Ten seconds appears to be the limit readers will wait before they get annoyed and click away to another site. Answer this question by using different access methods. Load the site over a 56K modem and over a T1 line. The differences are often large. Some programs (such as Front Page) provide a menu item that gives this information.
- Does the browser used affect whether the features appear? The two major browsers are Internet Explorer and Netscape Communicator. In most cases, but not all, a site will appear exactly the same regardless of which browser the viewer uses. For various program coding reasons, more sophisticated elements such as tables, frames, and videos sometimes work in one browser but not in the other. Checking a site with both browsers will ensure that

readers see the items that you intended in the manner in which you intended.

If you must include features that only one browser supports, alert viewers to that effect ("Use Internet Explorer in order to view all the features of this site."). If you are using an application that viewers can download a version of for free (e.g., Shockwave), include a link to that site.

Clarity 清晰度

The site or document must appear clearly on the screen. A viewer must be able to read all the elements.

To check for clarity, answer the following questions:

- Do all the visual aids appear? If not, edit the Web document to make sure that they do.
- Can all the text be read? Sometimes, inexperienced Web authors use color combinations that make text hard to read (black text on a blue background, yellow text on a white background).
- Are the visual aids clear? If visual aids are fuzzy or illegible, edit them in a software program (such as Photoshop) that allows you to resample the image.

Worksheet for Planning a Website or Document
设计网站或文件工作表

- ☐ Identify the audience and the role they will play.
- ☐ Identify questions the audience will have about the content.
- ☐ Identify probable nodes for the site or document.
- ☐ Create a flow chart that indicates hierarchy and paths.
- ☐ Plan paths that give readers the freedom they need.
- ☐ Plan features of site (both screen and text items) that will facilitate the way readers find the information that they need.
- ☐ Create a screen template that groups similar information into distinct locations, including placement of visual aids.
- ☐ Choose font and color for heads and text.
- ☐ Determine which visual aids you need to convey your information.
- ☐ Choose a neutral background (light blues are good).
- ☐ Write text in manageable chunks.

Worksheet for Evaluating a Website

网站评估
工作表

Homepage
- Does the title make the content clear?
- Does the introduction tell you the purpose of the site?
- Can the homepage fit on one screen only?
- Did the site load quickly?

Navigation/Links
- Does every link work?
- Does every link have the same wording as the title of the page it links to?
- Are links coded or designed so that similar links look the same?
- Are all links of the same type always in the same location on each page?
- Do readers have sufficient freedom to access sections?
- Is the level of freedom too restrictive or annoying?
- Did you get lost navigating the site? If so, where?

Style
- Does the word choice indicate an exact awareness of the audience's knowledge and expectations?
- Are all the words spelled correctly?
- Is the grammar correct?

Text/Screen
- Is the background the same color in each document?
- Is the title of the page in the largest type on that page?
- Are all similar objects placed in the same place and do they have the same size?
- Are items on the page "clumped" so that the most important are together, set in bigger type and placed higher up?
- Can an audience easily read each document or is the font too small or too big or too busy?
- Does every document have the same font, including size?
- Is the text always aligned left?
- Is the format of each page consistent with every other page in the site?

Information
- Can readers easily figure out your plan of organization?
- Is the plan easy to find in the visual design you present?
- Does each section use appropriately convincing examples to inform the reader?
- Does each section start with a clear introduction that lists both the purpose and the parts of that section?
- Does each section contain a list of references with title of page, URL, and date visited?

(continued)

(continued)

Visual Aid Design
- Does each image load?
- Does the picture or table add a dimension of detail or interest not available in words?
- Is each visual aid in the same relative place on the page?
- Is the visual aid one that really helps a reader (and is not a waste of space and reader time)?
- Is there a clear cross-reference to each visual aid from the text?
- Does each visual aid have a caption?
- Is each visual aid roughly the same size?

Examples 例 子

Here are the report sections from the homepage presented in Figure 13.4, another informational Web report, and two sets of instructions. Note that Example 13.3 contains links to many other sections that are lower in the report's hierarchy. Those sections are not reproduced here.

Example 13.1

Report Sections That Can Be Linked to Homepage

List of links includes all sections, except planning.

> PLANNING IS THE KEY TO SUCCESS
>
> Much like any other project that you may tackle, creating a good website involves a little bit of planning. Many things have to be taken into account when you begin writing your own webpage.
>   The following should be considered:
>
> 1. Appearance
> 2. Actual size
> 3. Links
> 4. Visuals
> 5. Audience
> 6. Design
>
> Go to other sections of this report:
>
> *Establishing a Purpose*—Before you embark on this voyage . . .
> *Implementing Links*—In order to make your site easy to use . . .
> *Handling Visuals and Text*—These seem to spice up your website, but . . .
> *Interactive Websites*—People do not just want to see a webpage, they want to . . .

ESTABLISHING A PURPOSE FOR YOUR WEBSITE

Before you decide what you are going to put up on your webpage, it is important that you define what purpose your website intends to serve. A lot of people have a webpage just for the sake of having one. Their homepage is just kind of there for others to look at. There is no way to interact with the webpage. Webpages should have the purpose clearly stated on them, so the reader knows what they are getting into.

Go to other sections of this report:

Planning Is the Key—Planning is essential in order for you to . . .
Implementing Links—In order to make your site easy to use . . .
Handling Visuals and Text—These seem to spice up your website, but . . .
Interactive Websites—People do not just want to see a webpage, they want to . . .

> Wording of links repeats keywords in titles of other sections.

IMPLEMENTING LINKS IN YOUR WEBPAGE

People need to be able to navigate their way around your website once they are in it. They should be able to move back, forward, and to other sites if they want to. The more links a webpage has, the more freedom the reader has to pick and choose whatever it is he or she wants to read.

One of the biggest complaints I've heard from Web users is the fact that they often feel "trapped" inside of webpages, with no way out except to use the "Back" key. However, one must decide carefully the number of links to include, and which ones to exclude as well.

Go to other sections of this report:

Planning Is the Key—Planning is essential in order for you to . . .
Establishing a Purpose—Before you embark on this voyage . . .
Handling Visuals and Text—These seem to spice up your website, but . . .
Interactive Websites—People do not just want to see a webpage, they want to . . .

HANDLING VISUALS AND TEXT

Much like the traditional medium of written communication, webpages, too, benefit from visual aids. Visuals tend to catch the eye of the reader and take the place of text as well. However, when placing visuals on the Web, they must be planned just as carefully as they are when they are placed on paper. The same technical writing rules apply to visuals on the Web.

(continued)

Example 13.1
(continued)

> Text needs to be thought about, too. Especially on the Web, short "chunks" are necessary to keep the reader's interest. Because a computer screen seems to be smaller than what we would actually see on a regular sheet of paper, readers seemed to be turned off by large blocks of text on the Web. They are forced to keep scrolling down in order to get everything. Also, the bolding of heads and increasing their font sizes makes these items dominant over all other text, as they should be.
>
> Go to other sections of this report:
>
> *Planning Is the Key*—Planning is essential in order for you to . . .
> *Establishing a Purpose*—Before you embark on this voyage . . .
> *Implementing Links*—In order to make your site easy to use . . .
> *Interactive Websites*—People do not just want to see a webpage, they want to . . .

> **INTERACTIVE WEBSITES**
>
> It is nice to have a webpage that allows readers to interact with the webpage somehow. Some examples of this may include a webpage that allows readers to e-mail the authors with questions or comments. Including your e-mail address on your webpage allows others to give you some input and constructive criticism about your website.
>
> Another way a webpage could be interactive is through links that allow you to order something or inquire about something. Many companies today have their catalogs on the Web, and people can order things directly from the Internet. It is amazing what kind of feedback you can receive, or how your sales can increase, if you make your website interactive.
>
> Go to other sections of this report:
>
> *Planning Is the Key*—Planning is essential in order for you to . . .
> *Establishing a Purpose*—Before you embark on this voyage . . .
> *Implementing Links*—In order to make your site easy to use . . .
> *Handling Visuals and Text*—These seem to spice up your website, but . . .

Example 13.2

Informational Web Report, Using Anchor Link Strategy

Links that jump reader to appropriate section.

> **IMRD: RESEARCH REPORT**
>
> Introduction / Method / Results / Discussion
>
> **Introduction**
>
> With the advanced use of the electronic job-search, it is becoming difficult to ignore the increasingly important role of the on-line résumé. Since com-

puters are becoming increasingly user-friendly, even those with relatively little computer experience are becoming familiar with this technique. One eminent problem, however, is the question of how users can get the information they need to the end they desire. This page will focus on how to translate a current résumé into one that is readily accessible for use in this type of a search. We aim to overcome the problem that there are limitless ways for an employer to request such résumés: as an attachment, as text format, as HTML, and still others limiting the characters per line to 80. A solution is a résumé done in HTML, since anyone with Web access can get it open—in most cases, if the reader is getting your e-mail, he or she also has a browser installed. The only problem that remains is that of the fonts you choose—the user may have different default fonts set. Add a line "Best read in xxx font"—is there another way? **Top**

> "Top" links return reader to links at beginning of document.

Method

I went on to create an electronic résumé, to be either included or posted on the Web. To do this, I saved my résumé, which was previously in Word format, as HTML. I inserted horizontal lines, as well as targets and anchors. Then I reopened the copy of my résumé that had been saved in Word and saved it this time in .txt format. I then changed the page layout from a contemporary design to a more standardized paragraph form. **Top**

Results

Attempt	Result
Word to HTML	When I changed my résumé from Word to HTML format, the result was that I lost much of the formatting I had done, because HTML does not support it. To force my résumé to look essentially the same, I inserted tables. Moreover, the targets and anchors were inserted to help eliminate the problem of not being able to view all of the information on the screen, as you would if the résumé were in front of you. The horizontal lines further helped to separate each section of information for the reader's understanding.
Word to text	When I changed my résumé from Word to .txt format, the result was that I lost much of the formatting I had done. In this case, I had even fewer options and ended up deciding on a different layout for my résumé altogether, simplifying it greatly. This, however, includes the issue of having 80 characters per line, as it was easy to change the page layout so that, despite any line specification, it would match. **Top**

(continued)

Example 13.2

(continued)

> Discussion
>
> Because specifications vary from employer to employer, there are limitless ways of sending a résumé electronically. Hence, there is no perfect or universal résumé—a relatively frustrating result of this process. However, it is useful at this time to have a copy of your résumé in multiple formats so that they are readily available despite the request—particularly in .txt format, as this can be attached, sent as an e-mail, and easily translated to HTML. A solution to this problem is, just as a paper résumé has standards, to have standards for the electronic résumé. This will take time and the acceptance of the résumé in this medium. The best way to be safe right now is to save your résumé as text.   <u>Top</u>

Example 13.3

Instructions on a Webpage

Links lead to more detailed discussions.

> DEVELOPING ELECTRONIC RÉSUMÉS
>
> Developing an electronic résumé is a useful technique, particularly when doing electronic job searches. It gets your credentials across to the reader, as well as allowing the freedom to move around efficiently. These instructions will lead you step by step through the process of creating an electronic résumé.
>
> **RECOMMENDATIONS**
>
> - *It is recommended that you create your résumé before beginning this process*. Typically, résumés require a great deal of information, and the beginner will find it simpler to understand the contents of these instructions without being concerned with this information. <u>Traditional résumé sections</u>
>
> **ASSUMPTIONS**
>
> These instructions assume that the user
>
> - Has a basic knowledge of how to operate a personal computer.
> - Has a basic knowledge of how to operate basic features of a word processor program.
> - Has not previously created an HTML-formatted résumé.
> - Has a basic concept of a résumé.
>
> Operational assumptions:
>
> - The user is currently operating in Microsoft Word.
> - The user has previously saved a copy of the résumé in Word format.
>
> **DIRECTIONS**
>
> 1. Open your résumé as you would normally.
>   - Check to assure that you have it saved in <u>Word format</u>.

Examples

Links lead to more detailed discussions.

2. Save your résumé as an HTML document.
3. As a result of the previous step, *your document will lose all formatting* that was in place in the Word document. To get the results of formatting in your new HTML document,
   a. Insert a table.
   b. Insert horizontal lines to visually separate section bodies of the résumé.
4. Insert a horizontal menu between your name and the first section of your résumé. This menu should be horizontal, with the main sections of your résumé and index items. See example.
5. Create internal hyperlinks from each index item in the menu to the respective section body within the résumé.
   - This will let the user view the sections of your résumé that they wish to see.
6. Other formatting to enhance your résumé:
   a. Horizontal menus at the end of each résumé section (example)
      - Add internal hyperlinks for usability.
7. Add a Letter of Application.
   a. Save as a separate HTML document.
   b. Insert a hyperlink at the bottom of each page
      - So that the reader can move back and forth between your Résumé and Letter of Application.
8. Open a copy of a Web browser. Open your document and view it to assure that it is functioning properly.
9. *Your resume is now ready!* You can now
   - Send it as an attachment to anyone with a browser that can view it.
   - Contact your local Web administrator to post it on your website.
   - Do an electronic job search and post your résumé on the employers' sites.

Example 13.4

Instruction Set

This short document uses the "scroll" strategy.

DOWNLOADING AND SAVING IMAGES OFF THE WEB

1. Open an Internet browser program like Microsoft Internet Explorer or Netscape Navigator, and "surf" the Internet until you find an image that you would like to download.
2. Using the mouse, move the pointer arrow until it is on the image that you wish to download, and click on the right mouse button. A pop-up menu will appear next to the image you have selected.

(continued)

Example 13.4
(continued)

The pop-up menu that appears will let you choose several options:

Save Picture lets you save the picture as a .gif file to your disk or the computer's hard drive.

Set as Wallpaper lets you use the picture as the "wallpaper" or background on your computer's desktop screen.

Copy lets you copy the picture into another program or document (e.g., Microsoft Word) using the program's edit and paste features.

Add to Favorites lets you bookmark the webpage that the image is on into the "favorites" section of your Internet browser software.

Properties will tell you the name of the picture file, the address of the webpage on which it is found, the type of file the picture is (e.g., .gif), and the size of the picture file.

3. Click on Save Picture. A Save Picture dialogue window will open that looks like this (Figure 1):

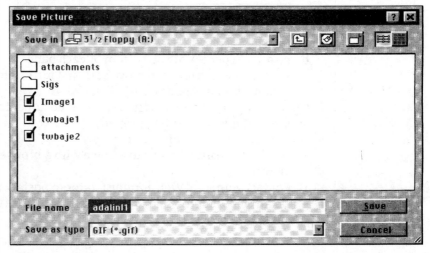

Figure 1

Highlighted terms duplicate wording and look of terms in Figure 1.

Save in allows you to choose the disk drive that you want the picture to be saved on.

File name allows you to type in the name you wish the picture to be saved as.

Save as type lets you choose what type of file you wish the picture to be saved as. Image or picture files are usually saved as .gif files or .jpg files. Notice that the .gif file type popped up in the "Save as type" box as a default.

4. Fill in the appropriate information in the "Save in," "File name," and "Save as type" dialogue boxes and then click Save.

Crop an Image / Resize an Image / Change Image Resolution

全球化/本地化和网站
Globalization/Localization and Websites

As Internet use grows worldwide, so does the number of non-English-speakers who use it. According to International Data Corporation (IDC), by 2005 non-English speakers will represent 70 percent of all Web users ("Globalization"). In order to reach a wider audience and/or client base, websites written in English must be able to be translated for use in non-English-speaking countries. Preparing a website for localization in other countries, languages, and cultures presents certain challenges.

One of the most common problems in website translation is the expansion and contraction of text. European languages often take up as much as 30 percent more space than English on a webpage. For example, Italian, Czech, German, and Greek will all expand to over 100 percent of English text, whereas Arabic, Hebrew, and Hindi will contract to less than 100 percent (Hoft). The languages that rely on characters (e.g., Japanese, Chinese, Korean—referred to as "double-byte" languages) can take up more or less space. It is difficult to predict exactly how a double-byte translation will affect your screen design until the actual translation is in place. This in turn interferes with spacing in the text and effective positioning of visual aids. Keep this contraction and expansion in mind when designing your screens, composing content, setting table properties, and creating graphics. Give extra space around items such as control buttons, menu trees, and dialog boxes (Macromedia).

When creating tables on your websites, base the properties on the longest translation that will be used on your site. If you use percentages rather than pixels, you can set your tables to 100 percent width. This will allow the table and the text to expand according to the user's browser—the text and the graphics will appear the same to users viewing it in French as it will to those using the English-language version (Macromedia).

The symbols you choose are critical also. Avoid culturally specific symbols. Graphics with multiple meanings, pictures of body parts, religious symbols (e.g., a cross), or even symbols such as a stop sign may cause confusion, misunderstanding, and may even be construed as offensive ("Globalization"). Both the American A-Okay sign (thumb and forefinger forming a circle) and the thumbs-up sign are considered obscene gestures in parts of Europe, Middle Eastern countries, Brazil, and Australia. A website that utilized these symbols would signal to users in those areas that you hadn't done any research on their culture and customs.

Be sure to budget time for adjustments, even if you think you've optimized the site for localization.

For further reference:
Nancy Hoft Consulting at <www.world-ready.com> is a training and consulting firm that specializes in effective techniques for communicating with multilingual and multicultural audiences. Look here for their advice on writing and designing for a global community and for links to other helpful sites.

(continued)

(continued)

> The Macromedia DreamWeaver Support Center at <www.macromedia.com/support/dreamweaver/manage/localization_design/localization_design03.html> has a great example, based on a French chocolate manufacturer's website, of text expansion and contraction and other issues with website design.
>
> **Works Cited**
> "Globalization, Internationalization, Localization: An Overview." 2001–2004. Globalization.com. 7 Feb. 2004 <www.globalization.com/index.cfm?MycatID=1&MysubCatID=1&pageID=1322>.
> Hoft, Nancy. "Writing and Designing for an International Audience." 5 Apr. 2002. 7 Feb. 2004 <www.world-ready.com/stcorlando.htm>.
> Macromedia Dreamweaver Support Center. "Accounting for text expansion and contraction." 27 Aug. 2001. 7 Feb. 2004. <www.macromedia.com/support/dreamweaver/manage/localization_design/localization_design03.html>.

Exercises 练 习

These exercises assume that they will occur in a computer lab where it is possible to project a site onto many screens or one large one. In that situation, small groups of two or three and oral reporting seem most effective. However, if individual work and written reports work better in the local situation, use that approach.

▶ You Create

1. Create a simple webpage that includes a title, text about yourself, and at least one visual aid.
2. Using the page you created in Exercise 1, create two other versions of it. Keep the content the same, but change the design.
3. Create a series of paragraphs that presents the same information in promotional, concise, and scannable text.
4. Create or download an image. Present it on a webpage in three different sizes. In groups of two or three, discuss how you achieved the differences and the effect of the differences. Report your findings orally to the class.
5. Using the page you created in Exercise 1, make several different backgrounds. In groups of three or four, review the effectiveness of the background (Is it distracting? Does it obscure the text?), and demonstrate both a good and bad version to the class.

▶ You Analyze/Group

6. Go to any website. In groups of two or three, assess the role the reader is asked to assume. Orally report your findings to the class. Alternative: Write a brief analytical report in which you identify the role and present support for your conclusion.

7. Go to any website. In groups of two or three, assess the style of the text. Is it promotional, concise, or scannable? Present your findings orally to the class. Or, as in Exercise 6, write a brief analysis.

8. Go to any website. In groups of two or three, assess the use of visuals at the site. Review for clarity, length of time to load, physical placement on the site. Present an oral report to the class, or write an information analysis.

9. Go to any website. In groups of two or three, assess the template. Are types of information effectively grouped? Is it easy to figure out where the links will take you? Report orally or in writing as your instructor requires.

10. In groups of two or three, critique any of the Examples (pp. 330–336) or use one of the samples in the website that accompanies this text. Judge them in terms of style, screen design, and audience role. Explain where you think the examples are strong and where they could be improved.

Writing Assignment 写作任务

Create an informational website; if possible, load it onto the Web so that others may review it. Determine a purpose and an audience for the site. Create a homepage and documents that carry out the purpose. The site should have at least three nodes. Before you create the site, fill out the planning sheet on page 328. Your instructor will place you in a "review group"; set up a schedule with the other group members so that they can review your site for effectiveness at several points in your process. To review the site, use the points in the section "Testing" (pp. 324–328) or use the Worksheet for Evaluating a Website (pp. 329–330).

Web Exercise 网络练习

Review two or three websites of major corporations in order to determine how they use the elements of format. Review the homepage, but also review pages that are several layers "in" (e.g., Our Products/Cameras/UltraCompacts) in the Web; typically, pages further "in" look more like printed pages. Write a brief analytical or IMRD report discussing your results.

Works Cited and Consulted 引用或参考的作品

Brooks, Randy M. "Principles for Effective Hypermedia Design." *Technical Communication* 40.3 (August 1993): 422–428.

Coney, Mary, and Michael Steehouder. "Role Playing on the Web: Guidelines for Designing and Evaluating Personas Online." *Technical Communication* 47.3 (August 2000): 327–340.

December, John. "An Information Development Methodology for the World Wide Web." *Technical Communication* 43.4 (November 1996): 369–376.

Farkas, David K., and Jean B. Farkas. "Guidelines for Designing Web Navigation." *Technical Communication* 47.3 (August 2000): 341–358.

Gallagher, Susan. "Your First Web Page." *intercom* 44.4 (May 1997): 13–15.

Grice, Roger A., and Lenore S. Ridgway. "Presenting Technical Information in Hypermedia Format: Benefits and Pitfalls." *Technical Communication Quarterly* 4.1 (Winter 1995): 35–46.

Horton, William. *Designing and Writing Online Documentation: Hypermedia for Self-Supporting Products.* 2nd ed. New York: Wiley, 1994.

Hunt, Kevin. "Establishing a Presence on the World Wide Web: A Rhetorical Approach." *Technical Communication* 43.4 (November 1996): 376–387.

Nielson, Jakob. "How Users Read the Web." 1 Oct. 1997. 24 April 2004 <www.useit.com/alertbox/981129.html>.

Pearrow, Mark. *Web Site Usability Handbook.* Rockland, MA: Charles River Media, 2000.

Spyridakis, Jan. "Guidelines for Authoring Comprehensible Web Pages and Evaluating Their Success." *Technical Communication* 47.3 (August 2000): 359–382.

Tatters, Wes. *Teach Yourself Netscape Web Publishing in a Week.* Indianapolis: Samsnet, 1996.

Wilkinson, Theresa A. "Web Site Planning." *intercom* 44.10 (December 1997): 14–15.

Williams, Thomas R. "Guidelines for Designing and Evaluating the Display of Information on the Web." *Technical Communications* 47.3 (August 2000): 383–396.

 关注HTML

HTML (*H*yper*t*ext *M*arkup *L*anguage) is the invisible structure of the Web. Viewers can see a Web document because the browser (e.g., Netscape Communicator or Internet Explorer) "reads" an HTML document and displays the results on the screen. Actually, HTML is a code, a series of typed orders placed in the document. For instance, to make a word appear boldfaced on the screen, the writer places a "start bold" () and an "end bold" () command in the HTML document:

I want you to read this book.

The browser displays the sentence

I want you to **read** this book.

HTML code exists for everything that makes a document have a particular appearance on screen. If the item appears on screen, it appears because the code told the browser to display it. Codes exist for paragraphing, fonts, font sizes, color, tables, and all other aspects of a document. Codes tell which visual aid should appear in a particular place in a document. Figures 1 and 2 show the HTML code for a simple document and the document as it displays on a browser.

| ``` <html> <head> <title> Sample Display Techniques Illustrated </title></head> <body> <b><h3>Sample Display Techniques Illustrated </b></h3> by Dan Riordan <p>These pages illustrate several techniques for displaying information. I have illustrated ways to use lists, the align command, the anchor command, and escape links. <p><b>List</b> I like to teach, especially <ul> <li>in groups and <li>using technology.</ul> <p><b>Align Center</b> My wife and I often visit a cabin up north. Here is what the cabin looks like: <center><img src="twridal.gif" width=100 height=167></center> <p><b>Anchor</b> This device allows you to "link" inside a document. I illustrate the device by letting you read a series of <a href="twrida5.htm">letters</a> my family's immigrants wrote in the 1850s. <p><b>Escape Links</b> Here are "escape links" to sites connected to this one:
<b><i><small>Return to
<a href="http://www.uwstout.edu/english/riordan/ techwrit/techwrit.htm">Technical Writing </a>|</b> <b><i> <a href="http//www.uwstout.edu/english/ projects.htm">English Department Student Projects</a>|</b> <b><i> <a href="http//www.uwstout.edu/english/ english.htm">English Department</a></p></b></i> </small> </body> </html> ``` | browser title

title

text

list

visual aid

"escape links" |

Figure 1
HTML Code for a Web Document

(continued)

(continued)

The classic way to develop a site is to create material using an ASCII text editor like Notepad (DOS) or SimpleText (Mac). The method for creating it is easy.

- Open a file in one of these two programs.
- Type in certain HTML commands.
- Type in your text.

But typing in code is time consuming and susceptible to errors. If, for instance, one of the brackets (>) is omitted in the boldface code, the word will not appear as boldfaced. As a result, most Web authors use a Web authoring program that creates the code as the writer designs the webpage on screen. Many such programs exist. Some of the most frequently used are Front Page, DreamWeaver, AdobeGoLive, and Netscape Composer. Instructions on using such programs are beyond the scope of this book; however, many good instruction books are available, and all the programs have help menus and training tutorials. The best advice is to begin to practice with the programs to learn their features and to develop enough proficiency so that you can achieve the effects that you visualize.

Sample Display Techniques Illustrated

by Dan Riordan

These pages illustrate techniques for displaying information. I have illustrated ways to use lists, the align command, the anchor command, and escape links.

List I like to teach, especially

- in groups and
- using technology

Align My wife and I often visit a <u>cabin</u> up north. Here is what the cabin looks like:

Anchor This device allows you to "link" inside a document. I illustrate the device by letting you read a series of <u>letters</u> my family's immigrants wrote in the 1850s.

Escape Links Here are the "escape links" to sites connected to this one:

Return to

<u>Technical Writing</u> | <u>English Department Student Projects</u> | <u>English Department</u>

Figure 2
Browser Display of the Code in Figure 1

Chapter 14 Formal Reports
正式报告

Chapter Contents
Chapter 14 In a Nutshell
The Elements of a Formal Report
Front Material
The Body of the Formal Report
End Material

Chapter 14 In a Nutshell 概 要

Formal format presents documents in a way that makes them seem more "official." Often the format is used with longer (10 or more pages) documents, or else in documents that establish policy, make important proposals, or present the results of significant research.

Formal format requires a title page, a table of contents, a summary, and an introduction, in that order.

The *title page* gives an overview of the report—title, author, date, report number if required, and report recipient if required. Place all these items, separated by white space, at the left margin of the page.

The *table of contents* lists all the main sections and subsections of the report and the page on which each one begins.

The *summary*—often called "executive summary" and sometimes "abstract"—presents the report in brief. The standard method is to write the summary as a "proportional reduction"; each section of the summary has the same main point and the relative length as the original section. After your readers finish the summary, they should know your conclusions and your reasons.

The *introduction* contains all the usual introductory topics but gives each of them a head—background, scope, purpose, method, and recommendations.

Chapter 14 Formal Reports

Formal reports are those presented in a special way to emphasize the importance of their contents. Writers often use formal reports to present recommendations or results of research. Other reasons for using a formal approach are length (over 10 pages), breadth of circulation, perceived importance to the community, and company policy. Although a formal report looks very different from an informal report, the contents can be exactly the same. The difference is in the changed perception caused by the formal presentation. This chapter explains the elements of formal reports and discusses devices for the front, body, and end material.

The Elements of a Formal Report 正式报告的组成

To produce a formal report, the writer uses several elements that orient readers to the report's topics and organization. Those elements unique to the formal report are the front material and the method of presenting the body. Other elements—appendixes, reference sections, introductions, conclusions, and recommendations—are often associated with the formal report but do not necessarily make the report formal; they could also appear in an informal report.

The formal front material includes the title page, the table of contents, and the list of illustrations. Almost all formal reports contain a summary at the front, and many also have a letter of transmittal. The body is often presented in "chapters," each major section starting at the top of a new page.

Because these reports often present recommendations, they have two organizational patterns: traditional and administrative (Freeman and Bacon; ANSI). The traditional pattern leads the reader through the data to the conclusion (Freeman and Bacon). Thus conclusions and recommendations appear at the end of the report. The administrative pattern presents readers with the information they need to perform their role in the company, so conclusions and recommendations appear early in this report.

Traditional	Administrative
Title page	Title page
Table of contents	Table of contents
List of illustrations	List of illustrations
Summary or abstract	Summary or abstract
Introduction	Introduction
Discussion—Body Sections	Conclusions
Conclusions	Recommendations/Rationale
Recommendations/Rationale	Discussion—Body Sections
References	References
Appendixes	Appendixes

Front Material 前面的材料

Transmittal Correspondence 沟通函件

Transmittal correspondence is a memo or letter that directs the report to someone. A memo is used to transmit an internal, or in-house, report. An external, or firm-to-firm, report requires a letter. (See Chapter 19 for a sample letter.) In either form, the information remains the same. The correspondence contains

- The title of the report.
- A statement of when it was requested.
- A very general statement of the report's purpose and scope.
- An explanation of problems encountered (for example, some unavailable data).
- An acknowledgment of those who were particularly helpful in assembling the report.

Sample Memo of Transmittal

Date: May 1, 2005
To: Ms. Elena Solomonova, Vice-President, Administrative Affairs
From: Rachel A. Jacobson, Human Resources Director
Subject: Proposal for the Spousal Employment Assistance Program

Title of report / *Cause of writing*
Attached is my report "Proposal for the Implementation of a Spousal Employment Assistance Program," which you requested after our March 15 meeting.

Purpose of report / *Statement of request*
The report presents a solution to the problems identified by our large number of new hires. In brief, those new hires all had spouses who had to leave careers to move to Rochester. This proposal recommends initiating a spousal employment assistance program to deal with relocation problems.

Praise of coworkers
Compiled by the Human Resources staff, this report owes a significant debt to the employees and their spouses who agreed to be interviewed as part of its preparation.

Title Page 标题页

Well-done title pages (see Figure 14.1, p. 346) give a quick overview of the report, while at the same time making a favorable impression on the reader. Some firms have standard title pages just as they have letterhead stationery for business letters. Here are some guidelines for writing a title page:

Figure 14.1

Title Page for a Formal Report

PROPOSAL FOR THE IMPLEMENTATION
OF A SPOUSAL EMPLOYMENT
ASSISTANCE PROGRAM

By
Rachel A. Jacobson
Director, Human Resources

May 1, 2005

Corporate Proposal
HRD 01-01-2005

Prepared for
Elena Solomonova
Vice-President, Administrative Affairs

- Place all the elements at the left margin (ANSI). (Center all the elements if local policy insists.)
- Name the contents of the report in the title.
- Use a 2-inch left margin.
- Use either all caps or initial caps and lowercase letters; use boldface when appropriate. Do not use "glitzy" typefaces, such as outlined or cursive fonts.
- Include the writer's name and title or department, the date, the recipient's name and title or department, and a report number (if appropriate).

Table of Contents 目 录

A table of contents lists the sections of the report and the pages on which they start (see Figure 14.2). Thus it previews the report's organization, depth, and emphasis. Readers with special interests often glance at the table of contents, examine the abstract or summary, and turn to a particular section of the report. Here are some guidelines for writing a table of contents:

- Title the page *Table of Contents*.
- Present the name of each section in the same wording and format as it appears in the text. If a section title is all caps in the text, place it in all caps in the table of contents.
- Do not underline in the table of contents; the lines are so powerful that they overwhelm the words.

Front Material

Figure 14.2
Table of Contents for an Administrative Report

TABLE OF CONTENTS	
Summary	2
Introduction	3
Conclusion	4
Recommendation	4
Discussion	5
Nature of the Problem	6
Description of the Program	7
Advantages	9
Costs vs. Benefits	10
Implementation	13

- Do not use "page" or "p." before the page numbers.
- Use only the page number on which the section starts.
- Set margins so that page numbers align on the right.
- Present no more than three levels of heads; two is usually best.
- Use *leaders*, a series of dots, to connect words to page numbers.

List of Illustrations 插图列表

Illustrations include both tables and figures. The list of illustrations (Figure 14.3) gives the number, title, and page of each visual aid in the report. Here are guidelines for preparing a list of illustrations:

- Use the title *List of Illustrations* if it contains both figures and tables; list figures first, then tables.
- If the list contains only figures or only tables, call it *List of Figures* or *List of Tables*.
- List the number, title, and page of each visual aid.
- Place the list on the most convenient page. If possible, put it on the same page as the table of contents.

Figure 14.3
List of Illustrations for a Formal Report

LIST OF ILLUSTRATIONS	
Figure 1. Schedule for Program Implementation	10
Table 1. Special Features of the Program	7
Table 2. Cost/Employee Investment Comparison	8

Summary or Abstract 总结或摘要

A summary or an abstract (or executive summary) is a miniature version of the report. (See Chapter 8 for a full discussion of summaries and abstracts.)

In the summary, present the main points and basic details of the entire report. After reading a summary, the reader should know

- The report's purpose and the problem it addresses.
- The conclusions.
- The major facts on which the conclusions are based.
- The recommendations.

Because the summary "covers" many of the functions of an introduction, recent practice has been to substitute the summary for all or most of the introductory material, placing the conclusions and recommendations last. Used often in shorter (10- to 15-page) reports, this method eliminates the sense of overrepetition that is sometimes present when a writer uses the entire array of introductory elements.

Follow these guidelines to summarize your formal report:

- Concentrate this information into as few words as possible—one page at most.
- Write the summary *after* you have written the rest of the report. (If you write it first, you might be tempted to explain background rather than summarize the contents.)
- Avoid technical terminology (most readers who depend on a summary do not have in-depth technical knowledge).

SUMMARY

Recommendation given first
Background

This report recommends that the company implement a spousal assistance program. Swift expansion of the company has brought many new employees to us, most of whom had spouses who left professional careers. Because no assistance program exists, our employees and their spouses have found themselves involved in costly, time-consuming, and stressful situations that in several instances have affected productivity on the job.

Basic conclusions

Benefits

A spousal assistance program will provide services that include home- and neighborhood-finding assistance, medical practitioner referrals, and employment-seeking assistance. Advantages include increased employee morale, increased job satisfaction, and greater company loyalty.

Cost

Implementation

Cost is approximately $54,000/year. The major benefit is productivity of the management staff. The program will take approximately six months to implement and will require hiring one spousal employment assistance counselor.

Introduction 介 绍

The introduction orients the reader to the report's organization and contents. Formal introductions help readers by describing purpose, scope, procedure, and background. Statements of purpose, scope, procedure, and background orient readers to the report's overall context.

To give readers the gist of the report right away, many writers now place the conclusions/recommendation right after the introduction. Recently, writers have begun to combine the summary and the introductory sections to cut down on repetition. Example 14.1 (pp. 356–359) illustrates this approach.

Purpose Statement

State the *purpose* in one or two sentences. Follow these guidelines:

- State the purpose clearly. Use one of two forms: "The purpose of this report is to present the results of the investigation" or "This report presents the results of my investigation."
- Use the *present* tense.
- Name the alternatives if necessary. (In the purpose statement in the example below, the author names the problem [lack of a spousal assistance program] and the alternatives that she investigated.)

Scope Statement

A *scope statement* reveals the topics covered in a report. Follow these guidelines:

- In feasibility and recommendation reports, name the criteria; include statements explaining the rank order and source of the criteria.
- In other kinds of reports, identify the main sections, or topics, of the report.
- Specify the boundaries or limits of your investigation.

Procedure Statement

The *procedure statement*—also called the *methodology statement*—names the process followed in investigating the topic of the report. This statement establishes a writer's credibility by showing that he or she took all the proper steps. For some complex projects, a methodology section appears after the introduction and replaces this statement. Follow these guidelines:

- Explain all actions you took: the people you interviewed, the research you performed, the sources you consulted.
- Write this statement in the *past tense*.

- Select heads for each of the subsections. Heads help create manageable chunks, but too many of them on a page look busy. Base your decision on the importance of the statements to the audience.

Brief Problem (or Background) Statement

In this statement, which you can call either the *problem* or *background statement*, your goal is to help the readers understand—and agree with—your solution because they view the problem as you do. You also may need to provide background, especially for secondary or distant readers. Explain the origin of the problem, who initiated action on the problem, and why the writer was chosen. Follow these guidelines:

- Give basic facts about the problem.
- Specify the causes or origin of the problem.
- Explain the significance of the problem (short term and long term) by showing how new facts contradict old ways.
- Name the source of your involvement.

In the following example, the problem statement succinctly identifies the basic facts (relocating problems), the cause (out-of-state hires), the significance (decline in productivity), and the source (complaints to Human Resources). Here are the purpose, scope, procedure, and background statements of the proposal for Spousal Employment Assistance:

INTRODUCTION

Purpose

Two-part purpose: to present and to recommend

This proposal presents the results of the Human Resources Department's investigation of spousal employment assistance programs and recommends that XYZ Corp. implement such a program.

Scope

Lists topics covered in the report

This report details the problems caused by the lack of a spousal employment assistance program. It then considers the concerns of establishing such a program here at XYZ. These concerns include a detailed description of the services offered by such an office, the resources necessary to accomplish the task, and an analysis of advantages, costs, and benefits. An implementation schedule is included.

Procedure

Enough information given to establish credibility

The Human Resources Department gathered all the information for this report. We interviewed all 10 people (8 women and 2 men) hired within the past 12 months and 6 spouses (4 men and 2 women). We gathered information from professional articles on the subject. The human resources office provided all the salary and benefits figures. We also interviewed the director of a similar program operating in Arizona and a management training consultant from McCrumble University.

Problem

Background (cause)

Basic facts

Source of impetus to solve problem

Possible solution

In the past year, XYZ has expanded swiftly, and this expansion will occur throughout the near future. In the past year, 10 new management positions were created and filled. Seven of these people moved here from out of state. Several of these people approached the Human Resources Department for assistance with the problems involved in relocating.

Some of these problems were severe enough that some decline in productivity was noted and was also brought to the attention of Human Resources. Four of the managers left, citing stress as a major reason. That turnover further affected productivity. A spousal employment assistance office is one common way to handle such concerns and offset the potential bad effects of high turnover.

Lengthy Problem (or Background) Statements

Some reports explain both the problem and its context in a longer statement called either *Problem* or *Background*. A *background statement* provides context for the problem and the report. In it you can often combine background and problem in one statement.

Some situations require a lengthier treatment of the context of the report. In that case, the background section replaces the brief problem statement. Often this longer statement is placed first in the introduction, but practices vary. Place it where it best helps your readers.

To write an effective background statement, follow these guidelines:

- Explain the general problem.
- Explain what has gone wrong.
- Give exact facts.
- Indicate the significance of the problem.
- Specify who is involved and in what capacity.
- Tell why you received the assignment.

BACKGROUND

General problem

Management increases have brought many new persons into the XYZ team in the past year. This increase in personnel, while reflecting an excellent trend in a difficult market, has had a marked down side. The new personnel have all experienced significant levels of stress and some slide in productivity as a result of the move. All 10 of the recent hires had spouses who left professional career positions to relocate in Rochester. These people have experienced considerable difficulty finding career opportunities in our smaller urban region, and all the families have reported a certain amount of stress related to everything from finding a home to finding dentists. Four of these managers subsequently left our employ, citing stress as the major reason to leave. These departures caused us to undertake costly, time-consuming personnel searches.

After interviews revealed the existence of such stress, the Executive Committee of Administrative Affairs discussed the issue at length and authorized Human Resources to carry out this study. The Director of Human Resources chaired a committee composed of herself, one manager who did not leave, and a specialist on budget. HR staff conducted the data gathering.

Data on what is wrong

Significance

Why the author received the assignment

Conclusions and Recommendations/Rationale 结论和建议/基本原理

Writers may place these two sections at the beginning of the report or at the end. Choose the beginning if you want to give readers the main points first and if you want to give them a perspective from which to read the data in the report. Choose the end if you want to emphasize the logical flow of the report, leading up to the conclusion. In many formal reports, you present only conclusions because you are not making a recommendation.

Conclusions

The conclusions section emphasizes the report's most significant data and ideas. Base all conclusions only on material presented in the body. Follow these guidelines:

- Relate each conclusion to specific data. Don't write conclusions about material you have not discussed in the text.
- Use concise, numbered conclusions.
- Keep commentary brief.
- Add inclusive page numbers to indicate where to find the discussion of the conclusions.

CONCLUSIONS

This investigation has led to the following conclusions. (The page numbers in parentheses indicate where supporting discussion may be found.)

1. The stresses experienced by the new hires are significant and are expected to continue as the company expands (6).

Conclusions presented in same order as in text

2. Stress is not related to job difficulties but instead is related more to difficulties other family members are experiencing as a result of the relocation (6).
3. Professionals exist who are able to staff such programs (7).
4. The program will result in increased employee morale, increased job satisfaction, and greater company loyalty (9).
5. A program could begin for a cost of $54,000 (10).
6. The major benefits of the program will be increased productivity of the management staff and decreased turmoil created by frequent turnover (11).
7. A program would take six months to initiate (13).

Recommendations/Rationale

If the conclusions are clear, the main recommendation is obvious. The main recommendation usually fulfills the purpose of the report, but do not hesitate to make further recommendations. Not all formal reports make a recommendation.

In the rationale, explain your recommendation by showing how the "mix" of the criteria supports your conclusions. Follow these guidelines:

- Number each recommendation.
- Make the solution to the problem the first recommendation.
- If the rationale section is brief, add it to the appropriate recommendation.
- If the rationale section is long, make it a separate section.

RECOMMENDATIONS

Solution to the basic problem

1. XYZ should implement a spousal employment assistance program. This program is feasible and should eliminate much of the stress that has caused some of the personal anxiety and productivity decreases we have felt with the recent expansion.

Other recommendations on implementation

2. The Executive Committee should authorize Human Resources to begin the procedure of writing position guidelines and hiring an SEA counselor.

The Body of the Formal Report 正式报告的主体

The body of the formal report, like any other report, fills the needs of the reader. Issues of planning and design, covered in other chapters, all apply here. You can use any of the column formats displayed in Chapter 6 for laying out pages. Special concerns in formal reports are paginating and indicating chapter divisions.

Paginating 分页

Be consistent and complete. Follow these guidelines:

- Assign a number to each piece of paper in the report, regardless of whether the number actually appears on the page.
- Assign a page number to each full-page table or figure.
- Place the numbers in the upper right corner of the page with no punctuation, or center them at the bottom of the page either with no punctuation or with a hyphen on each side (-2-).
- Consider the title page as page 1. Do not number the title page. Most word processing systems allow you to delete the number from the title page.
- In very long reports, use lowercase roman numerals (i, ii, iii) for all the pages before the text of the discussion. In this case, count the title page as page i, but do not put the i on the page. On the next page, place a ii.
- Paginate the appendix as discussed in "End Material" (below).
- Use headers or footers (phrases in the top and bottom margins) to identify the topic of a page or section.

Indicating Chapter Divisions 标示章节安排

To make the report "more formal," begin each new major section at the top of a page (see Example 14.2, which starts on p. 360).

End Material 后面的材料

The end material (glossary and list of symbols, references, and appendixes) is placed after the body of the report.

Glossary and List of Symbols 术语表和符号列表

Traditionally, reports have included glossaries and lists of symbols. However, such lists tend to be difficult to use. Highly technical terminology and symbols should not appear in the body of a report that is aimed at a general or multiple audience. Place such material in the appendix. When you must use technical terms in the body of the report, define them immediately; informed readers can simply skip over the definitions. Treat the glossary as an appendix. If you need a glossary, follow these guidelines:

- Place each term at the left margin, and start the definition at a tab (2 or 3 spaces) farther to the right. Start all lines of the definition at this tab.
- Alphabetize the terms.

References   参考书目

The list of references (included when the report contains information from other sources) is discussed along with citation methods in Appendix B.

Appendix   附 件

The appendix contains information of a subordinate, supplementary, or highly technical nature that you do not want to place in the body of the report. Follow these guidelines:

- Refer to each appendix item at the appropriate place in the body of the report.
- Number illustrations in the appendix in the sequence begun in the body of the report.
- For short reports, continue page numbers in sequence from the last page of the body.
- For long reports, use a separate pagination system. Because the appendixes are often identified as Appendix A, Appendix B, and so on, number the pages starting with the appropriate letter: A-1, A-2, B-1, B-2.

Worksheet for Preparing a Formal Report   准备正式报告的工作表

- ☐ **Determine the audience for this report.**
  Who is the primary audience and who the secondary? How much does the audience understand about the origins and progress of this project? How will they use this report? Will it be the basis for a decision?
- ☐ **Plan the visual aids that will convey the basic information of your report.**
- ☐ **Construct those visual aids.**
  Follow the guidelines in Chapter 7.
- ☐ **Prepare a style sheet for up to four levels of heads and for margins, page numbers, and captions to visual aids.**
- ☐ **Decide whether each new section should start at the top of a new page.**
- ☐ **Create a title page.**
- ☐ **Prepare the table of contents.**
  How many levels of heads will you include? (Two is usual.) Will you use periods for leaders?

(continued)

(continued)

- ☐ Prepare the list of illustrations.
  Present figures first, then tables.
- ☐ **Determine the order of statements (purpose, scope, procedure, and so forth) in the introduction.**
  In particular, where will you place the problem and background statements? in the introduction? in a section in the body?
- ☐ Prepare a glossary if you use key terms unfamiliar to the audience.
- ☐ List conclusions.
- ☐ List recommendations, with most important first.
- ☐ Write the rationale to explain how the mix of conclusions supports the recommendations.
- ☐ Write the summary.
- ☐ Prepare appendixes of technical material.
  Use an appendix if the primary audience is nontechnical or if you have extensive tabular or support material.

Examples 练 习

Example 14.1 is the body of the report whose introduction is explained in this chapter. Example 14.2 is a brief formal report.

Example 14.1

Formal Report Body

DISCUSSION

In this section, I will describe spousal employment assistance (SEA), discuss the advantages and benefits of it, and develop a time schedule for the implementation of it.

NATURE OF THE PROBLEM

Many complex issues arise when relocating a dual-career family. Issues such as a new home, a new mortgage, two new jobs in the family, a new and reliable child care service—to name only a few. These issues, if not dealt with in an efficient manner, can create tremendous stress in the new employee—stress that dramatically affects productivity on the job.

Productivity and protection of our company's human resources investment are the key issues we are dealing with in this program. The intention is that the more quickly the employee can be productive and settled in a new area, the less costly it will be for our company.

DESCRIPTION OF THE PROGRAM

I am proposing a separate office within the company for the SEA program. It would be staffed by a consultant who would research and develop the following areas:

- Home-finding counseling
- Neighborhood finding
- Mortgage counseling
- Spouse and family counseling
- Spouse employment assistance
- Child care referrals
- School counseling
- Cost-of-living differences
- Doctor and dentist referrals

All counseling services would be handled by our SEA office employee except for formal employment assistance, which would be contracted with a third-party employment firm. A third-party firm can provide the advantage of objectivity as well as a proper level of current employment information.

ADVANTAGES OF THE PROGRAM

The program is a service provided by us, and paid for by us, that is for the sole purpose of assisting the new employee. The advantages are increased employee morale, increased job satisfaction, and greater company loyalty. The employee feels that the company is concerned with the problems he or she is facing in the relocation process. The assistance the employee receives makes the move easier, so adjusting to the new job is quicker. The result is a more productive employee.

WHAT ARE THE COSTS VERSUS THE BENEFITS?

Costs

The comprehensive program will cost the company approximately $54,500 per year. As illustrated in Table 1, this includes $2,500 for research and

(continued)

Example 14.1 (continued)

development, $27,000 for the SEA consultant, and $25,000 for the third-party employment firm (10 contracts at $2,500 each). This figure doesn't include the cost of office completion, which would run about $1,100 to finish the first-floor office space (room 120), which isn't currently occupied.

Also in Table 1, I have estimated the dollar amount our company invests yearly on new relocating managers. $54,500 is a drop in the bucket when you realize that we spend at least $290,000 yearly on new hires alone.

Table 1
Cost/Employee Investment Comparison

	Estimated Yearly Cost of Program*	Estimated Value of Human Resource Investment	
Research/development	$ 2,500	New relocating managers	
SEA consultant	27,000	Approx. 10 @ $29,000 each	
			$290,000
Employment firm contracts			
10 @ approx. $2,500 each	25,000		
TOTAL	$ 54,500	TOTAL	$290,000

*Doesn't include the one-time cost of office completion (about $1,100).

Benefits

The benefit to our company is the increase in productivity of the management staff. The cost to our company shouldn't be considered a luxury or frill expense, but a way to protect and enhance the company's human resources investment. The yearly cost of the program ($54,500) compared with the estimated yearly cost of new employees who would use it ($290,000) shows that the expense is far outweighed by the investment we've made in new management hires

WHAT ABOUT IMPLEMENTATION?

Implementation time is estimated at six to seven months depending on when the SEA consultant is hired. This is because, after a three-month hiring and selection period, the new consultant would be given three months to begin the research and development of the program. After these three months, research would continue, but client consultation would also begin (refer to Figure 1).

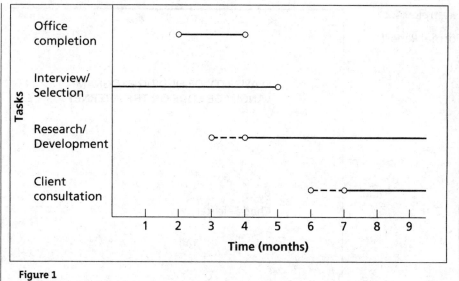

Figure 1
Schedule for Program Implementation

Example 14.2

Formal Report

FEASIBILITY OF FINDING PROGRAM
LANGUAGE CODE ON THE INTERNET

By
Chad Seichter

May 8, 2003

Prepared for
Kim O'Neil
Program Director

TABLE OF CONTENTS

EXECUTIVE SUMMARY 1
Abstract 2
Introduction 3
Discussion 4
    Finding Java Code Sites on the Web 4
    Finding Smalltalk Code Sites on the Web 6
List of Tables
    Java Code Sites on the Internet 4
    Smalltalk Code Sites on the Internet 6

(continued)

Example 14.2

(continued)

ABSTRACT

This report determines whether or not it is feasible for Applied Mathematics majors to find program language code on the Internet. To make this judgment, I looked for two separate programming languages: Java and Smalltalk. The pages I looked at were evaluated according to how current they were, if the source was credible, and if there actually was code on them. I found that I was easily able to find code for both of these languages and therefore have concluded that the Internet is a feasible source of information for my major.

INTRODUCTION

Background

Goal   The goal of this project was to decide if the Internet is a feasible source of information for Applied Math majors. I researched to see if I could find source code for Java and Smalltalk. Because of my research, I have come to the conclusion that the Internet is a good source for information for Applied Math majors. The purpose of this report is to explain my research and tell how I came to this decision.

Rationale   For my study I chose two different programming languages to try to find information on. The two languages were Java and Smalltalk. I picked these because writing computer programs is a large part of the Applied Math program. I chose the Java language because it is an up-and-coming language that is very popular right now. I figured it would be easy to find information on this. On the other hand, Smalltalk is a lot less known and used in the present day. I didn't know how much I would find on a language that is not very popular. I figured that choosing languages on the opposite ends of the popularity spectrum would give me a good look at not only these two languages but also all the other ones.

Method

Choosing Topics   My topics of study were whether or not I could find source code for programming languages on the Internet. I focused my search on two separate languages. One was a popular language, Java, and one less popular, Smalltalk. I figured that these two languages would give me a good overview about finding code for all of the different computer languages there are.

Determining Feasibility   I had to research my topics in order to figure out if the Internet was a feasible source of information. I used two separate search engines to do this: WebCrawler and Dogpile. Both of these search engines seemed to give me good information on my topics. Once I did the search, I evaluated the websites that came up and based my evaluation on my criteria (see "Explanation of Criteria" section below). In order to conclude that the Internet was useful for me, I needed to find websites that met most of the criteria for each topic.

Explanation of Criteria   I used the following criteria to come up with a conclusion:

1. Current   For the Java language, I chose that the pages had to have been updated sometime within the last six months because many changes are still being done to this language. For the Smalltalk language, I decided that anything within the last two years was good because it is an older language with fewer revisions still taking place.
2. Credible   In order for the source to be credible, it couldn't be someone's personal webpage. I also tried out the code myself to see if the page was credible. If it didn't work for me, then I considered it noncredible.
3. Was there code?   To meet this criterion, the webpage had to have actual examples of source code on it that could be used by others.

Conclusion

After doing my searches using WebCrawler and Dogpile, I am able to conclude that the Internet is a feasible source of information for Applied Math majors. I was able to find numerous webpages that met my three criteria for both the Java language and the Smalltalk language.

DISCUSSION

Finding Java Code on the Web

Introduction   I am an Applied Math major and am trying to figure out if the Internet and my major are interrelated. The purpose of this search is to find code that I could use to assist me in making computer programs. The language of code I would like to find is Java code. Specifically, I want to find Java applets that can be inserted into my programs. To help answer my question, I used the WebCrawler search engine. I checked the first five sites and evaluated them according to my criteria. If I could find at least five sites that had code, I could come to the conclusion that the Web is useful for finding Java code.

(continued)

Example 14.2
(continued)

Findings Using the WebCrawler search engine, I typed in the keywords "java applets" and then looked at the sites that came up. Over 45,000 sites came up using this search, so I started looking at them starting at the beginning. I found that all of the first five sites met my criteria. Table 1 below shows my results using my criteria.

Table 1
Java Code Sites on the Internet

	Current	Credible	Were There Applets?
http://java.sun.com/starter.html	Yes	Yes	No, but had links to some
http://www.javasoft.com/applets/index.html	Yes	Yes	Yes
http://javapplets.com/	Yes	Yes	Yes
http://www.conveyor.com/conveyor-java.html	Yes	Yes	Yes
http://javaboutique.internet.com/	Yes	Yes	Yes

Conclusion After doing this search and going through these top five sites, I have concluded that the Internet is very helpful for me to find applets for Java. All these pages appeared to be very recent. Most of them had a copyright in the year 2000, so I know they would still be useful now. I wanted to check to see if the code was correct, so I moved some of the applets off these webpages onto one that I had created, and they all worked in my code as well. Therefore I knew that these sites were credible.

Java has become such a big language to program that there appears to be an almost unlimited amount of code on the Web for it. I think that the sites that I checked out were probably above-average sites, because all the code I used worked correctly. I'm sure that there are some sites that aren't as good as these and could have bad code. If I was ever to use any of these pages, I would make sure I understood the code and made sure it was an efficient way to do the task. At worst, there are many examples to give you an idea of how to create an applet, so this search was very helpful to me.

Finding Smalltalk Code on the Web

Introduction I am an Applied Math major and am trying to figure out if the Internet and my major are interrelated. The purpose of this search is to find code that I could use to assist me in making computer programs. The language of code I would like to find is Smalltalk. I chose this language because it isn't very popular, so I figure if I can find this, then I should be able to find almost any other language. To help answer my question, I used the Dogpile search engine. I checked the first five sites and evaluated them according to my criteria. If I could find at least five sites that had code, I could come to the conclusion that the Web is useful for finding Java code.

Findings Using the Dogpile search engine, I typed in the keywords "Smalltalk example code" and then looked at the sites that came up. There weren't a whole lot of sites, but the ones that came up usually had good information and links to other good pages. Table 2 below shows my results from the five websites I looked at.

Table 2
Smalltalk Code Sites on the Internet

	Current	Credible	Code on the Page?
www.site.gmu.edu	1995, but information was still useful	Yes	Yes
www.mk.dmu.ac.uk	No date given	Yes	Yes
www.ics.hawaii.edu	Yes	Yes	Yes
www.phaidros.com	Yes	Yes	Yes
www.objectconnect.com	No date given	Yes	Yes

Conclusion After doing this search and going through these top five sites, I have concluded that the Internet is helpful for me to find Smalltalk code. Some of the pages weren't very current or didn't have a date, but because there haven't been too many changes to this language recently, that isn't a big issue. Most of them were within the last couple of years, so that was sufficient. I wanted to check to see if the code was correct, so I used some of the code in other programs I have written in the past, and it all seemed to work. Therefore, I knew that these sites were credible. Also, because Smalltalk isn't a popular language to program in, I feel that because I can use the Internet as a tool for this language, I can probably also use it for almost any other. Besides having code, I found several other helpful tools while using the Web that related to the programming language that could help me in writing my own programs.

Exercises 练 习

▶ You Create

1. For Exercise 10, Chapter 6 (pp. 161–162), create one or all of the following: a title page, table of contents, summary, conclusion, and recommendation.
2. For Exercise 10, Chapter 6 (pp. 161–162), create a page layout.

▶ You Revise

3. Redo this table of contents to make it more readable.

Introduction	2–3	chefmate		6
LIST OF FIGURES	2	conclusion	page 5	
recommendation		4	table 1 cost	page 6
discussion	5–12	cost	7–8	
width of front panel		5	hitachi 7	
hitachi 5				

4. Edit the following selection, which is taken from the discussion section of a formal report. Add at least two levels of heads, and construct one appropriate visual aid. Write a one- or two-sentence summary of the section.

    > The cost of renting a space will not exceed $150. Our budget allows $140 per month investment at this time for money available from renting space. The cost of renting a space is $175 per month for 100 square feet of space at Midtown Antique Mall. This exceeds the criteria by a total of $25 per month. The cost for renting 100 square feet of space at Antique Emporium is $100 per month, which is well within our criteria based on our budget. Antique Emporium is the only alternative that meets this criterion. The length of the contract cannot exceed 6 months because this is what we have established as a reasonable trial period for the business. Within this time, we will be able to calculate average net profit (with a turnover time no longer than 3 months) and determine if it is worth the time invested in the business. We will also be able to determine if we may want to continue the business as it is or on a larger scale by renting more floor space. The Midtown Antique Mall requires a 6-month contract. The Antique Emporium requires an initial 6-month contract which continues on a month-to-month basis after the contract is fulfilled. Both locations fulfill the contract length desired in the criteria. The possibility of continuing monthly at the Antique Emporium is an attractive option compared with renewing contracts bi-yearly.

▶ Group

5. In groups of two to four, discuss whether the conclusions and recommendations in Examples 15.2 or 15.3 (pp. 385–395) should appear at the beginning. Be prepared to give an oral report to the class. If your instructor requires, rewrite the introductory material so it follows the pattern of the human resources proposal (pp. 349–350) Alternate: Rewrite the human resources introduction by using the executive summary method.

6. Your instructor will hand out a sample report from the *Instructor's Manual*. In groups of two to three, edit it into a formal report. Change introductory material as necessary.

7. If you are working on formal format elements, bring a draft of them to class. In groups of two or three, evaluate each other's material. Use the guidelines (for Title Page, Table of Contents, Summary, Introduction, Conclusion, Recommendation) in this chapter as your criteria. Rewrite your material as necessary.

Writing Assignments 写作任务

1. Create a formal report that fulfills a recommendation, feasibility, proposal, or research assignment, as given in other chapters of this book.
    a. Create a template for your formal report. Review Chapter 6, pages 151–153, and Chapter 17, pages 435–437.
    b. Choose an introductory combination and write it.
    c. Write the conclusions and recommendations/rationale sections.
    d. Divide into pairs. Read each other's draft from the point of view of a manager. Assess whether you get all the essential information quickly. If not, suggest ways to clarify the material.
2. Write a learning report for the writing assignment you just completed. See Chapter 5, Writing Assignment 7, pages 133, for details of the assignment.

Web Exercise 网络练习

Review two or three websites of major corporations in order to determine how they use the elements of format. Review the homepage, but also review pages that are several layers into the site (e.g., Our Products/Cameras/Ultra-Compacts); typically, pages further "in" look more like hard copy. Write a brief analytical or IMRD report discussing your results.

Works Cited 引用的作品

American National Standards Institute (ANSI). *Guidelines for Format and Production of Scientific and Technical Reports.* ANSI 239. 18-1974. New York: ANSI, 1974.

Freeman, Lawrence H., and Terry R. Bacon. *Writing Style Guide.* Rev. ed. GM1620. Warren, MI: General Motors, 1991.

Chapter 15
Recommendation and Feasibility Reports
推荐和可行性报告

Chapter Contents
Chapter 15 In a Nutshell
Planning the Recommendation Report
Drafting the Recommendation Report
Planning the Feasibility Report
Writing the Feasibility Report

Chapter 15
In a Nutshell 概 要

Feasibility studies and recommendations present a position based on credible criteria and facts. *Feasibility studies* use criteria to investigate an item in order to tell the reader whether or not to accept the item. *Recommendations* use criteria to compare item A to item B in order to tell the reader which one to choose. To decide whether or not to air condition your house is a feasibility issue; to decide which air conditioning system to purchase is a recommendation issue.

Report strategy. In the introduction, *set the context*: tell the background of the situation, explain the methods you used to collect data, and state why you chose these criteria. In the body, *deal with one criterion per section*. A helpful outline for a section is

▶ Brief introduction to set the scene
▶ Discussion of data, often subdivided by alternative
▶ A helpful visual aid
▶ A brief, clear conclusion

Based on criteria. Criteria are the framework through which you and the reader look at the subject.

▶ Select topics that an expert would use to judge the situation. (For the air conditioner, a criterion is cost.)
▶ Select a standard, to limit the criterion. (The limitation is "the system may not cost more than $6000.")
▶ Apply the criteria. (Look at the sales materials of two reputable systems.)
▶ Present the data and conclusion clearly. Report the appropriate facts from your investigation, create a useful visual aid, and use heads and chunks to guide the reader through the subsections.

Professionals in all areas make recommendations. Someone must investigate alternatives and say "choose A" or "choose B." The "A" or "B" can be anything: which type of investment to make, which machine to purchase, whether to make a part or buy it, whether to have a sale, or whether to relocate a department. The decision maker makes a recommendation based on *criteria:* standards against which the alternatives are judged.

For professionals, these choices often take the form of *recommendation reports* or *feasibility reports.* Although both present a solution after alternatives have been investigated, the two reports are slightly different. Recommendation reports indicate a choice between two or more clear alternatives: this distributor or that distributor, this brand of computer or that brand of computer (Markel). Feasibility reports investigate one option and decide whether it should be pursued. Should the client start a health club? Should the company form a captive insurance company? Should the company develop this prototype? (Alexander and Potter; Angelo; Bradford). This chapter explains how to plan and write both types of reports.

Planning the Recommendation Report 设计推荐报告

In planning a recommendation, you must consider the audience, choose criteria for making your recommendations, use visual aids, and select a format and an organizational principle.

Consider the Audience 考虑读者

In general, many different people with varying degrees of knowledge (a multiple audience) read these reports. A recommendation almost always travels up the organizational hierarchy to a group—a committee or board—that makes the decision. These people may or may not know much about the topic or the criteria used as the basis for the recommendation. Usually, however, most readers will know a lot about at least one aspect of the report—the part that affects them or their department. They will read the report from their own point of view. The human resources manager will look closely at how the recommendation affects workers, the safety manager will judge the effect on safety, and so on. All readers will be concerned about cost. To satisfy such readers, the writer must present a report that enables them all to find and glean the information they need.

Choose Criteria 选择标准

To make data meaningful, analyze or evaluate them according to criteria. Selecting logical criteria is crucial to the entire recommendation report because you will make your recommendation on the basis of those criteria and because your choice of the "right" criteria establishes your credibility.

The Three Elements of a Criterion

A *criterion* has three elements: a name, a standard, and a rank (Holcombe and Stein). The *name* of the criterion, such as "cost," identifies some area relevant to the situation. The *standard* is a statement that establishes the limit of the criterion—for instance, "not to exceed $500.00." The standard heavily influences the final decision. Consider two very different standards that are possible for cost:

1. The cost of the water heater will not exceed $500.
2. The cheapest water heater will be purchased.

If the second standard is in effect, the writer cannot recommend the more expensive machine even if it has more desirable features.

The *rank* of the criterion is its weight in the decision relative to the other criteria. "Cost" is often first, but it might be last, depending on the situation.

Discovering Criteria

Criteria vary according to the type of problem. In some situations, a group or individual will have set up all the criteria in rank order. In that case, you show how the relevant data for the various alternatives measure up to these criteria.

When criteria have not been set up, you need to discover them by using your professional expertise and the information you have about needs and alternatives in the situation. One helpful way of collecting relevant data is to investigate appropriate categories: technical, management/maintenance, and financial criteria (Markel).

Technical criteria apply to operating characteristics such as the necessary heat and humidity levels in an air-moving system. *Management/maintenance criteria* deal with concerns of day-to-day operation, such as how long it will take to install a new air-moving system. *Financial criteria* deal with cost and budget. How much money is available, and how big a system will it purchase?

Applying Criteria

Suppose you were to investigate which of two jointers to place in a high school woods lab. To make the decision, you need to find the relevant data and create the relevant standards. To find relevant data, answer questions derived from the three categories.

- Technical—Does the jointer have appropriate fence size? table length? cutting capacity?

- Financial—How much does each jointer cost? How much do optional features cost? How much money is available? What is the standard?
- Management/Maintenance—Which one is safer? Will we need to reconfigure the lab or its electrical service? Will the jointers be available by the start of school in August?

To create standards, you must formulate statements that turn these questions into bases for judgment. You derive these standards from your experience, from an expert authority (such as another teacher), or from policy. For instance, because you know from your own experience the length of your typical stock, your standard will read "Must be able to handle up to 52 inches." Another teacher who has worked with these machines can tell you which features must be present for safety. School policy dictates how you should phrase the cost standard.

Use Visual Aids 利用视图

Although you might use many kinds of visuals—maps of demographic statistics, drawings of key features, flow charts for procedures—you will usually use tables and graphs. With these visuals you can present complicated information easily (such as costs or a comparison of features). For many sections in your report, you will construct the table or figure first and then write the section to explain the data in it. Visual aids help overcome the problem of multiple audiences. Consider using a visual with each section in your report.

In the following example, the author first collected the data, then made the visual aids, and *then* wrote the section. Note that the table combines data from several criteria; this technique avoids many small, one-line tables. (The entire report appears as Example 15.1 at the end of the chapter.)

Fence Size

The fence serves as a guide for planing face and edge surfaces. The size of the fence, width and length, is directly related to cutting efficiency. The fence size of the jointer currently in operation is 3" × 28". In purchasing a new jointer the fence size should be increased for improved accuracy and squaring efficiency.

- Delta DJ-20. As Table 1 shows, the Delta fence size is 5" × 36". These dimensions represent a 2" × 8" increase, which will result in more efficient operations.
- Powermatic-60. The Powermatic fence is 4" × $34^{1/2}$", a 1" × $6^{1/2}$" increase over that of the existing fence (see Table 1).

Conclusion. Both machines exceed the fence size criterion of 3" × 28". Delta DJ-20 has the greatest increase, 2" × 8", and will result in greater squaring accuracy and longitudinal control when jointing edge surfaces.

Table 1

8″ Jointer Capabilities Comparison

Criteria	Standard	Delta DJ-20	Powermatic-60
Fence size	Minimum of 3″ wide × 28″ long	5″ × 36″	4″ × 34$\frac{1}{2}$″
Table length	Minimum of 52″	76$\frac{1}{2}$″	64″
Cutting capacity	Minimum depth of $\frac{3}{8}$″	$\frac{5}{8}$″	$\frac{1}{2}$″
Cost	Not to exceed $2300	$2128.00	$2092.00

Select a Format and an Organizational Principle 选择格式和组织原则

As you plan your report, you must select a format, an organizational principle for the entire report, and an organizational principle for each section.

Select a Format

Your choice of format depends on the situation. If the audience is a small group that is familiar with the situation, an informal report will probably do. If your audience is more distant from you and the situation, a formal format is preferable. The informal format is explained in Chapter 12, the formal format in Chapter 14.

In addition to selecting format type, create a style sheet of heads and margins. Review Chapter 6 and the examples in Chapters 12 and 14. Your style sheet should help your audience find what they need to do their job.

Organize the Discussion by Criteria

Organize the discussion section according to criteria, with each criterion receiving a major heading. Review Examples 15.1 and 15.2; each major section is the discussion of one criterion. Your goal is to present comparable data that readers can evaluate easily.

Organize Each Section Logically

Each section deals with one criterion and evaluates the alternatives in terms of that criterion. Each of these sections should contain three parts: an introduction, a body, and a conclusion. In the introduction, define the criterion and discuss its standard, rank, and source, if necessary. (If you discuss the standard, rank, and source somewhere else in the report, perhaps in the introduction, do not repeat that information.) In the body, explain the relevant facts about each alternative in terms of the criterion; in the conclusion, state the judgment you have made as a result of applying this criterion to the facts. You will find a sample section on page 377.

Drafting the Recommendation Report 起草推荐报告

As you draft the recommendation report, carefully develop the introduction, conclusions, recommendations/rationale, and discussion sections.

Introduction 介绍

After you have gathered and interpreted the data, develop an introduction that orients the readers to the problem and to the organization of the report. Your goal is to make readers confident enough to accept your recommendation. In recommendation reports, as in all reports, you can mix the elements of the introduction in many ways. Always include a purpose statement and add the other statements as needed by the audience. Four common elements in the introduction are

- Statement of purpose.
- Explanation of method of investigation.
- Statement of scope.
- Explanation of the problem.

Purpose

Begin a recommendation report with a straightforward statement, such as "The purpose of this report is . . . " or, more simply, "This report recommends. . . . " You can generally cover the purpose, which is to choose an alternative, in one sentence.

Method of Gathering Information

State your method of gathering information. As explained in Chapter 5, the four major methods of gathering data are observing, testing, interviewing, and reading. Stating your methodology not only gives credit where it is due but also lends authority to your data and thus to your report.

In the introduction, a general statement of your model of investigation is generally sufficient: "Using lab and catalog resources here at the university and after discussion with other Industrial Arts teachers in this area, I have narrowed my choices to two: Delta Model DJ-20 and Powermatic Model 60."

Scope

In the scope statement, cite the criteria you used to judge the data. You can explain their source or their rankings here, especially if the same reasons apply to all of them. Name the criteria in the order in which they appear in your report. If you have not included a particular criterion because data are unavailable or unreliable, acknowledge this omission in the section on scope so that your readers will know you have not overlooked that criterion. Here is an example:

Drafting the Recommendation Report

Each machine has been evaluated using the following criteria, in descending order of importance:

1. Fence size
2. Table length
3. Cutting capacity
4. Cost

Background

In the background, discuss the problem, the situation, or both. To explain the problem, you must define its nature and significance: "Considering that the machine has been under continuous student use for 27 years and has reduced accuracy because of the small table and fence size, I indicated I would contact you regarding a new jointer." Depending on the audience's familiarity with the situation, you may have to elaborate, explaining the causes of various effects (Why does it have reduced accuracy? Just what is the relationship of the table and the fence? What *are* tables and fences?).

To explain the situation, you may need to outline the history of the project, indicate who assigned you to write the report, or identify your position in the corporation or organization.

The following informal introduction effectively orients the reader to the problem and to the method of investigating it.

Sample Informal Introduction

Memo head	Date: December 2, 2006
	To: Joseph P. White, Superintendent of Schools
	From: David Ayers
	Subject: Purchase recommendation for 8" jointer
Situation and background	Recently, Jim DeLallo and I discussed at length the serious problems he was having in operating the jointer at the high school. Considering that the machine has been under continuous student use for 27 years and has reduced accuracy because of the small table and fence size, I indicated I would contact you regarding a new jointer. You asked that I forward
Cause of writing	2007–2008 budget requests by December 15.
Method	Therefore, I have prepared this recommendation report for choosing a new 8" jointer. Using lab and catalog resources here at the university and after discussion with other Industrial Arts teachers in this area, I have narrowed my choices to two: Delta Model DJ-20 and Powermatic Model 60. Each machine has been evaluated using the following criteria, in descending order of importance:
Scope	1. Fence size
	2. Table length

3. Cutting capacity
4. Cost

Preview　　　　　　　　The remainder of the report will compare both machines to the criteria.

Conclusions　结　论

Your conclusions section should summarize the most significant information about each criterion covered in the report. One or two sentences about each criterion are usually enough to prepare the reader for your recommendation. Writers of recommendation and feasibility reports almost always place these sections in the front of the report. Remember, readers want the essential information quickly.

All elements in the criteria have been met. The slightly higher cost of the Delta, $36.00, is more than offset by increased efficiency and capacity as noted below:

1. A larger fence size—for better control of stock when squaring
2. A larger table size—resulting in more efficient planing
3. A greater depth of cutting capacity—for improved softwood removal and increased rabbeting capacity

Recommendations/Rationale Section　推荐/基本原理部分

The recommendation resolves the problem that occasioned the report. For short reports like the samples presented here, one to four sentences should suffice. For complex reports involving many aspects of a problem, a longer paragraph (or even several paragraphs) may be necessary.

Recommendation

Possible negative factor explained

It is recommended that the district budget for capital purchase of the Delta Model DJ-20 8" Jointer in 2007–2008. Selection of the Delta jointer is a departure from the practice of purchasing Powermatic equipment for the woodworking shop. It is my feeling that the Delta Jointer is best suited for the current and future needs of the woodworking program. Service and repair will not be a problem in changing equipment manufacturers, since N. H. Bragg services both lines of equipment.

Discussion Section　讨论部分

As previously noted, you should organize the discussion section by criteria, from most to least important. Each criterion should have an introduction, a body discussing each alternative, and a conclusion. Here is part of the discussion section from the recommendation report on ink-jet printers.

DISCUSSION

A. Impressions Per Hour

Definition For a press to be economically efficient it should be able to print a minimum of 8000 impressions per hour. Most of the presses on the market today are capable of this speed, but some produce at even faster speeds.

Comparison

Press	Impressions Per Hour
AB Dick 9840	10,000
Multigraphic 1860	8000

As you can see, both of the proposed presses are rated as acceptable according to the criterion set in this area. As the comparison shows, the AB Dick 9840 is capable of printing 2000 more impressions per hour than the Multigraphic 1860. With impressions per hour being the most important criterion, the AB Dick would be the best choice.

Planning the Feasibility Report   设计可行性报告

Feasibility reports investigate whether to undertake a project. They "size up a project before it is undertaken and identify those projects that are not worth pursuing" (Ramige 48). The project can be anything: place a golf course at a particular site, start a capital campaign drive, or accept a proposal to install milling machines. The scope of these reports varies widely, from analyses of projects costing millions of dollars to informal reviews of in-house proposals. Your goal is to investigate all relevant factors to determine whether any one factor will prevent the project from continuing. Basically you ask, "Can we perform the project?" and you provide the rationale for answering yes or no. Follow the same steps as for planning recommendation reports. In addition, consider the following guidelines:

- Consider the audience.
- Determine the criteria.
- Determine the standards.
- Structure by criteria.

Consider the Audience   考虑读者

Generally, the audience is familiar with the situation in broad outline. Your job is to give specific information. They know, for example, that in any project a certain time frame is allowed for cost recovery, but they do not know how much time this project needs. Your goal is to make them confident enough of you and the situation to accept your decision.

Determine the Criteria   确定准则

Criteria are established either by a management committee or by "prevailing practice." Either a group directs investigators to consider criteria such as cost and competition level, or "prevailing practice"—the way knowledgeable experts investigate this type of proposed activity—sets the topics. For instance, cost recovery is always considered in the evaluation of a capital investment project.

If you have to discover the topics yourself, as you often do with small projects, use the three categories described on page 371—technical, management/maintenance, and financial criteria. The criteria you choose will affect the audience's sense of your credibility.

Determine the Standards   制定标准

To determine standards is to state the limits of the criteria. If the topic is reimbursement for acceptable expenses, you must determine the standards to use to judge whether the stated expenses fall within the acceptable limit. These standards require expert advice unless they exist as policy. If the policy is that a new machine purchase must show a return in investment of 20 percent, and if the machine under consideration will return 22 percent, buying the machine is feasible.

Structure by Criteria   按标准排序

The discussion section of a feasibility report is structured by criteria. The reimbursement report could include sections on allowable growth, time of recovery of investment, and disposal costs.

Writing the Feasibility Report   撰写可行性报告

To write the feasibility report, choose a format and write the introduction and the body.

Choose a Format   选择一个格式

The situation helps you determine whether to use a formal or an informal format for your feasibility studies. As a rule of thumb, use the formal format for a lengthy report intended for a group of clients. The informal format is suitable for a brief report intended to determine the feasibility of an internal suggestion.

Write the Introduction and Body　撰写介绍和主体

In the introduction, present appropriate background, conclusions, and recommendations. Treat this introduction the same as a recommendation introduction. In the discussion, present the details for each topic. As in the recommendation report, you should present the topic, the standard, relevant details, and your conclusion. Organize the material in the discussion section from most to least important. As with all reports, use appropriate visual aids, including tables, graphs, and even maps, to enhance your readers' comprehension.

The following section from an informal internal feasibility report presents all four discussion elements succinctly:

Sample Feasibility Section

WHOLESALE COST

Introduction

This section examines the wholesale costs associated with producing the Heaven 'n Nature Sticker Christmas Card Kit. The standard set for this criterion was, "The wholesale cost of the product should not exceed $6.00 per set."

Analysis

A list of potential suppliers was provided by Illuminated Ink. These sources were then reviewed by searching through wholesale supply catalogs, visiting local vendors, and searching on-line sources. After an acceptable supplier had been located for each component of the kit, the total price of the kit was calculated and compared to the standard set for this criterion. See Table 1.

Table 1

Breakdown of Wholesale Component Costs

Component	Description	Qty	Supplier	Cost/Unit
Card base	Cranberry Red, Forest Green, and Midnight Blue cardstock	3	Picture This (1)	$0.54
Card insert	white 20# bond, green ink	3	Picture This (1)	$0.12
Winter friends stickers	Frances Meyer	3	Picture This (1)	$2.64
Snowflake stickers	silver, gold, & white	24	Picture This (1)	$0.48
Brads	gold minibrads	6	Picture This (1)	$0.24

(continued)

Table 1 (continued)

Component	Description	Qty	Supplier	Cost/Unit
Cotton ball	small, white	3	Wal-Mart (2)	$0.03
Envelope	white fiber A2 envelope	3	Impact Images (3)	$0.72
Soft fold box	6" × 9"	1	Impact Images (3)	$0.28
Instruction sheet	white 20# bond paper, black ink	1	Illuminated Ink (4)	$0.04
Mailing labels	1" × 2⁵⁄₈", white	8	Sam's Club (5)	$0.04
			Total Cost Per Kit	**$5.13**

CONCLUSION

This research reveals that it is possible for Illuminated Ink to produce this kit for $5.13 per kit, a price that is lower than the standard required.

Several brief informal feasibility reports appear in the examples and exercises of this chapter. In addition, you can find a wide range of examples by searching Google with the keyword phrases "feasibility report" or "feasibility study."

Worksheet for Preparing a Recommendation/Feasibility Report

准备推荐/可行性报告的工作表

- ☐ **Analyze the audience.**
  Who will receive this report?
  Who will authorize the recommendation in this report?
  How much do they know about the topic?
  What is your purpose in writing to them? How will they use the report?
  What will make you credible in their estimation?

- ☐ **Name the two alternatives or name the course of action that you must decide whether to take.**

- ☐ **Determine criteria.**
  Ask technical, management/maintenance, and financial questions.

- ☐ **For each criterion, provide a name, a standard, and a rank.**

- ☐ **Rank the criteria.**

- ☐ **Prepare background for the report.**
  Who requested the recommendation report? Name the purpose of the report. Name the method of investigation. Name the scope. Explain the problem. What is the basic opposition (such as need for profit versus declining sales)?
  What are the causes or effects of the facts in the problem?

- [ ] Select a format—formal or informal.
- [ ] Prepare a style sheet including treatment of margins, headings, page numbers, and visual aid captions.
- [ ] Select or prepare visual aids that illustrate the basic data for each criterion.
- [ ] Select an organizational pattern for each section, such as introduction, alternative A, alternative B, visual aid, conclusion.

Worksheet for Evaluating Your Report
评估报告的工作表

- [ ] Evaluate the introduction.
  - Does the introduction give you the gist of the report?
  - Does the introduction give you the context (situation, criteria, reason for writing) of the report?
  - Do you know the recommendation after reading 5 to 10 lines?
- [ ] Evaluate the criteria.
  - Do they seem appropriate?
  - Are all the appropriate ones included? If not, which should be added?
  - Can you find a statement of the standard for each one? If no, which ones?
  - Can you really evaluate the data on the statement of standard?
  - Do you understand why each criterion is part of the discussion?
  - Do you understand the rank of each criterion?
- [ ] Evaluate the discussion.
  - Is the standard given so you can evaluate?
  - Are there enough data so you can evaluate?
  - Do you agree with the evaluation?
  - Do you understand where the data came from?
- [ ] Evaluate the visual aid and the paper's format.
  - Are the two levels of heads different enough? See pages 142–144.
  - Is the discussion called "discussion"?
  - Does a visual appear in each spot where one would help communicate the point?
  - Are any of the visuals more or less useless; that is, they really do not interact with any points in the text?
  - Is the visual clearly titled and numbered?
  - Is the visual on the same page as the text that describes it?
  - Does the text tell you what to see in the visual?

Worksheet for Evaluating a Peer's Report

评估同行报告的工作表

☐ Interview a peer. Ask these questions:
1. Why did you include each sentence in the introduction? (Your partner should explain the reason for each one.)
2. Why did you use the head format you used?
3. Why did you choose each criterion?
4. Why did you write the first sentence you wrote in each criterion section?
5. Why did you organize each section the way you did? Do you think a reader would like to read it this way?
6. What one point have you made with the visual aid? Why did you construct it the way you did and place it where you did?
7. If you had to send this paper to someone who paid you money regularly for doing a good job, would you? If not, what would you do differently? Why don't you do that for the final paper?
8. Are you happy with the level of writing in this paper? Do you think these sentences are appropriately professional, the kind of thing you could bring forward as support for your promotion? If not, how will you fix them? If you try to fix them, do you know what you're doing?

Examples 例 子

Examples 15.1–15.3 illustrate informal recommendation and feasibility reports. For other recommendation examples, see "Brief Analytical Reports," Chapter 12, pages 285–289. For another feasibility example, see "Feasibility of Finding Program Language Code on the Internet," Chapter 14, Example 14.2, pages 360–365.

Example 15.1

Informal Recommendation Report

Date: December 2, 2006
To: Joseph P. White, Superintendent of Schools
From: David Ayers
Subject: Purchase recommendation for 8" jointer

Recently, Jim DeLallo and I discussed at length the serious problems he was having in operating the jointer at the high school. Considering that the machine has been under continuous student use for 27 years and has reduced accuracy because of the small table and fence size, I indicated I would contact you regarding a new jointer. You asked that I forward 2006–2007 budget requests by December 15.

Therefore, I have prepared this recommendation report for choosing a new 8" jointer. Based on lab and catalog resources and after discussion with other Industrial Arts teachers in this area, I have narrowed my choices to two: Delta Model DJ-20 and Powermatic Model 60. Each machine has been evaluated using the following criteria, in descending order of importance:

1. Fence size
2. Table length
3. Cutting capacity
4. Cost

RECOMMENDATION

It is recommended that the district budget for capital purchase of the Delta Model DJ-20 8" jointer in 2006–2007. Selection of the Delta jointer is a departure from the practice of purchasing Powermatic equipment for the woodworking shop. It is my feeling that the Delta jointer is best suited for the current and future needs of the woodworking program. Service and repair will not be a problem in changing equipment manufacturers, since N. H. Bragg services both lines of equipment.

All elements in the criteria have been met. The slightly higher cost of the Delta, $36.00, is more than offset by increased efficiency and capacity, as noted below.

1. A larger fence size—for better control of stock when squaring
2. A larger table size—resulting in more efficient planing
3. A greater depth of cutting capacity—for improved softwood removal and increased rabbeting capacity

The remainder of the report will compare both machines to the criteria.

CRITERIA

Fence Size

The fence serves as a guide for planing face and edge surfaces. The size of the fence, width and length, is directly related to cutting efficiency. The fence size of the jointer currently in operation is 3" × 28". In purchasing a new jointer the fence size should be increased for improved accuracy and squaring efficiency.

- Delta DJ-20. As Table 1 shows, the Delta fence size is 5" × 36". This represents a 2" × 8" increase, which will result in more efficient operations.
- Powermatic-60. The Powermatic fence is 4" × 34½", a 1" × 6½" increase over that of the existing fence (see Table 1).

(continued)

Example 15.1
(continued)

Conclusion Both machines exceed the fence size criterion of 3" × 28". Delta DJ-20 has the greatest increase, 2" × 8", and will result in greater squaring accuracy and longitudinal control when jointing edge surfaces.

Table 1
8" Jointer Capabilities Comparison

Criteria	Standard	Delta DJ-20	Powermatic-60
Fence size	Minimum of 3" wide × 28" long	5" × 36"	4" × 34½"
Table length	Minimum of 52"	76½"	64"
Cutting capacity	Minimum depth of ⅜"	⅝"	½"
Cost	Not to exceed $2300	$2128.00	$2092.00

Table Length

In-feed and out-feed tables are combined and referred to as table length. Increased table length improves accuracy when jointing and provides greater stability when planing face surfaces. On the existing machine, the table length is 52". When planing and jointing stock over 40", it is difficult to maintain accuracy. To realize improved handling and accuracy on a new jointer, the table length should be above 52".

- Delta DJ-20. As Table 1 shows, the table length of the Delta is 76½", a 24½" increase. This increased size will allow for greater efficiency when planing stock to approximately 60".
- Powermatic-60. As Table 1 shows, the table length of this jointer exceeds the minimum length by 12". Improved planing can be increased to approximately 50".

Conclusion Both jointers exceed the 52" minimum table length size. The significant increase in the Delta jointer table length will offer improved planing and jointer accuracy and increased handling capacity.

Cutting Capacity (Depth of Cut)

Jointer cutting capacity is determined by the maximum depth of cut. This depth of cut is created when the in-feed table is lowered. For production work with softwoods and edge rabbeting, a large depth of cut is desired. The existing jointer has a ⅜" maximum depth of cut. This is a limiting factor when doing softwood production work and constructing edge rabbets over ⅜". When purchasing a new machine, the depth of cut should be at least ⅜".

- Delta DJ-20. As Table 1 shows, the depth of cut on this machine is $5/8''$, $1/4''$ above the minimum standard. This will be an important feature when edge rabbeting and doing softwood production work.
- Powermatic-60. As Table 1 shows, the depth of cut for this machine is $1/2''$, a $1/8''$ increase above the minimum standard.

Conclusion Both machines exceed the $3/8''$ minimum criterion set. The Delta jointer has the greatest depth of cut, $5/8''$, which will allow for greater softwood removal and maximum rabbeting.

Cost

The jointer is a capital equipment item and the cost cannot be department budgeted if in excess of $2300, unless prior approval is granted by the secondary committee. Costs (including shipping, stand, and three-phase conversion) are

- Delta DJ-20: $2128.00
- Powermatic-60: $2092.00

Conclusion Both machines meet the fourth criterion. The Powermatic is slightly lower in cost, but does not have all the capacity and features of the Delta model. The additional cost of the Delta jointer ($6.80 on a 20-year depreciation schedule) is more than offset by the increase in table and fence size and improved cutting depth.

Example 15.2

Informal Recommendation Report

Date: December 3, 2006
To: Steve Zubek, President/Widgit Printing
From: Mark Jezierski, Production Manager
Subject: Which of the proposed printing presses we should purchase

I am writing in response to your recent request to determine which of the proposed printing presses, the Multigraphic 1860 or the AB Dick 9840, would best satisfy our needs. The age and inefficiency of the current equipment used in production have prompted this report. I have thoroughly researched these machines through trade journals and with other printers who currently use these machines to determine which of these machines best fit the criteria set by upper management.

My recommendation to you is that the Widget Printing Company purchase the AB Dick 9840. The criteria I have used to determine the feasibility of this purchase according to their rank and importance consist of:

1. Machine must be able to print a minimum of 8000 impressions per hour.
2. The press must be able to print an area image up to $11.5'' \times 17.25''$.

(continued)

Example 15.2 (continued)

3. The press must be able to print a paper size of 12" × 17.5".
4. The cost to purchase the new machine must be under $25,000.

DISCUSSION

A. Impressions Per Hour

Definition For a press to be economically efficient it should be able to print a minimum of 8000 impressions per hour. Most of the presses on the market today are capable of this speed, but some produce at even faster speeds.

Comparison

Press	Impressions Per Hour
AB Dick 9840	10,000
Multigraphic 1860	8000

As you can see, both of the proposed presses are rated as acceptable according to the criterion set in this area. As the comparison shows, the AB Dick 9840 is capable of printing 2000 more impressions per hour than the Multigraphic 1860. With impressions per hour being the most important criterion, the AB Dick would be the best choice.

B. Maximum Image Area

Definition The press purchased must be able to print an image up to 11.5" × 17.25". This image area will allow the printing of 8.5" × 11" and 11" × 17" jobs that have from one side to four sides that bleed.

Comparison

Press	Maximum Image Area
Multigraphic 1860	13.19" × 17.50"
AB Dick 9840	12.50" × 17.25"

Again you can see both of the presses meet the suggested criterion of 11.5" × 17.25". However, the Multigraphic 1860 is capable of the largest maximum image area (13.19" × 17.50"). This gives a considerable excess amount of image area to be used to print jobs that require larger image areas than the specified maximum of the criterion. The AB Dick 9840 is capable of an image area of 12.5" × 17.25", which is acceptable according to the standards we have set. When considering only image area, the Multigraphic 1860 would be the best choice.

C. Paper Size

Definition The press purchased must be able to print a paper size of 12" × 17.5". This paper size will allow the printing of 8.5" × 11" and 11" × 17" jobs that have from one side to four sides that bleed.

Comparison

Press	Maximum Paper Area
Multigraphic 1860	15.00" × 18.00"
AB Dick 9840	13.50" × 17.25"

Again, as you can see, both of the proposed presses meet the criterion established for this area. The Multigraphic 1860 is capable of printing on the largest size paper. It can print on paper up to 15" × 18", which by far exceeds the paper size requirement needed by Widget Printing. This capability, however, will allow us a greater flexibility in projects that require larger than specified paper sizes. The AB Dick 9840 also exceeds the established criterion, although by a smaller margin than the Multigraphic 1860, but it will also allow us a degree of flexibility in the undertaking of larger projects. When considering only paper size, the Multigraphic 1860 would be the best choice.

D. Price

Definition The price of the press purchased is not a major criterion. The capabilities of the press are more important factors. However, a price range has been set and cannot be overlooked when deciding on which press to purchase. We have established a price ceiling of $25,000.

Comparison

Press	Price
AB Dick 9840	$17,395
Multigraphic 1860	$20,000

Once again both of the proposed machines meet the established criterion. Both of these presses are well within the price range set. Based on only price as a criterion, the AB Dick would be the best choice.

RECOMMENDATION

After comparing the AB Dick 9840 and the Multigraphic 1860 presses, I feel the AB Dick 9840 is the press that the Widget Printing Company should purchase. The AB Dick meets all of the established criteria and has the largest capabilities in the area of impressions per hour, which is the most important criterion established. It also is the best press per dollar of purchase available. Therefore I feel that it is in our best interest to purchase the AB Dick 9840.

Example 15.3

Informal
Feasibility Report

NEW PRODUCT DEVELOPMENT FEASIBILITY REPORT

Heaven 'n Nature Sticker Christmas Card Kit

October 28, 2005

Frances Butek

Product Development Specialist

Prepared for
Illuminated Ink
15825 - 160th Ave.
Bloomer, WI 54724

REPORT ABSTRACT

This feasibility report addresses the question, "Should Illuminated Ink produce Heaven 'n Nature Sticker Christmas Card kits?" The criteria used to answer this question are wholesale cost, component availability, and product desirability. Our conclusion is that Illuminated Ink should go forward with production plans.

INTRODUCTION

Question

This feasibility report addresses and answers the question, "Should Illuminated Ink produce Heaven 'n Nature Sticker Christmas Card kits?"

Purpose

The purpose of this report is to provide the co-owners of Illuminated Ink with information on if they should invest their time, effort, and resources into the development of a particular new product. Illuminated Ink is a small, faith-based business specializing in developing, designing, and marketing educational toys, games, crafts, and curriculum.

Product Description

The Heaven 'n Nature Sticker Christmas Card Kit is a product designed to encourage a child to create six unique Christmas cards that display a beautiful winter scene of realistic woodland animals decorating a majestic Christmas tree. The interior of the card is preprinted with the greeting, "Joy to the World, the Lord is come! Let every heart prepare Him room, while Heaven and Nature sing the wonders of His love!"

CRITERIA AND STANDARDS

Three criteria were considered to make an informed decision. The standards set for each criteria were determined by the co-owners of Illuminated Ink. These criteria and standards were:

1. **Wholesale Cost.**   The wholesale cost of the product should not exceed $6.00 per set.
2. **Component Availability.**   All of the components of the kit must be received within 10 days of ordering.
3. **Product Desirability.**   The product must be deemed desirable by 75 percent or more of Illuminated Ink's customers.

(continued)

Example 15.3
(continued)

METHOD

Two lists were supplied by Illuminated Ink. These lists contained the names and contact information for potential customers and wholesale suppliers. The lists were reviewed, customers and suppliers were contacted, and an analysis performed on the information provided. The results of the analysis were compared to the criterion standards, and a decision was made.

CONCLUSION

The results of all three criteria were positive. First, the final wholesale cost of the components was determined to be $5.13 per set. Second, the maximum amount of time Illuminated Ink must wait to receive the kit components was established to be 10 days. And third, the kit was rated as highly desirable by Illuminated Ink's customers. Thus, having met all three criteria standards, our conclusion to this feasibility question is a resounding "YES! Illuminated Ink should produce this product."

WHOLESALE COST

Introduction

This section examines the wholesale costs associated with producing the Heaven 'n Nature Sticker Christmas Card kit. The standard set for this criterion was, "The wholesale cost of the product should not exceed $6.00 per set."

Analysis

A list of potential suppliers was provided by Illuminated Ink. These sources were then reviewed by searching through wholesale supply catalogs, visiting local vendors, and searching on-line sources. After an acceptable supplier had been located for each component of the kit, the total price of the kit was calculated and compared to the standard set for this criterion. See Table 1.

CONCLUSION

This research reveals that it is possible for Illuminated Ink to produce this kit for $5.13 per kit, a price that is lower than the standard required.

COMPONENT AVAILABILITY

Introduction

This section examines the availability of the components required for the Heaven 'n Nature Sticker Christmas Card kit. The standard set for this criterion was, "All of the components of the kit must be received within ten days of ordering."

Analysis

A list of potential suppliers was provided by Illuminated Ink. These sources were then reviewed by searching through wholesale supply catalogs, visiting local vendors, and searching on-line sources. After an acceptable supplier had been located for each component of the kit, the amount of time required for delivery was noted. See Table 2.

Table 1
Breakdown of Wholesale Component Costs

Component	Description	Qty	Supplier	Cost / Unit
Card base	Cranberry Red, Forest Green, and Midnight Blue cardstock	3	Picture This (1)	$0.54
Card insert	white 20# bond, green ink	3	Picture This (1)	$0.12
Winter friends stickers	Frances Meyer	3	Picture This (1)	$2.64
Snowflake stickers	silver, gold, & white	24	Picture This (1)	$0.48
Brads	gold minibrads	6	Picture This (1)	$0.24
Cotton ball	small, white	3	Wal-Mart (2)	$0.03
Envelope	white fiber A2 envelope	3	Impact Images (3)	$0.72
Soft fold box	6" × 9"	1	Impact Images (3)	$0.28
Instruction sheet	white 20# bond paper, black ink	1	Illuminated Ink (4)	$0.04
Mailing labels	1" × 2⅝", white	8	Sam's Club (5)	$0.04
			Total Cost Per Kit	**$5.13**

Table 2
Breakdown of Component Supply Times

Component	Supplier	Description	Supply Time
Card base	Picture This (1)	Cranberry Red, Forest Green, and Midnight Blue cardstock	3 days
Card insert	Picture This (1)	white 20# bond, green ink	2 days
Winter friends stickers	Picture This (1)	Frances Meyer	7 days
Snowflake stickers	Picture This (1)	silver, gold, & white	3 days
Brads	Picture This (1)	gold minibrads	10 days
Cotton ball	Wal-Mart (2)	small, white	2 days
Envelope	Impact Images (3)	white fiber A2 envelope	4 days
soft fold box	Impact Images (3)	6" × 9"	4 days
instruction sheet	Illuminated Ink (4)	white 20# bond paper, black ink	2 days
mailing labels	Sam's Club (5)	1" × 2⅝", white	2 days
		Maximum Supply Time	**10 days**

(continued)

Example 15.3
(continued)

Conclusion

This research reveals that it is possible for Illuminated Ink to obtain the components for this kit within 10 days, a time frame that falls within the standard required.

PRODUCT DESIRABILITY

Introduction

This section examines the desirability of the Heaven 'n Nature Christmas Card kit. The standard set for this criterion was, "The product must be deemed desirable by 75 percent or more of Illuminated Ink's customers."

Analysis

A list of customers was provided by Illuminated Ink. These customers were sent an e-mail that requested that they fill out an on-line Product Desirability Survey (6) that was posted on the Illuminated Ink website. This survey displayed an illustration of the product and provided a detailed description of the kit and its contents. The survey then asked viewers if they found the product appealing, and what price range they felt was most appropriate for the product. The survey responses were recorded in a table and the results analyzed. See Table 3.

Table 3
Breakdown of Desirability Survey Responses

Question: Do you find this product appealing?	Yes	No
Total Responses	176	16

Conclusion

Of the 192 responses received, 92 percent of Illuminated Ink's customers found this product desirable. This finding is considerably higher than the standard that was set, and indicates that Illuminated Ink should strongly consider producing this product.

CHRISTMAS CARD KIT SURVEY

Card Description

A beautiful winter scene of realistic woodland animals decorating a majestic Christmas tree is created by a child from a selection of stickers and then applied to a white background. A Midnight Blue cardstock base with a hinged church window is folded in half, and the forest scene is placed "in" the window. The interior of the card is preprinted with the greeting, "Joy to the World, the Lord is come! Let every heart prepare Him room, while Heaven and Nature sing the wonders of His love!" The interior and exterior of the card are then decorated with additional snowflake and woodland animal stickers. Finally, two tiny gold brads are attached to the window frame as handles.

Kit Contents
(All materials needed to make six cards.)

6 die-cut card exteriors (2 each of Midnight Blue, Forest Green, and Cranberry Red)
6 white, interior sheets
6 white fiber, acid-free-paper envelopes
12 gold brads
Stickers (silver, gold, and white snowflakes, woodland animals)
3 cotton balls
Illustrated instructions

(continued)

Example 15.3

(continued)

Our Questions

Please answer the questions below. Your answers will not be used for any purpose other than to help us determine whether or not we should develop this product.

Please Note

We are confident that the design of this card kit will be well received by our customers. What we are concerned about is the cost involved in producing it. We are very cost conscious about our products and strive to make our products affordable to all. Please give special consideration to the question regarding the price you would be willing to pay for this kit, as this will most likely be the factor that ultimately determines whether or not we are able to produce this product.

First Name _____

Last Name _____

Email Address _____

As described above, does this product idea appeal to you?
○ Yes   ○ No

Would you be inclined to purchase such a product if it were available?
○ Yes   ○ No   ○ Maybe

What is the maximum price range that you would be willing to pay for this type of product?
○ $4.00 - $5.99   ○ $6.00 - $7.99   ○ $8.00 - $9.99
○ $10.00 - $11.99 ○ $12.00 - $13.99 ○ $14.00 - $15.99

Your Advice

We value your advice! Please use the space below to share with us any comments/suggestions/concerns that you feel might help us improve this product.

1. _____
2. _____
3. _____
4. _____
5. _____

Thank You for your help!

[Submit] [Clear]

REFERENCES

(1) Picture This
    6000 Hwy 93
    Eau Claire, WI
    Price Quote Date: October 28, 2005

(2) Wal-Mart
    3915 Gateway Drive
    Eau Claire, WI
    Visited On: October 28, 2005

(3) Impact Images
    4919 Windplay Drive Suite 7
    El Dorado Hills, CA 95762
    Price Quote Date: October 23, 2005

(4) Illuminated Ink
    15825 – 160th Ave.
    Bloomer, WI 54724
    Price Quote Date: October 23, 2005

(5) Sam's Club
    4001 Gateway Dr.
    Eau Claire, WI 54701
    Price Quote Date: October 28, 2005

(6) Christmas Card Kit Survey
    <www.illuminatedink.com/christmas_card_kit_survey.htm>
    Posted On: October 28, 2005

Exercises 练习

▶ Group

1. In groups of two to four, analyze the community attitudes that are addressed by the authors of Examples 15.1–15.3 or of the examples in Exercises 2 and 3 below. What factors have the writers obviously tried to accommodate? What kind of memo is expected? What length? Do they desire to prove conclusively that the material is accurate? Or is there an informal understanding that only a few words are necessary?

    Alternate: In the groups, role-play the sender and receiver of the reports. Receivers interview the senders to decide whether to implement the recommendation.

▶ You Analyze

2. Analyze this sample for organization, format, depth of detail, and persuasiveness. If necessary, rewrite the memo to eliminate your criticisms. Create the visual aid that the author mentions at the end of the report. Alternate: Rewrite the memo as a much "crisper," less chatty document. Alternate: Construct a table that summarizes the data in the report.

    The purpose of this report is to determine from which insurance company I should purchase liability insurance for my 2001 Chevrolet Cavalier. Data for this report were gathered from personal interviews with agents representing their companies. After comparing different companies, I narrowed my choice to decide which one I should buy. I evaluated Ever Safe and Urban Insurance using the following criteria, which are ranked in importance:

    1. Cost—Could annual insurance of liability be less than $250?
    2. Payments—Could it be paid semiannually?
    3. Service—Is the agent easily accessible?

    After this evaluation, I concluded that Ever Safe was the best company to purchase my liability insurance. First, this insurance company costs $245, which is less than the $250 limit that I proposed to spend. Second, it can be paid semiannually. And, third, Ever Safe offers toll-free claim service 24 hours a day.

    Ever Safe costs $245 a year, with Urban Insurance costing $240 a year, which both met my required criteria of purchasing liability insurance for under $250. Urban Insurance is $5 less; however, Ever Safe does have other options that are worth the extra money in means of purchasing.

    Ever Safe and Urban Insurance both offer semiannual payments. In terms of this aspect, they are both weighted the same.

Ever Safe offers toll-free claim service 24 hours a day. Urban Insurance is long distance with limited working hours. They are available after working hours but only through an answering machine that will record your message for the agent to get in touch with you on the following day.

In the decision of an insurance company, it is plain to see that Ever Safe meets the requirements of my criteria and that Urban Insurance does not. Urban Insurance is cheaper, allows semiannual payments, but does not fulfill the service that I was looking for. For the extra dollars of payment, the service in Ever Safe is worth it.

3. Analyze this section for organization, format, depth of detail, and persuasiveness. Rewrite the memo, if necessary, to eliminate your criticisms. Create a visual aid that the author mentions at the end of the report. Summarize the data that support the recommendation. Alternate: Rewrite the memo as a much "crisper," less chatty document. Alternate: Construct a table or figure that effectively summarizes the data in the report.

COST

INTRODUCTION

Since the 49'R Pulling Team does not have any sponsors, they can only spend money on parts that are necessary and feasible. It was proposed that a new supercharger should not cost more than $5000 after the trade-in of the 49'R Pulling Teams' current supercharger. Just the purchase of the supercharger minus the estimated value of the current supercharger would have been fine. But there would have been a cost associated with the equipment criterion that would push the total cost too high.

RESEARCH

The 49'R Pulling Team wanted to trade in their existing supercharger, so a sales representative would have to be contacted to negotiate a price. Since the 49'R Pulling Team has been in this sport for many years, they provided some information about who to contact about purchasing a new supercharger. The one person they have done business with is John Knox, who is with Sassy Engines in New Hampshire. It was estimated the value of the existing supercharger would be $1500.

Research from the Internet provided only a few companies that offer the style and size supercharger that the 49'R Pulling Team was looking for. The companies included Littlefield, SSI, SCS, Kobelco, and Kuhl. The cost for a new Kobelco 14-71 hi-helix supercharger was $5800. For a SSI 14-71 hi-helix supercharger, the outright cost was $5800 dollars. The cost for a Kuhl 14-71 hi-helix retro-fit supercharger was $5250. Those prices did not include any money from a trade-in or sale.

So far, all three superchargers were under $5000 and this criterion would have had a positive recommendation. But after looking into the equipment criterion and finding out there would be an additional $3500 cost, all three superchargers exceed the $5000 limit. The reason for the equipment cost can be found under the equipment link.

www.kuhlsuperchargers.com/cat_p02.htm
www.kocoa.com/2005_pricing_schedules.htm
www.sassyengines.com/Blowerdriveparts.html

CONCLUSION

This table gives the results that were accumulated and the cost after a trade-in or possible sale estimated at $1500 and with the $3500 equipment cost.

Supercharger Brand	Cost for New	Cost After Trade-In	Final Cost
Kobelco	$5800	$4300	$7800
Kuhl	$5250	$3750	$7250
SSI	$5800	$4300	$7800

After the estimated value of the existing supercharger was subtracted from the cost of a new 14-71 supercharger from three different companies and the addition of the equipment cost, all three were more than the $5000 that was set in this criterion. Under the restrictions of this criterion, the purchase of a new supercharger would not be recommended to the 49'R Pulling Team.

▶ You Revise

4. Rewrite this brief section. Create a table that illustrates the data.

INTRODUCTION

The University of Wisconsin—Stout has been submitted to a tremendous amount of budget cuts. The athletic department has been granted an estimated budget of $250,000 for updates of current facilities. For a new floor installation to be feasible, the total cost must not reach over $250,000.

FIGURES

According to Connors Flooring, the total installation cost of a maple sports floor is $81,300 with over 38 years of life expectancy. This is based on a 10,000-square-foot floor.

The Maple Floor Manufacturers Association has concluded that wood floors also require regular cleaning, sanding, lines repainted, and floor refinishing approximately every three years. This is a cost of approximately

$8,000.00 per three years, equaling $2,666.00 p/year. With a 38 year life expectancy, the total for cleaning, sanding, painting, etc. = $101,308.

CONCLUSION

The total cost of the floor is under $200,000, which meets the first criteria of not exceeding $250,000.

5. Rewrite this text for a more professional tone. Evaluate the table for effectiveness; if necessary create a new table.

HAS TO BE UNDER $75

INTRODUCTION

One of the biggest things for our team is going to be the fact of money and how much these sweat suits will be costing. First off none of us have much money to begin with and we also have limited funds for our sport as is. I feel that if you can set a limit that the whole team can agree is reasonable while at the same time getting a quality product. I feel that this is actually one of the most important criterion.

RESEARCH

First of all to get the price set at $75 was very easy, at practice one day when we were discussing the sweat suits, all I had to say was that price and everyone agreed right on the spot. The next part of the research was the tough part. The three places I ended up going to look for this price was eastbay.com, askjeeves.com, and to Fleet Feet. The research that I did turned out pretty helpful for this project although a lot more work then I had intended.

RESULTS

When I first started looking at sweat suits on eastbay, it was a big disappointment, the selection was really good and they had quite a bit of stuff but I knew that there was no way that anyone on our team could afford those. All the suits were at least $100 or more and I won't even mention some of the prices that were listed. When I went to askjeeves, I ran into basically the same problem. All that it was really giving me were links to really expensive name brand products. Although name brands are very dependable there is always another no name brand that can be just as durable for a cheaper price, so pushed on in my journey. When I went into Fleet Feet I just had a feeling that they would at least help me find something if they didn't have it there with them. Sure enough they gave me a catalog along with a website that I could visit. When I went to the website which is hollowayusa.com, I found what I was looking for right away. When I saw it, it was just too good to be true, the pants were listed at

$35.90 and the top is listed at $37.90. Which is a grand total of $73.80. You can see the different prices I ended up finding on the different sites located in Table 1 below.

Table 1
Different Price Options

Brand	Top	Bottom	Total
Nike	$55.00	$60.00	$115.00
Holloway	$37.90	$35.90	$73.80
Addidas	$52.50	$50.25	$102.75

CONCLUSION

When I saw the sweats and then saw the price of them I knew that they had a good shot of getting accepted. This price is a perfect price and a price that everyone on the team had agreed on before I even started looking for the suits. When I let the team know the price they were all very excited.

▶ You Create

6. As your instructor requires, perform the following exercises in conjunction with one of this chapter's Writing Assignments.

    a. Perform the actions required by the worksheet.

    b. Write a discussion section. Construct a visual aid that depicts data for each criterion. Write an introduction for the section: define the criterion and tell its significance, rank, and source. Point out the relevant data for each section. Write a one-sentence conclusion. Word it positively. (Say X is cheaper than Y, not Y is more expensive than X.)

    c. Write an introduction that orients the reader to the situation and to your recommendation. Choose one of the several methods shown in this chapter and Chapter 12.

    d. In groups of two or three, review each other's problem statements and the criteria derived from them. Make suggestions for improvement.

    e. In groups of two or three, read a body section from each other's reports. Assess whether it presents the data that support the conclusion.

    f. In groups of two or three, compare conclusions to the recommendations. Do the conclusions support the recommendations?

    g. In groups of two or three, assess each other's introductions. Do they contain enough information to orient the reader to the situation and the recommendation?

h. In groups of two or three, read the near-final reports for consistency of format. Are all the heads at the appropriate level? Are all the heads really informative? Is the style sheet applied consistently? Does it help make the contents easy to group? Do the visual aids effectively communicate key points?

Writing Assignments 写作任务

1. Assume that you are working for a local firm and have been asked to evaluate two kinds, brands, or models of equipment. Select a limited topic (for instance, two specific models of 10-inch table saws, the Black and Decker model 123 and the Craftsman model ABC), and evaluate the alternatives in detail. Write a report recommending that one of the alternatives be purchased to solve a problem. Be sure to explain the problem. Both alternatives should be workable; your report must recommend the one that will work better.

    Gather data about the alternatives just as you would when working in industry—from sales literature, dealers, your own experience, and the experience of others who have worked with the equipment. Select a maximum of four criteria by which to judge the alternatives and use a minimum of one visual aid in the report. Aim your report at someone not familiar with the equipment. Fill out the worksheet in this chapter, and perform the parts of Exercise 6 that your instructor requires.

2. Assume that you are working for a local firm that wants to expand to a site within 50 miles. Pick an actual site in your area. Then write a feasibility report on the site. Devise criteria based on the situation. Do all the research necessary to discover land values, transportation systems, governing agencies, costs, and any other relevant factors. Your instructor will provide you with guidance about how to deal with the local authorities and how to discover the facts about these topics. Use this chapter's worksheet, and perform those parts of Exercise 6 that your instructor requires.

3. Assume that you have been asked to decide on the feasibility of a proposed course of action. Name and describe the proposal. Then establish the relevant criteria to determine feasibility. Apply the criteria and write an informal report. Use this chapter's worksheet, and perform those parts of Exercise 6 that your instructor requires.

4. Find a firm or an agency in your locale that has a problem that it will allow you to solve. Research the problem, and present the solution in a report. The report may be either formal or informal, recommendation or feasibility. Your instructor will help you schedule the project. This project should not be an exercise in format and organization, but a solution that people need in order to perform well on their jobs. Use this chapter's worksheet, and perform those parts of Exercise 6 that your instructor requires.

5. Assume that your manager wants to create a webpage. Investigate the situation, and write a report explaining the feasibility of creating and maintaining a website.
6. Write a learning report for the writing assignment you just completed. See Chapter 5, Writing Assignment 7, page 133, for details of the assignment.

Web Exercises 网络练习

1. Assume that your manager wants to create a webpage. Investigate the situation and write a report explaining the feasibility of creating and maintaining a website.
2. Write a report on whether or not the Web is a feasible source of information that you can use to perform your duties as a professional in your field. For instance, is the Web a more feasible source than hard copy of OSHA regulations or ASTM standards?

Works Cited 引用的作品

Alexander, Heather, and Ben Potter. "Case Study: The Use of Formal Specification and Rapid Prototyping to Establish Product Feasibility." *Information and Software Technology* 29.7 (1987): 388–394.

Angelo, Rocco M. *Understanding Feasibility Studies.* East Lansing, MI: Educational Institute of the American Hotel and Motel Association, 1985.

Bradford, Michael. "Four Types of Feasibility Studies Can Be Used." *Business Insurance* (19 June 1989): 16.

Holcombe, Marya W., and Judith K. Stein. *Writing for Decision Makers: Memos and Reports with a Competitive Edge.* Belmont, CA: Lifelong, 1981.

Markel, Mike. "Criteria Development and the Myth of Objectivity." *The Technical Writing Teacher* 18.1 (1991): 37–47.

Ramige, Robert K. "Packaging Equipment, Twelve Steps for Project Management." *IOPP Technical Journal* X.3 (1992): 47–50.

Chapter 16 Proposals
提 案

Chapter Contents
Chapter 16 In a Nutshell
The External Proposal
Planning the External Proposal
Writing the External Proposal
The Internal Proposal
Planning the Internal Proposal
Ethics and Proposals
Writing the Internal Proposal

Chapter 16
In a Nutshell 概 要

The goal of a proposal is to persuade readers to accept a course of action as an acceptable way to solve a problem or fill a need. Internal proposals show that the situation is bad and your way will clearly make it better. External proposals show that your way is the best.

Basic proposal issues. Four issues for you to discuss convincingly in a proposal are

- The *problem*—how some fact negatively affects positive expectations (high absenteeism on manufacturing line 1 is causing a failure to meet production goals) and that you know the cause (workers are calling in sick because of sore backs).
- The *solution*—actions that will neutralize the cause (eliminate bending by reconfiguring the work tables and automating one material transfer point).
- The *benefits* of the solution—what desirable outcome each person or group in the situation will obtain.
- The *implementation*—who will do it and how, how long it will take.

Develop credibility. To accept your solution, your readers must feel you are credible. Your methods must be clear and sound—an expert's assessment of the situation. Your analyses of the problem, the cause, the benefits, how long it will take, the cost, etc., must show a reasoned regard of each concern, one that will not cause surprises later on.

Basic guidelines. Follow these guidelines:

- Use a top-down strategy.
- Describe the situation and use visual aids.
- Provide context in the introduction.
- Provide a summary that clearly states the proposed solution.

A proposal persuades its readers to accept the writer's idea. There are two kinds of proposals: external and internal. In an *external proposal,* one firm responds to a request—from another firm or the government—for a solution to a problem. Ranging from lengthy (100 pages or more) to short (4 or 5 pages), these documents secure contracts for firms. In an *internal proposal,* the writer urges someone else in the company to accept an idea or to fund equipment purchases or research.

The External Proposal 外部提案

A firm writes external proposals to win contracts for work. Government agencies and large and small corporations issue a *request for proposal (RFP),* which explains the project and lists its specifications precisely. For example, a major aircraft company, such as British Airlines, often sends RFPs to several large firms to solicit proposals for a specific type of equipment—say, a guidance system. The RFP contains extremely detailed and comprehensive specifications, stating standards for minute technical items and specifying the content, format, and deadline for the proposals.

The companies that receive the RFP write proposals to show how they will develop the project. A team assembles a document demonstrating that the company has the technical know-how, managerial expertise, and budget to develop the project.

After receiving all the proposals, the firm that requested them turns them over to a team of evaluators, some of whom helped write the original specifications. The evaluators rate the proposals, judging the technical, management, and cost sections in order to select the best overall proposal (Bacon).

Not all proposals are written to obtain commercial contracts. Proposals are also commonly written by state and local governments, public agencies, education, and industry. University professors often write proposals, bringing millions of dollars to campuses to support research in fields as varied as food spoilage and genetic research.

Discussion of a lengthy, 50- to 200-page proposal is beyond the scope of this book; it is a subject for an entire course. But brief external proposals are very common. They require the same planning and contain the same elements as a lengthy proposal. The following sections illustrate the planning and elements of a brief external proposal.

Planning the External Proposal 设计外部提案

To write an external proposal, you must consider your audience, research the situation, use visual aids, and follow the usual form for this type of document.

Consider the Audience 考虑读者

The audience for an external proposal consists of potential customers. These customers know that they have a need, and they have a general idea of how to fill that need. Usually they will have expressed their problem to you in a written statement (an RFP) or in an interview. Generally, a committee decides whether to accept your proposal. Assess their technical awareness and write in such a way that not only do they understand your proposal, but they also have confidence in it and in you. To write to them effectively, you should follow these guidelines:

- Address each need they have expressed.
- Explain in clear terms how your proposal fills their needs.
- Explain the relevance of technical data.

For instance, if you want to sell a computer system to a nonprofit arts organization, you cannot just drop terms for computer parts—say, 2 gigs of RAM—and expect them to know what that means. You need to explain the data so that the people who make the decision to commit their money will feel comfortable doing so.

Research the Situation 情况调研

To write the proposal effectively, understand your customer's needs as well as the features of your own product or service. Your goal is to show how the features will fill the needs. Discover this by interviewing the customer or by reading their printed material. Showing that you understand the situation and have taken proper research steps enhances your credibility.

Writers devise different ways to develop their research. To relate needs and features, many writers compile a two-column table like this:

Need	Feature That Meets Need
Director must be able to access latest financial data and public relations data.	Available in content management database.
Director must be able to access data at any time.	Director needs personal digital assistant with wireless capabilities.
Secretary enters data, but not continuously.	Secretary needs wireless access to workstation.
Secretary does accounting.	Secretary can use Accountant Inc. 2.1c and Excel.
Artist enters data.	Artist needs wireless access to workstation.

Need	Feature That Meets Need
Artist does desktop publishing.	Artist needs InDesign, Photoshop, Illustrator, and six-color laser printer.
$15,000 maximum.	Airport station, 2 laptop computers, 1 pda, software for artwork, word processing, accounting, and desktop publishing.

Once you establish the client's needs, you can easily point out a reasonable way to meet them.

Use Visual Aids 利用视图

Many types of visual aids may be appropriate to your proposal. Tables might summarize costs and technical features. Maps (or layouts), for instance, might show where you will install the workstation and the electrical lines in the office complex. Illustrations of the product with callouts can point out special features. Remember that your goal is to convince the decision makers that your way is the best; good visuals are direct and dramatic, drawing your client into the document.

Writing the External Proposal 撰写外部提案

To write an external proposal, follow the usual form for writing proposals. The four main parts of a proposal are an executive summary and the technical, managerial, and financial sections.

The Executive Summary 行政总结

The executive summary contains information designed to convince executives that the proposers should receive the contract. In short external proposals, this section should be reduced in proportion to the body (see Chapter 8). It should succinctly present the contents of the technical, managerial, and financial sections. Generally write this section last.

The Technical Section 技术部分

A proposal's technical section begins by stating the problem to be solved. The proposers must clearly demonstrate that they understand what the customer expects. The proposal should describe its approach to solving the problem and present a preliminary design for the product, if one is needed. Sometimes the

The Management Section 管理部分

The management section describes the personnel who will work directly on the project. The proposal explains the expertise of the people responsible for the project. In a short proposal, this section usually explains qualifications of personnel, the firm's success with similar projects, and its willingness to service the product, provide technical assistance, and train employees. This section also includes a schedule for the project, sometimes including deadlines for each phase.

The Financial Section 财务部分

The financial section provides a breakdown of the costs for every item in the proposal. This section varies in depth. Often a brief introduction and table may be sufficient, but if you need to explain the source or significance of certain figures, do so.

The Internal Proposal 内部提案

The internal proposal persuades someone to accept an idea—usually to change something, or to fund something, or both. Covering a wide range of subjects, internal proposals may request new pieces of lab equipment, defend major capital expenditures, or recommend revised production control standards. The rest of this chapter explains the internal proposal's audiences, visual aids, and design.

Planning the Internal Proposal 设计内部提案

The goal of a proposal is to convince the person or group in authority to allow the writer to implement his or her idea. To achieve this goal, the writer must consider the audience, use visual aids, organize the proposal well, and design an appropriate format.

Consider the Audience 考虑读者

The audience profile for a proposal focuses on the audience's involvement, their knowledge, and their authority.

firm offers alternative methods for solving the problem and invites the proposal writer to select one. In the computer network example, the proposal might explain three different configurations that fulfill needs slightly differently but still stay within the $15,000 maximum cost.

Ethics and Proposals 撰写提案的注意事项

> Proposals are an attempt to persuade an audience to approve whatever it is that is being proposed. Whether the proposal is internal or external, solicited or unsolicited, it is a kind of contract between the technical writer (or company) and the audience. Because proposals often deal with time and money, your trustworthiness and accountability are at stake. Consider your audience's needs and write sympathetically and knowledgeably for them. The ethical writer considers the audience's requirements, not what he or she can get out of the situation.

How Involved Is the Audience?

In most cases, readers of a proposal either have assigned the proposal and are aware of the problem or have not assigned the proposal and are unaware of the problem. For example, suppose a problem develops with a particular assembly line. The production engineer in charge might assign a subordinate to investigate the situation and recommend a solution. In this assigned proposal, the writer does not have to establish that a problem exists, but he or she does have to show how the proposal will solve the problem.

More often, however, the audience does not assign the proposal. For instance, a manager could become aware that a new arrangement of her floor space could create better sales potential. If she decides to propose a rearrangement, she must first convince her audience—her supervisor—that a problem exists. Only then can she go on to offer a convincing solution.

How Knowledgeable Is the Audience?

The audience may or may not know the concepts and facts involved in either the problem or the solution. Estimate your audience's level of knowledge. If the audience is less knowledgeable, take care to define terms, give background, and use common examples or analogies.

How Much Authority Does the Audience Have?

The audience may or may not be able to order the implementation of your proposed solution. A manager might assign the writer to investigate problems with the material flow of a particular product line, but the manager will probably have to take the proposal to a higher authority before it is approved. So the writer must bear in mind that several readers may see and approve (or reject) the proposal.

Use Visual Aids 利用视图

Because the proposal is likely to have multiple audiences, visual aids are important. Visuals can support any part of the proposal—the description of the problem, the solution, the implementation, and the benefits. In addition to the tables and graphs described in Chapter 7, Gantt charts (see Chapter 17) and diagrams can be very helpful.

Gantt Charts

As described in Chapter 7, Gantt charts visually depict a schedule of implementation. A Gantt chart has an X axis and a Y axis. The horizontal axis displays time periods; the vertical axis, individual processes. Lines inside the chart show when a process starts and stops. By glancing at the chart, the reader can see the project's entire schedule. Figure 16.1 is an example of a Gantt chart.

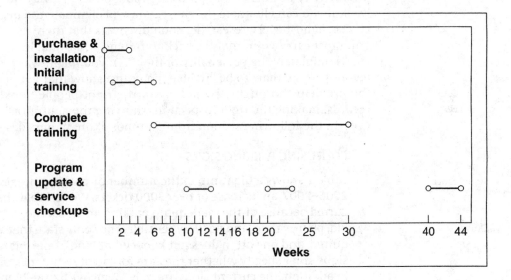

Figure 16.1

Gantt Chart

Diagrams

Many kinds of diagrams, such as flow charts, block diagrams, organization charts, and decision trees, can enhance a proposal. Layouts, for instance, are effective for proposals that suggest rearranging space.

Organize the Proposal 组织提案

The writer should organize the proposal around four questions:

1. What is the problem?
2. What is the solution?
3. Can the solution be implemented?
4. Should the solution be implemented?

What Is the Problem?

Describing the problem is a key part of many proposals. You must establish three things about the problem:

- The data
- The significance
- The cause

The *data* are the actual facts that a person can perceive. The *significance* is the way the facts fail to meet the standard you hope to maintain. To explain the significance of the problem, you show that the current situation negatively affects productivity or puts you in an undesirable position. The *cause* is the problem itself. If you can eliminate the cause, you will eliminate the negative effects. Of course, almost every researcher soon discovers that there are chains of causes. You must carry your analysis back to the most reasonable cause. If the problem is ultimately the personality of the CEO, you might want to stop the chain before you say that. To be credible, you must show that you have investigated the problem thoroughly by talking to the right people, looking at the right records, making the right inspection, showing the appropriate data, or whatever. In the following section from a proposal, the writers describe a problem:

CONFUSING PARKING SIGNS

Significance — Table 1 shows a big jump in the number of parking tickets given out in 2006–2007, an increase of over 3000 tickets. We feel that the increase occurred because of the inadequate parking lot signs. The current signs are *Cause* old, plain, vague, and not very sensible. They only state that a permit is re-*Data* quired, and one often does not know what kind of permit is needed. The signs don't specify whether they are for faculty, students, or commuters. In addition, the current signs are only 12 inches by 18–24 inches and can be overlooked if people are unaware of them.

Significance — In our survey of some West Central University students, we found that many students who received tickets either did not know that they could not park in the specific lot, were unsure of which lot they were able to park in, or did not see any specific signs suggesting that they could not park there.

Table 1

Tickets Given Out per 2500 Parking Stalls at West Central University

Year	No. of Tickets
2004–2005	13,202
2005–2006	13,764
2006–2007	16,867

What Is the Solution?

To present an effective solution, explain how it will eliminate the cause, thus eliminating whatever is out of step with the standard you hope to maintain. If the problem is causing an undesirable condition, the solution must show how that condition can be eliminated. If the old signage for parking lots gives insufficient information, explain how the solution gives better information. A helpful approach is to analyze the solution in terms of its impact on the technical, management/maintenance, and financial aspects of the situation.

NEW SIGNS FOR ENTRANCE

Solution named

Details show how the solution solves the problem.

Benefits

Our solution is to create new permanent signs to be installed at the entrance of each parking lot. The new signs (in their entirety) will measure 3 feet by 4 feet so they will be visible to anyone entering the lot. Each sign will include the name of the lot; a letter to designate if the lot is for students (S), faculty (F), or administration (A); a color code for the particular permit needed; and the time and the days that the lot is monitored. The signs will not only present the proper information but will also look nice, making the campus more appealing. See Figure 1 for the proposed design.

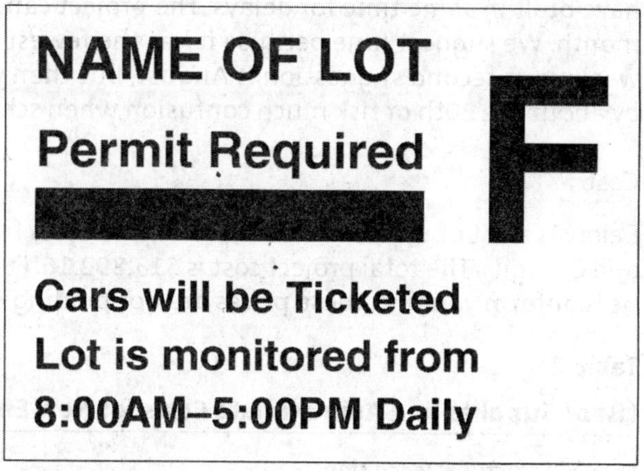

```
┌─────────────────────────────┐
│ NAME OF LOT                 │
│                          F  │
│ Permit Required             │
│ ▬▬▬▬▬▬▬▬▬▬▬▬               │
│                             │
│ Cars will be Ticketed       │
│ Lot is monitored from       │
│ 8:00AM–5:00PM Daily         │
└─────────────────────────────┘
```

Figure 1
Entrance Sign

Can the Solution Be Implemented?

The writer must show that all the systems involved in the proposal can be put into effect. To make this clear to the audience, you would explain

- The cost
- The effect on personnel
- The schedule for implementing the changes

This section may be difficult to write because it is hard to tell exactly what the audience needs to know.

IMPLEMENTATION

Agents involved in implementation

The businesses we suggest that you deal with are Fulweil Structures, CE Signs, and University Grounds Services. The reason for choosing these businesses is that you will please the community of Menomonie by doing business in town and these businesses have good prices for a project like this. Also, these companies can provide services over the summer.

Schedule

Implementation of the new signs will take approximately one summer. A suggested schedule is

1. Order signs from Fulweil.   1 week
2. Fulweil constructs signs.   1 week
3. CE paints signs.   1 week
4. Grounds crew erects signs.   2 weeks

Schedule explained

If you compare this schedule to the estimates below, you will see that we have built in some time for delays. The project can be easily finished in a month. We suggest June because it has the fewest students for the most weeks; our second suggestion is August, but then you will have to finish by about the 20th or risk much confusion when school starts on the 25th.

Cost

Cost background

Below is a list of supplies and approximate costs from Fulweil Structures and CE Signs. The total project cost is $13,892.16. Fulweil Structures asked us to inform you that these prices are not binding quotes.

Table 2
List of Supplies and Approximate Costs for New Entrance Signs

Table presents all cost figures

Fulweil Structures (each sign)

6' × 2" × 2" solid bar aluminum (2 in quantity)	$118.91
3'4" × 3'4" aluminum sheet (1 in quantity)	64.93
3 hours of labor at $25/hour	75.00
Total cost	$ 258.84

CE Signs (each sign)

3' × 3' Reflective Scotchguard	$ 50.00
10–15 letters painted	125.00
2½ hours labor at $34/hour	85.00

Total cost		$ 260.00
Total cost of each sign		518.84
Total cost of 24 signs		12,452.16
Projected cost of erecting signs		
2 hours/sign @ 25.00/hr (24 signs)	$1200.00	
Materials/sign @ 10.00 (24 signs)	240.00	
Total cost of erecting signs		1440.00
Total cost of project (24 signs)		$13,892.16

Should the Solution Be Implemented?

Just because you can implement the solution does not mean that you should. To convince someone that you should be allowed to implement your solution, you must demonstrate that the solution has benefits that make it desirable, that it meets the established criteria in the situation, or both.

THE BENEFITS OF THIS PROJECT

List of people who benefit

Discussion of each area of benefit

The benefits of the signs will be felt by you, the students, the faculty, and the administration. You will see the number of appeals decline because the restrictions will be clearly visible, saving much bookwork and time for appeals. You will also answer fewer phone calls from persons needing to know where to park and you will write fewer tickets, thus saving much processing time.

    The students, faculty, and administration will be happier because they will know exactly where and when they can and cannot park. Students will not receive as many parking tickets and will save money. Faculty and administration will also benefit by not having students park in their reserved parking spots (or at least not as often).

Design the Proposal 设计提案

To design a proposal, select an appropriate format, either *formal* or *informal*. A formal proposal has a title page, table of contents, and summary (see Chapter 14). An informal proposal can be a memo report or some kind of preprinted form (see Chapter 12). The format depends on company policy and on the distance the proposal must travel in the hierarchy. Usually the shorter the distance, the more informal the format. Also, the less significant the proposal, the more informal the format. For instance, you would not send an elaborately formatted proposal to your immediate superior to suggest a $50 solution to a layout problem in a workspace.

Writing the Internal Proposal 撰写内部提案

Use the Introduction to Orient the Reader 利用介绍来引导读者

The introduction to a proposal demands careful thought because it must orient the reader to the writer, the problem, and the solution. The introduction can contain one paragraph or several. You should clarify the following important points:

- Why is the writer writing? Is the proposal assigned or unsolicited?
- Why is the writer credible?
- What is the problem?
- What is the background of the problem?
- What is the significance of the problem?
- What is the solution?
- What are the parts of the report?

An effective way to provide all these points is in a two-part introduction that includes a context-setting paragraph and a summary. The context-setting paragraph usually explains the purpose of the proposal and, if necessary, gives evidence of the writer's credibility. The summary is a one-to-one miniaturization of the body. (Be careful not to make the summary a background; background belongs in a separate section.) If the body contains sections on the solution, benefits, cost, implementation, and rejected alternatives, the summary should cover the same points.

A sample introduction follows.

DATE:	April 8, 2006
TO:	Jennifer Williamson
FROM:	Steve Vinz
	Mike Vivoda
	Michele Welsh
	Marya Wilson
SUBJECT:	Installing new parking lot signs

Reason for writing: sets context

Parking on campus has been a topic of many discussions here at West Central University and one of much concern. The topics on parking include what lots students are able to park in, when students can park in the lots, and the availability of parking on campus. We believe that students do not know exactly when and where they can park in the campus lots because of the vague and confusing signs.

Summary

We feel that the school should post at each entrance new, more informative, and more readable signs containing all the rules and regulations. These signs would say exactly who can and cannot park in the lot, the times when the lots are patrolled, and what type of permit is needed. The project could be completed in 5 weeks and would cost $13,892.16. Major

Preview of sections

benefits include fewer administrative hassles and happier university community members. This memo will first discuss the problem, then the solution, implementation, and the benefits.

Use the Discussion to Convince Your Audience 利用讨论来说服读者

The discussion section contains all the detailed information that you must present to convince the audience. A common approach functions this way:

The problem

- Explanation of the problem
- Causes of the problem

The solution

- Details of the solution
- Benefits of the solution
- Ways in which the solution satisfies criteria

The context

- Schedule for implementing the solution
- Personnel involved
- Solutions rejected

In each section, present the material clearly, introduce visual aids whenever possible, and use headings and subheadings to enhance page layout.

Which sections to use depends on the situation. Sometimes you need an elaborate implementation section; sometimes you don't. Sometimes you should discuss causes, sometimes not. If the audience needs the information in the section, include it; otherwise, don't.

The section above (pp. 410–413) illustrates one approach to the body. Other examples appear in the examples.

Worksheet for Preparing a Proposal

准备提案的工作表

☐ Determine the audience for the proposal.
Will one person or group receive this proposal?
Will the primary audience decide on the recommendations in this proposal?
How much do they know about the topic?
What information do you need to present in order to be credible?

(continued)

(continued)

- ☐ Prepare background.
  Why did the proposal project come into existence?
- ☐ Select a format—formal or informal.
- ☐ Prepare a style sheet of margins, headings, page numbers, and visual aid captions.

External Proposal

- ☐ Write a statement of the customer's needs.
- ☐ Prepare a two-column list (pp. 405–406) of the customer's needs and the ways your proposal meets those needs.
- ☐ Present your features in terms of the customer's needs, using the customer's terminology.
- ☐ Clearly explain the financial details.
- ☐ Explain in detail why your company has the expertise to do the job.
- ☐ Prepare a schedule for implementing. Assess any inconveniences implementation may cause.

Internal Proposal

- ☐ Define the problem.
  Tell the basic standard that you must uphold (we must make a profit). Cite the data that indicate that the standard is not being upheld (we lost $5 million last quarter). Explain the data's causes (we lost three large sales to competitors) and significance (we cannot sustain this level of loss for another year).
- ☐ Construct a visual aid that illustrates the problem or the solution.
  Write a paragraph that explains this visual aid.
- ☐ List all the parameters within which your proposal must stay.
  Examples include cost restrictions, personnel restrictions (can you hire more people?), and space restrictions.
- ☐ Outline your methodology for investigating the situation.
- ☐ Prepare a list of the dimensions of the problem, and show how your proposed solution eliminates each item.
  (This list is the basis for your benefits section.)
- ☐ Write the solution section.
  Explain the solution in enough detail so that a reader can fully understand what it entails in terms of technical aspects, management/maintenance, and finances. Also clearly show how it eliminates the causes of the undesirable condition.

Examples

- ☐ **Construct the benefits section.**
  Clearly relate each benefit to some aspect of the problem. A benefit eliminates causes of the problem (the bottleneck is eliminated) or causes the solution to affect something else positively (worker morale rises).

- ☐ **Prepare a schedule for implementation.**
  Assess any inconveniences.

- ☐ List rejected alternatives, and in one sentence tell why you rejected them.

Worksheet for Evaluating a Proposal
评估提案的工作表

- ☐ Answer these questions about your paper or a peer's. You should be able to answer "yes" to all of the following questions. If you receive a "no" answer, you must revise that section.
  a. Is the problem clear?
  b. Is the solution clear?
  c. Do you understand (and believe) the benefits?
  d. Does the implementation schedule deal with all aspects of the situation?
  e. Does the introduction give you the basics of the problem, the solution, and the situation?
  f. Is the style sheet applied consistently? Does it help make the contents clear?
  g. Do the visual aids communicate key ideas effectively?

Examples 例子

Examples 16.1, 16.2, and 16.3 illustrate three different methods of handling internal proposals.

Example 16.1
Internal Proposal

Date:	November 7, 2007
To:	George Schmidt, Chief Engineer
From:	Greg Fritsch, Assistant Engineer
Subject:	Unnecessary shearing from joint welds

After talking to you on the phone last week, I mentioned that the Block Corporation is having difficulties with shearing on their engine mount supports. I contacted Mr. Jackson, a research expert, who said the stress

(continued)

Example 16.1
(continued)

from the weight of the engine causes the weld to shear. The shearing then causes the motor to collapse onto the engine mount supports. He advised me to purchase a higher-tensile-strength weld. The new weld I propose will reduce the defect rate from 10% to 0%. This memo includes the following information: weld shearing, weld constraints, and shearing solution.

WELD SHEARING

Unnecessary weld shearing of the engine mount supports has been a problem for the Block Corporation since 2004. The company is suffering a 10% defective rate on every 100 engine mounts welded.

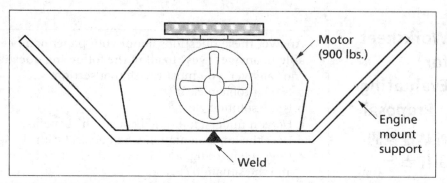

Figure 1
Engine Mount Weld

As seen in Figure 1, the weld must hold together when 900 lbs. of force are applied to the motor mount supports. A quality weld with a high tensile strength should withstand temperature fluctuation without shearing.

WELD CONSTRAINT

The Block Corporation listed the following constraints for implementing a new weld:

1. Material costs must increase by less than .01¢ per engine mount support welded.
2. Welding machines must not exceed 240 volts.
3. Current welding machines have to be used.
4. Each electrical outlet has to have a separate transformer.

SHEARING SOLUTION

The solution to the company's problem is to implement a higher-tensile-strength weld. The weld is projected to increase material and electrical costs, but is not expected to exceed the company's 1% budget increase for the 2008 fiscal year.

Cost

New welding wire with a higher tensile strength will increase 2¢ for every 100 yards of wire. All engine mount welds require 3 yards of wire to secure a solid weld. The overall cost increase per engine mount welded will be only .006¢.

Voltage

There will be an increase in the amount of electricity used in the new welding process. The welding machines will be required to switch from 120 to 240 volts.

Use of Current Machines

The welders will use the same welding machines as in the past. The welding machines are compatible with the new welds and do not need to be replaced.

Separate Transformers

An electrical hookup from 120 to 240 volts will be needed at each electrical outlet. A transformer will be required at each individual box to ensure an increase in voltage flow.

Example 16.2

Internal Proposal

Date: February 14, 2006
To: Irene Gorman
From: Chris Lindblad
Subject: Replacing Voltage Buss Bars

INTRODUCTION

Right now, the voltage buss bars on the C90 modules are not ohmed until after all of the option chips have been bonded to the circuit board. If a voltage buss-to-ground short is found after the bonding process, the short must be located, which takes an average of over 10 hours.

RECOMMENDATION

Based on time savings, cost, space available on the bonders, training involved, and savings to the company, I recommend installing a Fluke model 73 multimeter at each bonding station and to have operators ohm the buss bars after each option is bonded to the circuit board.

(continued)

Example 16.2
(continued)

TIME SAVINGS WILL RESULT

Installing a Fluke model 73 multimeter at each bonding station would have a positive effect on the time spent on locating voltage buss-to-ground shorts, as shown in Table 1. It also shows that ohming the voltage buss bars after each bond would increase the bonding process time but would result in a time savings of 7.1 hours per module.

Table 1
Time Savings with Ohming Capabilities Installed at Bonding Stations

Time	Without Using a Fluke 73 (in hours)	Using a Fluke 73 (in hours)
Average time required to bond all options on circuit board	49.5	51.9
Average time required to locate buss-to-ground shorts	10.0	0.5
Total time required	59.5	52.4
Time savings	—	7.1

WITHIN ALLOWED BUDGET

Currently the budget allows for $5000.00 in bonder improvements. The cost of equipping each bonding machine with a Fluke model 73 multimeter and associated test leads would amount to $350.00. The total cost of equipping the four option bonders would be $1400.00. This cost is well within the allowed budget and would also allow any future bonders to be installed with this equipment.

THE SPACE IS AVAILABLE

The space required for the installation of the ohming equipment is minimal, and it can easily be installed at the base of the bonder at the buss bar end of the module without any loss of mobility of the bonding head. It would also be within easy reach of the operator and cause no safety hazards. Also, no special power requirements are necessary because the Fluke 73 operates on an internal battery source.

TRAINING IS MINIMAL

The training required by the operator to learn how to use the Fluke 73 could be handled by the company's training department, which already has training in place for its use. Only one hour of class time is required with three hours on-the-job training to become proficient in its use.

SAVINGS ARE SIGNIFICANT

By installing a Fluke model 73 multimeter at each of the option bonding stations, the company could save a considerable amount of money. The current cost of troubleshooting a voltage buss-to-ground short is $130.00. This cost, with ohming equipment installed, would drop to around $13.00 per voltage buss-to-ground short, with a savings of $117.00.

CONCLUSION

If you require any further information or documentation on my recommendation, please contact me at the module test department.

Example 16.3

Internal Proposal

REPLACEMENT OF PRESENT SINGLE-PHASE VENTILATION MOTOR WITH A NEW THREE-PHASE INDUCTION MOTOR

INTRODUCTION

The purpose of this report is to inform you of the inadequacies of the present ventilation system, and the benefits of replacing the current motor. In this report I will first give you a quick summary of the proposal, followed by the necessary background information required. I will then discuss in detail the following: the problems with the present system, the proposed solution to correct the problem, the implementation of the new system, the rationale behind the decision, followed by the conclusion.

Summary of Proposal

The problem in the ventilation system came to light during a routine inspection. I noticed the following problems with the present system:

1. Insufficient air flow at the southern end of plant
2. Current motor wastes too much electricity

The combination of these two problems creates both an unsafe and an inefficient system. Fortunately, the solution is quite simple and inexpensive. To correct the problem, the present single-phase motor in the system must be removed and replaced with a new three-phase induction motor. This new motor will not only correct the problems of the present system, it will also produce the following benefits:

1. Longer life
2. Decreased power factor
3. Expandability
4. Minimal downtime at installation

(continued)

Example 16.3

(continued)

Background Information

One must know the difference between a single-phase and a three-phase motor. A single-phase motor runs on only one electrical phase, but requires additional starting circuitry. Three-phase motors, on the other hand, require all three electrical phases, but do not need any starting circuitry. It is also important to know that the amount of air flow in a system is measured in cubic yards per hour.

DISCUSSION

This section covers problems with the present system, a proposed solution, implementation of the new system, rationale, and benefits of the system.

Problems with the Present System

Air Flow The main problem with the present ventilation system is that it is unable to produce enough air flow to the southern end of the plant. During my inspection, I took various measurements of air flow throughout the plant using an air flow meter. I noticed that the southern end is receiving only 1800 cubic yards ventilation an hour. OSHA standards require that 2000 cubic yards must be replaced every hour. If this situation is not corrected, we may be endangering the well-being of our employees, not to mention being slapped with a possible fine from OSHA. After closer examination of the ventilation system, I discovered that the only thing wrong with the system is the motor driving the fan. The motor is old and worn out, and therefore unable to produce the necessary air flow.

Electrical Consumption The other problem with the present system is its abnormally high power-consumption, which I discovered while taking measurements on the present motor with a digital VOM meter. With these measurements, I calculated that the motor is running at only 50% peak efficiency. An average three-phase induction motor runs at approximately 90% peak efficiency. Over the course of a year, the company loses about $900 from the inefficiency of the present motor.

Proposed Solution

After careful analysis of all information, I have come to the following conclusion: replace the present single-phase motor in the ventilation system with a new three-phase induction motor. A new three-phase motor will not only increase air flow, it will also do it more efficiently.

Air Flow If a three-phase induction motor were installed in place of the single-phase motor, it would increase air flow by almost 20%. I calculated this by using the torque and speed characteristics of a three-phase motor.

This would boost the air flow to the southern end of the plant from 1800 cubic yards to over 2100 cubic yards per hour. This is well within OSHA standards.

Electrical Consumption One of the biggest advantages of a three-phase motor over a single-phase motor is the efficiency. An average new three-phase motor can run at up to 90% efficiency. An average single-phase motor of the same horsepower could achieve only 80% efficiency at best. The more efficient a device, the less expensive it is to run. See Figure 1.

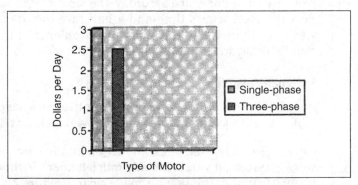

Figure 1
Electrical Running Cost of a Single-Phase Motor vs. a Three-Phase Motor

As you can see from this figure, a three-phase motor requires much less electricity to run per day than the single-phase motor. The reason a three-phase is more efficient than the single-phase motor is that it needs no additional starting circuitry. The addition of this starting circuitry in a single-phase motor is what robs it of maximum efficiency.

Implementation of the New System

The installation of a new three-phase induction motor should pose no problems. In this section, I will concentrate on the main aspects of installation: cost, time, and inconvenience.

Cost The overall cost of replacing and installing the new motor should not exceed $500. The motor and control box together are $300. The wiring must be done by a certified electrician and overall labor cost should not exceed $150. The remaining $50 will buy new motor mountings, brackets, and wire. A three-phase junction box is within 20 feet of the ventilation system and should pose no installation difficulties for the electrician.

(continued)

Example 16.3
(continued)

Time The installation time from start to finish should be no more than five hours. It will take one hour for us to remove the old single-phase motor. Installing the three-phase motor should take no more than an hour and a half. The remaining hour would be used for cleanup work and initial start-up of the system. I received all of these time and cost figures from a certified electrician.

Inconveniences The new three-phase motor could be installed with only a few slight inconveniences, the most obvious of which is the shutdown of the ventilation system. This cannot be done during working hours, so it will have to be done on a Saturday. The labor costs I have stated earlier reflect the electrician's time-and-a-half rate imposed by working on the weekend. There is also the minor inconvenience of having someone here that Saturday to let the electrician into the building.

Rationale/Benefits

A three-phase induction motor in a ventilation system will provide three main benefits: longer life, decreased power factor, and expandability.

Longer Life If a three-phase induction motor were installed into the ventilation system, it would provide much longer life than an equivalent single-phase motor. This point is made clear in Figure 2.

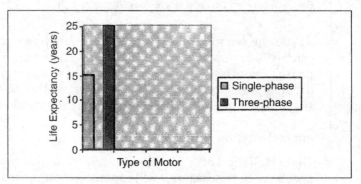

Figure 2
Expected Life of a Single-Phase Motor vs. a Three-Phase Motor

As you will notice from Figure 2, a three-phase motor will last much longer than will a single-phase motor doing the same task. The reason for this is the simplicity of operation of a three-phase motor; the single-phase requires starting circuitry, which has a tendency to break down more quickly.

Decreased Power Factor Power factor is a confusing factor involved with the use of any inductive device, including motors. Power factor, if left unchecked, alters the electricity we receive. Although both single-phase and three-phase motors have some amount of power factor associated with them, a three-phase motor has less. A three-phase motor will reduce the amount we are charged for power factor.

Expandability   Another advantage of a three-phase motor is the expandability we would receive in our ventilation system. With the increase in air flow, we could easily add on to the ventilation system.

CONCLUSION

We cannot afford to let this problem continue. A three-phase motor in the ventilation system will best suit our needs both now and in the future.

Exercises 练 习

▶ You Create

1. Create a visual aid that demonstrates that a problem exists.
2. With the visual aid from Exercise 1, write a paragraph that includes the data, the significance, and the cause of the problem, and write a second paragraph that suggests a way to eliminate the problem.
3. Make a Gantt chart of a series of implementation actions. Write a paragraph that explains the actions.
4. Create two different page designs for the proposal about parking signs on campus (pp. 410–413).

▶ You Revise

5. Rewrite the following paragraphs. The writer is a recreation area supervisor who has discovered the problem; the reader is the finance director of a school district. Shorten the document. Make the tone less personal. Make a new section if necessary. Adopt the table or create new visual aids. If your instructor requires, also add an introduction and a summary.

DISCUSSION OF TRENDS

I have data that establish trends in the building's use (see Table 1). These data show peak adult and student use during the winter months. When school is out (June–August), we have more students and children using the building. Our slow months are in the Spring (April and May) and in the Fall (September and October). These trends coincide with what we know to be true about revenue loss. I have a more difficult time controlling the adult and student population using the building during the winter months. This results in a higher (25%) revenue loss for these months. On the other end, the children and students using the building during the summer are easier to control. This results in a lower (10%) revenue loss.

Table 1
Building Use for Open Recreation

	Adults	Students (Grades 7–12)	Children (Grade 6 & Under)	Total
January	621	583	412	1616
February	645	571	407	1623
March	597	545	393	1535
April	428	372	279	1070
May	210	330	239	779
June	365	701	587	1653
July	276	823	650	1749
August	327	859	718	1904
September	189	268	225	682
October	226	314	275	815
November	398	292	412	1102
December	589	494	384	1467

PROBLEM

The problem of revenue loss really involves two issues. The loss of revenue leads directly to a secondary issue, which is loss of control. When I cannot control the people entering the building, we lose revenue. When these people assume they can get in free, they also assume I cannot control their actions thereafter.

As a supervisor I have many duties. During open rec. I am expected to be at the office window collecting fees. This is all well and fine *if* I could stay there the entire time! Unfortunately, I must occasionally check activities in the weight room, the fieldhouse, the pool, and the locker rooms. At these times I am out of the office and cannot control people from just walking in. Even answering the phone causes problems. I must cross the office to the desk, and then I lose direct eye contact to the front entrance.

I really have no good explanation for why I have more problems with the adult-student users during the winter months as compared to the student-children users in the summer. All I know is that when these winter "bucket shooters" start pouring in for open rec., control goes right out the window. The only answer is a barrier to contain them in the lobby area until they have paid.

SOLUTION

The solution is a barrier that extends from the entrance door into the lobby, to the office wall. This is a length (open space) of about 14 feet. I suggest a chain as a temporary solution. Attached at the entrance door frame, it should extend $5\frac{1}{2}$ feet to a stationary post (nonpermanent support), feed through an opening at the top of this post, and continue on another $5\frac{1}{2}$ feet to another post. The remaining 3 feet to the office wall will be the entrance area. This will be chained off as well, and passage will be allowed only after paying the open rec. fee. A sign that reads "DO NOT ENTER" should be attached to the chain at the entrance area by the office. When I am out of the office, people may think twice and remain in the lobby until I return.

The cost in hardware for this barrier will be minimal, and I suggest it only as a temporary measure. I would like to establish the effectiveness of a simple barrier before considering a more permanent structure. There will always be some who ignore the barrier. There is never a perfect solution.

▶ You Analyze

6. Analyze Examples 16.1 and 16.2. Follow the instructions for Exercise 8. Alternate: If your instructor requires, rewrite and redesign one of the examples.

▶ Group

7. In groups of two to four, discuss one of the proposals given in this chapter. What do you like? dislike? Would you agree to implement the solution? Report your results to the class.

8. In groups of three or four, analyze Example 16.3. Prepare a memo to your class that pinpoints its weaknesses and strengths. Focus on depth of detail, appropriateness for audience, and unnecessarily included items.

9. In groups of three or four, write a proposal using the details given for a nonprofit organization's need for a computer system (pp. 405–406).

Writing Assignments 写作任务

For each of the following assignments, first perform the activities required by the worksheet (pp. 415–417).

1. Write a proposal in which you suggest a solution to a problem. Topics for the assignment could include a problem that you have worked on (and perhaps solved) at a job or a problem that has arisen on campus, perhaps involving a

student organization, or at your workplace. Explain the problem and the solution. Show how the solution meets established criteria or how it eliminates the causes of the problem. Explain cost and implementation. If necessary, describe the personnel who will carry out the proposal. Explain why you rejected other solutions. Use at least two visual aids in your text. Your instructor will assign either an informal or a formal format. Fill out the worksheet from this chapter, and perform the exercises that your instructor requires.

Your instructor may make this a group assignment. If so, follow the instructions for developing a writing team (Chapter 2), and then analyze your situation and assign duties and deadlines.

2. In groups of three or four, write a simple request for a proposal (RFP). Ask for a common item that other people in your class could write about. (If you've all taken a class in computerized statistics, for example, ask for a statistics software program.) Try to find a real need in your current situation. Interview affected people (such as the statistics instructor) to find out what they need. Then trade your RFP with that of another group. Your group will write a proposal for the RFP you receive. Your instructor will help you with the day-to-day scheduling of this assignment.

3. Write a learning report for the writing assignment you just completed. See Chapter 5, Writing Assignment 7, page 133, for details of the assignment.

Web Exercise 网络练习

Write a proposal suggesting that you create a website for a campus club or a company division (including a "special interest" site, such as for the company yoga club). Explain how you will do it, why you are credible, the cost, the benefits to the company, and the schedule for production.

Work Cited 引用的作品

Bacon, Terry. "Selling the Sizzle, Not the Steak: Writing Customer-Oriented Proposals." *Proceedings of the First National Conference on Effective Communication Skills for Technical Professionals.* Greenville, SC: Continuing Engineering Education, Clemson University, November 15–16, 1988.

Chapter 17 User Manuals
使用说明书

Chapter Contents
Chapter 17 In a Nutshell
Planning the Manual
Writing the Manual

Chapter 17
In a Nutshell 概 要

A manual should be written and designed so that readers are comfortable enough with the machine or object to confidently interact with it. Effective manuals teach readers that machines are objects that require humans to use and control them. Your readers can achieve this position as you help them relate to the machine.

Supply context. Help them see the machine from the designer's point of view. What does this machine or this part do, and why, and what kinds of concerns does that function imply? Once readers get the big picture, they will usually try to use the item for its intended purpose.

Explain what the parts do. List all the visible parts, and explain what they cause, how to stop or undo what they cause, what other parts work in sequence with them.

Explain how to perform the sequences. Think of readers as users or doers. What actions will they perform? Think of common ones like turning the machine on and off. Spend time working on the machine yourself so you can clearly explain how to work it.

Use visual logic. One major section should discuss each of the three areas mentioned above. Divide each section into as many subsections as needed. Use heads and white space so readers can easily find sections and subsections. Use clear text and visual aids so readers figure out how to do the actions confidently.

Develop credibility. Give brief introductions that tell the end goal of a series of steps; give warnings before you explain the step; state the results of actions or give clear visual aids so that readers can decide if they are progressing logically through the steps.

Companies sell not only their products but also knowledge of how to use those products properly. This knowledge is contained in manuals. Both the manufacturer and the buyer want a manual that will allow users safely and successfully to assemble, operate, maintain, and repair the product.

Very complex mechanisms have separate multivolume manuals for different procedures such as installation and operation. The most common kind of manual, however, is the user's manual, which accompanies almost every product.

User's manuals have two basic sections: descriptions of the functions of the parts and sets of instructions for performing the machine's various processes. In addition, the manual gives information on theory of operation, warranty, specifications, parts lists, and locations of dealers to contact for advice on parts. This chapter explains how to plan and write an operator's manual.

Planning the Manual   设计使用说明书

Your goal is for the manual to help readers make your product work. To plan effectively, determine your purpose, consider the audience, schedule the review process, discover sequences, analyze the steps, analyze the parts, select visual aids, and format the pages.

Determine Your Purpose   确定你的目的

The purpose of a manual is to enable its readers to perform certain actions. But manuals cannot include every detail about any system or machine. Decide which topics your readers will need, or can deal with. For example, you would choose to explain simple send and receive commands for e-mail beginners, but not complicated directory searching.

Decide the level of detail. Will you provide a sketchy outline, or will you "hand-hold," giving lots of background and explanation? To see the results of a decision to "hand-hold," follow the "Background Sound" instructions in Example 11.2, pages 266–267. Making these key decisions will focus your sense of purpose, allowing you to make the other planning decisions detailed in this chapter.

Consider the Audience   考虑读者

Who is your audience? Create an audience profile. Characterize your readers and their situation so that you can include text, visuals, and page design that give them the easiest access to the product. First, determine how much they know about general terms and concepts. Readers who are learning their first word processing program know nothing about "save," "cut," "paste," "open," "close," and "print." Readers learning their fifth program, however, already understand these basic word processing concepts. Early in the planning process, make a list of all the words the readers must understand.

Second, consider your goal for your readers. What should they be able to do as a result of reading the manual? A common answer, of course, is to be able to operate the product, but what are those key abilities they *must* have to do so? Those abilities will help you decide what sections to include and how to write them.

Third, consider how your readers will read the manual. Both beginning and expert audiences usually are "active learners." They do not want to read; instead, they want to accomplish something relevant quickly (Redish). When they do read, they do not read the manual like a story, first page to last. Instead, they go directly to the section they need. To accommodate these active learners who differ widely in knowledge and experience, use format devices—such as heads and tables of contents—that make information accessible and easy to find. This type of thinking will help you with the layout decisions you must make later and will help you decide what information to include in the text.

Fourth, consider where the audience will use the manual. This knowledge will help you with page design. For instance, manuals used in poor lighting might need big pages and typefaces, whereas manuals used in constricted spaces or enclosed in small packages need small pages and typefaces.

Fifth, consider your audience's emotional state. For various reasons, many, if not most, users do not like, or even trust, manuals (Cooper). Further, users are often fearful, hassled, or both. Your goal is to both allay their fears and develop their confidence. The presentation of your manual—its sequence and format—and of your identity as a trustworthy guide will develop a positive relationship.

Determine a Schedule   确定一个进度表

Early in your planning process, set up a schedule of the entire project. Typically, a manual project includes not just you, the writer, but also other people who will review it for various types of accuracy—technical, legal, and design. In industrial situations, this person might be the engineer who designed the machine. If you write for a client, it will be the client or some group designated by the client.

Think of each draft as a cycle. You write, and then someone reviews, and as a result of their review you rewrite or redesign. At the outset of the project, set dates for each of these reviews and decide who will be part of the review team. In addition, agree with your reviewers on when you expect them to return the draft and on what types of comments they are to make. You can handle the actual schedule in several ways, perhaps write in the actions you will perform during various weeks on a calendar. Or you could make a Gantt chart.

Suppose your tasks are to interview an engineer, create a design, write a draft, have a reader's review, write a second draft, have a second review, and print the manual. Suppose also that your schedule allows you 8 weeks. Your Gantt chart might look like Figure 17.1 (p. 432).

Figure 17.1

Gantt Chart

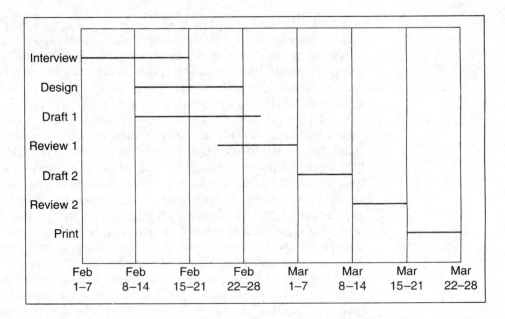

Discover Sequences 发现顺序

Discovering all the sequences means that you learn what the product does and what people do as they use it (Cohen and Cunningham). To learn what the product does, learn the product so thoroughly that you are expert enough to talk to an engineer about it. Because this process takes a good deal of time, you need to plan the steps you will take to gain all this knowledge. Schedule times to use the product. Talk to knowledgeable people—either users or designers, or both. Your goal is to learn all the procedures the product can perform, all the ways it performs them, and all the steps users take as they interact with the product.

For example, the writer of a manual for a piston filler, a machine that inserts liquids into bottles, must grasp how the machine causes the bottle to reach the filling point and how the machine injects the liquid into the bottle. Gaining this knowledge requires observing the machine in action, interviewing engineers, and assembling and disassembling sections.

But the writer must also know what people do to make the machine work. The most practical way to gain this knowledge is to practice with the product. These acts become the basis for the sections in the procedures section. As you practice, make flow charts and decision trees. In your flow charts, list each action and show how it fits into a sequence with other actions (see Figure 17.2).

The sequences your manual must teach the user typically include

- How to assemble it.
- How to start it.
- How to stop it.
- How to load it.

Figure 17.2

Flow Chart

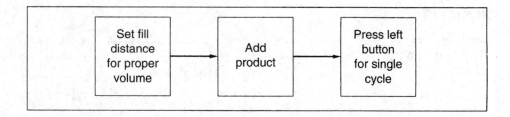

- How it produces its end product.
- How each part contributes to producing the end product.
- How to adjust parts for effective performance.
- How to change it to perform slightly different tasks.

Analyze the Steps 分析步骤

To analyze the steps in each sequence means to name each individual action that a user performs. This analysis is exactly the same as that for writing a set of instructions (review Chapter 11). In brief, determine both the end goal and the starting point of the sequence, and then provide all the intermediary steps to guide the users from start to finish. Try constructing a decision tree. Make a flow chart for the entire sequence, and then convert the chart into a decision tree.

For an example of such a conversion, compare Figures 17.2 and 17.3. In these steps, taken from a piston filler manual, the writer wants to explain how to insert a specified amount of liquid into a bottle. Figure 17.2 shows the flow chart; Figure 17.3 (p. 434) shows a decision tree based on the flow chart.

Here is the text developed from the two figures:

1. Set the fill distance for the proper volume.
   a. Check specifications for bottle volumes (p. 10).
   b. To determine this distance, find out the diameter of your piston.
   c. Go to the volume chart on p. 11.
   d. Find the piston diameter in the left column.
   e. Read across to the volume you need.
   f. Read up to determine the length you need.
   g. Adjust the distance from *A* to *B* (Figure 6 [not shown]) to the length you need.
2. Add the product to the hopper. If you are unsure of the product type, see specifications (p. 11).
3. Press the left button (*A* on Figure 6 [not shown]) for single cycle.

Analyze the Parts 分析组成部分

To analyze the parts, list each important part and explain what it does. Then convert these notes into a sentence. If you look at a few common user manuals, say, for a DVD player, you will always find this section in the front of the manual. A helpful method is to make a three-part row for each part. Name the

Figure 17.3

Decision Tree Based on Flow Chart

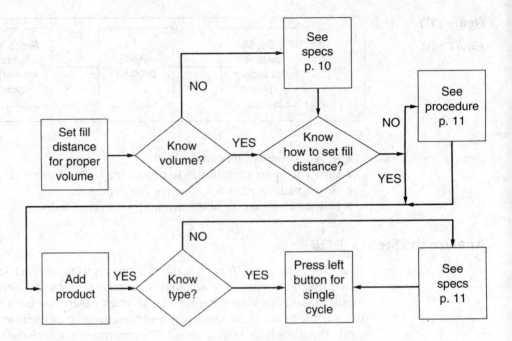

part, write the appropriate verb, and write the effect of the verb. Then turn that list into a comprehensible sentence. Here is the list for a stop button:

Name of Part	Verb	Effect
stop button	stops/ends	all functions stop

Here is the sentence for the button:

> The red emergency stop button immediately stops all functions of the machine.

Select Visual Aids 选择视图

Visual aids—photographs, drawings, flow charts, and troubleshooting charts—all help the reader learn about the product. In recent years, with the advent of desktop publishing and many graphics software and hardware programs, the use of visual aids has proliferated. Including many visuals is now the norm. Many manuals have at least one visual aid per page; many provide one per step.

Your goal is to create a text-visual interaction that conveys knowledge both visually and textually. Consider this aspect of your planning carefully. If you can use a visual aid to eliminate text, do so. Notice one key use of visual aids in manuals. Visuals give permission. Although many visual aids are logically unnecessary because the text and the product supply all the knowledge, they are still useful. Consider, for instance, Figure 5.3 on page 442 of the video camera manual or the phone visuals on pages 448–451 of the telephone manual.

Planning the Manual

Neither of these is strictly needed because the user could read the text and look at the machine and see what is described in the text. But the visual reassures the readers that they are "in the right place." Use visuals liberally in this manner. Your readers will appreciate it.

You must decide whether each step needs a visual aid. Most manual writers now repeat visual aids. As a result, the reader does not have to flip back and forth through pages. To plan the visual image needed to illustrate a step, decide which image to include and from which angle users will view it. If they will see the part from the front, present a picture of it from the front. Use a storyboard (Riney), such as the one shown in Figure 17.4, to plan the visual aid. Storyboards are discussed in Chapter 18.

Figure 17.4

Storyboard

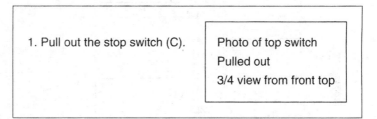

Format the Pages 设置页面

The pages of a manual must be designed to be easy to read. Create a style sheet with a visual logic (see Chapters 6 and 7) that associates a particular look or space with a particular kind of information (all figure captions italic, all page numbers in the upper outside corner, and all notes in a different typeface). You must also design a page that moves readers from left to right and top to bottom. (Review Chapter 6 for format decisions.) This process is more complex than you might think, so carefully consider your options. You might review several consumer manuals that accompany software products or common home appliances.

To produce effectively laid out pages, use a grid and a template. A *grid* is a group of imaginary lines that divide a page into rectangles (see Figure 17.5, p. 436). Designers use a grid to ensure that similar elements appear on pages in the same relative position and proportion. One common grid divides the page into two unequal columns. Writers place text in the left column and visual aids in the right column, as shown on page 436.

A *template* is an arrangement of all the elements that will appear on each page, including page numbers, headers, footers, rules, blocks of text, headings, and visual aids. Figure 17.6 (p. 437) is a template of a page. The arrows indicate all the spots at which the author made a deliberate format decision. Create a tentative template before you have gone very far with your writing because your visual logic is part of your overall strategy (see p. 437) and will influence your word choice dramatically.

Figure 17.5

Page Grids

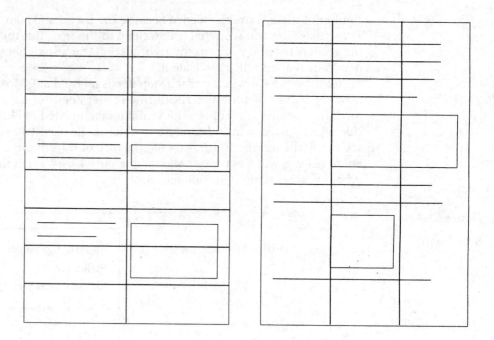

The following notes list all the format decisions that the author made for Figure 17.6:

1. Type, font, size, position of header text
2. Position, width, length of header rule
3. Size, type, font, position, and grammatical form (*-ing* word) of level 1 heads
4. Size, type, font, and position of instructional text; space between head and next line of text (leading)
5. Size, type, font, and position of numeral for instructional step
6. Punctuation following the numeral
7. Position of second line of text
8. Space between individual instructions
9. Punctuation and wording of reference to figure
10. Size, type, font, position of notes or warnings
11. Space between text and visual aid
12. Width (in points) and position of frame for visual aid
13. Size, type, font, and position of figure number and brief explanatory text
14. Position, width, length of footer rule
15. Type, font, size, position of footer text
16. Type, font, size, position of page number

Figure 17.6

Page Template with Decision Points

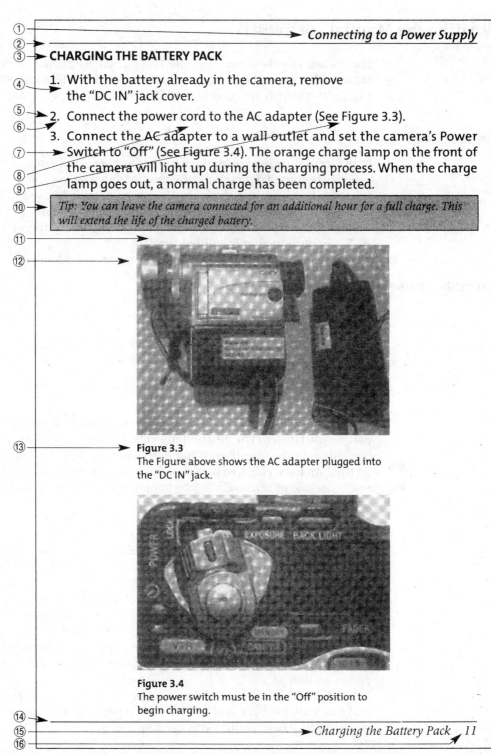

Writing the Manual 撰写说明书

The student sample shown in Figure 17.7 is taken from a user's manual for a video camera. This manual uses a one-column page; instructions are aligned on the left margin and visuals are centered. All the visual aids are clear digital photographs.

Introduction 介 绍

In the introduction explain the manual's purpose and whatever else the reader needs to become familiar with the product: how to use the manual, the appropriate background, and the level of training needed to use the mechanism.

The introduction tells the purpose of the machine, states the purpose and divisions of the manual, and explains why a user needs the machine. In Figure 17.7, the introduction is entitled "Preface."

Arrange the Sections 安排内容

A manual has two major sections:

- Description of the parts (see Figure 17.7, "Identifying Parts of the Camera")
- Instructions for all the sequences (see Figure 17.7, "Recording Video")

The Parts Section

The parts and functions section provides a drawing of the machine with each part clearly labeled. The description explains the function of each item. This section answers the question: What does this part do? or What happens when I do this? An easy, effective way to organize the parts description is to key the text to a visual aid of the product. Most appliance manuals have such a section.

The Sequences Section

The sequences section enables users to master the product. Arrange this section by operations, not parts. Present a section for each task. Usually the best order is chronological, the order in which readers will encounter the procedures. Tell first how to assemble, then how to check out, then how to start, to perform various operations, and to maintain. However, be aware that readers seldom read manuals from beginning to end, so you must enable them to find the information they need. Make the information easy to locate and use by cross-referencing to earlier sections. Never assume that readers will have read an earlier section.

In addition, as mentioned earlier, repeat key instructions or visuals. Do not make readers flip back and forth between pages. Rather, place the appropriate information where readers will use it (Rubens).

Figure 17.7

Excerpts from an Operator's Manual for a Digital Mini Video Camera

Table of Contents

TABLE OF CONTENTS

Preface	ii
Tips for Camera Use	v
Warnings	vi
Chapter 1: Identifying Parts of the Camera	**1**
Chapter 2: Identifying the Camera's Accessories	**6**
Chapter 3: Connecting to a Power Source	**9**
Using the Power Cord	10
Using the Battery Pack	10
Charging the Battery Pack	11
Chapter 4: Loading the Video Tape	**12**
Opening the Cassette Housing	13
Inserting the Video Cassette	14
Chapter 5: Recording Video	**15**
Preparing the Camera	16
Shooting Footage	17
Chapter 6: Tips on Shooting Video	**18**
Using the Zoom Feature	19
Using the LCD Screen Outdoors	19
Using and Adjusting the Viewfinder	20
Shooting Backlit Objects	20
Shooting in the Dark	21
Using the Manual Focus	21
Chapter 7: Recording Video	**22**
Using the Camera for Playback	23
Connecting the Camera to Your TV or VCR	24
Chapter 8: Dubbing to a VHS Tape	**25**
Preparing the Equipment	26
Clearing the Display Screen	26
Connecting to Your VCR	27
Recording the Tape	28
Index	**29**
A–I	30
L–S	31
S–Z	32

iii

(continued)

Figure 17.7
(continued)

Identifying Parts of the Camera

IDENTIFYING PARTS OF THE CAMERA

LCD Screen   Projects camera image for recording or camcorder image for review. Swivels to any position.

LCD Open Button   Opens LCD screen when pushed

Lens Cap   Covers lens; protects lens from scratches

Microphone   Records sound during recording

Viewfinder   Shows image as it will be recorded

Open/Eject Button   Opens tape cover and ejects tape after being pushed

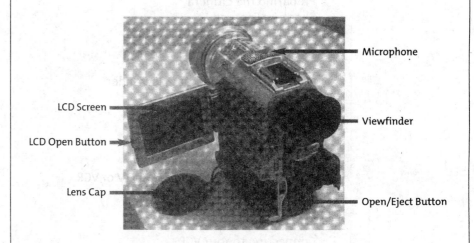

Tip: While using the LCD screen is easier to use than the viewfinder, it does consume more power from the battery pack.

2

Preparing the Camera

RECORDING VIDEO
PREPARING THE CAMERA

This camera uses DV Mini Video Cassette Tape. They can be purchased in two-packs from either the campus bookstore or local department stores.

1. Remove the lens cap.
2. Connect the power source.
3. Insert a video cassette.
4. Press the small green button on the Power Switch and slide it to the "CAMERA" position (see Figure 5.1).
5. Press "OPEN" on the LCD panel and open the LCD screen to 90 degrees (see Figures 5.2 and 5.3).

Figure 5.1
The power switch is in the "CAMERA" position. The start/stop button is also circled.

Figure 5.2
The "OPEN" button for the LCD screen is located just below the Power Switch.

(continued)

Figure 17.7
(continued)

Recording Video

SHOOTING FOOTAGE

1. Press the round Start/Stop button with the red dot in the center of the Power Switch to start recording.

> *Tip: As soon as you press the Start/Stop button, the red recording lamp on the front of the camera will light up to indicate that the camera is recording (see Figure 5.4).*

2. Press the red Start/Stop button again to stop recording (see Figure 5.1).

Figure 5.3
The image above shows the LCD screen fully opened.

Figure 5.4
The recording lamp is located next to the A/V jack cover. The lamp turns red while recording.

Assume Responsibility

All manual writers have an ethical responsibility to be aware of the dangers associated with running a machine. Keep in mind that if you leave out a step, the operator will probably not catch the error, and the result may be serious. Also, you must alert readers to potentially dangerous operations by inserting the word WARNING in capital letters and by providing a short explanation of the danger. These warnings should always appear before the actual instruction. Sometimes generic warnings, which apply to any use of the mechanism, are placed in a special section at the front of the manual.

Other Sections

Manuals traditionally have several other sections, although not all of them appear in all manuals or in the exact arrangement shown here. These sections are the front matter, the body, and the concluding section. The front matter could include such elements as

- Title page
- Table of contents
- Safety warnings
- A general description of the mechanism
- General information, based on estimated knowledge level of the audience
- Installation instructions

The body could include this element:

- A theory of operation section

The concluding section could include such elements as

- Maintenance procedures
- Troubleshooting suggestions
- A parts list
- The machine's specifications

Test the Manual 测试说明书

Usability testing helps writers find the aspects of the manual that make it easier or harder to use, especially in terms of the speed and accuracy with which users perform tasks (Craig). You need to plan, conduct, and evaluate a usability test (Brooks).

Planning a Usability Test

Planning the test is selecting what aspects of the manual you want to evaluate, what method you will use, and who will be the test subjects.

Select the aspects of the manual that you want to study. The most important question is, Does this manual allow the readers to use the object easily and confidently? Consider using some or all of these questions (Bethke et al.; Queipo):

- *Time*
  How long did it take to find information? to perform individual tasks? to perform groups of tasks?
- *Errors*
  How many and what types of errors did the subject make?
- *Assistance*
  How often did the subject need help?
  At what points did the subject need help?
  What type of help did the subject need?
- *Information*
  Was the information easy to find? easy to understand? sufficient to perform the task?
- *Format*
  Is the format consistent?
  Are the top-down areas (headings, introductions, highlighters) helpful?
  Is the arrangement on the page helpful?
- *Audience Engagement*
  Is the vocabulary understandable?
  Is the text concrete enough?
  Is the sequence "natural"? Does it seem to the learner that this is the "route to follow" to do this activity?

Select the method you will use to find the answers to your questions. Some questions need different methods. One method often is not sufficient to derive all the information you want to obtain. Test methods (Sullivan) include

- *Informal observation*—watching a person use the manual and recording all the places where a problem (with any of the topic areas you selected to watch for) arose.
- *User protocols*—the thoughts that the user speaks as he or she works with the manual and that an observer writes down, tapes, or video records.
- *Computer text analysis*—subjecting the text to evaluation features that a software program can perform, including word count, spelling, grammar, and readability scores (i.e., at what "grade level" is this material?)
- *Editorial review*—knowledgeable commentary from a person who is not one of the writers of the text.
- *Surveys and interviews*—a series of questions that you ask the user after he or she has worked with the manual.

Your goal is to match the test method with the kind of information you want. For instance, an editorial review would produce valuable information on consistency. User protocols or survey/interviews would help you determine if the vocabulary was at the appropriate level or if the page arrangement was helpful. Observation would tell you if the information given was sufficient to perform the task.

Select the test subjects. The test subjects are most often individuals who are probable members of the manual's target audience but who have not worked on developing the manual.

Conducting a Usability Test

Conducting the test is administering it. The key is to have a way to record all the data—as much feedback as possible as quickly as possible. You can use several methods:

- If you do an informal observation, you can use a tally sheet (Rubin) that has three columns—Observation, Expected Behavior or User Comment, and Design Implications. Fill out the observation column as you watch and the other two columns later.
- For user protocols, you can design a form like the one you use for informal observations, or you can audio or video record, although the difficulties with taping methods—setup procedure, use of the material after the session—require a clear decision on your part of whether you will really use the data you record.
- Computer and editorial analysis will tell you about the features of the text but will not tell the audience's reaction; these tests are relatively simple to set up, although telling an editor what to look for and setting a grammar checker to search for only certain kinds of problems are essential.
- For surveys and interviews, you can design a form (as outlined in Chapter 5) and administer it after the subject has finished the session. Sample questions include:

    Were you able to find information on X quickly?
    Did the comments in the left margin help you find information?
    Did you read the introductions to the sequences?
    Did the introduction to each sequence make it easier for you to grasp the point of sequence?

A typical way to record the answers is either yes/no/comments or some kind of recording scale (1 = highly agree, 5 = highly disagree).

Evaluating a Usability Test

Evaluating the test is determining how to use the results of the test (Sullivan). Your results could indicate a problem with

- The text (spelling, grammar, sufficiency of information)
- The text's design (consistency, usefulness of column arrangement or highlighting techniques)
- The "learning style" of the audience (sequence of the text, basic way in which they approach the material)

If you have determined beforehand what is an acceptable answer (e.g., this procedure should take X minutes; this word is the only one that can be used to refer to that object), you will be able to make the necessary changes. For more help on this topic, consult John Craig (see Works Cited).

Worksheet for Preparing a Manual 准备说明书的工作表

- ☐ **Consider the audience.**
  How much do readers know about the general terms and concepts?
  Where and when will they use the manual?
  What should they be able to do after reading the manual?
  List all the terms a user must comprehend. Define each term.

- ☐ **Determine a schedule.**
  On what date is the last version of the manual due? By what date must each stage be completed?
  Who will review each stage?
  How long will each review cycle take?

- ☐ **List where you can obtain the knowledge you need to write the manual.**
  a person? reading? working with the mechanism?

- ☐ **Analyze the procedures a user must follow to operate the product.**
  What must be done to install it, to turn it on, to turn it off, and to do its various tasks?
  List the sequence for presenting the processes.
  Choose an organizational pattern for the sequence—chronological or most important to least important.
  Create a flow chart for each procedure the machine follows.
  Create a decision tree for each procedure the user follows.
  Name each part and its function.
  For a complicated product, you will discover far too many parts to discuss. Group them in manageable sections. Decide which ones your audience needs to know about.

- ☐ **Choose a visual aids strategy.**
  Will you use drawings or photographs?
  Will you use a visual aid for each instruction?
  Will you use a visual aid on each page?
  Will you use callouts?

> ☐ Create a storyboard for your manual.
>
> ☐ **Design pages by preparing a style sheet of up to four levels of heads, captions for visual aids, margins, page numbers, and fonts (typefaces).**
> Select rules, headers, and footers as needed to help make information easy to find on pages.
>
> ☐ **Write step-by-step instructions.**
> Clearly label any step that could endanger the person (WARNING!) or the machine (CAUTION!).
>
> ☐ **Field-test the manual.**
> Select the features of the manual you want to field-test.
> Select a method of testing those features. Be sure to create a clear method for recording answers. Determine what you think are acceptable results for each feature (e.g., How long should it take to perform the process?).
> Select subjects to use the manual.

Examples 例 子

The excerpts shown in Example 17.1 are several sections of an operator's manual for a telephone. The entire manual is a one-page foldout, with seven sections including one in Spanish. Presented here are the table of contents, the parts and functions section (1-B, "Location of Controls"; 3, "Speed Dialer"; and 4, "One-Touch Dialer,"), two sections of operating instructions (3B and 4B), and one page of troubleshooting. These pages represent sections you will find in almost all manuals written for consumers. Example 17.2 is a usability report, written to explain the results of a usability test on a website.

Example 17.1

Excerpts From an Operator's Manual

Source: Reprinted by permission of Panasonic.

Examples

1 Getting Started

1-B Location of Controls

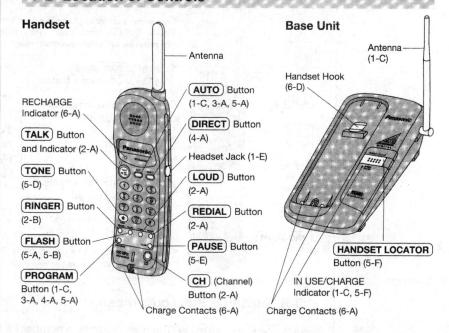

(continued)

Example 17.1
(continued)

3 Speed Dialer
Section 3

3-A Storing Phone Numbers in Memory

You can store up to 10 phone numbers in the handset. The dialing buttons ((0) to (9)) function as memory stations. **The TALK indicator light must be off before programming.**

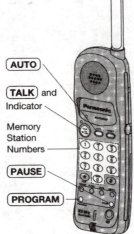

1 Press (PROGRAM).
• The TALK indicator flashes.

2 Enter a phone number up to 22 digits.

3 Press (AUTO).

4 Press a memory station number ((0) to (9)).
• A beep sounds.
• To store other numbers, repeat steps 1 through 4.

If you misdial
Press (PROGRAM) to end storing. ➡ Start again from step 1.

To erase a stored number
Press (PROGRAM) ➡ (AUTO) ➡ the memory station number ((0) to (9)) for the phone number to be erased.
• A beep sounds.

• If a pause is required for dialing, press (PAUSE) where needed. Pressing (PAUSE) counts as one digit (5-E).

3-B Dialing a Stored Number

Press (TALK) ➡ (AUTO) ➡ The memory station number ((0) to (9)).
• If your line has rotary or pulse service, any access numbers stored after pressing (TONE) will not be dialed.

Examples

4 One-Touch Dialer

4-A Storing a Phone Number in the DIRECT Button

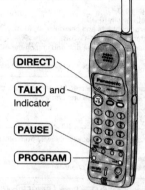

A phone number stored in the (DIRECT) button can be dialed with a one-touch operation. **The TALK indicator light must be off before programming.**

1. Press (PROGRAM).
   - The TALK indicator flashes.

2. Enter a phone number up to 22 digits.
   - If you misdial, press (PROGRAM), and start again from step 1.

3. Press (DIRECT).
   - A beep sounds.

- If a pause is required for dialing, press (PAUSE) where needed. Pressing (PAUSE) counts as one digit (5-E).

4-B Dialing the Stored Number in the DIRECT Button

Press (TALK) ➡ (DIRECT).
- If your line has rotary or pulse service, any access numbers stored after pressing (TONE) will not be dialed.

To erase a stored number: press (PROGRAM) ➡ (DIRECT).

(continued)

Example 17.1
(continued)

Things You Should Know — Section 6

6-E Before Requesting Help

Problem	Remedy
The unit does not work.	• Check the settings (1-C). • Charge the battery fully (6-A). • Clean the charge contacts and charge again (6-A). • Install the battery properly (1-C, 6-B). • Place the handset on the base unit and unplug the AC adaptor to reset. Plug in and try again. • Re-insert the battery and place the handset on the base unit. Try again.
An alarm tone sounds.	• You are too far from the base unit. Move closer and try again. • Place the handset on the base unit and try again. • Plug in the AC adaptor. • Raise the base unit antenna.
Static, sound cuts in/out, fades. Interference from other electrical units.	• Locate the handset and the base unit away from other electrical applicances (6-C). • Move closer to the base unit. • Raise the base unit antenna. • Press (CH) to select a clearer channel.
The unit does not ring.	• To ringer volume is set to OFF. Press (RINGER) while the TALK indicator light is off (2-B).
While storing a number, the unit starts to ring.	• To answer the call, press (TALK). The program will be cancelled. Store the number again.
You cannot store a phone number in memory.	• You cannot store a number while the unit is in the talk mode. • Do not pause for over 60 seconds while storing. • Move closer to the base unit.
Previously programmed information is erased.	• If a power failure occurs, programmed information may be erased. Reprogram if necessary.
You cannot redial by pressing (REDIAL).	• If the last number dialed was more than 32 digits long, the number will not be redialed.
(HANDSET LOCATOR) does not function.	• The handset is too far from the base unit or is engaged in an outside call.
The RECHARGE indicator flashes or the unit beeps intermittently.	• Charge the battery fully (6-A).
You charged the battery fully, but the RECHARGE indicator flashes.	• Clean the charge contacts and charge again (6-A). • Install a new battery (6-B).
The IN USE/CHARGE indicator light does not go out while charging	• This is normal.
If you cannot solve your problem	• Call our customer call center at 1-800-211-PANA (7262).

Example 17.2

Report on NALC Branch 728 Website Usability

1. EXECUTIVE SUMMARY

This report contains the results of a usability test for NALC Branch 728 website created by Hilary Peterson. I performed the test with three participants, all of whom indicated that they have at least a moderate familiarity with the Internet and with website use in general. All the test subjects are members of the target audience for the site, but had not seen the website before the test. I gave the test subjects a time limit of 15 minutes to complete three specific tasks; during that time, I observed the subjects and made careful notes of their actions and comments for later analysis. After the test, each subject completed a survey to express his overall response to the experience.

Analysis of the data I collected shows that the website is very effective overall. It is easy to navigate, and the page layout allows for easy scanning of the pages for important information. There is a need, however, to rethink the name of one of the lines, Get Smart!, and how it relates to the Letter Carrier Perfect Page to which it connects.

I make recommendations for the problem area.

2. INTRODUCTION

The goal of this report is to document the findings of a usability test of NALC Branch 728's website, created by Hilary Peterson. As the author of the report, I also conducted the usability test. The website is available at the following URL: http://fp1.centurytel.net/nalcbranch728. To serve and inform the members of Branch 728 and of other NALC branches in the area, there is a need for a useful, well-written website that includes an on-line version of the Branch's newsletter as well as a wealth of information for its users.

This report will interest the Web master, since it will indicate any improvements that should be made to the website. It will also interest my client, the editor of *The Sawdust Cities Satchel* and vice president of Union Branch 728. He will use this report to determine whether or not to request funding for the website.

These pages include a brief description of my methodology along with summaries of my test results, observations, and results of the post-test survey. I express my conclusions based on these data as well as my recommendations for improvement where I found problem areas during the test.

3. METHODOLOGY

3.1 Participant Selection

The primary audience for NALC Branch 728's website is members of Branch 728 who have at least a moderate familiarity with the Internet and with

(continued)

Example 17.2
(continued)

website use in general. The website was designed with this type of user in mind, so the pages are meant to be clean, simple, and easy to navigate.

My client chose three members of Branch 728 to participate in the usability test. The subjects possess varying levels of computer skills, but all of the subjects indicated that they were at least fairly familiar with the Internet. None of the subjects had ever seen or used the Branch 728 website before.

3.2 Task Selection

I gave each of the test subjects three test scenarios and three tasks to complete; these appear in Appendix A.

With question 1 of Task One, I aimed to test the readability of the homepage, where the answer to question 1 is found.

With question 2 of Task One, my goal was to test the usefulness of the bookmarking feature on the Constitution and By-Laws page.

Task Two tested the "scannability" of a very long page of text, the Get Smart! page. I also wanted to find out whether or not I could reasonably assume that most of my audience members were aware that "Get Smart!" is the new name for the Letter Carrier Perfect handbook.

Task Three tests the function and visibility of the Outside Links page.

3.3 Test Procedure

I scheduled 15 minutes for each participant to complete the assigned tasks. The subjects performed the test individually. Before the test, I gave an introduction to the test, emphasized the subject's role, and told each participant what to expect during the test. This introduction appears in Appendix A.

Next, I gave each subject scenarios and instructions for completing the tasks, encouraging them to talk aloud while they were performing the test. Hearing the participants say why they chose to click on a particular link helped to show the effectiveness of the links.

As the test's administrator, I did not interact with the test subjects or give hints when they were lost. Instead, I took careful notes on the subjects' behavior, demeanor, comments, and activities on screen.

3.4 Post-Test Survey

To obtain each participant's overall feelings about his experience, I administered a short post-test survey, shown in Appendix B.

4. RESULTS

4.1 Observations

All three of the test subjects completed the assigned tasks within the time limit of 15 minutes. The subjects completed the tasks in four minutes, six minutes, and nine minutes. The fastest test participant completed the tasks in the fewest possible number of steps. The slowest participant completed the tasks within the 15 minute time limit, but he did not use the most efficient path through the site.

All three of the subjects stayed on the homepage at the beginning of the test. The answer to the first question in Task One was there, and two of the three subjects found it within one minute. One subject did not find the answer right away, and he browsed unsuccessfully through a different page before returning to the homepage and finding the answer.

Question 2 of Task One was answered successfully by all three subjects within an appropriate amount of time. The subjects started by immediately clicking on the link that would take them to the correct page. However, two of the three subjects skipped over the bookmarking feature at the top of the Constitution and By-Laws page, which would have been the quickest way to complete the task. Of the two that did not immediately use the bookmarks, one scanned the long page of text and found the answer to the question. The other participant started to scan the page and then went back to the top and successfully used the bookmark to more quickly find the desired information.

4.2 Survey Results

The results of the post-test survey indicate that, overall, the website was easy to navigate, well designed, and easy to scan for important information. All of the test subjects indicated that they felt comfortable when using the site. All three test participants commented on the easy-to-use navigation bars. Two of the participants mentioned that "Get Smart!" and "Letter Carrier Perfect" are not yet synonymous for all of the people who will use this site, and that the links to the Get Smart! page should also indicate a connection to Letter Carrier Perfect. The post-test survey appears in Appendix B.

5. CONCLUSIONS

5.1 Positive Aspects

Two of the three test subjects found the answer to question 1 of Task One within a minute. They did this by scanning the homepage for the necessary information. I suspect that the subject who did not find the answer immediately felt pressured during the test and would have been more successful in a different situation. Question 2 of Task One went well for all of the test subjects. On a scale of 1–5 (1 = difficult; 5 = easy), two participants rated Task One a 5.

Task Three also went well for all of the participants. On a scale of 1–5 (1 = difficult; 5 = easy), completing Task Three was a 5 for all participants.

(continued)

Example 17.2
(continued)

On the post-test survey, organization of the site, moving from page to page, ease of reading and scanning text, and page layout were rated at very easy or very effective by all subjects. All three participants indicated that they felt comfortable using the site and that it is a site that they would use often.

5.2 PROBLEM AREAS

The main problem the participants had during the test was completing Task Two. The task instructions ask the participant to find the on-line version of "Letter Carrier Perfect," the name of which has recently been changed to "Get Smart!" I discovered during the test that this name change is not yet known to all of the website's audience members, and two of the subjects were not at all confident that clicking on the Get Smart! link would bring them to an on-line version of Letter Carrier Perfect.

6. RECOMMENDATIONS

Determine whether to continue using a link named "Get Smart!" to connect to a page that is an on-line version of "Letter Carrier Perfect."

Keeping the "Get Smart!" link is probably a good idea, because it will help to reinforce the name change of this handbook from "Letter Carrier Perfect" to "Get Smart!"

7. APPENDIX A

7.1 NALC Branch 728 Website Usability Test Introduction and Instructions

Thank you for participating in this project. Your input will help us to create a more useful website for Branch 728's members. You will be able to use this site in the near future to read *Satchel* articles and to take note of upcoming Branch meetings and activities, among other things.

The purpose of this test is to evaluate the usefulness and effectiveness of Branch 728's website.

To accomplish this, we will ask you to perform specific tasks. During the test, we will not make suggestions or be able to help in any way. Just use the site as you normally would to complete the tasks, and we will take notes for later analysis.

Please talk through your motions during the test. For example, let us know why you are choosing to click on a particular link. Then we'll have you fill out a short survey about your experience.

Please remember that the purpose of this test is to evaluate the usability of our website. We are not testing your personal abilities.

Examples

Task Scenarios and Instructions

Task One As a member of NALC Branch 728, you are preparing for the next union meeting. You have decided to use the Branch's new website to gather some information. These are the questions you need to answer:

1. When is the next union meeting?
2. According to the Branch By-Laws, how many members constitute a quorum?

Task Two As a Letter Carrier, you would like to find out more about your rights and responsibilities concerning safety, service, and mail security. The on-line version of Letter Carrier Perfect is arranged into three distinct sections. What are the three sections?

Task Three You have taken some time to view the new Branch 728 website, but you need some more information from the Wisconsin State AFL-CIO. Use the Branch 728 website to connect to the Wisconsin State AFL-CIO website.

8. APPENDIX B

8.1 Post-Test Survey (highlighted numbers reflect the most common participant response)

1. What would have helped you complete these tasks more successfully?

2. What parts of the website did you find most helpful?

Please circle the number that best corresponds to your feelings about each question.

1. Completing Task One (next union meeting/quorum questions) was
   difficult 1 2 3 4 5 **easy**
2. Completing Task Two (Get Smart!/Letter Carrier Perfect question) was
   difficult 1 2 3 4 5 **easy**
3. Completing Task Three (connecting to WI State AFL-CIO site) was
   difficult 1 2 3 4 5 **easy**

(continued)

Example 17.2
(continued)

> 4. Organization of the site was
>   **not effective** 1 2 3 4 5 **very effective**
> 5. Moving from page to page was
>   **confusing** 1 2 3 4 5 **easy**
> 6. The text on the website was generally
>   **difficult to read** 1 2 3 4 5 **easy to read**
> 7. Scanning the pages for important information was
>   **confusing** 1 2 3 4 5 **easy**
> 8. When I was looking for the pages I needed, I
>   **felt lost** 1 2 3 4 5 **felt I knew where I was**
> 9. While working on the tasks, I
>   **felt confused** 1 2 3 4 5 **felt comfortable**
> 10. I thought the layout of most of the pages was
>   **difficult to understand** 1 2 3 4 5 **easy to understand**
> 11. NALC Branch 728's webpage seems like a site that I would
>   **never use** 1 2 3 4 5 **use often**

Exercises 练 习

▸ You Analyze

1. Collect one or two professional (VCR, stereo, CD, automobile, appliance, or computer) manuals and bring to class. Analyze them for page design, visual logic, text-visual interaction, sequence of parts, and assumptions made about the audience. Discuss these topics in groups of two to four, and then report to the class the strategies that you find most helpful and are most likely to use in Writing Assignment 1.

▸ Group

2. In groups of two to four, analyze the page layout of one of the manuals that appears in this chapter. Write a brief description of and reaction to this layout and share your reactions with the group. Your instructor will ask some groups to report their results.

▸ You Create

3. Using any machine or software program you know well, write a parts description.
4. Using any machine or software program you know well, create a flow chart for the sequences you want a reader to learn. Convert that flow chart into step-by-step instructions.

5. Review the types of decisions included in creating a template (pp. 435–437). Then create your own design for what you wrote in Exercise 3 or 4.
6. For the manual you are creating for Writing Assignment 1 or for the section you wrote for Exercise 4, create a storyboard.
7. Write the introduction to the parts description and sequences you created in Exercises 3 and 4.
8. For the manual you are creating for Writing Assignment 1, complete the following exercises. Your instructor will schedule these steps at the appropriate time in your project.
   a. Consider how consistently it handles all details of format.
   b. Consider how precisely it explains how to perform an action. Read closely to see whether everything you need to know is really present.
   c. Conduct a field test by asking a person who knows almost nothing about the product to follow your manual. Accompany the tester, but do not answer questions unless the action is dangerous or the tester is hopelessly lost (say, in a software program). Note all the problem areas, and then make those changes. Discuss changes that would help the user.

Writing Assignments 写作任务

1. Write an operator's manual. Choose any product that you know well or one you would like to learn about. The possibilities are numerous—a bicycle, a sewing machine, part of a software program such as FrontPage® or Dreamweaver®, a computer system, any laboratory device, a welding machine. If you need to use high-quality photographs or drawings, you may need help from another student who has the necessary skills. Your manual must include at least an introduction, a table of contents, a description of the parts, and the instructions for procedures. You might also include a troubleshooting section. Give warnings when appropriate. Complete this chapter's worksheet or the appropriate exercises.
2. Write a learning report for the writing assignment you just completed. See Chapter 5, Writing Assignment 7, page 133, for details of the assignment.

Web Exercise 网络练习

Create a mini-manual to publish on a website. Use a simple machine, say, a flashlight. Include one section describing the parts and one section presenting the appropriate sequences for operating. Include several visual aids.

Works Cited 引用的作品

Bethke, F. J., W. M. Dean, P. H. Kaiser, E. Ort, and F. H. Pessin. "Improving the Usability of Programming Publications." *IBM Systems Journal* 20.3 (1981): 306–320.

Brooks, Ted. "Career Development: Filling the Usability Gap." *Technical Communication* 38.2 (April 1991): 180–184.

Cohen, Gerald, and Donald H. Cunningham. *Creating Technical Manuals: A Step-by-Step Approach to Writing User-Friendly Manuals.* New York: McGraw-Hill, 1984.

Cooper, Marilyn. "The Postmodern Space of Operator's Manuals." *Technical Communication Quarterly* 5.4 (1996): 385–410.

Craig, John S. "Approaches to Usability Testing and Design Strategies: An Annotated Bibliography." *Technical Communication* 38.2 (April 1991): 190–194.

Queipo, Larry. "Taking the Mysticism Out of Usability Test Objectives." *Technical Communication* 38.2 (April 1991): 185–189, 190–194.

Redish, Virginia. "Writing for People Who Are 'Reading to Learn to Do.'" *Creating Usable Manuals and Forms: A Document Design Symposium.* Technical Report 42. Pittsburgh, PA: Carnegie-Mellon Communications Design Center, 1988.

Riney, Larry A. *Technical Writing for Industry: An Operations Manual for the Technical Writer.* Englewood Cliffs, NJ: Prentice-Hall, 1989.

Rubens, Phillip M. "A Reader's View of Text and Graphics: Implications for Transactional Text." *Journal of Technical Writing and Communication* 16.1/2 (1986): 73–86.

Rubin, Jeff. "Conceptual Design: Cornerstone of Usability." *Technical Communication* 43.2 (May 1996): 130–138.

Sullivan, Patricia. "Beyond a Narrow Conception of Usability Testing." *IEEE Transactions of Professional Communication* 32.4 (December 1989): 256–264.

Section 3

Professional Communication
职场写作

Chapter 18　Oral Presentations　口头陈述

Chapter 19　Letters　信　函

Chapter 20　Job Application Materials　工作申请材料

Chapter 18 Oral Presentations
口头陈述

Chapter Contents
Chapter 18 In a Nutshell
Planning the Presentation
Making an Effective Presentation
Globalization and Oral Presentations

Chapter 18
In a Nutshell 概 要

Oral reports range from brief answers to questions at meetings, to hour-long speeches to large audiences. Follow these guidelines:

- Plan your presentation. Determine your audience. Determine whether your slides will carry information to explain or will function as a helpful outline. Use a simple template that does not draw attention to itself. Choose an organizational pattern, such as narrative or problem-solution, as appropriate.

- Speak in a normal voice. Help yourself speak normally by not memorizing—practice enough so you can speak from notes.

- Arrange your speech in a narrative fashion. Use topic sentences to begin sections so that you are constantly telling the audience where they are in the sequence.

- Practice with any technology (laptops, computer slide presentations) before you give the speech.

- Be presentable. Dress appropriately; if you don't know what a professional should wear in this situation, ask someone who does. Avoid irritating mannerisms (smacking lips, shaking keys in pockets, saying "um" repeatedly).

Throughout your career, you will give oral reports to explain the results of investigations, propose solutions to problems, report on the progress of projects, make changes to policy, create business plans, justify requests for such items as more employees and equipment, or persuade clients to purchase your services and merchandise. Sometimes these presentations are impromptu, but more often they are scheduled and therefore require careful planning. Since the introduction of PowerPoint presentational software, oral reports are almost always accompanied by a visual presentation. Edward Tufte says, "In corporate and government bureaucracies, the standard method for making a presentation is to talk about a list of points organized onto slides projected up on the wall" (3). Tufte calculates that trillions of slides are produced yearly (3).

This chapter explains how to plan and deliver an oral presentation.

Planning the Presentation   设计陈述

Planning includes decisions about audience, situation, organizational pattern, and presentation.

Plan for Your Audience   为读者作计划

Because of the popularity of the oral report, many listeners have been subjected to the same kind of presentation many times. Indeed, the use of PowerPoint is so common that most oral reports are simply called "PowerPoints" or "PowerPoint reports." Therefore, an audience may often anticipate that any presentation is likely to be another dreary time-waster (Miller; Tufte 23).

The key to preventing audience apathy or even a downright hostility is to focus on your audience, not on the technology of your presentation. The central goal for your presentation is, simply, that you be relevant. One speech expert says, "People will pay close attention to something they perceive as having relevance to their own lives and concerns" (Bacall). In order to remain aligned to your audience, consider differences between listeners and readers, and ask the same audience analysis questions that you ask in report writing.

Presenting to a Listening Audience

Speakers Use Personal Contact. A presentation allows you to have personal contact with listeners. You can make use of personality, voice, and gestures, as well as first-person pronouns, visuals, and feedback from listeners. If you are a person speaking to people, your audience will react positively

Listeners Are Present for the Entire Presentation. That listeners are present for the entire report may seem advantageous, but it also may make communication more difficult. Many listeners want to hear only selected parts of a report—the parts that apply directly to them. If, for instance, your listeners are the plant manager and her staff, the plant manager would probably prefer a capsule version of the report, which a short abstract would provide, and would rather leave the details for staff members to examine. The oral report gives her no choice but to listen to all of your detailed information, a situation that might put her in a negative frame of mind.

Ask Audience Analysis Questions

In speeches the audience analysis questions are the same as for reports or other documents. Ask these questions (based on Laskowski):

- Who are they?
- How many will be present?
- What is their knowledge level?
- What task will your presentation help them complete?
- What do they need?
- Why are they there?

Consider how you would give a speech on your new data analysis software to these two audiences: three experienced managers seated around a conference table, waiting to decide whether to place an order with you; and 50 sales reps seated in a lecture hall, eager to familiarize themselves with the product prior to making sales calls. Obviously, these situations would require two very different presentations. The answers to the audience analysis questions, then, will help you develop a presentation that keeps your audience attentive to your points, so that they walk away feeling that their time with you has been well spent and productive.

Plan for the Situation 视情况作计划

Presentations are made in many venues, from small rooms in which people sit around a conference table to large auditoriums packed with conference attendees. Spend time investigating the physical layout of the room. Follow these guidelines (based in part on Jacobs):

- Determine the size of the room and where you will stand in relation to the audience, the screen, and the computer controls.
- Determine the location of the electrical outlets and the electrical cords on the floor.
- Learn how sound carries in the room. Will you have to use a microphone? If so, do you know how to adjust it so that your voice carries well without ringing or buzzing?

- Determine whether you will have to bring a disk to use in a computer already present in the room, or whether you need to bring your laptop.
- If you have to bring your own laptop, determine how to hook it up to the overhead projector system located in the room.

Plan Your Organizational Pattern   设计安排模式

The organizational pattern that you choose depends on the needs of your audience and the actual content of the material. Common organizational patterns are problem-solution, goal-methods-results-discussion, narrative (see Shaw, Brown, and Bromiley), as well as the traditional approach of introduction, body and conclusion (Tracy).

The narrative approach, advocated by Shaw, Brown, and Bromiley, has three stages: set the stage, introduce the dramatic conflict, resolve the conflict. To set the stage, the speaker defines the current situation by analyzing factors that affect the situation—market forces, forces that affect change, company objectives and strengths. To introduce dramatic conflict, the speaker explains the challenges that face the company in the current situation. What are the obstacles (the bad guys) in this situation? poorly functioning technology? new competitor? market share losses? To resolve the conflict, the speaker must show how the audience can overcome the obstacles to win—This change will cause the technology to function correctly. This strategy will offset the new competitor's appeal. This strategy will induce the consumers to purchase again.

Shaw, Brown, and Bromiley (see also Tufte) feel that the story method is very effective, especially in contrast to "bullet-point" presentations. Bullet-point presentations have two problems: first, listeners tend to remember only the first and last items in a list; and second, listeners are unable to clarify the relationships of the items in a list. For instance, items in a list can have only three relationships: sequence (this point follows that point), priority (from most to least important or vice versa), and membership (all these items are the same kind of thing). Missing is the ability of the listeners to easily understand critical relationships such as cause or contrast.

The story structure "defines relationships, a sequence of events, cause and effect, and a priority among items—and those items are likely to be remembered as a complex whole" (4). As a result, the act of writing the speech will cause the speaker to think clearly about the complexity of the ideas, and so give the listeners access to the speaker's thought process. The upshot will be listeners who grasp the significance of the main point because they have been engaged by the story that expounds it.

Plan Your Presentation   设计你的陈述

To plan the presentation, determine your relationship to the slides, create a storyboard, and finally the series of slides.

Determine Your Relationship to the Slides

A presentation consists of two things—your voice and personal presence, and the information on the slides—and you need to determine their relationship. Because the slide can contain only a small amount of information, it is not the main source of information in the speech—you are. However, if you do not control the relationship, the slides can easily take over, basically drawing all the audience attention away from you and the points you have to make. To do so, use the advice of many experienced speakers—deliver quality content to the audience (Bacall; Stratten; Tufte 22). In order to deliver quality content, decide which combination of information from you and information from the slide will best convey the information to the audience.

What is the purpose of the information on the slide? Understand that it is not the slide that provides the complexity—You do. According to Tufte, people learn because information is placed into context. People need not just bits of information but also a narrative that interrelates them, explaining causal assumptions or analytical structure (6). The slide can provide the bits but you supply the context.

It is helpful to see the slide in either "the foreground" or "the background." If it is in the foreground, it provides information, either visual aid or text, that you explain. Project a visual in order to explain it. For instance, if you have a table of sales made during a quarter, you might show the table with its columns of numbers, and then point out items in the table and explain the relationships that are important to the audience. If you practice with the program, you will even be able to highlight the items that you wish to interrelate. Project text in order to emphasize. If, for instance, you want the audience to remember a certain point, you can project just that point on the screen and then discuss it.

With foreground material, then, you speak to the slide. The idea is that you will explain in some detail the implication of what the audience sees on screen, and the combination of the visual and your explanation is the point to get. For instance, Figure 18.1 illustrates the credentials of two researchers. The speaker projected the slide, then spoke for several minutes explaining in turn the various achievements of each researcher. The point of the slide is to establish the credibility of the researchers, and the speaker filled in details and context about the credentials listed.

When a slide is in the background, you do not speak to it. Instead it is present in order to summarize key points, either what is about to be covered or what has just been covered (Glenn Miller). At its best, this method helps the audience stay on track and follow and remember the points that have been made. If you have four subpoints to make about a topic, projecting them on a slide, then discussing each in turn will help the listeners follow along.

Figure 18.2 shows a slide that functioned as an outline. The speaker projected a point, addressed it, then moved on to the next point. The slide functions to keep the audience aware of their place in the presentation.

Understanding this relation to your slides will help you create a presentation that delivers content to audiences effectively.

Figure 18.1

Slide of Credentials

Reprinted by permission of Dr. Scott Zimmerman.

Figure 18.2

Slide Showing an Outline

Reprinted by permission of Dr. Scott Zimmerman.

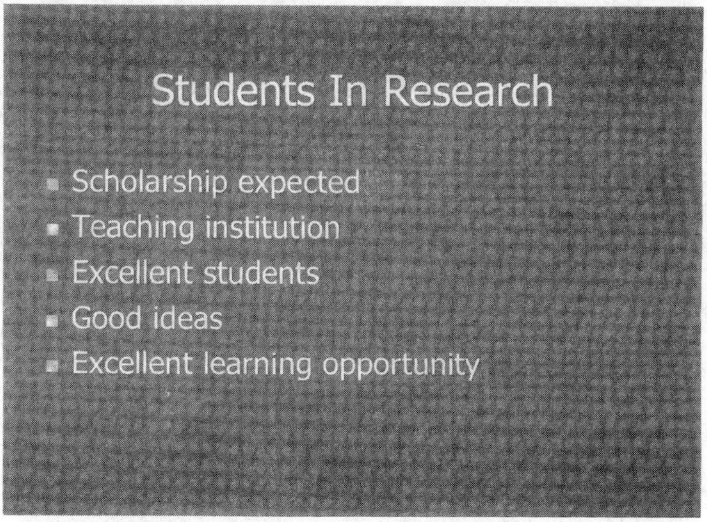

Create a Storyboard

A storyboard is a text and graphics outline of your presentation. A storyboard can be as simple as a two-column table that lists topics on the left and visuals on the right (Figure 18.3, p. 468). A storyboard can also be a three-column sequence of lines, boxes, and comments. Place the slide's text in the line; sketch the look of the slide in the box, and add explanatory material in the **comments** space (Figure 18.4, p. 469). Variations of storyboards also exist in **presentation programs**. PowerPoint, for instance, has an outline function **and a slide sorter** function that allow you to see the entire sequence of your presentation (Figure 18.5, p. 469).

Figure 18.3

Sample Text Storyboard

Topic	Visual Aid
Introduction	
Source of assignment	
Recommendation	List of recommendations
Preview	Outline of main topics
	List of main methods for each type (use of a two-column slide)
Section 1	
Method of researching	Cross-sectional view
Section 2	
Three types of laminates	
Advantages of each	List of advantages
Section 3	
Cost	Table of costs
Conclusion	
Summary	

Use storyboards as an integrated outline that shows both the sequence of the topics and the content of the slide or slides devoted to that topic (Korolenko 151–153; Lindstrom 110; "Web").

Create the Slides or Other Visual Aids

After you have the storyboard outline of your presentation, create the slides. A well-designed presentation will help convey your point pleasingly to an attentive audience. But, as Edward Tufte points out, "If your words or images are not on point, making them dance in color won't make them relevant" (22). The following guidelines (based in part on Scoville; Tessler; Welsh) will help you create pleasing slides and sequences that help to convey information rather than to distract attention from the main points. As you create slides, understand the parts of a slide, pay attention to helping your reader, and make effective use of fonts, colors, animations, sound effects, and slide transitions.

Understand the Parts of a Slide. The parts of the slide are the title, the text or graphics, the border, and the background (see Figure 18.6, p. 470).

- The title appears at the top, usually in the largest type size. Use it to explicitly identify the contents of the visual. A rule ($\frac{1}{2}$ or 1 point in size) separates the title from the text or graphic.
- The text makes the points you want to highlight. Use phrases that convey specific content rather than generic topics.
- The graphic consists of a table, chart, or drawing.
- The border is a line that provides a frame around the visual.
- The background is the color or design that appears behind the text or graphics.

Planning the Presentation

Figure 18.4

Sample Three-Column Storyboard

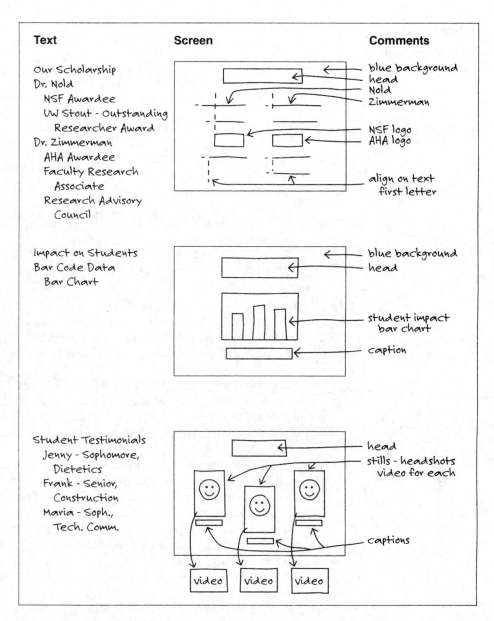

Figure 18.5

PowerPoint Outline View and Slide Sorter View

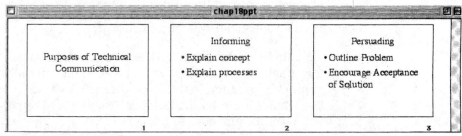

Figure 18.6

Parts of a Visual

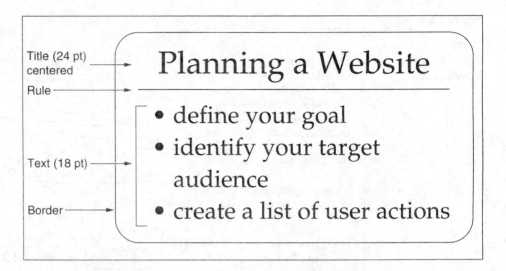

Help the Reader. The most important part of any presentation is the content, but do not try to put all of your ideas on slides. Too much text will cause viewers to read slides, deflecting attention from you. Display only text that the audience should read carefully. Follow these guidelines to design your slides:

- Use a landscape (horizontal) layout for your text rather than a portrait (vertical) layout. Landscape makes the longer lines of text easier to read, and columns easier to use.
- Title each slide so your audience will have a quick reference to the topic at hand.
- Create (or choose) a template or "master" to establish a visual logic. A template establishes rules for consistently presenting parts of the slide—the title, the text, the visual aids, the background. For instance, make all titles 24-point Arial, black, and centered at the top. Make all text 18-point Arial, black, flush left. Center all visuals with a caption in 14-point Arial below the visual. Figure 18.7 illustrates a template in action. Notice that slices a and c, which function as section introductions, use one sentence, a question, with a yellow font. However, slides b and d, the content of the section, have a title and a bulleted list, in a white font. Notice that the template used for Figure 18.8, a version of slide d, undercuts the seriousness of the content with its use of unbusiness-like fonts.

For visual aids (tables, graphs, pictures):

- Simplify the graph so that it makes only one point.
- Use graphs for dramatic effect. A line graph that plunges sharply at one point calls attention to the drop. Your job is to interpret it.
- Use tables for presenting numbers. Be prepared to point out the numbers you want the audience to notice.

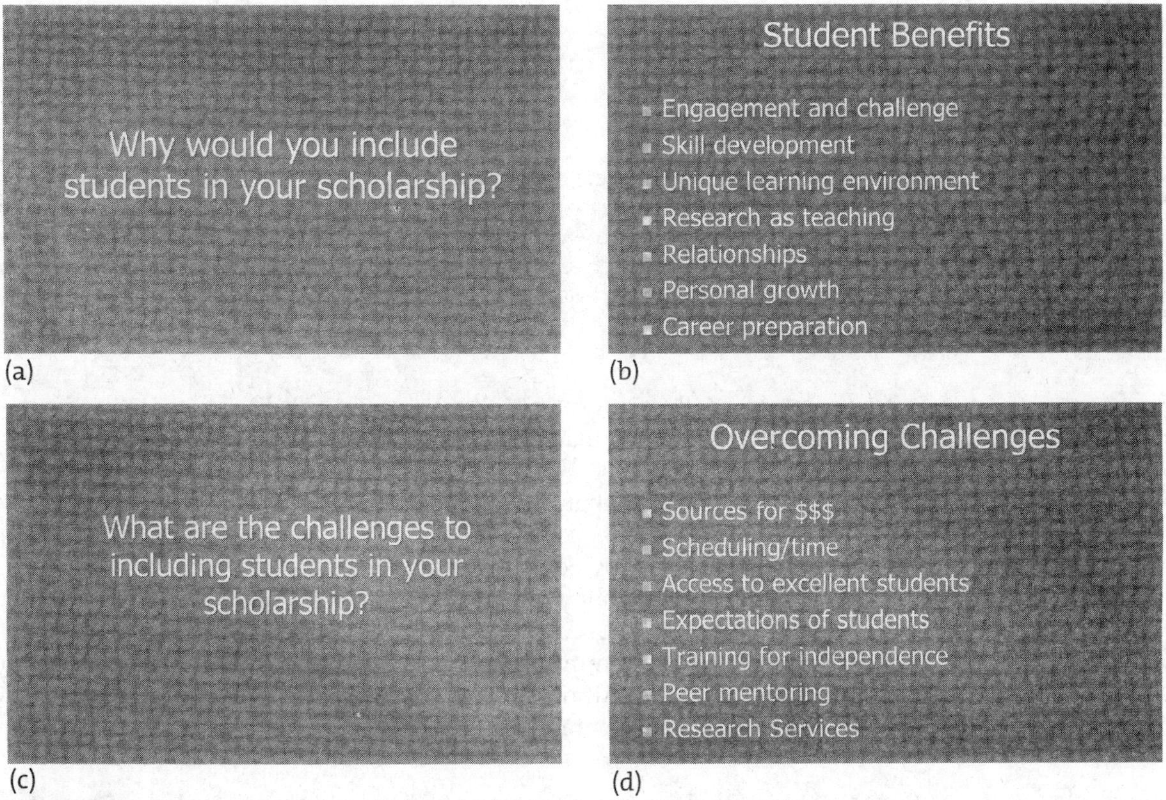

Planning the Presentation

(a) Why would you include students in your scholarship?

(b) **Student Benefits**
- Engagement and challenge
- Skill development
- Unique learning environment
- Research as teaching
- Relationships
- Personal growth
- Career preparation

(c) What are the challenges to including students in your scholarship?

(d) **Overcoming Challenges**
- Sources for $$$
- Scheduling/time
- Access to excellent students
- Expectations of students
- Training for independence
- Peer mentoring
- Research Services

Figure 18.7
Slide Template

Figure 18.8
Font May Change Meaning

Overcoming Challenges
- Sources for $$$
- Scheduling time
- Access to excellent students
- Expectations of students
- Training for independence
- Peer mentoring
- Research Services

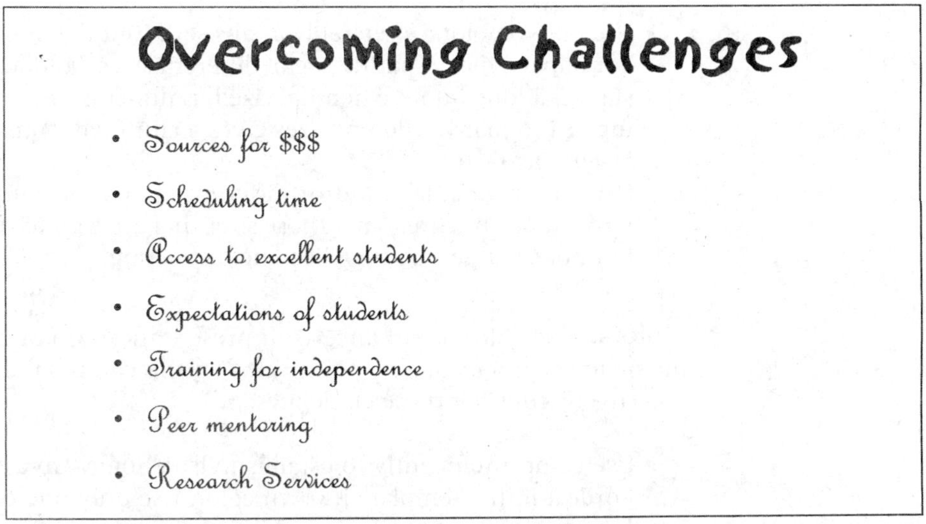

> **TIP**
> ## Line Length in Visuals
>
> Many texts (see George Miller) encourage using no more than seven lines and limiting lines to seven words. It is more helpful to think about whether you want the audience to read a long quote or to present a group of short lines, summarizing what you are saying. Shorter text lines keep the words in the background as you speak, focusing attention on you.

- Use pictures to illustrate an object that you want to discuss, for instance, the control panel of a new machine.

For text visuals (visuals that use only words):

- Use initial capitals followed by lowercase letters.
- Use 18-point type for body text, 24-point type for titles.

Keep running text to a minimum. Try to keep text to no more than six to eight lines per slide, fewer if possible. If you project a long quote, stop speaking and let people read it themselves (Stratten).

Fonts. Keep your text font simple yet elegant, subtle yet striking. Fonts can portray a wide range of emotions, from casual to authoritative, from serious to comic. Selecting and using a font that will elicit the desired response from your audience is important. Follow these three guidelines when selecting fonts:

- Use only one font, preferably a sans serif font like Helvetica or Arial.
- For impact, make sparing use of different sizes, boldfacing, or italics. For instance, a long quote when italicized, is difficult to read. Too much boldfacing or too many different sizes gives a cluttered, "ransom note" effect that is very distracting.
- Use larger font sizes and/or different colors for your titles. When using larger fonts, be sure to use those sizes that are easy to read (18 to 24 points), but not so large that they become distracting.

Colors. Use color to enhance your presentation. Color combinations should help viewers focus on key points, not on the combination itself. To use color effectively, consider these guidelines:

- Use color intelligently to establish visual logic. Give each item (title, test, border) in the template its own color. Use only one color for emphasizing key words.

- Use a background color; blue is commonly used.
- Use contrasting colors—white or yellow text on green or blue background.
- Use green and red sparingly. Ten percent of the population is color blind, and can't distinguish between red or green. It is best to assume that at least one person in every ten of your audience will be limited in his or her ability to translate color.
- Avoid hard-to-read color combinations, such as yellow on white and black on blue. Violet can also be very hard to read.
- Select combinations with an awareness of technology. Colors that look well together in a sign or in print, as in a magazine or newspaper, will probably not work the same way projected onto a screen. For example, ambient light, which is what is produced by an LCD projector, will affect contrast greatly; it will turn a dark color, such as burgundy or a deep green, into a pastel.
- Use what is known to work well. Yellow backgrounds with black lettering work well in most situations (think about school buses). Other good combinations are deep-blue backgrounds with yellow letters, or gray backgrounds with black letters.
- Evaluate templates before using them. Programs such as PowerPoint have a variety of background templates with color schemes that are handsome and exciting at first glance, but when you make your selection, always try to keep your audience in mind. Look at it from their standpoint—will this combination help them understand your point? If you're not certain about the combination, don't use it.

Animation. Animation is making text move. In slides, text can appear and depart from the slide by many animated routes—for instance, text can slide to the left or right, up or down, or disintegrate or blossom out from the center. Animation can emphasize important points visually while you explain them verbally. However, the idea is to enhance the production, not provide gimmicky entertainment. Follow these guidelines:

- Use only one text animation. Remember that the audience should be tracking as closely as possible with the presenter. To keep the audience tracking, pick only one primary reading transition. For example, a simple "wipe-right" text animation—the text appears to move off the screen left to right—will keep the reader's eye going in the normal reading direction.
- Treat previous lines carefully. Fading or subduing the previous bullets when the new information appears will help to keep the audience focused, but select a subdued tone for the previous bullets. Using an entirely different color will only draw attention away from the new text you are trying to introduce.
- Use animated graphics to make complex points. The multimedia, electronic presentation can use graphics effectively to show the progression of complicated points. Process steps, time lines, and flow charts all benefit from animated graphics. Keep in mind that being consistent is important when

using animated graphics. Your audience will appreciate consistent use of color contrast and special effects.

Sound Effects. Sound effects can accompany animation. As the word appears on the screen, audiences can hear sounds such as the clacking of an old typewriter or brakes squealing. Remember, the point is to enhance the contents of the slides, not distract the audience from them. Use these guidelines:

- Use no sound at all.
- Use the same sound for each transition. In other words, develop an audio logic so that each instance of the sound indicates a repetition of a step in the sequence (new slide or new line of text).
- Use subdued, undramatic sounds for transition. The first time you use a ricocheting bullet sound, you may get a reaction from your audience, but the second time you use it, the reaction may be greatly diminished, and the third time may have no effect at all.
- If you have a special point that you want to emphasize, or if you want to use a sound effect for some comic relief in a deadly serious situation, go ahead, but use these strategies sparingly.

Slide Transitions. Slide transitions are like animations. Like scene cuts in a movie, they help move one set of visual data out of view and move a new set into view. The goal of using this device is to create a sequence logic—each instance of the event means that another type of data is about to appear. If your audience concentrates on the transition rather than on the message, you've lost your audience. Follow these guidelines:

- Be consistent. Use the same transition for the same kind of event. Make each slide move off to the left or right or whatever you've chosen.
- Use only one or two simple transitions.
- Select transitions in order to aid the viewer. For example, a transition that "wipes up" will help to guide the watcher's eye back to the top of the slide so that the subject of the slide is immediately identified. A simple fade-to-black between sections of a presentation signals that a new topic is being considered.

Visual Aids and Slides. The visual aids that you use on your slides are the same that you would use in a hardcopy report: outlines; slides or drawings; tables and graphs. In addition, consider paper handouts.

Many slides are, in effect, outlines. They are lists of words in some kind of hierarchy (level 1, level 2, etc.). Like all outlines, this type of slide shows listeners the sections and subsections of the presentation. And like all outlines, they project very little depth or indication of relationship of ideas. This device, while common, is a background device (see above).

Tables and graphs can present data in a way that enables listeners to grasp relationships right away. An oral explanation of the relationship among the percentages that affect a pay increase is hard to follow, but a table or graph makes it clear. Note, however, that the space on a slide is restricted, so complex tables (as are often produced as part of scientific experiments) can be hard to project. (See Chapter 7 for more on tables and graphs.)

Paper handouts are often useful for a presentation. PowerPoint has a function that allows a speaker to print out and distribute the entire presentation in a series of "thumbnails," small versions of the actual slide. This device, although commonly used, is essentially just an outline, with none of the attendant contextualization that the speaker provides. You can supply some of that context by using PowerPoint's Notes function and handing out copies of the slides with your commentary in the note window. One speech expert suggests this: "If what you say when you expand the bullet points is useful for the audience to take away, put it in the handout" (Stratten).

In addition, paper handouts can more effectively show complex text, numbers, and data graphics (Tufte 22). A handout can replace or supplement projected visual aids. Pass out copies of a key image, perhaps a table. Listeners can make notes on it as you speak.

Making an Effective Presentation 作有效的陈述

To make an effective presentation, develop your introduction, navigate the body, develop your conclusion, rehearse your presentation, and deliver your presentation.

Develop the Introduction 展开介绍

The introduction establishes both the tone and the topic of the speech. Your tone is your attitude toward the listeners and the subject matter. Use the introduction to establish the relevance of the presentation to the audience. Be serious, but not dull. Avoid being so intense that no one can laugh, or so flip that the topic seems insignificant. Be explicit about your purpose and the sections of the presentation. In other words, follow the old advice of "Tell 'em what you are going to tell 'em" (Bacall; Tracy).

Follow these guidelines:

- You do not need to begin your report with a joke, a quotation by an authority, or an anecdote, but a well-chosen light story often helps relax both you and the audience.
- Explain why your report is important to your audience.
- Present your conclusions or recommendations right away. Then the audience will have a viewpoint from which to interpret the data you present.
- Explain how you assembled your report.
- Indicate your special knowledge of or concern with the subject.

- Identify the situation that required you to prepare the report (or the person who requested it).
- Preview the main points so your listeners can understand the order in which you will present your ideas.

Navigate the Body   主体导航

Many studies have shown that listeners simply do not hear everything the speaker says. Therefore, you should give several minutes to each main idea—long enough to get each main point across, but not long enough to belabor it.

Use Transitions Liberally

Clear transitions are very helpful to an audience of listeners. Your transitions remind them of the report's structure, which you established in the preview. Indicate how the next main idea fits into the overall report and why it is important to know about it. For instance, a proposal may seem very costly until the shortness of the payback period is emphasized.

Emphasize Important Details

Presumably, if you have created a storyboard, you know the details that you want to emphasize for the audience, and you have placed them on slides. Choose details that are especially meaningful to the audience. Explain any anticipated changes in equipment, staff, or policy, and show how these changes will be beneficial.

Impose a Time Limit

Find out how long the audience expects the presentation to last and fit your speech into that time frame. If they expect 15 minutes and you talk for 15 minutes, they will feel very good. Generally, speak for less time than is required. It is much better to present one or two main ideas carefully than to attempt to communicate more information than your listeners can comfortably grasp.

Develop a Conclusion   提出结论

The conclusion section restates the main ideas presented in the body of the report. Follow these guidelines:

- As you conclude your report, you should actually say, "In conclusion . . ." to capture (or recapture) your listeners' interest.
- For a proposal, stress the main advantages of your ideas, and urge your listeners to take specific action.
- For a recommendation report, emphasize the most significant data presented for each criterion, and clearly present your recommendations.

- Use a visual to summarize the important data.
- End the report by asking whether your listeners have any questions.

Rehearse Your Presentation 陈述预演

During rehearsals, go straight through the speech, using note cards. If it is a formal presentation, when you practice, wear the same clothes you will wear in the actual presentation.

Practice Developing a Conversational Quality

When you make your speech, sound like a person speaking to people, and use both voice and gestures to emphasize important points. Even the best information will fall on deaf ears if it is delivered like a robotic time-and-weather announcement. Rehearse until you feel secure with your report, but always stop short of memorizing it. If you memorize, you will tend to grope for memorized words rather than concentrating on the listeners and letting the words flow.

Practice Handling Your Technology and Visual Aids

Understand how to open and navigate your presentation. If necessary, have the presentation on several media. Often, speakers have the same file both on a disk and on their laptops. If you are unfamiliar with the technology, practice opening the files from both a disk and a laptop. Because technological arrangements in new places can be difficult to navigate, have a backup plan in case your technology does not work. Practice giving the presentation so that you know how to open the software program and advance and reverse the slides. Practice talking to the audience and looking at the screen only for those slides that you will use as foreground slides.

If you have paper visual aids or overhead transparencies, arrange these in the order they will be needed, and decide where you will place them when you are finished with them. If a listener asks you to return to a visual, you want to be able to find it easily. If you are using handouts, decide whether to distribute them before or during the presentation. Distributing them before the presentation eliminates the need to interrupt your flow of thought later, but because the listeners will flip through the handouts, they may be distracted as you start. Distributing them during the presentation causes an interruption, but listeners will focus immediately on the visual.

Rehearse

Practice your presentation at least once under conditions similar to those in which you will make the presentation, particularly for reports to large groups. Use a room of approximately the same size, with the same type of equipment for projecting your voice and your visuals. If you have never used a microphone, now is the time to practice with one.

Deliver Your Presentation　发表陈述

You will increase your effectiveness if you use notes and adopt a comfortable extemporaneous style.

Use Notes

Experienced speakers have found that outlines prepared on a few large note cards (5 by 8 inches, one side only) are easier to handle than outlines on many small note cards. Some speakers even prefer outlines on one or two sheets of standard paper, mounted on light cardboard for easier handling.

The outline should contain clear main headings and subheadings. Make sure your outline has plenty of white space so you can keep your place.

Adopt a Comfortable Style

The extemporaneous method results in natural, conversational delivery and helps you concentrate on the audience. Using this method, you can direct your attention to the listeners, referring to the outline only to jog your memory and to ensure that ideas are presented in the proper order. Smile. Take time to look at individual audience members and to collect your thoughts. Instead of rushing to your next main point, check whether members of the audience understood your last point. Your word choice may occasionally suffer when you speak extemporaneously, but reports delivered in this way still communicate what you want to say better than those memorized or read.

The following suggestions will help as you face your listeners and deliver the presentation:

1. Look directly at each listener at least once during the report. With experience, you will be able to tell from your listeners' faces whether you are communicating well. If they seem puzzled or inattentive, repeat the main idea, give additional examples for clarity, or solicit questions. Don't proceed in lockstep through your notes. Adapt.

2. Make sure you can be heard, but also try to speak conversationally. You should feel a sense of your voice as a round, full tone, projecting with conviction. You should also feel that your voice fills the space of the room, with the sound of your voice bouncing back slightly to your own ears. The listeners should get the impression that you are talking to them rather than just presenting a report. Inexperienced speakers often talk too rapidly.

3. Try to become aware of—and to eliminate—your distracting mannerisms. No one wants to see speakers brush their hair, scratch their arms, rock back and forth on the balls of their feet, smack their lips. If the mannerism is pronounced enough, it may be all the audience remembers of your presentation. Stand firmly on both feet without slumping or swaying.

全球化和口头陈述
Globalization and Oral Presentations

Giving a presentation to a foreign or non-English-speaking audience is easier if you give some thought to relating to an audience whose culture is not your own. A key idea for your planning is that although English is commonly studied as a second language, "English proficiency within a given audience can vary widely, so the best approach is to simplify and clarify content at every turn" (Zielinski). In order to simplify and clarify content, follow these tips: Use simple sentences, make clear transitions, avoid digressions, reduce use of potentially confusing pronouns, restate key points, pause periodically, use subject-verb-object word order, repeat phrases using the exact wording. If you call it a "plan" the first time, continue to use that word; don't switch to "proposal" or "map" or "vision" (Zielinski).

Also, be aware that the international audience's reaction to you may differ greatly from what you are used to. For example, in Japan, it is not unusual for audience members to close their eyes in order to convey concentration and attentiveness, while in the United States closed eyes are a sign that you are lulling the audience to sleep. Applause is a generally universal sign of approval, but whistling in Europe is a negative reaction to your presentation. Finally, know that other cultures have a different sense of acceptable personal space than Americans have. Middle Easterners and Latin Americans tend to stand much closer than Americans find comfortable, while many Asian cultures stand quite far away from each other. Keep this in mind if you have others onstage with you or if you will be going into the audience for your presentation (McKinney, "International").

Be aware of body language conventions. Hand gestures that are accepted in the United States, such as the A-OK symbol (the circle formed with your index finger and thumb), or the thumbs-up gesture, are considered obscene in some countries. Pointing with a finger can be impolite; use a fully extended hand. In some countries, emphatic gestures are poorly received. Body language that is unwittingly offensive can cause an audience to focus on what is inappropriate and lose the content of your presentation (Zielinski).

Plan for differences in technology. Bring pictures of the equipment that you will need during your presentation. Bring a voltage converter. Remember that many countries have differently sized standard paper and may use a two-hole instead of a three-hole punch. Most importantly, have a backup plan and keep a sense of humor (McKinney, "Public," "Professional").

For further reference, check out these websites:

Executive Planet at <www.executiveplanet.com/> is a guide to all aspects of conducting international business: etiquette, customs, and culture. If you'll be presenting in a foreign country, you can find out the details of greetings, business attire, and meeting formalities as well as general information for many different countries.

(continued)

(continued)

> For insight into the cultural dynamics of other countries and regions and how this may impact your business dealings abroad, refer to "International Business Etiquette and Manners" at <www.cyberlink.com/>. Your presentations will be more effective if you know of the appropriate way you should act.
>
> Although addressed to potential conference speakers, this article offers an invaluable overview of preparing to give a presentation to an international audience: Gagnon, Michael, and Raymond Wallace. "Making a Presentation in English at a European Conference." Federation of European Chemical Societies. Division of Chemical Education. July 2001. 7 Feb. 2004 <http://216.239.37.104/search?q=cache:df8EOxSS4-8J:www.chemsoc.org/pdf/enc/fecs/fecsedgagan.pdf+%22visual+aids%22+tips+%22international+audience%22&hl=en&ie=UTF-8>.
>
> **Works Cited**
>
> McKinney, C. "Public Speaking: Bilingual Help." 2003. Advanced Public Speaking Institute. 31 Jan. 2004 <www.public-speaking.org/public-speaking-bilingual-article.htm>.
>
> ———. "Public Speaking: International Perspective on Humor." 2003. Advanced Public Speaking Institute. 31 Jan. 2004 <www.public-speaking.org/public-speaking-international-article.htm>.
>
> ———. "Public Speaking: Professional Photographs." 2003. Advanced Public Speaking Institute. 31 Jan. 2004 <www.public-speaking.org/public-speaking-equipmentphotos-article.htm>.
>
> Zielinski, Dave. "Going Global, Part I." 3M United States. *Presentation* (n.d.) 6 Feb. 2004 <www.3m.com/meetingnetwork/presentations/pmag_going_global_1.html>.

4. To point out some aspect of a visual projected by an overhead projector, lay a pencil or an arrow made of paper on the appropriate spot of the transparency.

5. When answering questions, make sure everyone hears and understands each question before you begin to answer it. If you cannot answer a question during the question-and-answer session, say so, and assure the questioner that you will find the answer and provide it at a later time.

Worksheet for Preparing an Oral Presentation

准备口头陈述的工作表

- ☐ Identify your audience.
  What is your listeners' level of knowledge about the topic?
  What is their level of interest in the entire speech?
  Why are they attending?
  What do they need?

- ☐ Create an outline showing the main point and subpoints.
  Which strategy will best help the audience? Problem-solution? Narrative? IMRD?

- ☐ Assign a time limit to each point.

- ☐ Create a storyboard.
  What visual aid will illustrate each point most effectively?

- ☐ Decide whether you need any kind of projection or display equipment.
  laptop? LCD projector? flip chart?

- ☐ Review the speaking location. Do you know how to make your technology (laptop, disk, projector) interact with the technology resident at the site?

- ☐ Determine your relationship to the slides. Will they be foreground or background for you?

- ☐ Prepare clearly written note cards—with just a few points on each.

- ☐ Rehearse the speech several times, including how you will actually handle the technology.

Worksheet for Evaluating an Oral Presentation

评估口头陈述的工作表

- ☐ Answer these questions:
  1. Clarity
     Did the speaker tell you the point early in the speech? Could you tell when the speaker moved to a new subpoint?
  2. Tone
     Did the speaker sound conversational? Did the speaker go too fast? go too slow? speak in a monotone?
  3. Use of technology
     Did the speaker interact effectively with the slides?
     Did the slides help you understand the content, or were they distracting?

Exercises 练 习

▶ You Create

1. Create a PowerPoint presentation of two or three slides that illustrates a problem in one of your current projects. Give a brief speech (2 to 3 minutes) explaining the problem. Alternate 1: Prepare two or three PowerPoint slides that illustrate the solution or its effects, and present the entire problem and solution to the class in a 4- to 5-minute speech. Alternate 2: Prepare the PowerPoint presentation in groups of two to four. Select a speaker for the group. Give the speech.

2. Report on a situation with which you are involved. Your work on an assignment for this class is probably most pertinent, but your instructor will provide his or her own requirements. Depending on the available time, draw a visual on the board, make a transparency, create a handout, or prepare one or two PowerPoint slides. In 2 minutes, explain the point of the visual aid. Class members will complete and/or discuss the evaluation questions above.

3. For Exercises 1 and 2, each member of the audience should prepare a question to ask the speaker. Conduct a question-and-answer session. When the session is finished, discuss the value and relevance of the questions that were asked. What constitutes a good question? Also evaluate the answers. What constitutes a good answer?

4. Make a storyboard for the speech you will give for the following Speaking Assignment. Divide a page into these three columns and fill them in, following this example:

Point	Visual Aid	Time
Method of extrusion	Cross section of laminate	2 minutes

5. Use the generic graph on page 483 to make a 2-minute speech. Title the graph and explain its source, its topic, and the significance of the pattern. Choose any topic that would change over time.

6. Give a brief speech in which you freely use technical terms. The class will ask questions that will elicit the definitions. If there is time, redeliver the speech at a less technical level.

▶ Speaking Assignment 演讲任务

Your instructor may require an oral presentation of a project you have written during the term. The speech should be extemporaneous and should conform to an

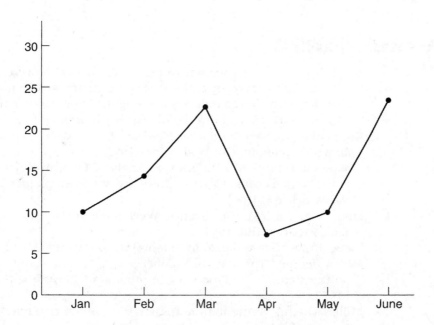

agreed-upon length. Outline the speech, construct a storyboard, make your visuals, and rehearse. Follow your presentation with a question-and-answer session.

Writing Assignment 写作任务

Write a learning report for the speaking assignment you just completed. See Chapter 5, Writing Assignment 7, page 133, for details of the assignment.

Web Exercises 网络练习

1. Create a PowerPoint version of a document you have previously written for this class. Upload the PowerPoint to the Web. Give a 4- to 5-minute speech using the on-line slides. Alternate: Upload the PowerPoint presentation created above. Have classmates, as assigned by your teacher, read and evaluate the report. Use the evaluation sheet for the appropriate type of report in the appropriate chapter.

2. Using screens that you download from the Web, create a PowerPoint presentation to your classmates in which you do either of the following:
    a. Explain the effective elements of a well-designed screen.
    b. Explain how to use the screen to perform an activity (order plane tickets, contact a sales representative, perform an advanced search).

Works Cited 引用的作品

Bacall, Robert. "How Attention Works for Audiences." PowerPointAnswers.com. 13 Oct. 2003 <www.powerpointanswers.com/article1035.php>.

Jacobs, Kathryn. "Overcoming Stage Fright." 2002. PowerPointAnswers.com. 14 Nov. 2003 <www.powerpointanswers.com/article1002.html>.

Korolenko, Michael. *Writing for Multimedia: A Guide and Sourcebook for the Digital Writer.* Belmont, CA: Wadsworth, 1997.

Laskowski, Lenny. "A.U.D.I.E.N.C.E. Analysis: It's Your Key to Success." 2001. PowerPointers.com 13 Oct. 2003 <www.powerpointers.com/showarticle.asp?articleid=248>.

Lindstrom, Robert L. *The* Business Week *Guide to Multimedia Presentations.* New York: McGraw-Hill, 1994.

Meng, Brita. "Get to the Point." *Macworld* 5.4 (1988): 136–143.

Miller, George. "The Magical Number Seven, Plus or Minus Two: Some Limits on Our Capacity for Processing Information." *Psychological Review* 63 (1956): 81–97.

Miller, Glenn. "Presentation Disasters: Conference Style." 08 Mar. 2004. PowerPointAnswers.com. 1 May 2004 <www.powerpointanswers.com/article1036.php>.

Scoville, Richard. "Slide Rules." *Publish!* 4.3 (1989): 51–53.

Shaw, Gordon, Robert Brown, and Philip Bromiley. "Strategic Stories": How 3M Is Rewriting Business Planning." *Harvard Business Review* 76 (May–June 1998): 42–44. Reprint 98310.

"Storyboard" WWWNetSchool. 13 Oct. 2003 <www.thirteen.org/edonline/software/earthinflux/orgc.html>.

Stratten, Scott. "Business Tip: Giving Effective PowerPoint Presentations." 13 Oct. 2003 <http://virtual.yosemite.ce.ea.s/itolhurst/ESGIS/Presentational/Business_Tip.htm>.

Tessler, Franklin. "Step-by-Step Slides." *Macworld* 5.12 (1988): 148–153.

Tracy, Larry. "Preparing a Presentation." 2000. PowerPointers.com. 11 Oct. 2003 <www.powerpointers.com/showarticle.sap?articleid=216>.

Tufte, Edward. *The Cognitive Style of PowerPoint.* Cheshire, CT: Graphics Press, 2003.

"Web Resources in Multimedia Storyboards." 1999–2003. Teacher Resource Center. Georgia Department of Education. 2 May 2004 <www.glc.k12.ga.us/trc/cluster.asp?mode=browse&intPathID=7801>.

Welsh, Theresa. "Presentation Visuals: The Ten Most Common Mistakes." *intercom* 43.6 (1996): 22–43.

Chapter 19: Letters
信 函

Chapter Contents
- Chapter 19 In a Nutshell
- Three Basic Letter Formats
- Elements of a Letter
- Planning Business Letters
- Globalization and Letters
- Ethics and Letters
- Types of Business Letters

Chapter 19
In a Nutshell 概 要

Letters are presented in an agreed-upon set of ways. Study Figure 19.1 on page 487 to find out what these conventions are and how they fit on the page. That figure presents the parts in block format, which arranges all the items at the left margin. Using block format is an easy way to present yourself as a credible professional.

Letters represent you or your company in professional, often legal and emotional, situations. The key to all types of letters is to treat the reader appropriately, using the "you" attitude and speaking to readers in clear, understandable, nonconfrontational words. Write several short paragraphs rather than fewer long ones. Treat readers as you would want yourself or people close to you treated.

Business letters are an important—even a critical—part of any professional's job and are written for many reasons to many audiences. They may request information from an expert, transmit a report to a client, or discuss the specifications of a project with a supplier. Letters represent the firm, and their quality reflects the quality of the firm. This chapter introduces you to effective, professional letter writing by explaining the common formats, the standard elements, the planning required, and several common types of business letters.

Three Basic Letter Formats 信函的三种基本格式

The three basic formats are the block format, the modified block format, and the simplified format (*Merriam; Webster's*).

Block Format 齐头式

In the *block format,* place all the letter's elements flush against the left margin. Do not indent the first word of each paragraph. The full block format, shown in Figure 19.1 or Example 20.3 (p. 524), is widely used because letters in this format can be typed quickly.

Modified Block Format 混合式

The *modified block format* (an example appears in Figure 19.3, p. 496) is the same as the full block format with two exceptions: The date line and closing signature are placed on the right side of the page. The best position for both is five spaces to the right of the center line, but flush right is acceptable. A variation of this format is the *modified semiblock.* It is the same as the modified block, except that the first line of each paragraph is indented five spaces.

Simplified Format 简化型格式

The *simplified format* (see Figure 19.4, p. 497, for an example) contains no salutation and no complimentary close, but it almost always has a subject line. It is extremely useful for impersonal situations and for situations where the identity of the recipient is not known. In personal situations, writers start the first paragraph with the recipient's name.

Elements of a Letter 信函的组成部分

Internal Elements 内部组成部分

This section describes the elements of a letter from the top to the bottom of a page.

Elements of a Letter

Figure 19.1
Block Format

Heading	4217 East Eleventh Avenue Post Office Box 2701 Austin, TX 78701 　　*(skip 2 lines)*
Date	February 24, 2005 　　*(skip 2 lines)*
Inside address	Ms. Susan Wardell Director of Planning Acme Bolt and Fastener Co. 23201 Johnson Avenue Arlington, AZ 85322 　　*(double-space)*
Salutation, mixed punctuation	Dear Ms. Wardell: 　　*(double-space)*
Subject line	SUBJECT: ABC CONTRACT (optional) 　　*(double-space)*
Body paragraphs flush left	_____ _____ 　　*(double-space between paragraphs)* _____ _____ 　　*(double-space)*
Closing, mixed punctuation	Sincerely yours,
Signature	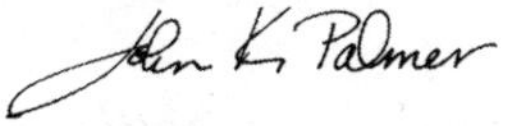 *John K. Palmer*　　*(skip 3 lines)*
Typed name Position in company	John K. Palmer Treasurer 　　*(double-space)*
Typist's initials Enclosure line	abv enc: (2) 　　*(skip 1 or 2 lines; depends on letter length)*
Copy line	c: Ms. Louise Black

TIP: Punctuation

Letter items are punctuated by either *open* or *mixed* patterns. You may choose either. Be consistent. In open format, put no punctuation after the salutation and complimentary close. In mixed format, put a colon after the salutation and a comma after the complimentary close.

Heading

The heading is your address.

> 4217 East Eleventh Avenue
> Post Office Box 2701
> Austin, TX 78701

- Spell out words such as *Avenue, Street, East, North,* and *Apartment* (but use *Apt.* if the line would otherwise be too long).
- Put an apartment number to the right of the street address. If, however, the street address is too long, put the apartment number on the next line.
- Spell out numbered street names up to *Twelfth*.
- To avoid confusion, put a hyphen between the house and street number (1021-14th Street).
- Either spell out the full name of the state or use the U.S. Postal Service Zip Code abbreviation. If you use the Zip Code abbreviation, note that the state abbreviation has two capital letters and no periods and that the Zip Code number follows one space after the state (NY 10036).
- Note on letterhead: place the date two lines below the last line of the letterhead, in the position required by the format (e.g., flush left for block).

Date

Dates can have one of two forms: February 24, 2006, or 24 February 2006.

- Spell out the month.
- Do not use ordinal indicators, such as 1st or 24th.

Inside Address

The inside address is the same as the address that appears on the envelope.

> Ms. Susan Wardell
> Director of Planning
> Acme Bolt and Fastener Co.
> 23201 Johnson Avenue
> Arlington, AZ 85322

- Use the correct personal title (Mr., Ms., Dr., Professor) and business title (Director, Manager, Treasurer).
- Write the firm's name exactly, adhering to its practice of abbreviating or spelling out such words as *Company* and *Corporation*.
- Place the reader's business title after his or her name or on a line by itself, whichever best balances the inside address.
- Use the title *Ms.* for a woman unless you know that she prefers to be addressed in another way.

Attention Line

Attention lines are generally used only when you cannot name the reader ("Attention Human Resources Manager"; "Attention Payroll Department").

- Place the line two spaces below the inside address.
- Place the word *Attention* against the left margin. Do *not* follow it by a colon.

Salutation

The salutation always agrees with the first line of the inside address.

- If the first line names an individual (Ms. Susan Wardell), say, "Dear Ms. Wardell:" If the name is "gender neutral" (Robin Jones), say "Dear Robin Jones:"
- If the first line names a company (Acme Bolt and Fastener Co.), use the simplified format (see Figure 19.4, p. 497) with a subject line or repeat the name of the company ("Dear Acme Bolt and Fastener Co.:").
- If the first line names an office (Director of Planning), address the office, use an attention line, or use a subject line.

  Dear Director of Planning: (*or*)
  Attention Director of Planning (*or*)
  SUBJECT: ABC CONTRACT

- If you know only the first initial of the recipient, write "Dear S. Wardell," or use an attention line.
- If you know only a Post Office box (say, from a job ad), use a subject line.

  Box 4721 ML
  The Daily Planet
  Gillette, WY 82716
  Subject: APPLICATION FOR OIL RIG MANAGER

Subject Line

Use a subject line to replace awkward salutations, as explained above, or to focus the reader's attention.

SUBJECT: **Request to Extend Deadline**

- Follow the word *Subject* with a colon.
- For emphasis, capitalize or boldface the phrase.
- Use of the word *Subject* is optional, especially in simplified format. If you do not use *Subject,* capitalize the entire line.

Body

Single-space the body, and try to balance it on the page. It should cover the page's imaginary middle line (located 5½ inches from the top and bottom of the page). Use several short paragraphs rather than one long one. Use 1-inch margins at the right and left.

Complimentary Closing and Signature

Close business letters with "Sincerely" or "Sincerely yours." Add the company name if policy requires it.

Sincerely yours,
ACME BOLT AND FASTENER CO.

John K. Palmer

John K. Palmer
Treasurer

- Capitalize only the first word of the closing.
- Place the company's name immediately below the complimentary closing (if necessary).
- Allow three lines for the handwritten signature.
- Place the writer's title or department, or both, below his or her typed name.

Optional Lines

Place optional lines below the typed signature.

- Place the typist's initials in lowercase letters, flush left.
- Add an enclosure line if the envelope contains additional material. Use "Enclosure:" or "enc:". Place the name of the enclosure (résumé, bid contract) after the colon, or put the number of enclosures in parentheses.

  enc: (2)
  Enclosure: résumé

- If copies are sent to other people, place "c:" (for copy) at the left margin and place the names to the right.

  c: Joanne Koehler

Succeeding Pages

For succeeding pages of a letter, place the name of the addressee, the page number, and the date in a heading.

Susan Wardell   -2-   February 24, 2006

Envelopes 信 封

The standard business envelope is 9½ by 4³⁄₁₆ inches. Place the stamp in the upper right corner. Place your address (the same one that you used in the heading) in the upper left corner.

Place the address anywhere in the "read area" of the U.S. Postal Service's optical character recognition (OCR) machines (Figure 19.2). The U.S. Postal Service (USPS) recommends the following descending order:

- Attention line
- Company name
- Street address; on the street address line, also add directions (N, NE, S, etc.), designator (St., Ave., Rd.), and sublocation (Apt., STE [suite], RM [room]). *Note:* The postal service will deliver the mail to the address directly above the city and state.
- City and state
- Zip Code to the right of the state; use all 9 digits if you know them

Figure 19.2

OCR Area of Envelope

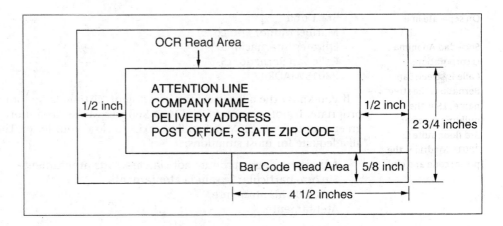

Planning Business Letters 设计商务信函

In planning your letter, you must consider your audience, your tone, and your format.

Globalization and Letters 全球化和信函

Basically, writing letters to a foreign audience requires that you be clear and direct. Jargon, idioms, and humor can all be misinterpreted or misunderstood, so keep your writing free of them. In most countries, any business communication is formal, so keep your tone professional. Refrain from sounding casual and what may seem to an international audience as overly familiar.

Letter-writing conventions differ from country to country; make an effort to learn what format your audience expects. For example, outside the United States, the date is usually written as day/month/year. So, March 9, 2004, would be 9/3/04 or 9 March 2004. In France, Spain, and Italy, the months are not capitalized when they are written out.

Also, salutations differ from country to country. In Germany, business is kept on a formal level and you should not use given names unless you are directly invited to do so. You would address a letter to Herr Schmidt and refer to him as Herr Schmidt throughout the letter. In China, people are addressed with their family (last) names preceding their given (first) names. They do use Mr. or Ms. at all times, so make sure that you are using the correct last name. And in Japan, it is customary to address a letter using a person's last name and their job title, or else with a –san at the end for a more general salutation ("International").

Let's say that you need to write a letter to a colleague in Spain. Using this sample format from "Writing Letters in Spanish," you would address the letter to either Señor (Sr.) or Señora (Sra.) and could add Don or Doña as an additional title of respect:

> On separate line

Sra. Doña
Maribel Muñoz Franco
Editores Internacionales S.A.
Calle San Bernado, 15-3°-C
28015 MADRID

> Sociedad Anonima is corporation; Calle is street; San Bernado is the street name; 15 is the building number, 3rd floor, suite C; 28015 Madrid is the postal code and city

If you know the addressee, the greeting of "Estimada Señora Muñoz:" is appropriate. If not, you may use "Muy Señores Mios:" as a more formal way to greet your colleagues. Many endings exist to close your letter. The following are all adequate for most situations:

A la espera de sus prontaa noticias, le saluda atentamente,
Sin otro particular, le saluda atentamente,
Le saluda atentamente,
Atentamente,

For further reference, check out this website: *The Business Start Page*, at www.bspage.com, contains much general business information. Under the Addresses, you will find the elements of international addresses and gives tips on the correct salutations. The site also has a section for international e-mail etiquette.

> **Works Cited**
> "International Addresses and Salutations." The Business Start Page. 6 Feb. 2004 <www.bspage.com/address.html>.
> "Writing Letters in Spanish." 2004. AskOxford.com. 6 Feb. 2004 <www.askoxford.com/languages/es/spanish_letters/?view=uk>.

Consider Your Audience   考虑你的读者

Before you begin to write, consider the audience's knowledge level and its specific need for the information. The audience could be a customer who can identify the defective part but who may not know much about how the part fits into the larger system in the machine. The audience could be an expert engineer or a manager who understands the general theory of this kind of project (say, constructing a commercial building) but knows little about this particular project.

Also be aware that the audience has various reasons for needing your letter. Assessing that need allows you to write a more effective letter. Your letter may be shown to someone other than just the recipient, usually a person more distant from the situation. And your letter could be used as a basis for decisions, even legal action.

Consider Your Tone   考虑你的基调

Use Plain English

You want to sound natural; you are, after all, one human being addressing another. Plain conversational English makes your point better than "businessese." Even if your letter has legal implications, you should use a relaxed, clear tone. Consider this brief passage:

> Pursuant to our discussion of February 3 in reference to the L-19 transistor, please be advised that we are not presently in receipt of the above-mentioned item but expect to have it in stock within one week. Enclosed herewith please find a brochure regarding said transistor as per your request.

Here is the paragraph rewritten in a more direct, conversational style that makes the contents much easier to grasp.

> I've enclosed a brochure on the L-19 transistor we talked about on February 3. Our shipment of L-19s should arrive within a week.

Use the "You" Approach

The "you" approach is based on the writer's recognition that the recipient is a person who appreciates being approached in a personal way. Applying this approach requires only that you use "I," "we," and "you." Consider the following example, and note how the writer addresses the customer's dissatisfaction both by showing empathy and by proposing solutions to the problem.

Dear Mr. Hillary:

After my January 27th visit to your complex to investigate the poorly performing laser printers, I talked to our technical support and to Megacorp's customer representative. We have several suggestions for solving the problem. If they do not work, we will investigate the relatively more difficult task of replacing all ten printers.

Technical support suggests that you discontinue using the printer driver in your desktop publishing program. Hold the shift key down while you select print and you will default to the word processing print driver. In tests we performed here we found that the word processor driver prints about 8–10 times faster. This simple procedure change should solve most of the problems.

The difficulty you have in printing eps images in your desktop publishing program is more complicated. Our simple recommendation is that you convert them to GIF images. We tried this and the documents printed about 3 times faster. Our more involved recommendation is that we upgrade the RAM in the printers to 4 MB. Because of the difficulties you have experienced and because of the length of time you have been our customer, we will install them free and charge only our cost.

If none of these suggestions works, we will have to begin to negotiate to return the printers to Megacorp or trade them in. My brief contact with the customer rep at Mega indicates that this option will be more difficult.

I will contact you next week on Tuesday to see if our suggestions have had any effect.

Sincerely,

Marian Goodrich

Marian Goodrich
District Sales Manager

Consider Format 考虑格式

Format can affect the way your audience accepts your message. Use one of the basic formats or one that your company requires. Readers expect you to be a knowledgeable professional; using the correct form helps reinforce that impression. Make careful design decisions. Choose several short paragraphs rather than one long paragraph. Use bullets and indentations to help readers grasp key points easily. Review Chapter 6 to see how format can help presentation.

Ethics and Letters 撰写信函的注意事项

Letters are written to communicate something in a more formal way than is an e-mail or a memo. Understanding the letter's format and audience is essential if the writer is to establish his or her *ethos* (the character that the reader perceives). Business letters are written for a specific purpose and therefore are to the point. Sometimes this terseness can be misconstrued, so the letter's structure directly affects how the information it contains is interpreted. Letters containing good news are, not surprisingly, easier to write than letters with bad news and structuring it is simple: Start with the good news. However, relaying bad news makes considering the audience reaction much more important. Communicating bad news in a way that develops an effective *pathos* (sense of the emotional impact of the letter) also creates a positive *ethos* (perception of the character of the writer) for the sender. The letter writer must take ethical responsibility for his or her epistolary communication.

Types of Business Letters 商务信函的类型

The rest of this chapter examines several types of business letters and suggests how to structure their contents.

Transmittal Letters 商务沟通信函

A *transmittal letter* (Figure 19.3, p. 496) conveys a report from one firm to another. (Transmittal correspondence is explained in Chapter 14.) To write a transmittal letter, follow these guidelines:

- Identify the report enclosed.
- Briefly explain the report's purpose and scope.
- Explain any problems encountered.
- Acknowledge the people who helped.

General Information Letters 通用信函

General information letters can deal with anything. They serve to keep the writer in touch with the reader (a common public relations device), to send information, or to reply to requests. Figure 19.4 (p. 497) shows an example. To write such a letter, follow these guidelines:

- Use a context-setting introduction.
- If there is an acceptance or rejection, state it clearly.
- Use formatting to highlight the main point.
- Add extra information as needed, but keep it brief.

Figure 19.3

Transmittal Letter in Modified Block Format with Closed Punctuation

VINZ CONSULTING
EVERYTHING ABOUT THE SHOP
1021 Portland Drive
East Pines, MD 20840-1461
(307) 432-8866

October 27, 2006

Mr. Charles Lindsay
Mountain Milling
3266 Crestview Drive
Charleston, WV 25301

Dear Mr. Lindsay:

Attached is my final report on the type of milling machine you should purchase for your plant. I recommend that you purchase Ironton's #02119-BTUA.

As we discussed on my site visit last month, I have researched the appropriate literature on this subject, talked to several sales reps, and observed three different demonstrations of the 02119 and its two competitors. You were particularly concerned about size and power—the 02119 will do the job for you.

I have enjoyed our work together and look forward to working with you in the future. I have found your staff particularly helpful in filling my several requests about your plant's capacity and materials flow.

Sincerely,

Steve Vinz

Steve Vinz
Project Manager

Closing and signature set near middle of page

Figure 19.4

General Information Letter in Simplified Format

Maxwell and Goldman
3227 Girard Avenue South
Minneapolis, Minnesota 55408
608-385-1944 / fax 608-385-1945
www.maxgold.com

July 14, 2006

Mr. Duwan James
James Corporation
4810 River Heights Drive
St. Paul, Minnesota 55106

No salutation

Duwan, here is the background information on the Adjustable Speed Drive. The cost of this system, as we discussed earlier, is $1000.00 installed.

1. The Adjustable Speed Drive can operate as a clutch to inch and jog your conveyor to the exact assembly position. The operator can control the speed instantly from zero to maximum speed, and any speed in between.

2. The conveyor speed can be varied simply and easily while the motor remains at a constant operating speed. The operator controls the speed by hand with the control lever.

3. This speed drive system offers a speed range of 0 to 160 feet per minute (fpm) for the conveyor. This is approximately 2 miles per hour (mph). You indicated that your average speed is 60 fpm. This speed can be locked in for normal runs or sped up for resupplying the line, and again, slowed down for positioning.

4. The drive system is a compact package weighing 45 pounds and having overall dimensions of 10" x 12" x 32". It won't overload or clutter the conveyor frame. The whole system operates from one power cord and requires no special maintenance. The unit is sealed and prelubricated. The only maintenance necessary would be a periodic check of mounting hardware.

Duwan, if you need more information or have any more questions, call or fax to the numbers above, or email me at goldmans@maxgold.com.

Shana Goldman

No closing or typed name

Worksheet for Writing a Business Letter

撰写商务信函的工作表

Planning

☐ **Analyze the audience.**
Who will receive this letter?
Why do they need it? What will they do as a result of receiving it?

☐ **Name your goal for the reader.**
What do you want to happen after the reader reads the letter?

☐ **Choose a format for the reader.**
Use the simplified format for more impersonal or more routine situations.

Generating

☐ **State your main points succinctly.**

☐ **Compose with a "you" attitude.**

Finishing

☐ **Reread the letter slowly, word for word, to weed out any errors in spelling and grammar or problems with style (wrong tone, "garden path" sentences, see Chapter 4).**

☐ **Reread the letter to make sure your facts are accurate.**

☐ **Review each of the following for standard form:**
Your address. Do not use abbreviations, except for the state.
The recipient's name, title, corporation title, and address.
The salutation. Repeat the recipient's name.
If you do not know the recipient's name, use a subject line.
The complimentary closing.
Your typed signature (three spaces below the closing).
Your signature (between the closing and the typed signature).

Exercises 练 习

▶ You Revise

1. Rewrite this passage using plain English and a "you" attitude.

   There was a question asked to me in regard to the complete fulfillment of contract 108XB (Manual Effector Arm Robot A). Complete documentation of same has not been fulfilled. The specifications are interpreted by this office to mean that no such documentation was required.

▶ You Analyze

2. Analyze this letter.

    A shredded conveyor belt? What a disaster! And here we were, so happy the last time we talked. Well, while it's always something, there's a silver lining in every cloud, so let's talk about what happened.

    Why did this happen? We haven't had a conveyor belt shred at a customer site in 31 years. You're the first. Have you checked your operating procedures? What do you do for training? These things are practically indestructible—who runs your machines? What do you know about them?

    Anyhow, if that's the cloud, the silver lining is that you get one free. It's in the mail. COD.

    Then I reviewed the problem with our design engineer. She feels that the belt exactly fills the specifications and that the fault probably is with your staff, but there is a slight possibility that there could be a problem with the metal "hooks" that join the two ends of the rubber. As your employees install the new belt, make them check those hooks. They should not "wobble." If they do, call me.

    Our sales representative can get to your place on Friday, June 19. If anything else strange comes up, let her know; she can fix anything—she's a great gal.

    Hope there's no hard feelings. Your business is important to us.

▶ You Create

3. a. Write two passages. In the first passage, try to be overtechnical, acting as if you expect that anyone would know the terms and concepts you use. In the second passage, rewrite your text so that it assumes that the technical language is foreign to the reader.

    b. In groups of two to four, read your two versions, then discuss your results with the class.

    c. Write a memo that tells what you learned from this assignment.

Writing Assignments 写作任务

1. Write a general information letter to your instructor to give her or him the background details of a report you will write. Explain items that the instructor needs to know to read the report as a knowledgeable member of the corporate community.

2. As part of a research project, write a letter of inquiry to a professional. Ask him or her for information about your topic. Your questions should be as specific as you can make them. Ask questions such as "How does Wheeler Amalgamated extrude the plastic used in the cans for Morning Bright orange juice?"

Avoid questions such as "Can you send me all the information you have on the extruding process and any other processes of interest?"

3. As part of an assignment that requires a formal report, write a transmittal letter. Follow Figure 19.3.
4. Write a learning report for the writing assignment you just completed. See Chapter 5, Writing Assignment 7, page 133, for details of the assignment.

Web Exercise 网络练习

Analyze two or three company homepages for the "you" attitude. What happens (or doesn't happen) on the screen to make readers feel that they are being addressed personally?

Works Cited 引用的作品

Merriam Webster's Secretarial Handbook. Ed. Sheryl Lindsell-Roberts. 3rd ed. Springfield, MA: Merriam, 1993.

United States Postal Service (USPS). *Addressing for Optical Character Recognition.* Notice 165. June 1981.

United States Postal Service (USPS). *Here's How to Address Your Mail for the Best Mail Service.* Notice 36SUC380. Washington, DC, n.d.

Webster's New World Office Professionals' Desk Reference. Ed. Anthony S. Vlamis. New York: Macmillan, 1999.

Chapter 20 Job Application Materials
求职材料

Chapter Contents

Chapter 20 In a Nutshell
Analyzing the Situation
Planning the Résumé
Writing the Résumé
Planning a Letter of Application
Ethics and Résumés
Writing a Letter of Application
Globalization and Job Applications
Interviewing
Writing Follow-Up Letters
Focus on Electronic Résumés

Chapter 20
In a Nutshell 概　要

The goal of the *letter of application* and the résumé is to convince someone to offer you a job *interview*.

Basic letter strategies. Relate to the potential employer's needs. Show how you can fill those needs. If, in the job announcement, an employer lists several requirements, your letter should include a paragraph on each. In those paragraphs, present a convincing and memorable detail: "At Iconglow I was in charge of the group that developed the on-line Help screens. Under my direction, we analyzed what topics were needed and which screen design would be most effective."

Write in small chunks, putting the employer's keywords at the beginning of each chunk. Pay close attention to spelling and grammar—mistakes could cost you an interview.

Basic résumé strategies. Design your *résumé* so that key topics jump out. Include sections on

- Your objective (one brief line).
- How to contact you.
- Your education (college only).
- Your work history (most relevant jobs at the top; list job title, employer, relevant duties, and responsibilities).

Most résumés place the major heads at the left margin and indent the appropriate text about one inch.

Basic interview strategies. At the *interview*, you talk to people who have the power to offer you the job. Impress them by knowing about their company and by telling the truth—if you don't know the answer, say so.

This chapter explains the process of producing an effective résumé and letter. You must analyze the situation, plan the contents of the résumé and letter, present each in an appropriate form, and perform effectively at an interview.

Analyzing the Situation 情况分析

To write an effective résumé and letter of application, you must understand your goals, your audience, the field in which you are applying for work, your own strengths, and the needs of your employers.

Understand Your Goals 明白你的目标

Your goals are to get an interview and to provide topics for discussion at that interview. If you present your strengths and experiences convincingly in the letter and résumé, prospective employers will ask to interview you. To be convincing, you must explain what you can do for the reader, showing how your strengths fill the reader's needs.

The letter and résumé also provide topics for discussion at an interview. It is not uncommon for an interviewer to say something like "You say in your résumé that you worked with material requirements planning. Would you explain to us what you did?"

Understand Your Audience 了解你的读者

Your audience could be any of several people in an organization—from the human resources manager to a division manager, one person or a committee. Whoever they are, they will have only a limited amount of time to read your letter and résumé and so will want to see immediately your qualifications stated in a professional manner.

The Reader's Time

Employers read letters and résumés quickly. A manager might have 100 résumés and letters to review. On the initial reading, the manager spends only 30 seconds to 3 minutes on each application, quickly sorting them into "yes" and "no" piles.

Skill Expectations

Managers want to know how the applicant will satisfy the company's needs. They look for evidence of special aptitudes, skills, contributions to jobs, and achievements at the workplace (Harcourt and Krizar). Suppose, for instance, that the manager placed an ad specifying that applicants need "experience in materials resource planning." Applications that show evidence of that experience probably will go into the "yes" pile, but those without evidence will go into the "no" pile.

Professional Expectations

Managers read to see if you write clearly, handle details, and act professionally. Clean, neat documents written in clear, correct English and formatted on high-quality paper demonstrate all three of these skills.

Assess Your Field 评估你的领域

Find out what workers and professionals actually do in your field, so that you can assess your strengths and decide how you may fill an employer's needs. Answer the following questions:

1. What are the basic activities in this field?
2. What skills do I need to perform them?
3. What are the basic working conditions, salary ranges, and long-term outlooks for the areas in which I am interested?

Talk to professionals, visit your college placement office, and use your library. To meet professionals, set up interviews with them, attend career conferences, or join a student chapter or become a student member of a professional organization. Your college's placement service probably has a great deal of career and employer information available.

In your library two helpful books, among many that describe career areas, are the *Dictionary of Occupational Titles (DOT)* and the *Occupational Outlook Handbook (OOH),* both issued by the U.S. Department of Labor. The *DOT* presents brief but comprehensive discussions of positions in industry, listing the job skills that are necessary for these positions. You can use this information to judge the relevance of your own experience and course work when considering a specific job. Here, for instance, is the entry for manufacturing engineer:

> **012.167-042 MANUFACTURING ENGINEER (profess. & kin.)** Plans, directs, and coordinates manufacturing processes in industrial plant: Develops, evaluates, and improves manufacturing methods, utilizing knowledge of product design, materials and parts, fabrication processes, tooling and production equipment capabilities, assembly methods, and quality control standards. Analyzes and plans work force utilization, space requirements, and workflow, and designs layout of equipment and workspace for maximum efficiency [INDUSTRIAL ENGINEER (profess. & kin.) 012.167-030]. Confers with planning and design staff concerning product design and tooling to ensure efficient production methods. Confers with vendors to determine product specifications and arrange for purchase of equipment,

materials, or parts, and evaluates products according to specifications and quality standards. Estimates production times, staffing requirements, and related costs to provide information for management decisions. Confers with management, engineering, and other staff regarding manufacturing capabilities, production schedules, and other considerations to facilitate production processes. Applies statistical methods to estimate future manufacturing requirements and potential.
GOE: 05.01.06 STRENGTH: L GED: R5 M5 L5 SVP: 8 DLU: 89

The *OOH* presents essays on career areas. Besides summarizing necessary job skills, these essays contain information on salary ranges, working conditions, and employment outlook. This type of essay can help you in an interview. For instance, you may be asked, "What is your salary range?" If you know the appropriate figures, you can confidently name a range that is in line with industry standards.

Assess Your Strengths   评估你的强项

To analyze your strengths, review all your work experience (summer, part-time, internship, full-time), your college courses, and your extracurricular activities to determine what activities have provided specific background in your field.

Prepare this analysis carefully. Talk to other people about yourself. List every skill and strength you can think of; don't exclude any experiences because they seem trivial. Seek qualifications that distinguish you from your competitors. Here are some questions (based in part on Harcourt and Krizar) to help you analyze yourself.

1. What work experience have you had that is related to your field? What were your job responsibilities? In what projects were you involved? With what machinery or evaluation procedures did you work? What have your achievements been?

2. What special aptitudes and skills do you have? Do you know advanced testing methods? What are your computer abilities?

3. What special projects have you completed in your major field? List processes, machines, and systems with which you have dealt.

4. What honors and awards have you received? Do you have any special college achievements?

5. What is your grade point average?

6. How have you paid for your college expenses?

7. What was your minor? What sequence of useful courses have you completed? A sequence of three or more courses in, for example, management, writing, psychology, or communication might have given you knowledge or skills that your competitors do not possess.

8. Are you willing to relocate?
9. Are you a member of a professional organization? Are you an officer? What projects have you participated in as a member?
10. Can you communicate in a second language? Many of today's firms are multinational.
11. Do you have military experience? While in the military, did you attend a school that applies to your major field? If so, identify the school.

Assess the Needs of Employers　评估雇主的需求

To promote your strengths, study the needs of your potential employers. At your college's library or placement service, you can find many helpful volumes that describe individual firms. Read annual reports and company brochures, and visit company websites. You can easily discover the names of persons to contact for employment information and details describing the company, as well as its location(s) and the career opportunities, training and development programs, and benefits it offers.

Planning the Résumé　设计简历

Your résumé is a one-page (sometimes two-page) document that summarizes your skills, experiences, and qualifications for a position in your field. Plan it carefully, selecting the most pertinent information and choosing a readable format.

Information to Include in a Résumé　简历需包含的信息

The information to include in a résumé is that which fills the employer's needs. Most employers expect the following information to appear on applicants' résumés (Harcourt and Krizar; Hutchinson and Brefka):

- Personal information: name, address, phone number
- Educational information: degree, name of college, major, date of graduation
- Work history: titles of jobs held, employing companies, dates of employment, duties, a career objective
- Achievements: grade point average, awards and honors, special aptitudes and skills, achievements at work (such as contributions and accomplishments)

Résumé Organization　简历内容的安排

Traditionally, the information required on a résumé has usually been arranged in chronological order, emphasizing job duties. Because employers are accustomed to this order, they know exactly where to find information they need and can focus easily on your positions and accomplishments (Treweek).

The chronological résumé has the following sections:

- Personal data
- Career objective
- Summary (optional)
- Education
- Work experience

Personal Data

The personal data consist of name, address, telephone number (always found at the top of the page), place to contact for credentials, willingness to relocate, and honors and activities (usually found at the bottom of the page). If appropriate add an e-mail address and personal website url.

List your current address and phone number. Tell employers how to acquire credentials and letters of reference. If you have letters in a placement file at your college career services office, give the appropriate address and phone numbers. If you do not have a file, indicate that you can provide names on request.

Federal regulations specify that you do not need to mention your birth date, height, weight, health, or marital status. You may give information on hobbies and interests. They reveal something about you as a person, and they provide topics of conversation at a surprising number of interviews.

Career Objective

The career objective states the type of position you are seeking or what you can bring to the company. A well-written objective reads like this: "Management Consulting Position in Information Systems" or "Position in Research and Development in Microchip Electronics" or "To use my programming, testing, and analysis skills in an information systems position."

Summary

The summary, an optional section, emphasizes essential points for your reader (Parker). In effect, it is a mini-résumé. List key items of professional experience, credentials, one or two accomplishments, and one or two skills. If you don't have room for the summary in the résumé, consider putting it into your accompanying letter.

SUMMARY OF QUALIFICATIONS

Strong operations and client relationship management background with proven expertise in leading an operations team for multimillion-dollar retail organization. Well-developed customer relations skills that build lasting client loyalty. Proven new business development due to excellent prospecting and client rapport building skills. Able to develop processes that increase productivity, profitability, and employee longevity.

Education

The education section includes pertinent information about your degree. List your college or university, the years you attended it, and your major, minor, concentration, and grade point average (if good). If you attended more than one school, present them in reverse chronological order, the most recent at the top. You can also list relevant courses (many employers like to see technical writing in the list), honors and awards, extracurricular activities, and descriptions of practicums, co-ops, and internships. You do not need to include your high school.

EDUCATION

Bachelor of Science, University of Wisconsin–Stout, May 2002.
Major: Food Systems and Technology; Emphasis: Food Science
Minor: Chemistry

Associate of Applied Science Degree, Georgia Military College, Brunswick, Georgia 1995.

ACADEMIC ACCOMPLISHMENTS

Phi Theta Kappa—International Honor Society of the Two Year College Academic National Honor Society

Work Experience

The work experience section includes the positions you have held that are relevant to your field of interest. List your jobs in reverse chronological order—the most recent first. In some cases, you might alter the arrangement to reflect the importance of the experience. For example, if you first held a relevant eight-month internship and then took a job as a dishwasher when you returned to school, list the internship first. List all full-time jobs and relevant part-time jobs—as far back as the summer after your senior year in high school. You do not need to include every part-time job, just the important ones (but be prepared to give complete names and dates).

Each work experience entry should have four items: job title, job description, name of company, and dates of employment. These four items can be arranged in several ways, as the following examples show. However, *the job description is the most important part* of the entry. Describe your duties, the projects you worked on, and the machines and processes you used. Choose the details according to your sense of what the reader needs.

Write the job description in the past tense, using "action" words such as *managed* and *developed*. Try to create pictures in the reader's mind (Parker). Give specifics that he or she can relate to. Arrange the items in the description in order of importance. Put the important skills first. The following example illustrates a common arrangement of the four items in the entry:

PROFESSIONAL EXPERIENCE

Job title / Company details
Sales/Marketing Director, Information Services Group, LLC, Milwaukee, WI
2000–2001

Duties and accomplishments
Established client database that led to strong relationships with key accounts.

Extensive coordination over all advertising including: writing, proofreading, detail organization, layouts, designs, and productions.

Personally responsible for several major accounts, doubling sales revenues for fiscal year 2000.

Developed new accounts due to excellent prospecting and follow-through abilities.

Extensive telemarketing, cold calls, and sales presentations.

Organized, developed, and implemented new employee handbook; responsible for material and design.

Order of Entries on the Page

In the chronological résumé, the top of any section is the most visible position, so you should put the most important information there. Place your name, address, and career objective at the top of the page. In general, the education section comes next, followed by the work section. However, if you have had a relevant internship or full-time experience, put the work section first. Figure 20.1 shows a chronological résumé.

Writing the Résumé   撰写简历

Drafting your résumé includes generating, revising, and finishing it. Experiment with content and format choices. Ask a knowledgeable person to review your drafts for wording and emphasis. Pay close attention to the finishing stage, in which you check consistency of presentation and spelling.

The résumé must be easy to read. Employers are looking for essential information, and they must be able to find it on the first reading. To make that information accessible, use highlight strategies explained in Chapter 6: heads, boldface, bulleting, margins, and white space. Follow these guidelines (and compare them to the sample résumés in this chapter):

- Usually limit the résumé to one page.
- Indicate the main divisions at the far left margins. Usually, boldface heads announce the major sections of the résumé.

Figure 20.1

Sample Résumé

Michelle L. Stewart

2837 Main Street (715) 421-8765
Eau Claire, WI 54701 michstew27@yahoo.com

CAREER OBJECTIVE

To obtain a position in the food industry as a Consumer Scientist.

SUMMARY OF QUALIFICATIONS

Strong operations and client relationship management background with proven expertise in leading an operations team for multimillion-dollar retail organization. Well-developed customer relations skills that build lasting client loyalty. Proven new business development due to excellent prospecting and client rapport building skills. Able to develop processes that increase productivity, profitability, and employee longevity.

EDUCATION

Bachelor of Science Degree, University of Wisconsin—Stout, May 2002
Major: Food Systems and Technology; Emphasis: Food Science
Minor: Chemistry
Associate of Applied Science Degree, Georgia Military College, Brunswick, Georgia 1995.

ACADEMIC ACCOMPLISHMENTS

Phi Theta Kappa—International Honor Society of the Two Year College Academic National Honor Society

PROFESSIONAL EXPERIENCE

Sales/Marketing Director, Information Services Group, LLC, Milwaukee, WI 2000–2001

Established client database that led to strong relationships with key accounts.

Extensive coordination over all advertising including: writing, proofreading, detail organization, layouts, designs, and productions.

Personally responsible for several major accounts, doubling sales revenues for fiscal year 2000.

Developed new accounts due to excellent prospecting and follow-through abilities.

(continued)

Figure 20.1
(continued)

Extensive telemarketing, cold calls, and sales presentations.

Organized, developed, and implemented new employee handbook; responsible for material and design.

Sales Professional, IKON Technology Services, Milwaukee, WI 1999–2000

Responsible for maintaining client relationships with several key business accounts.

Coordinated delivery of products and services to ensure on-time completion of projects.

Operations/Merchandise Manager, Best Buy Co., Inc, Madison, WI 1997–1999

Managed the daily processes of operations team including: development for three-person staff, flow delegation, implementation of new systems, processing of all transactions, and effective cost management.

Managed major departmental merchandising reorganizations according to company standards.

Created new performance standards and assessment tools that ranked employee performance and provided training and employee coaching to help employees meet new goals.

Primarily responsible for scheduling staff of 105+ and maintaining monthly labor budgets based on sales volume/store performance/job functions resulting in improved productivity.

Trained staff on company procedures to increase their ability to provide excellent customer service resulting in an increase in team morale, customer loyalty, and profitability.

Coordinated human resource activities including: hiring, training, performance evaluations, and team development.

Administered employee benefits, compensation, and payroll; mediated employee legal conflict/disputes; and dealt with employee terminations.

Developed new processes to reduce controllable expenses, resulting in an increase in net profit.

RELATED EXPERIENCE

Front End Operations Manager, Sam's Club, Madison, WI 1996–1997

Pharmacy Department Manager, Wal-Mart Corporation, St. Mary's, GA 1992–1996

- Boldface important words such as job titles or names of majors; use underlining sparingly.
- Use bulleted lists, which emphasize individual lines effectively.
- Single-space entries, and double-space above and below. The resulting white space makes the page easier to read.
- Control the margins and type size. Make the left margin 1 inch wide.
- Use 10- or 12-point type.
- Treat items in each section consistently. All the job titles, for example, should be in the same relative space and in the same typeface and size.
- Print résumés on good-quality paper; use black ink on light paper (white or off-white). Avoid brightly colored paper, which has little positive effect on employers and photocopies poorly.
- Consider using a résumé software program. Actually a database, it provides spaces for you to fill with appropriate data and offers several designs for formatting the page.

Planning a Letter of Application 申请信的设计

The goal of sending a letter of application is to be invited to an interview. To write an effective letter of application, understand the employer's needs, which are expressed in an ad or a job description. Planning a specific letter requires you to analyze the ad or description and match the stated requirements with your skills.

Analyze the Employer's Needs 分析雇主的需求

To discover an employer's needs, analyze the ad or analyze typical needs for this kind of position. To analyze an ad, read it for key terms. For instance, a typical ad could read, "Candidates need 1+ years of C++. Communication skills are required. Must have systems analysis skills." The key requirements here are 1+ years of C++, communication skills, and systems analysis.

If you do not have an ad, analyze typical needs for this type of job. A candidate for a manufacturing engineer position could select pertinent items from the list of responsibilities printed in the *Dictionary of Occupational Titles* (see pp. 515–516).

Match Your Capabilities to the Employer's Needs 将你的能力和雇主需求匹配

The whole point of the letter is to show employers that you will satisfy their needs. If they say they need 1+ years of C++, tell them you have it.

As you match needs with capabilities, you will develop a list of items to place in your letter. You need not include them all; discuss the most important or interesting ones.

Ethics and Résumés 撰写简历的注意事项

In writing a résumé, you want to engender confidence in your abilities, and avoid either underselling or overselling your experience. Recruiters are often looking through scores of résumés in search of measurable accomplishments that sound relevant for the position being filled. Using creative words to enhance the sound of an otherwise mundane job may result in your résumé being passed over, as the manager spends extra seconds trying to decipher the hidden meanings. What you say about your experience should be defensible and logical, and can be creative, but not outlandish. The résumé that honestly and straightforwardly presents the candidate's experience with a positive spin has the best chance of being read and landing you an interview (Truesdell). For example, stretching dates of employment to cover a jobless period is lying, and can cost you the offer or get you fired later on. Saying that you "specialized in retail sales and assisted in a 10 percent increase in sales at the store level," when you worked at the local video store and the store saw a 10 percent increase in sales is embellishing, but is not a lie. Claiming that you were store manager when you were not is lying (Trunk).

Résumé padding, telling lies on résumés, is becoming more and more common. Lying about experience or accomplishments on a résumé is risky. Résumé padding may get you a job for the short term if the employer hiring you does not check your résumé carefully, but résumé padding can come back to haunt you later (Callahan). *Inventing experiences, educational degrees, and accomplishments shouldn't be done due to the damage it can cause the writer down the road, even if the writer does not have a moral problem with lying.* False information on your résumé sits like a land mine waiting to explode (Callahan). In the recent past, lies on résumés ruined prestigious and lengthy careers. Companies have fired successful CEOs upon discovering they had misrepresented university credentials (Callahan). When share prices plummet as a result, investors may even sue the CEO for fraud. An otherwise stellar career that may never have needed a made-up degree can be brought to an unceremonious and humiliating end. Being a candidate without a master's degree or with a gap in employment is not out of the ordinary. Being a candidate who got caught stretching dates of employment to cover gaps or inventing a degree that never existed is inexcusable, ruinous, and unethical (Callahan; Truesdell).

Works Cited

Callahan, David. "Résumé Padding." *The Cheating Culture*. 26 Feb. 2004 <www.cheatingculture.com/resumepadding.htm>.

Truesdell, Jason. "Honesty." *Tech.Job.Search*. 26 Feb. 2004 <www.jagaimo.com/jobguide/resume/g-honest.htm>.

Trunk, Penelope. "Resume Writing: Lies v. Honesty." 2 June 2003. *The Brazen Careerist*. 26 Feb. 2004 <www.bankrate.com/smm/news/career/20030602a1.asp?prodtype=advice>.

Writing a Letter of Application   申请信的撰写

A letter of application has three parts: the introductory application, the explanatory body, and the request conclusion. You may organize the letter in one of two ways—by skills or by categories. This section first reviews the parts of a letter of application and then presents the same letter organized by skill and by category.(See Figure 20.2, pp. 516–517.)

Apply in the Introduction   在介绍部分申请

The introductory application should be short. Inform the reader that you are applying for a specific position. If it was advertised, mention where you saw the ad. If someone recommended that you write to the company, mention that person's name (if it is someone the reader knows personally or by name). You may present a brief preview that summarizes your qualifications.

Apply	I am interested in applying for the patient services manager position recently advertised in your Web homepage. I will complete a bachelor's
Tell source	degree in Dietetics in May 2003 from the University of Wisconsin–Stout. The skills I have developed from my academic background support my strong interest in working with your leading food and facility manage-
Qualification preview	ment services. I feel that my career goals and strong beliefs in assisting others to achieve a higher quality of life make me an excellent candidate for this position.

Convince in the Body   在主体部分说服

The *explanatory body* is the heart of the letter. Explain, in terms that relate to the reader, why you are qualified for the job. This section should be one to three paragraphs long. Its goal is to show convincingly that your strengths and skills will meet the reader's needs. Write one paragraph or section for each main requirement.

Base the content of the body on your analysis of the employer's needs and on your ability to satisfy those needs. Usually the requirements are listed in the ad. Show how your skills meet those requirements. If the ad mentioned "experience in software development," list details that illustrate your experience. If you are not responding to an ad, choose details that show that you have the qualifications normally expected of an entry-level candidate.

The key to choosing details is "memorable impact." The details should immediately convince readers that your skill matches their need. Use this guideline: In what terms will they talk about me? Your details, for instance, should show that you are the "development person." If you affect your reader that way, you will be in a positive position.

Globalization and Job Applications 全球化和工作申请

Applying for a job overseas may open the way for an exciting professional and personal adventure. Understanding how to reformat your résumé to fit the needs of your potential employers will make the process faster and easier.

The term *curriculum vitae* (CV) is often used in other countries. A CV is generally the same as a résumé—a document detailing your education and work experience. However, different countries, employers, and cultures call for different areas of information and different levels of detail. Most countries have specific formats that they find acceptable. If you are unsure about which format you should use, ask; or use the standard, reverse-chronological format—put the most recent job highest in the list and work backward. Many countries expect information on résumés and CVs considered unprofessional or illegal in the United States: date of birth, marital status, and nationality ("Résumés").

When applying to a Japanese company, you may submit either a two-page, standard format résumé in Japanese, called a *rirekisho*, or a cover letter and résumé in English. Center your name and contact information at the top of the page and begin your résumé with a summary of your major qualifications. Your next section will be Employment Experience, followed by Education. Finally, you will end your résumé with personal information—date of birth, marital status, and nationality (Thompson).

If you are interested in working and living in the United Kingdom, you will format your résumé a bit differently. Include a cover letter addressed to a specific person. Your résumé will start with your personal information: name, contact information, date of birth, marital status, and nationality. Three major sections follow. The Profile section describes your professional designation, your immediate ambitions, and, in bulleted list form, your relevant skills and work-related achievements. Your Employment History section begins with your current position and then provides the name, location, and focus of the companies you have worked for. In the Education section, list your schools in reverse chronological order and include degrees awarded, additional courses and training, and any special skills (Thompson).

If you do write your résumé in the language of the country to which you are applying, find a native speaker of the language to review it. If it is written in a language other than English, one of your goals is to show that you are familiar with culturally appropriate language. Furthermore, if you e-mail your résumé, keep in mind that the American standard paper size is 8½ by 11 inches, whereas the European A4 standard is 210-297 mm. Be sure to reformat your document in your word processing program for those parameters to ensure that the receiver doesn't lose any of your information.

For further reference, check out these websites:
Goinglobal at <www.goinglobal.com> contains lots of information on applying, interviewing, and working abroad. You can find advice on how you can expect to fit into the culture whether you want to work in Australia, Belgium, or China.

> Jobweb at <www.jobweb.com> is the on-line complement to the *Job Choices* magazine series. It has good, general information on all aspects of your job search, including an international search. It includes sample résumés and CVs and has articles written by professionals.
>
> Monster Workabroad at <http://workabroad.monster.com> includes practical advice on getting a job overseas. You'll find specific job information as well as general information on your country of choice. You can also receive newsletters and chat with other international job hunters.
>
> **Works Cited**
> "Résumés/CVs." Goinglobal.com. 7 Feb. 2004 <www.goinglobal.com/topic/resumes.asp>.
> Thompson, Mary Anne. "Writing Your International Résumé." Jobweb. 31 Jan. 2004 <www.jobweb.com/Resources/Library/International/Writing_Your_185_01.htm>.

Skills Section

Source of skill

As a student, I have learned many cost control methods. The courses Institutional Food Purchasing and Food Beverage Cost Controls have allowed me to become familiar with proper operating techniques, accounting for the monitoring of costs in relation to patient food service. I understand the qualities that a good manager possesses and believe that it is essential to strive to achieve and maintain a high level of patient satisfaction.

Convince

I have also had experience in food safety. Through the educational aspects of Microbiology and Food Science, I've developed a strong background in microorganisms and deciphering what control methods to use that will ensure the quality of the organization and its services. I have acquired a solid background in relation to Hazard Analysis Critical Control Point (HACCP) practices and methods.

Use of skill
Skill activities

I am knowledgeable about menu delivery systems and the proper procedures that must be followed to assure compliance with regulations. After completing my JACHO certification, I am aware that this organization sets the standards by which health care quality is measured. I will thus work to continuously improve the safety and quality of care provided to the public through the health care accreditation standards of JACHO.

Request an Interview 请求面试

In the final section, ask for an interview and explain how you can be reached. The best method is to ask, "Could I meet with you to discuss this position?" Also explain when you are available. If you need two days' notice, say so. If you can't possibly get free on a Monday, mention that. Most employers will try to

Figure 20.2

Response to Ad for Patient Services Manager

1427 Crestview Street
Menomonie, WI 54751

November 5, 2006

Johnson-United Hospital
2715 Jamestown Avenue
Gaithersburg, Maryland 20878

Subject: Patient Services Manager Position

> **Clear application**
> Use of key words at the beginning of the paragraph.

I am interested in applying for the patient services manager position recently advertised in your Web homepage. I will complete a bachelor's degree in Dietetics in May 2007 from the University of Wisconsin–Stout. The skills I have developed from my academic background support my strong interest in working with your leading food and facility management services. I feel that my career goals and strong beliefs in assisting others to achieve a higher quality of life make me an excellent candidate for this position.

> **Details of work experience and classes used to create interest.**

As a student, I have learned many cost control methods. The courses Institutional Food Purchasing and Food Beverage Cost Controls have allowed me to become familiar with proper operating techniques, accounting for the monitoring of costs in relation to patient food service. I understand the qualities that a good manager possesses and believe that it is essential to strive to achieve and maintain a high level of patient satisfaction.

> **Use of key words at the beginning of the paragraph.**

I have also had experience in food safety. Through the educational aspects of Microbiology and Food Science, I've developed a strong background in microorganisms and deciphering what control methods to use that will ensure the quality of the organization and its services. I have acquired a solid background in relation to Hazard Analysis Critical Control Point (HACCP) practices and methods.

I am knowledgeable about menu delivery systems and the proper procedures that must be followed to assure compliance with regulations. After completing my JACHO certification, I am aware that this organization sets the standards by which health care quality is measured. I will thus work to continuously improve the safety and quality of care provided to the public through the health care accreditation standards of JACHO.

> Asks for interview.
>
> I would welcome the opportunity to meet with you and discuss my qualifications for the position. I have enclosed a copy of my résumé. If you have any questions or would like to talk with me, I can be reached by phone at (715) 555-1224 or e-mail at michshan@uw.edu. Thank you for considering me for this position. I look forward to hearing from you soon.
>
> Sincerely,
>
> *Shannon M. Michaelis*
>
> Shannon M. Michaelis, R.D.
>
> Enclosure: résumé

work around such restrictions. If no one is at your house or dorm in the morning to answer the phone, tell the reader to call in the afternoon. A busy employer would rather know that than waste time listening to a phone ring. Thank your reader for his or her time and consideration. Readers appreciate the gesture; it is courteous and it indicates that you understand that the reader has to make an effort to fulfill your request.

Request

How to contact writer

Thank you

I would welcome the opportunity to meet with you and discuss my qualifications for the position. I have enclosed a copy of my résumé. If you have any questions or would like to talk with me, I can be reached by phone at (715) 555-1224 or e-mail at michshan@uw.edu. Thank you for considering me for this position. I look forward to hearing from you soon.

Select a Format   选择一种格式

To make a professional impression, follow these guidelines:

- Type the letter on 8½-by-11-inch paper.
- Use white, 20-pound, 100 percent cotton-rag paper.
- Use black ink.
- Use block or modified block format explained in Chapter 19.
- Sign your name in black or blue ink.
- Proofread the letter carefully. Grammar and spelling mistakes are irritating at best; at worst, they are cause for instant rejection.
- Mail the letter, folded twice, in a business envelope.

Examples 20.1–20.3 (pp. 522–525) show three application letters organized by skills. Examples 20.4 and 20.5 on pages 525–526 show two résumé styles.

Interviewing 面　试

The employment interview is the method employers use to decide whether to offer a candidate a position. Usually the candidate talks to one or more people (either singly or in groups) who have the authority to offer a position. To interview successfully, you need to prepare well, use social tact, perform well, ask questions, and understand the job offer (Stewart and Cash).

Prepare Well 做好准备

To prepare well, investigate the company and analyze how you can contribute to it (Spinks and Wells). To investigate the company, read company literature, annual reports, descriptions in *Moody's*, items from *Facts on File*, *F&S Index*, *Wall Street Journal Index*, or *Corporate Report Fact Bank*, and the company's website. After you have analyzed the company, assess what you have to offer. Answer these questions:

- What contributions can you make to the company?
- How do your specific skills and strengths fit into its activities or philosophy?
- How can you further your career goals with this company?

Use Social Tact 运用社交技巧

To use social tact means to behave professionally and in an appropriate manner. Acting too lightly or too intensely are both incorrect. First impressions are extremely important; many interviewers make up their minds early in the interview. Follow a few common sense guidelines:

- Shake hands firmly.
- Dress professionally, as you would on the job.
- Arrive on time.
- Use proper grammar and enunciation.
- Watch your body language. For instance, sit appropriately; don't lounge or slouch in your chair.
- Find out and use the interviewers' names.

Perform Well 好好表现

Performing well in the interview means to answer the questions directly and clearly. Interviewers want to know about your skills. Be willing to talk about yourself and your achievements; if you respond honestly to questions, your answers will not seem like bragging. For a successful interview, follow these guidelines:

- Be yourself. Getting a job based on a false impression usually ends badly.
- Answer the question asked.

- Be honest. If you don't know the answer, say so.
- If you don't understand a question, ask the interviewer to repeat or clarify it.
- In your answers, include facts about your experience to show how you will fit into the company.

Ask Questions   提出问题

You have the right to ask questions at an interview. Make sure you have addressed all pertinent issues (Spinks and Wells). If no one has explained the following items to you, ask about them:

- Methods of on-the-job training
- Your job responsibilities
- Types of support available—from secretarial to facilities to pursuit of more education
- Possibility and probability of promotion
- Policies about relocating, including whether you get a promotion when you relocate and whether refusing to relocate will hurt your chances for promotion
- Salary and fringe benefits—at least a salary range, whether you receive medical benefits, and who pays for them

Understand the Offer   了解录用职位

Usually a company will offer the position—with a salary and starting date—either at the end of the interview or within a few days. You have the right to request a reasonable amount of time to consider the offer. If you get another offer from a second company at a higher salary, you have the right to inform the first company and to ask whether they can meet that salary. Usually you accept the offer verbally and sign a contract within a few days. This is a pleasant moment.

Writing Follow-Up Letters   撰写跟进信函

After an interview with a particularly appealing firm, you can take one more step to distinguish yourself from the competition. Write a follow-up letter. It takes only a few minutes to thank the interviewer and express your continued interest in the job.

> Thank you for the interview yesterday. Our discussion of Ernst and Young's growing MIS Division was very informative, and I am eager to contribute to your team.
> I look forward to hearing from you.

Worksheet for Preparing a Résumé

准备简历的工作表

- ☐ Write out your career objective; use a job title.
- ☐ List all the postsecondary schools you have attended.
- ☐ List your major and any minors or submajors.
- ☐ List your GPA if it is strong.
- ☐ Complete this form. Select only relevant courses or experiences.

College Courses	Skills Learned	Projects Completed

- ☐ List extracurricular activities, including offices held and duties.
- ☐ Complete this form for all co-ops, internships, and relevant employment.

Job Title	Company	Dates	Duties	Achievements

- ☐ List your name, phone number, current address, and permanent address if it is different. If appropriate, add e-mail address and personal website url.
- ☐ Review standard résumé format. See pages 521–522.
- ☐ Choose a layout design.

Worksheet for Writing a Letter of Application

撰写申请信的工作表

- ☐ State the job for which you are applying.
- ☐ State where you found out about the job.
- ☐ Complete this form:

Employer Need (such as "program in C++")	*Proof That You Fill the Need* (show yourself in action: "developed two C++ programs to test widget quality")

- ☐ Select a format; the block format is suitable.

- [ ] Write compelling paragraphs:
  An introduction to announce that you are an applicant
  A body paragraph for each need, matching your capabilities to the need
  Select details that cause "measurable impact"—ones that cause readers to remember you because you can fill their needs
  A conclusion that asks for an interview
- [ ] Purchase good-quality paper and envelopes, and get a new cartridge for your printer if you produce the letter yourself.

Worksheet for Evaluating a Letter of Application 评估申请信的工作表

Answer these questions about your letter or a peer's:
  a. Are the inside address and date handled correctly? Are all words spelled out?
  b. Do the salutation and inside address name the same person?
  c. Is there a colon after the salutation?
  d. Does the writer clearly apply for a position in paragraph 1?
  e. Does each paragraph deal with an employer need and contain an "impact detail"?
  f. Does the closing paragraph ask for an interview? in an appropriate tone?
  g. Would you ask this person for an interview? Why or why not?

Examples 例子

The following examples illustrate ways in which applicants can show how their skills meet the employers' needs.

Example 20.1

Letter Organized by Skills

Slightly modified block format uses indented paragraphs to save space.

Specific application

Each body paragraph has in first line a key word or phrase from the ad.

Brief narrative demonstrates skills.

Two examples illustrate skills.

Narrative illustrates skills.

Request for contact

1503 West Second Street
Menomonie, WI 54751

ABC Global Services
1014 Michigan Avenue
Chicago, IL 60605

November 3, 2007

SUBJECT: I/T Specialist—Programmer Position

    I would like to apply for the I/T Specialist—Programmer Position for ABC Global Services in Chicago. I learned of this position through the University of Wisconsin–Stout Placement and Co-op Office. Because of my past co-op experiences and educational background, I feel I am an ideal candidate for this position.

    I am very familiar with all the steps of the application life cycle and processes involved in each of these steps. In my Software Engineering course, I and four other students developed a Math Bowl program that is used at the annual Applied Math Conference. We analyzed the problem through an analysis document, created a design document, coded the Math Bowl program from the design document, and maintained the software. In my past co-op with IBM, I also was involved in requirements planning, design reviews, coding, testing, and maintenance for my team's projects.

    I have experience with low-level languages such as C++ and Assembler Language through my work experience and course study. In my Computer Organization class, I developed a CPU simulator in C++, which manipulated the Assembler Language. During my Unisys co-op in the Compiler Products department, I developed test programs in C, which manipulated the low-level compiler code.

    I have strong customer relations and communication skills. Every day I deal with students and faculty at my job as a Lab Assistant at the Campus Computer Lab. It is my job to help them learn the available software and troubleshoot user's problems.

    Enclosed is my résumé for your consideration. I am interested in talking with you in person about this position and a possible interview. Please call me at (715) 233-3341 at your convenience. Thank you for your consideration.

Sincerely,

Heather Miller

Heather Miller

enc: résumé

Example 20.2

Letter Organized by Skills

Standard block format

Dana Runge
461-19th Avenue West Apt. 1
Menomonie, WI 54751

October 29, 2006

Rachel Rizzuto
Campus Relations Specialist
Target Headquarters
1000 Nicollet Mall
Minneapolis, MN 55403

Dear Ms. Rizzuto:

Specific application

I would like to apply for the Business Analyst position registered at the University of Wisconsin–Stout Placement and Co-op Office. I believe that my past retail experience and education make me an ideal candidate for the position.

Each body paragraph has in first line a key word or phrase from the ad.

I have excellent analytical skills that were developed further from my education and work experience. In my Managerial Accounting course, my group researched the Pepsi Corporation's performance through their 2005 Annual Report. We applied that research by converting numbers and statistics into financial ratios and analysis. We then compared that information to industry norms and made conclusions. Our results were reported to the class as a PowerPoint presentation.

Narrative demonstrates skills.

I have great experience with planning and organizing. As the Events Coordinator for the Stout Retail Association, I researched, planned, and implemented a three-day trip to Chicago. I organized everything, from the hotel and transportation to the tours and activities. I had to make several contacts and reservations, as well as create a detailed time and activity agenda. I was responsible for the schedule of sixty members.

Narrative demonstrates skills.

I demonstrated clear and effective communication for a group country report in my Environmental Science class. I led the group in outlining what each member was responsible for doing, as well as the time line for completion dates. We set up meetings and exchanged communication channels, such as phone numbers and e-mail addresses. Our group had a clear understanding of what each needed to do as an individual, as well as in a group. We then compiled our information into a class presentation.

Request for contact

A copy of my résumé is enclosed for your review. I am available for an interview at your convenience. If you have any questions, please feel free to call

(continued)

Example 20.2 (continued)

(715-237-1421) or e-mail me (rungdan@uws.edu). Thank you for your time and consideration. I look forward to your reply.

Sincerely,

Dana Runge

Dana Runge

Enclosure: résumé

Example 20.3

Letter Organized by Skills

Standard block format

421 Main Street North
Apartment 12
Menomonie, WI 54751

November 5, 2006

Kelly Services
370 Wabasha Street North
St. Paul, MN 55102-1306

ATTENTION: Human Resources Department

SUBJECT: KSW/260A/SDA

Specific application

I would like to apply for the Human Resource Assistant Position for Ecolab in St. Paul. I learned of this position from the Monster.com website on the Internet. I will graduate in August 2007 from the University of Wisconsin–Stout with a Bachelor of Science degree in Service Management.

First line of each body paragraph contains key word or phrase from the ad.

I have obtained strong organizational and process management skills as an office assistant for the University of Wisconsin–Stout Dining Services. As an aid to the Director, Assistant Director, and Accounts Payable Specialist, I have gained the ability to multitask and maintain excellent communication skills.

Examples demonstrate skills.

My day-to-day experience with Microsoft Office Suite involves creating and maintaining reports in Excel, planning and preparing presentations in PowerPoint, and designing various documents in Word.

I have extensive experience in preparing and maintaining presentation and other collateral recruiting materials for the annual Resident Advisor Resource

Examples

Examples demonstrate skills.	Fair and the Employee Orientations for Dining Services. I have created informational documents, designed motivational brochures, and prepared electronic presentations in order to enhance employees' and students' views of Dining's available services. By explaining the services we offer and recruiting students for employment at these events, I have developed excellent interpersonal and communication skills.
Request for interview	A copy of my résumé is enclosed for your consideration. Through my work experience and educational background, I am confident that I can be an asset to your company. Could I meet with you at your convenience to discuss my qualifications for this position? You may contact me during the evening at (715) 237-1142. Thank you for your time and consideration. I look forward to hearing from you.

Sincerely,

Cara Robida

Cara Robida

Enclosure: résumé |

Example 20.4

Résumé for an Internship

Rodney C. Dukes
4807 Oknol Street
Colfax, WI 54703
(715) 477-0012
dukrod@uw.edu

Brief, specific objective	**OBJECTIVE**	To obtain an Internship as Training Document Writer
Educational history, most recent listed at top	**EDUCATION**	University of Wisconsin–Stout (Recipient—Baldrige Award 2001), Menomonie, Wisconsin, Technical Communications Major, Junior, Applied Field—Biomedical Engineering, GPA 3.3, Financed 75% of Education
Education appears first because it contains most relevant skills.		Chicago Police Academy, Chicago Illinois, Officer Training Program
May 1991 State-Certified Peace Officer

(continued)

Example 20.4
(continued)

Courses chosen to demonstrate skills needed for position of training

Experience history, most recent job listed first

Consistent presentation of each job

Bulleted list begins with action verbs.

RELATED COURSES	Course Names and Titles • TRHRD-360—Training Systems in Business and Industry • GCM-141—Graphic Communications and Electronic Publishing • ENGL-415—Technical Writing • ENGL-247—Critical Writing • ENGL-207—Writing for the Media • PSYC-379—Public Relations • SPCOM-236—Listening
EXPERIENCE	**Technical Writer** (June 2003–August 2003), Luther Hospital, Eau Claire, Wisconsin • Researched current operational manuals • Developed specifications for manual • Communicated with superiors on a regular basis • Tested design samples and submitted prototypes for review • Evaluated the effectiveness of the tutorial • Created ACLS Manikin tutorial for the CPR Instructor training **Security Officer,** Luther Hospital, Eau Claire, WI (Jan. 2001–Present) • Employee, patient, and patron safety • Monitor and transport Behavioral Health patients • Secure Helipad for MAYO 2 • Patrol of hospital and property **Drug Enforcement Agent,** Ho Chunk Nation, Black River Falls, WI • (Oct. 1999–Sept. 2000) • Enforced the Drug and Alcohol Policies • Conducted and supervised urinalysis testing and training of employees • Submitted reports to the Compliance Director and Justice Department
STRENGTHS	**Computer Skills,** Microsoft Word, Excel, FrontPage, PowerPoint
REFERENCES	Available upon request.

Example 20.5

Résumé Emphasizing Job Experience of Working Professional

Source: Reprinted by permission of Amy Reid.

Objective indicating skills she can bring to position

Experience history listed first because it is most relevant to objective.

Most recent job at top of section

Longer paragraphs typical of experienced professionals who have many skills

---

Amy Reid
N687 W28471 Harness Avenue
Germantown, WI 53022
262-555-3801
reids@graphdes.com

OBJECTIVE To acquire a position that utilizes my copywriting, editing, and proofing skills in a print- or Web-based graphic design, advertising, or publishing environment.

EXPERIENCE **GS Design, Inc.—Milwaukee, Wisconsin**

Project Manager, November 1996 to present
Coordinate production of *Hog Tales*® magazine—a 48-page bimonthly publication for members of the Harley Owners Group. Responsibilities include meeting with the editor, who works for Harley-Davidson Motor Company: prepping the photographs and provided copy; meeting with in-house copywriters to have them write new content or edit the provided; edit the copywriters' copy, and prep it for the designers and layout staff; do simple layouts; review and proof all layouts; coordinate the layouts and original materials to be turned over to the editor for review; coordinate multiple rounds of revisions and proof them; coordinate final production of all pages; work closely with pre-press and the printer; review and final proof the color proofs from pre-press; attend the press checks at Perry-Judd's, Inc. in Baraboo; and archive all the proofs and materials upon completion of the edition.

Proofreader, December 1988 to present
Review all in-house projects and proposals for accurate grammar, punctuation, spelling, and content prior to being printed or posted on the Web. Edit copy as needed, or critique and meet with copywriters when more in-depth editing is required.

Production Manager, November 1996 to April 1999
Scheduled and assigned projects with in-house copywriters, designers, and production staff, and monitored progress to meet deadlines throughout process to completion. Met with clients and vendors to coordinate production schedules and kept tasks on track through project delivery. Coordinated bilingual and trilingual translations for projects as required.

(continued)

Example 20.5 (continued)

Graphic Designer, December 1988 to November 1996
Managed projects from concept through final print production. Responsibilities included designing, critiquing, typesetting, illustrating, and coordinating photography.

Econoprint—Milwaukee, Wisconsin
Desktop Publisher, May 1988 to September 1988
Met with customers, typeset projects per specs, and pasted-up galley copy and graphics. Occasional tasks included bindery work and customer service.

Education placed lower in résumé because job skills are more important for an experienced professional.

EDUCATION AND SKILLS

University of Wisconsin–Stout, Menomonie, Wisconsin
Bachelor of Science, May 1988
Major: Art
Concentration: Graphic Design
Minor: Technical Writing

American Management Association, Keye Productivity Center
"How To Be A Better Proofreader," September 1997

Proficient in Macintosh-based Quark XPress and Microsoft Word; limited working knowledge of Adobe Photoshop, Adobe Illustrator, Microsoft Excel, and Clients & Profits.

Professional honors

HONORS

ADDY Award, Milwaukee Ad Club

Collateral Material—Invitation (design and production of personal wedding invitation and collateral), March 2001

Featured in article in *Publishing & Production Executive*, April 2000

Professional coworkers or managers

REFERENCES

Jeff Prochnow
GS Design, Inc.
414-555-9821
proch@graphdes.com

Marc Tebon
GS Design, Inc.
414-555-8436
Tebon@graphdes.com

Additional references available upon request.

Exercises 练 习

▶ Group

1. Your instructor will arrange you in groups of two to four by major. Each person should photocopy relevant material from one source in the library. Include at least the *Dictionary of Occupational Titles* and the *Occupational Outlook Handbook*. In class, make a composite list of basic requirements in your type of career. Use that list as a basis for completing the Writing Assignments that follow.

▶ You Analyze

2. Analyze one of the letters in the Sample Documents section of the Instructor's Resource Manual (Examples 46–51). Comment on format and effectiveness of tone, detail, and organization.

3. Analyze this letter. It responded to an ad for a consumer scientist. The general requirements included abilities to evaluate and analyze new products; to write reports; and to assist with training, test kitchen organization, cooking demonstrations, and developing recipes and guides.

> 2837 Main Street
> Eau Claire, WI 54701
>
> April 9, 2006
>
> Wolf Appliance Company, LLC
> Attention: Human Resources
> P.O. Box 44848
> Fitchburg, Wisconsin 53719
>
> Subject: Consumer Scientist Position
>
> I am extremely interested in becoming a part of Wolf Appliance Company as a Consumer Scientist. In May 2006, I will be graduating from the University of Wisconsin—Stout with a Bachelor of Science degree in Food Systems and Technology, with a concentration in Food Science. I am also knowledgeable in the development and design of marketing tools for new products.
>
> My background includes extensive experience with analyzing data, evaluating results, and developing reports. Through course work, I have had to collect, analyze, and develop scientific reports in various formats utilizing MS Office, adapting the report to the specific situation. As an

operations manager, I also had the responsibility of gathering data, reporting the information, and explaining variances to the Corporate Office for profit and loss statements.

I developed excellent organizational, training, and evaluating techniques as an operations manager for a $40-million-a-year business. With an average staff of 105 employees, I was responsible for ensuring the training and evaluations were done promptly and accurately.

As a merchandise manager, I was responsible for managing several re-merchandising projects simultaneously. The projects I was responsible for were successful because of my organization and leadership abilities. The enclosed résumé outlines my credentials and accomplishments in further detail.

If you are seeking a Consumer Scientist who is highly self-motivated and is a definite team player wanting to be a part of a successful team, then please consider what I have to offer. I would be happy to have a preliminary discussion with you or member of your committee. You can reach me at (715) 421-8765. I look forward to talking with you and exploring this opportunity further.

Sincerely,

Michelle Stewart

4. Analyze an ad and yourself by filling out the third point in the Worksheet for Writing a Letter of Application (pp. 520–521).
5. Analyze yourself by using the fifth and seventh points in the Worksheet for Preparing a Résumé (p. 520).
6. After completing Writing Assignment 2, read another person's letter. Ask these questions: What do you like about this letter? What do you dislike about this letter? How would you change what you dislike?
7. After completing Writing Assignment 1, read the ad and résumé of a classmate. Read the ad closely to determine the employer's needs. Read the résumé swiftly—in a minute or less. Tell the author whether he or she has the required qualifications. Then switch résumés and repeat. This exercise should either convince you that your résumé is good or highlight areas that you need to revise.

▶ You Revise

8. Revise this rough draft.

1221 Lake Avenue
Menomonie WI 54751

March 21, 2006

Human Resources
Polaris Industries Inc.
301 5th Avenue SW
Roseau MN 54826

Subject: Inquiring about a summer co-op in the mechanical design area.

My name is Josh Buhr and I am a junior at UW—Stout majoring in Mechanical Design. I would like this co-op to learn and grow in my field.

Working with your company as a design engineer, I would be able to fulfill many of the requirements that you have listed in your ad. I am able to design and lay out drawings on AutoCAD in 3-D so I can easily verify that there is freedom of movement between the parts. With AutoCAD 14 I can even animate the object to see even clearer the movement between parts.

If I find a problem with one of the designs I will be able to talk to the people necessary and bring up the topic in a productive manor. The course at Stout "discussion," has taught me how to work in groups and even how to seat people to get the most out of everyone's mind, in a positive atmosphere.

I also need to mention that the AutoCAD experience at Stout has given me many needed skills for design. In the second semester of AutoCAD, I learned and used geometric tolerancing on a complete assembly and layout of a two cycle engine. This engine was fully dimensioned to clearance fits and I even made the piston and a few other parts animated to see that everything was in a freedom of movement.

If you like the qualifications that I have listed above please feel free to call me at (715) 235-4037 to set up an interview. I would be more that happy to meet with you. I have wanted to work with your company for several years after I bought my 95 500; and was never passed since.

Sincerely,

Josh Buhr

9. Revise this rough draft.

871 17th Avenue East
Menomonie, WI 54751
February 12, 2005

Parker Hannifin Corporation
Personnel Department
2445 South 25th Avenue
Broadway, IL 60513

Dear Personnel Department:

I wrote to apply for the entry level Plant Engineering position that you advertised in the Minneapolis Star Tribune January 27, 2005.

I will graduate from the University of Wisconsin—Stout in December with a Bachelor of Science degree in Industrial Technology with a concentration in Plant Engineering.

I have been in charge of projects dealing with capital equipment justification and plant layout while on my co-op with Kolbe and Kolbe Millwork, Company. Some specific work that I completed include: installation of a portable blower system and light design of jigs, conveyor beds and machines. I worked in the machine shop my first month there and have a working knowledge of equipment and procedures in that environment.

I am a self-motivated individual who prides in excelling in everything I take on. This quality is reflected in my résumé through my increased job responsibilities topping with my co-op "experience" and my 3.5 cumulative grade point average.

I would appreciate an opportunity to interview with you. Please contact me at the above address or call me at (715) 471-1627 after 2:00 p.m. on weekdays, or I can return your call. Thank you for your time and consideration. I look forward to hearing from you.

Sincerely,

Keith Munson

▶ You Create

10. Create a work experience résumé entry (pp. 527–528) for one job you have held. Select an arrangement for the four elements. Select details based on the kind of position you want to apply for. Alternate: Create a second version of the entry but focus one version on applying for a technical position and one version on applying for a managerial position.
11. Write a paragraph that explains a career skill you possess.

Writing Assignments 写作任务

1. Using the worksheet on page 520 as a guide, write your résumé following one of the two formats described in this chapter.
2. Find an ad for a position in your field of interest. Use newspaper Help Wanted ads or a listing from your school's placement service. On the basis of the ad, decide which of your skills and experiences you should discuss to convince the firm that you are the person for the job. Then, using the worksheet on pages 532–533 as a guide, write a letter to apply for the job.
3. Write a learning report for the writing assignment you just completed. See Chapter 5, Assignment 7, page 133, for details of the assignment.

Web Exercise 网络练习

Visit at least two websites at which career positions are advertised relative to your expertise. Do one or more of the following, depending on your instructor's directions:
   a. Apply for a position. Print a copy of your application before you send it. Write a brief report explaining the ease of using the site. Include comments about any response that you receive.
   b. Analyze the types of positions offered. Is it worth your time and energy to use a site like this? Present your conclusions in a memo or an oral report, as your instructor designates. Print copies of relevant screens to use as visual aids to support your conclusions.
   c. As part of a group of three or four, combine your research in part b into a large report in which you explain to your class or to a professional meeting the wide range of opportunities available to the job seeker.

Works Cited 引用的作品

Dictionary of Occupational Titles. 4th ed. Rev. Washington, DC: U.S. Dept. of Labor, 1991. On-line version available: <www.oalj.dol.gov/libdot.htm>.

Harcourt, Jules, and A. C. "Buddy" Krizar. "A Comparison of Résumé Content Preferences of Fortune 500 Personnel Administrators and Business Communication Instructors." *Journal of Business Communications* 26.2 (1989): 177–190.

Hutchinson, Kevin L., and Diane S. Brefka. "Personnel Administrators' Preferences for Résumé Content: Ten Years After." *Business Communication Quarterly* 60.2 (1997): 67–75.

Parker, Yana. *The Résumé Catalog: 200 Damn Good Examples.* Berkeley, CA: Ten Speed Press, 1996.

Spinks, Nelda, and Barron Wells. "Employment Interviews: Trends in the Fortune 500 Companies—1980–1988." *The Bulletin of the Association for Business Communications* 51.4 (1988): 15–21.

Stewart, Charles J., and William B. Cash, Jr. *Interviewing Principles and Practices* 8th ed. Dubuque, IA: Brown, 1997.

Treweek, David John. "Designing the Technical Communication Résumé." *Technical Communications* 38.2 (1991): 257–260.

Focus on 关注电子简历
Electronic Résumés

Electronic résumés are changing the job search. The candidate still submits a résumé, and the employer still reads it, but the "electronic way" has a key difference—technology intervenes to do much of the initial sorting. As a result, "keyword strategies" are very important. This section explains briefly how the sorting works, keyword strategies, and on-line, scannable, and ASCII résumés.

How the Sorting Works
Using one of the methods explained below, the candidate submits a résumé that, because it is electronic, is put into a searchable database. When an employer wants to find candidates to interview, he or she searches the database with a software program that seeks those keywords that the employer says are important. For example, the employer might want someone who can design websites and who knows Dreamweaver and HTML programming. Every time the search program finds a résumé with those words in it, it pulls the résumé into an electronic "yes" pile, which the human can then read.

Gonyea and Gonyea explain the process this way: "If the computer finds the same word or words [that describe the candidate the company is attempting to find] anywhere in your résumé, it considers your résumé to be a match, and will then present your résumé, along with others that are also considered to be a match, to the person doing the searching" (62).

Thus, your use of effective keywords is the key to filling out such a form. As Gonyea and Gonyea say, "To ensure that your résumé will be found, it is imperative that you include as many of the appropriate search words as are likely to be used by employers and recruiters who are looking for someone with your qualifications" (62).

Keyword Strategies
Keywords require a radical change in presenting your résumé. Your odds of being one of the "hits" in the search are increased by including a lot of keywords in your résumé. In addition to using keywords as you describe yourself in the education and work history sections of your résumé, you should also include a keyword section right in your résumé. Some of the major on-line résumé services, such as Monster.com, require you to add one.

Put the keyword section either first or last in your résumé, or in the box supplied by the résumé service. Use words that explain skills or list aspects of a job. The list should include mostly nouns of the terms that an employer would use to determine if you could fill his or her need—job titles, specific job duties, specific machines or software programs, degrees, major, and subjective skills, such as communication abilities. You can include synonyms; for instance, in the list below, Web design and DreamWeaver are fairly close in meaning, because you use one to do the other, but including both increases your chances of the scanner's choosing your résumé.

A short list might look like this:

> C++, software engineering, HTML, programmer, needs analysis, client interview, team, Web design, Photoshop, AuthorIT, design requirements.

Remember, the more "hits" the reading software makes in this list, the more likely that your résumé will be sent on to the appropriate department.

On-Line Résumés/Job Searches
The Web has dramatically changed the methods of advertising jobs and responding to advertisements. Job-posting sites allow employers to post employment opportunities; résumé-posting sites allow candidates to post their information. The exact way in which sites work varies, but all of them work in one of two ways. On job-posting sites, like America's Job Bank, employers post ads, listing job duties and candidate qualifications, and candidates respond to those ads. On résumé-posting sites, like

(continued)

(continued)

Monster.com, candidates post résumés in Web-based databases, and employers search them for viable applicants.

You have two options. You can begin to read the "Web want ads," and you can post your résumé.

"Web Want Ads" are posted at the job-posting site. For instance, America's Job Bank <www.ajb.dni.us> lists job notices posted by state employment offices, and Internet Career Connection: Help Wanted-USA <http://iccweb.com/HelpWantedUSA/hwusa.asp> posts ads for companies around the world in all lines of work. You simply access the site and begin to read. In addition, many of the résumé-posting services have a want ad site. For instance, Monster.com <www.monster.com> has an extensive listing of jobs in all categories. In all of these sites, job seekers can search by city, by job type, by level of authority (entry level, manager, executive). Candidates can search free of charge, but companies pay the sites to post the ads.

Post Your Résumé

Many sites provide this service; usually, it is free. Each site has you create your résumé at the site. You open an account, then fill in the form that the site presents to you. For instance, you will be asked for personal information (e.g., name and address) and also such typical items as job objective, work experience, desired job, desired salary, and special skills. Usually, filling out the form takes about 30 minutes. The site creates a standard-looking format (like the ones discussed in Chapter 19), which is sent to prospective employers when they ask for it.

Scannable Résumés

Many companies use optical character recognition (OCR) software (McNair; Quible) to scan résumés. First, paper résumés are scanned, turning them into ASCII files, which are entered into a database. Second, when an opening arises, the human resources department searches the database for keywords.

Those résumés that contain the most keywords are forwarded to the people who will decide whom to interview. This development means that job seekers must now be able to write résumés that are scannable and that effectively use keywords.

Scannable résumés are less sophisticated looking than traditional ones, because scanners simply cannot render traditional résumés correctly. These documents contain all the same sections as traditional résumés but present them differently:

- Use one column. Many scanners scramble two-column text. Start all heads and text at the same left-hand margin.

- Use 10- to 14-point fonts. For "fine" fonts like Times and Palatino, use 11 to 12 points; for "thick" fonts like New Century Schoolbook, use 10 or 11 points. For heads, use 12 to 14 points.

- Use the same font throughout the document.

- Place your name and address at the top of the page, centered. If you include two addresses (campus and home), place them under each other.

- Avoid italics, underlining, and vertical lines.

- Do not fold your résumé. Mail it in an envelope that will hold the 8½-by-11-inch page.

ASCII Résumés

Often companies ask you to send your résumé by e-mail. The best way to do so is to send the résumé as an ASCII file, one that contains only letters, numbers, and a few punctuation marks but does not contain formatting such devices as boldfacing and italics (Skarzenski).

Like scannable résumés, ASCII résumés maintain all the traditional sections; you just present them so that they will interact smoothly with whatever software program is receiving them.

The key items to be aware of are:

- Keep the line length to fewer than 65 characters. Some software systems have difficulty with longer lines.

- Use spaces, not tabs. Some software programs misinterpret tabs.

- Send the file to the receiver in two ways. You can send a file as part of an e-mail message or as an attachment to an e-mail message. Some programs can read the message both ways, some only one way. If the recipient's program does not have the capabilities, it will not be able to read your message.

To practice sending an ASCII file with your e-mail program, send yourself and a friend your résumé. You and the friend should be able to print out the résumé easily.

Works Consulted

Besson, Taunee. *Résumés*. 3rd ed. New York: Wiley, 1999.

Gonyea, James C., and Wayne M. Gonyea, *Electronic Résumés: A Complete Guide to Putting Your Résumé On-Line*. New York: McGraw-Hill, 1996.

McNair, Catherine. "New Technologies and Your Résumé." *intercom* 44.5 (1997): 65–75.

Quible, Zane K. "Electronic Résumés: Their Time Is Coming." *Business Communication Quarterly* 58.3 (1995): 5–9.

Skarzenski, Emily. "Tips for Creating ASCII and HTML Résumés." *intercom* 43.6 (1996): 17–18.

Yate, Martin. *Résumés That Knock 'Em Dead*. Holbrook, MA: Adams Media, 1998.

Appendix A: Brief Handbook for Technical Writers
专业文档撰写简要手册

Appendix Contents
Problems with Sentence Construction
Punctuation
Abbreviations, Capitalization, and Numbers

This appendix presents the basic rules of grammar and punctuation. It contains sections on problems with sentence construction, agreement of subjects and verbs, agreement of pronouns with their antecedents, punctuation, abbreviations, capitalization, and numbers.

Problems with Sentence Construction 句子结构的问题

The following section introduces many common problems in writing sentences. Each subsection gives examples of a problem and explains how to convert the problem into a clearer sentence. No writer shows all of these errors in his or her writing, but almost everyone makes several of them. Many writers have definite habits: They often write in fragments, or they use poor pronoun reference, or they repeat a word or phrase excessively. Learn to identify your problem habits and correct them.

Identify and Eliminate Comma Splices 识别并删除逗号拼凑句

A *comma splice* occurs when two independent clauses are connected, or spliced, with only a comma. You can correct comma splices in four ways:

1. Replace the comma with a period to separate the two sentences.

Splice
> The difference is that the NC machine relies on a computer to control its movements, a manual machine depends on an operator to control its movements.

539

Correction	The difference is that the NC machine relies on a computer to control its movements. A manual machine depends on an operator to control its movements.

2. Replace the comma with a semicolon only if the sentences are very closely related. In the following example, note that the word *furthermore* is a conjunctive adverb. When you use a conjunctive adverb to connect two sentences, always precede it with a semicolon and follow it with a comma. Other conjunctive adverbs are *however, also, besides, consequently, nevertheless,* and *therefore*.

Splice	The Micro 2001 has a two-year warranty, furthermore the magnetron is covered for seven years.
Correction	The Micro 2001 has a two-year warranty; furthermore, the magnetron is covered for seven years.

3. Insert a coordinating conjunction (*and, but, or, nor, for, yet,* or *so*) after the comma, making a compound sentence.

Splice	The engines of both cranes meet OSHA standards, the new M80A has an additional safety feature.
Correction	The engines of both cranes meet OSHA standards, but the new M80A has an additional safety feature.

4. Subordinate one of the independent clauses by beginning it with a subordinating conjunction or a relative pronoun. Frequently used subordinating conjunctions are *where, when, while, because, since, as, until, unless, although, if,* and *after*. The relative pronouns are *which, that, who,* and *what*.

Splice	Worker efficiency will increase because of lower work heights, lower work heights maximize employee comfort.
Correction	Worker efficiency will increase because of lower work heights that maximize employee comfort.

Exercises 练 习

Correct the following comma splices:

1. Different models of computers, software programs, and text formats are incompatible, data processing and information retrieval is slow and inefficient.
2. Web content development is becoming more necessary as businesses rely on the Internet to provide product information, advertising, and purchasing options for consumers, good writers can convey all this information accurately, stylishly, and in a concise manner.

3. For example, a millimeter is one-thousandth of a meter, therefore, a nanometer is one million times smaller.
4. Positive displacement pumps produce a pulsating flow, their design provides a positive internal seal against leakage.
5. In the printing business there are two main ways of printing, the first is by using offset and the second is by using flexography.
6. Two methods currently exist to enhance fiber performance, one method is to orient the fibers.

Identify and Eliminate Run-On Sentences   识别并删除流水句

Run-on, or fused, sentences are similar to comma splices but lack the comma. The two independent clauses are run together with no punctuation between them. To eliminate run-on sentences, use one of the four methods explained in the preceding section and summarized here.

- Place a period between the two clauses.
- Place a semicolon between them.
- Place a comma and a coordinating conjunction between them.
- Place a relative pronoun or subordinating conjunction between them.

Exercises   练 习

Correct the following run-on sentences:

1. Biology is not the only field of science that nanotechnology will permeate this revolution can quite possibly influence all sciences and most likely create more.
2. Nonpositive displacement pumps produce a continuous flow because of this design, there is no positive internal seal against leakage.
3. Offset is also known as offset lithography or litho printing the offset process uses a flat metal plate with a smooth printing surface that is not raised or engraved.
4. The countries that import OCC at the highest rates often produce corrugated board of 100% recycled fibers due to the lessened performance of bogus board, a dilemma may be created.
5. Images are engraved around the cylinder the plate is not stretched and distorted like traditional plates.

Identify and Eliminate Sentence Fragments   识别并删除句子碎片

Sentence fragments are incomplete thoughts that the writer has mistakenly punctuated as complete sentences. Subordinate clauses, prepositional phrases, and verbal phrases often appear as fragments. As the following examples show, fragments must be connected to the preceding or the following sentence.

1. Connect subordinate clauses to independent clauses.

    a. The fragment below is a subordinate clause beginning with the subordinating conjunction *because*. Other subordinating conjunctions are *where, when, while, since, as, until, unless, if,* and *after*.

Fragment	We should accept the proposal. Because the payback period is significantly less than our company standard.
Correction	We should accept the proposal because the payback period is significantly less than our company standard.

    b. The following fragment is a subordinate clause beginning with the relative pronoun *which*. Other relative pronouns are *who, that,* and *what*.

Fragment	The total cost is $425,000. Which will have to come from the contingency fund.
Correction	The total cost of $425,000 will have to come from the contingency fund.

2. Connect prepositional phrases to independent clauses. The fragment below is a prepositional phrase. The fragment can be converted to a subordinate clause, as in the first example below, or made into an *appositive*—a word or phrase that means the same thing as what precedes it.

Fragment	The manager found the problem. At the conveyor belt.
Correction 1	The manager discovered that the problem was the conveyor belt.
Correction 2	The manager found the problem—the conveyor belt.

3. Connect verbal phrases to independent clauses.

    a. Verbal phrases often begin with *-ing* words. Such phrases must be linked to independent clauses.

Fragment	The crew will work all day tomorrow. Installing the new gyroscope.
Correction	Tomorrow the crew will work all day installing the new gyroscope.

    b. Infinitive phrases begin with *to* plus a verb. They must be linked to independent clauses.

Fragment	I contacted three vendors. To determine a probable price.
Correction	I contacted three vendors to determine a probable price.

Exercises 练 习

Correct the following sentence fragments:

1. The National Nanotechnology Initiative 247 million dollars in federal funding in 1999.
2. The fourth aspect of the quality control function making adjustments to the process, in order to bring specifications into line.
3. Thickness availability of Celotex from ½" to 2¼".
4. Through orientation and the alkali process secondary fiber performance enhanced to levels above current performance.
5. While cost savings initiatives and quality have become critical for businesses to remain competitive today.
6. The virgin fiber sought by foreign corrugated producers to supply their customers with a higher quality product.

Place Modifiers in the Correct Position 把修饰语放在正确的位置

Sentences become confusing when modifiers do not point directly to the words they modify. Misplaced modifiers often produce absurd sentences; worse yet, they occasionally result in sentences that make sense but cause the reader to misinterpret your meaning. Modifiers must be placed in a position that clarifies their relationship to the rest of the sentence.

1. In the sentence below, *that is made of a thin, oxide-coated plastic* appears to refer to *the information*.

Misplaced modifier	The magnetic disk is the part that contains the information that is made of a thin, oxide-coated plastic.
Correction	The magnetic disk, which is made of a thin, oxide-coated plastic, is the part that contains the information.

2. In the sentence below, the modifier says that the horizontal position must be tested, but the meaning clearly is something different.

Misplaced modifier	Lower the memory module to the horizontal position that requires testing.
Correction	Lower the memory module that requires testing to the horizontal position.

Exercises 练 习

Correct the misplaced modifiers in the following sentences:
1. ADA noted that VCLDs reduced energy endurance without carbohydrate supplementation.
2. Three topic areas related to printing were formulated to determine Web feasibility.
3. Although EPA legislation contains strong support, it cannot make up for the lack of information in the two other areas for oil field service engineers.
4. Technology must continue to improve in order to fully benefit economically in the recovery and preparation processes.

Use Words Ending in -ing Properly 正确使用以ing结尾的词

A word ending in -ing is either a present participle or a gerund. Both types, which are often introductory material in a sentence, express some kind of action. They are correct when the subject can perform the action that the -ing word expresses. For instance, in the sentence below, the *XYZ computer table* cannot *compare* cost and durability.

Unclear	Comparing cost and durability, the XYZ computer table is the better choice.
Clear	By comparing cost and durability, you can see that the XYZ computer table is the better choice.

Exercises 练 习

In the following sentences, the participle (the -ing word) is used incorrectly; revise them.
1. While walking across the parking lot, the red convertible had its hood raised.
2. When filling out an on-line document, personal data always appear first.
3. When using a laptop computer, the mouse can be difficult to manage.
4. After comparing the weight and the features of the two laptops, both laptops seem to be of equal value.
5. Reviewing the internship, visual displays floor plans, and merchandising were my main duties.
6. By eliminating unnecessary wording, this would decrease cost by $10.00 per book.

Make the Subject and Verb Agree 主谓要一致

The subject and the verb of a sentence must both be singular or both be plural. Almost all problems with agreement are caused by failure to identify the subject correctly.

1. When the subject and verb are separated by a prepositional phrase, be sure you do not inadvertently make the verb agree with the object of the preposition rather than with the subject. In the following sentence, the subject *bar* is singular; *feet* is the object of the preposition *of*. The verb *picks* must be singular to agree with the subject.

Faulty	A bar containing a row of suction feet pick up the paper.
Correction	A bar containing a row of suction feet picks up the paper.

2. When a *collective noun* refers to a group or a unit, the verb must be singular. Collective nouns include such words as *committee, management, audience, union,* and *team*.

Faulty	The committee are writing the policy.
Correction	The committee is writing the policy.

3. Indefinite pronouns, such as *each, everyone, either, neither, anyone,* and *everybody*, take a singular verb.

Faulty	Each of the costs are below the limit.
Correction	Each of the costs is below the limit.

4. When compound subjects are connected by *or* or *nor*, the verb must agree with the nearer noun.

Faulty	The manager or the assistants evaluates the proposal.
Correction	The manager or the assistants evaluate the proposal.

Exercises 练 习

Correct the subject-verb errors in the following sentences:
1. Everybody in both classes were late in arriving to the classroom.
2. All the books in the bookstore is available for purchase.
3. When writing a technical manual, analysis of various audiences are very important.

4. The reasons the flat screen monitor should be used is well-documented in research.
5. Hypertext (HTML) is a method in which punctuation markings, spaces, and coding is used to create pictures on a webpage.

Use Pronouns Correctly   正确使用代词

A pronoun must refer directly to the noun it stands for, its *antecedent*.

As in subject-verb agreement, a pronoun and its antecedent must both be singular or both be plural. Collective nouns generally take the singular pronoun *it* rather than the plural *they*. Problems result when pronouns such as *they, this,* and *it* are used carelessly, forcing the reader to figure out their antecedents. Overuse of the indefinite *it* (as in "*It* is obvious that") leads to confusion.

Problems with Number   数字的问题

1. In the following sentence, the pronoun *It* is wrong because it does not agree in number with its antecedent, *inspections*. To correct the mistake, use *they*.

Vague	The inspections occur before the converter is ready to produce the part. It is completed by four engineers.
Clear	The inspections occur before the converter is ready to produce the part. They are completed by four engineers.

2. In current practice, it is now acceptable to deliberately misuse collective pronouns in an effort to avoid sexist writing.

Technically correct	Everyone must bring his or her card.
Correct for informal situations	Everyone must bring their card.

Problems with Antecedents   先行词的问题

If a sentence has several nouns, the antecedent may not be clear.

1. In the following case, *It* could stand for either *pointer* or *collector*. The two sentences can be combined to eliminate the pronoun.

Vague	The base and dust *collector* is the first and largest part of the lead *pointer. It* is usually round and a couple of inches in diameter.
Clear	The base and dust collector, which is the largest part of the lead pointer, is usually round and several inches in diameter.

2. In the following case, *It* could refer to *compiler* or *software*.

Problems with Sentence Construction

Vague   The new *compiler* requires new *software*. *It* must be compatible with our hardware.

Clear   The new compiler, which requires new software, must be compatible with our hardware.

Problems with *This*   使用This的问题

Many inexact writers start sentences with *This* followed immediately by a verb ("*This* is," "*This* causes"), even though the antecedent of *this* is unclear. Often the writer intends to refer to a whole concept or even to a verb, but because *this* is a pronoun or an adjective, it must refer to a noun. The writer can usually fix the problem by inserting a noun after *this*—and so turn it into an adjective—or by combining the two sentences into one. In the following sentence, *this* probably refers either to the whole first sentence or to *virtually impossible*, which is not a noun.

Vague   Ring networks must be connected at both ends—a matter that could make wiring virtually impossible in some cases. This would not be the case in the Jones building.

Clear   Ring networks must be connected at both ends—a matter that could make wiring virtually impossible in some cases. We can easily fill this requirement in the Jones building.

Exercises 练 习

Revise the following sentences, making the pronoun references clear:

1. Probably the computer will begin to have problems in three or four months. This is only an estimate but it would not be surprising, due to my experience with other computers. This would increase the amount of money spent on the computer.
2. The computers are in the warehouse and the boxes enter on a conveyor belt and then they load them into rail cars.
3. As more and more nodes are installed, it affects the time it takes for information to travel around the ring.
4. The pick-and-place robot places the part in the carton. It is sealed by an electronic heat seal device. [*Carton* is the intended antecedent.]
5. The computer malfunctions are generally minor problems that take 1 or 2 hours to fix. This costs the company about $1000.
6. As you can see, the IT department has a substantially higher absentee rate than any of the other departments. This shows a definite problem in this depart-

ment. This is the only department that requires such extreme on-call requirements with little or no extra compensation.

Punctuation 标点符号

Writers must know the generally accepted standards for using the marks of punctuation. The following guidelines are based on *The Chicago Manual of Style* and the U.S. Government's *A Manual of Style*.

Apostrophes 撇 号

Use the apostrophe to indicate possession, contractions, and some plurals.

Possession

The following are basic rules for showing possession:

1. Add an *'s* to show possession by singular nouns.

    a machine's parts   a package's contents

2. Add an *'s* to show possession by plural nouns that do not end in *s*.

    the women's caucus   the sheep's brains

3. Add only an apostrophe to plural nouns ending in *s*.

    three machines' parts   the companies' managers

4. For proper names that end in *s*, use the same rules. For singular add *'s;* for plural add only an apostrophe.

    Ted Jones's job   the Joneses' security holdings

    This point is quite controversial. For a good discussion, see *The Chicago Manual of Style*, 15th ed. (Chicago: University of Chicago Press, 2003): 283.

5. Do not add an apostrophe to personal pronouns.

    Theirs   ours   its

Contractions

Use the apostrophe to indicate that two or more words have been condensed into one. As a general rule, do not use contractions in formal reports and business letters.

I'll = I will   should've = should have   it's = it is   they're = they are

Plurals

When you indicate the plurals of letters, abbreviations, and numbers, use apostrophes only to avoid confusion. *Chicago* (p. 283) and U.S. (p. 118) disagree on this point.

1. Do not use apostrophes to form the plurals of letters.

    Xs   Ys   Zs

2. Do not use apostrophes to form the plurals of abbreviations and numbers.

    BOMs   1990s

3. Use apostrophes to form the possessive of abbreviations.

    OSHA's decision

Brackets 方括号

Brackets indicate that the writer has changed or added words or letters inside a quoted passage.

> According to the report, "The detection distance [5 cm] fulfills the criterion."

Colons 冒号

Use colons:

1. To separate an independent clause from a list of supporting statements or examples.

    The jointer has three important parts: the infeed table, the cutterhead, and the outfeed table.

2. To separate two independent clauses when the second clause explains or amplifies the first.

    The original problem was the efficiency policy: We were producing as many parts as possible, but we could not use all of them.

Commas 逗号

Use commas:

1. To separate two main clauses connected by a coordinating conjunction (*and, but, or, nor, for, yet,* or *so*). Omit the comma if the clauses are very short.

Two main clauses	The Atlas carousel has a higher base price, but this price includes installation and tooling costs.

2. To separate introductory subordinate clauses or phrases from the main clause.

Clause	If the background is too dark, change the setting.
Phrases	As shown in the table, the new system will save us over a million dollars.

3. To separate words or clauses in a series.

Words	Peripheral components include scanners, external hard drives, and external fax/modems.
Phrases	With this program you can send the fax at 5 P.M., at 11 P.M., or at a time you choose.
Clauses	Select equipment that has durability, that requires little maintenance, and that the company can afford.

4. To set off nonrestrictive appositives, phrases, and clauses.

Appositive	AltaVista, a Web search engine, has excellent advanced search features.
Phrase	The bottleneck, first found in a routine inspection, will take a week to fix.
Clause	The air flow system, which was installed in 1979, does not produce enough flow at its southern end.

Dashes and parentheses also serve this function. Dashes emphasize the abruptness of the interjected words; parentheses deemphasize the words.

5. To separate coordinate but not cumulative adjectives.

Coordinate	He rejected the distorted, useless recordings.

Coordinate adjectives modify the noun independently. They could be reversed with no change in meaning: *useless, distorted recordings.*

Cumulative	An acceptable frequency-response curve was achieved.

Cumulative adjectives cannot be reversed without distorting the meaning: *frequency-response acceptable curve.*

6. To set off conjunctive adverbs and transitional phrases.

Conjunctive adverbs	The vice-president, however, reversed the recommendation.
	The crane was very expensive; however, it paid for itself in 18 months.

Therefore, a larger system will solve the problem.

Transitional phrases

On the other hand, the new receiving station is twice as large.

Performance on Mondays and Fridays, for example, is far below average.

Dashes 破折号

You can use dashes before and after interrupting material and asides. Dashes give a less formal, more dramatic tone to the material they set off than commas or parentheses do. The dash has four common uses:

1. To set off material that interrupts a sentence with a different idea

   The fourth step—the most crucial one from management's point of view—is to ring up the folio and collect the money.

2. To emphasize a word or phrase at the end of a sentence

   The Carver CNC has a range of 175–200 parts per hour—not within the standard.

3. To set off a definition

   The total time commitment—contract duty time plus travel time—cannot exceed 40 hours per month.

4. To introduce a series less formally than with a colon

   This sophisticated application allows several types of instruction sets—stacks, queues, and trees.

Parentheses 圆括号

You can use parentheses before and after material that interrupts or is some kind of aside in a sentence or paragraph. Compared to dashes, parentheses have one of two effects: They deemphasize the material they set off, or they give a more formal, less dramatic tone to special asides. Parentheses are used in three ways:

1. To add information about an item.

Acronym for a lengthy phrase
A definition

This Computer Numerically Controlled (CNC) lathe costs $20,000.

The result was long manufacturing lead times (the total time from receipt of a customer order until the product is produced).

Precise technical data

This hard drive (20GB, 5400 rpm Ultra ATA/66) can handle all of our current and future storage needs.

2. To add an aside to a sentence.

> The Pulstrider has wheels, which would make it easy to move the unit from its storage site (the spare bedroom) to its use site (the living room, in front of the TV).

3. To add an aside to a paragraph.

> The current program provides the user with the food's fat content percentage range by posting colored dots next to the menu item on a sign in the serving area. To determine the percentage of fat in foods, one must match the colored dot to dots on a poster hanging in the serving area. The yellow dot represents a range of 30–60%. (The green dot is 0–29% and the red dot is 61–100%.) This yellow range is too large.

A Note on Parentheses, Dashes, and Commas 圆括号、破折号和逗号使用注意事项

All three of these punctuation marks may be used to separate interrupting material from the rest of the sentence. Choose dashes or parentheses to avoid making an appositive seem like the second item in a series.

Commas are confusing	The computer has an input device, a keyboard and an output device, a monitor.
Parentheses are clearer	The computer has an input device (a keyboard) and an output device (a monitor).
Commas are confusing	The categories that have the highest dollar sales increase, sweaters, outerware, and slacks, also have the highest dollar per unit cost.
Dashes are clearer	The categories that have the highest dollar sales increase—sweaters, outerware, and slacks—also have the highest dollar per unit cost.

Ellipsis Points 省略号

Ellipsis points are three periods used to indicate that words have been deleted from a quoted passage.

> According to Jones (1999), "The average customer is a tourist who … tends to purchase collectibles and small antiques" (p. 7).

Hyphens 连字号

Use hyphens to make the following connections:

1. The parts of a compound word when it is an adjective placed before the noun.

> high-frequency system   plunger-type device   trouble-free process

Do not hyphenate the same adjectives when they are placed after the word:

The system is trouble free.

2. Words in a prepositional phrase used as an adjective.

    state-of-the-art printer

3. Words that could cause confusion by being misread.

    energy-producing cell   eight-hour shifts   foreign-car buyers
    cement-like texture

4. Compound modifiers formed from a quantity and a unit of measurement.

    a 3-inch beam   an 8-mile journey

    Unless the unit is expressed as a plural:

    a beam 3 inches wide   a journey of 8 miles

    Also use a hyphen with a number plus *-odd*.

    twenty-odd

5. A single capital letter and a noun or participle.

    A-frame   I-beam

6. Compound numbers from 21 through 99 when they are spelled out and fractions when they are spelled out.

    Twenty-seven jobs required a pickup truck.   three-fourths

7. Complex fractions if the fraction cannot be typed in small numbers.

    1-3/16 miles

    Do not hyphenate if the fraction can be typed in small numbers.

    1½ hp

8. Adjective plus past participle (*-ed, -en*).

    red-colored table

9. Compounds made from *half-*, *all-*, or *cross-*.

    half-finished   all-encompassing   cross-country

10. Use suspended hyphens for a series of adjectives that you would ordinarily hyphenate.

    10-, 20-, and 30-foot beams

11. Do not hyphenate:

    a. *-ly* adverb-adjective combinations:

    recently altered system

    b. *-ly* adverb plus participle (*-ing, -ed*):

    highly rewarding positions   poorly motivated managers

    c. chemical terms

    hydrogen peroxide

    d. colors

    red orange logo

12. Spell as one word compounds formed by the following prefixes:

anti-	co-	infra-
non-	over-	post-
pre-	pro-	pseudo-
re-	semi-	sub-
super-	supra-	ultra-
un-	under-	

    Exceptions: Use a hyphen

    a. When the second element is capitalized (*pre-Victorian*).

    b. When the second element is a figure (*pre-1900*).

    c. To prevent possible misreadings (*re-cover, un-ionized*).

Quotation Marks 引号

Quotation marks are used at the beginning and at the end of a passage that contains the exact words of someone else.

> According to Jones (1999), "The average customer is a tourist who travels in the summer and tends to purchase collectibles and small antiques" (p. 7).

Semicolons 分号

Use semicolons in the following ways:

1. To separate independent clauses not connected by coordinating conjunctions (*and, but, or, nor, for, yet, so*).

    Our printing presses are running 24 hours a day; we cannot stop the presses even for routine maintenance.

Abbreviations, Capitalization, and Numbers

2. To separate independent clauses when the second one begins with a conjunctive adverb (*therefore, however, also, besides, consequently, nevertheless, furthermore*).

   Set-up time will decrease 10% and materials handling will decrease 15%; consequently, production will increase 20%.

3. To separate items in a series if the items have internal punctuation.

   Plans have been proposed for Kansas City, Missouri; Seattle, Washington; and Orlando, Florida.

Underlining (Italics)　下划线（斜体）

Underlining is a line drawn under certain words. In books and laser-printed material, words that you underline when typing appear in italics. Italics are used for three purposes:

1. To indicate titles of books and newspapers.

   Thriving on Chaos　　the San Francisco *Examiner*

2. To indicate words used as words or letters used as letters.

   That logo contains an attractive *M*.

   You used *there are* too many times in this paper.

   Note: You may also use quotation marks to indicate words as words.

   You used "there are" too many times in this paper.

3. To emphasize a word.

   Make sure there are no empty spaces on the contract and that all the blanks have been filled in *before* you sign.

Abbreviations, Capitalization, and Numbers　缩写、大写和数字

Abbreviations　缩写

Use abbreviations only for long words or combinations of words that must be used more than once in a report. For example, if words such as *Fahrenheit* or phrases such as *pounds per square inch* must be used several times in a report, abbreviate them to save space. Several rules for abbreviating follow (*Chicago*).

1. If an abbreviation might confuse your reader, use it and the complete phrase the first time.

   This paper will discuss materials planning requirements (MPR).

2. Use all capital letters (no periods, no space between letters or symbols) for acronyms.

   NASA   NAFTA   COBOL   HUD   PAC

3. Capitalize just the first letter of abbreviations for titles and companies; the abbreviation follows with a period.

   Pres.   Co.

4. Form the plural of an abbreviation by adding just *s*.

   BOMs   VCRs   CRTs

5. Omit the period after abbreviations of units of measurement. Exception: use *in.* for *inch*.

6. Use periods with Latin abbreviations.

   e.g. (for example)   i.e. (that is)   etc. (and so forth)

7. Use abbreviations (and symbols) when necessary to save space on visuals, but define difficult ones in the legend, a footnote, or the text.

8. Do not capitalize abbreviations of measurements.

   10 lb   12 m   14 g   16 cm

9. Do not abbreviate units of measurement preceded by approximations.

   several pounds per square inch   15 psi

10. Do not abbreviate short words such as *acre* or *ton*. In tables, abbreviate units of length, area, volume, and capacity.

Capitalization 大写

The conventional rules of capitalization apply to technical writing. The trend in industry is away from overcapitalization.

1. Capitalize a title that immediately precedes a name.

   Senior Project Manager Jones

But do not capitalize it if it is generic.

> The senior project manager reviewed the report.

2. Capitalize proper nouns and adjectives.

> Asia   American   French

3. Capitalize trade names, but not the product.

> Apple computers   Cleanall window cleaner

4. Capitalize titles of courses and departments and the titles of majors that refer to a specific degree program.

> The first statistics course I took was Statistics 1.

> I majored in Plant Engineering and have applied for several plant engineering positions.

5. Do not capitalize after a colon.

> The chair has four parts: legs, seat, arms, and back.

> I recommend the XYZ lathe: it is the best machine for the price.

Numbers 数 字

The following rules cover most situations, but when in doubt whether to use a numeral or a word, remember that the trend in report writing is toward using numerals.

1. Spell out numbers below 10; use figures for 10 and above.

> four cycles   1835 members

2. Spell out numbers that begin sentences.

> Thirty employees received safety commendations.

3. If a series contains numbers above and below 10, use numerals for all of them.

> The floor plan has 2 aisles and 14 workstations.

4. Use numerals for numbers that accompany units of measurement and time.

> 1 gram   0.452 minute
>
> 7 yards   6 kilometers

5. In compound-number adjectives, spell out the first one or the shorter one to avoid confusion.

   75 twelve-volt batteries

6. Use figures to record specific measurements.

   He took readings of 7.0, 7.1, and 7.3.

7. Combine figures and words for extremely large round numbers.

   2 million miles

8. For decimal fractions of less than 1, place a zero before the decimal point.

   0.613

9. Express plurals of figures by adding just *s*.

   21s   1990s

10. Place the last two letters of the ordinal after fractions used as nouns:

    $\frac{1}{10}$th of a second

    But not after fractions that modify nouns:

    $\frac{1}{10}$ horsepower

11. Spell out ordinals below 10.

    fourth part   eighth incident

12. For 10 and above, use the number and the last two letters of the ordinal.

    11th week   52nd contract

Works Cited 引用的作品

The Chicago Manual of Style: The Essential Guide for Writers, Editors, and Publishers. 15th ed. Chicago: University of Chicago Press, 2003.

U.S. Government Printing Office. *A Manual of Style.* 29th ed. New York: Gramercy, 2001.

Appendix B

Documenting Sources
记录来源

Appendix Contents
How Internal Documentation Works
The APA Method
The MLA Method
Numbered References

Documenting your sources means following a citation system to indicate whose ideas you are using. Three methods are commonly used: the American Psychological Association (APA) system, the Modern Language Association (MLA) system, and the numbered references system, shown here by the American Chemical Society (ACS) system. All three will be explained briefly. For more complete details, consult the *Publication Manual of the American Psychological Association* (5th ed.); the *MLA Handbook* (6th ed.); or *The ACS Style Guide* (2nd ed.).

How Internal Documentation Works 内部记录的运行方式

Each method has two parts: the internal citations and the bibliography, also called "References" (APA, ACS) or "Works Cited" (MLA). The internal citation works in roughly the same manner in all three methods. The author places certain important items of information in the text to tell the reader which entry in the bibliography is the source of the quotation or paraphrase. These items could be the author's last name, the date of publication, the title of an article, or the number of the item in the bibliography.

In the APA method, the basic items are the author's last name and the year of publication. In the ACS method, the basic item is the number of the item in the bibliography. In the MLA method, the basic item is the author's last name and sometimes the title of the work, often in shorthand form.

In each method, the number of the page on which the quotation or paraphrase appears goes in parentheses immediately following the cited material. Because the rest of the methods vary, the rest of this chapter explains each.

Here is an example of how each method would internally cite the following quotation from page 22 of the article "This Old Forest: The Home Depot Pitches in to Help Indonesia's Forests," by Katherine Sharpe and published in the magazine *Nature Conservancy* in Spring 2003.

> Most consumers have never heard of "certified" wood. Ron Jarvis, merchandising vice president for The Home Depot, knows this. Customers don't usually ask The Home Depot to carry wood products from forests that are sustainably managed and harvested—and independently verified as such.

APA Method   APA 方式

The APA method requires that you use just the author's last name and include the year of publication and a page number.

> According to Sharpe (2003), "Customers don't usually ask The Home Depot to carry wood products from forests that are sustainably managed and harvested—and independently verified as such" (p. 22).

To find all bibliographic information on the quotation, you would refer to "Sharpe" in the References section.

> Sharpe, K. (2003). This old forest: The Home Depot pitches in to help Indonesia's forests. *Nature Conservancy, 11,* 22.

MLA Method   MLA方式

The MLA method of citing the passage requires that you should include at least the author's last name with the page number.

> As the author noted, "Customers don't usually ask The Home Depot to carry wood products from forests that are sustainably managed and harvested—and independently verified as such" (Sharpe 22).

To find all the publication information for this quotation, you would refer to "Sharpe" in the Works Cited list.

> Sharpe, Karen. "This Old Forest: The Home Depot Pitches In to Help Indonesia's Forests." *Nature Conservancy* (Spring 2003): 22.

Numbered References Method   参考文献排序方式

The numbered references method does not require you to use a last name, although you may. Every time you cite the source, whenever the citation occurs in your text, you place in the text the item's number in the bibliography. So if "Sharpe" were the second item in the bibliography, you use the number 2 to cite the source in the text. You also include a page number:

As the author noted, "Customers don't usually ask The Home Depot to carry wood products from forests that are sustainably managed and harvested—and independently verified as such" (2, p. 22).

And the Reference entry looks like this:

2. Sharpe, K. This Old Forest: The Home Depot Pitches In to Help Indonesia's Forests. *Nature Conservancy* Spring 2003, *11*(1) 22.

Note: The ACS Style Guide (like all other style guides for the numbered method) does not present a way to handle quotations. The ACS assumes that references in scientific literature are to ideas in essays and that quotations are never used. However, because the method is commonly used in academia, the quotation method of the APA is added to it here.

The "Extension" Problem   "外延"的问题

A common problem with internal documentation is indicating where the paraphrased material begins and ends. If you start a paragraph with a phrase like "According to Sharpe," you need to indicate which of the sentences that follow come from Sharpe. Or if you end a long paragraph with a parenthetical citation (Sharpe, 2003, pp. 22–23), you need to indicate which preceding sentences came from Sharpe. To alleviate confusion, place a marker at each end of the passage. Either use the name at the start and page numbers at the end or use a term like "one authority" at the start and the citation at the end.

> According to Sharpe (2003), a "certified" wood product is one that comes from a "sustainable" forest. The maintenance and harvesting methods of such a forest must be independently verified. Marketing certified products is difficult because few consumers are aware enough of the products' existence to ask for them (22).

> One authority explains that a "certified" wood product is one that comes from a "sustainable" forest. The maintenance and harvesting methods of such a forest must be independently verified. Marketing certified products is difficult because few consumers are aware enough of the products' existence to ask for them (Sharpe, 2003, p. 22).

The APA Method   APA 方式

APA Citations   APA引用

Once you understand the basic theory of the method—to use names and page numbers to refer to the References—you need to be aware of the variations possible in placing the name in the text. Each time you cite a quotation or paraphrase, you give the page number preceded by *p.* or *pp.* Do not use *pg.* The following variations are all acceptable.

1. The author's name appears as part of the introduction of the quotation or paraphrase.

   As Sharpe (2003) noted, "Customers don't usually ask The Home Depot to carry wood products from forests that are sustainably managed and harvested—and independently verified as such" (p. 22).

2. The author is not named in the introduction to the quotation or paraphrase.

   It is noted that "customers don't usually ask The Home Depot to carry wood products from forests that are sustainably managed and harvested—and independently verified as such" (Sharpe, 2003, p. 22).

3. The author has several works listed in the References. If they have different dates, no special treatment is necessary; if an author has two works dated in the same year, differentiate them in the text and in the References with a lowercase letter after each date (2003a, 2003b).

   Sharpe (2003a) notes that "customers don't usually ask The Home Depot to carry wood products from forests that are sustainably managed and harvested—and independently verified as such" (p. 22).

4. Paraphrases are handled like quotations. Give the author's last name, the date, and the appropriate page numbers.

   Sharpe (2003) makes note that even though consumers don't ask for timber that is verified as sustainable, The Home Depot handles this type of wood (p. 22).

5. When citing block quotations, the period is placed *before* the page in parentheses. Do not place the quotation marks before and after a block quotation. Indent the left margin 5 spaces and double-space. Do not indent the right margin.

   According to Sharpe (2003),

   > Customers don't usually ask The Home Depot to carry wood products from forests that are sustainably managed and harvested—and independently verified as such. Despite the absence of significant consumer demand, The Home Depot recently threw its support behind a Nature Conservancy project that aims to create a supply of certified wood from Indonesia, where unlawfully harvested wood—including protected species and trees felled in national parks—account for two-thirds of the wood cut annually. "Part of our culture is doing the right thing," explains Jarvis. (p. 22)

6. If no author is given for the work, treat the title as the author and list the title first in the References.

To learn the Internet, it is useful to know that "the two most important parts are search engines and Boolean/logical operators" ("Tips," 2006, p. 78).

Tips for the Infohighway. (2006, July). *Cyberreal*, 78.

APA References   APA参考

The references list (titled "References") contains the complete bibliographic information on each source you use. The list is arranged alphabetically by the last name of the author or the first important word of the title. Follow these guidelines.

- Present information for all the entries in this order: Author's name. Date. Title. Publication information.
- Double-space the entire list. Entries should have a hanging indent, with the second and subsequent lines indented.
- Use only the initials of the author's first and middle names. *Note:* Many local style sheets suggest using the full first name; if this is the style at your place, follow that style.
- Place the date in parentheses immediately after the name.
- Capitalize only the first word of the title and subtitle and proper nouns.
- The inclusion of *p.* and *pp.* depends on the type of source. In general, use *p.* and *pp.* when the volume number does not precede the page numbers (or for a newspaper article).
- Place the entries in alphabetical order

    Berkenkotter, C. (1991). Paradigm debates, turf wars, and the conduct of sociocognitive inquiry in composition. *College Composition and Communication, 42*(2), 151–169.

    Bostic, H. (2002). Reading and rethinking the subject in Luce Irigaray's recent work. *Paragraph: A Journal of Modern Critical Theory, 25*, 22–31.

    Cooper, M., Lynch, D., & George, D. (1997). Moments of argument: Agonistic inquiry and confrontational cooperation. *College Composition and Communication, 48*, 61–85.

- If there are two or more works by one author, arrange them chronologically, earliest first.

    Berkenkotter, C. (1991).

    Berkenkotter, C. (1995).

Several common entries are shown below.

Book with One Author

Selfe, C. L. (1999). *Technology and literacy in the twenty-first century: The perils of not paying attention.* Carbondale: Southern Illinois University Press.

- Capitalize the first word after the colon.
- Use Zip Code abbreviations for states.

Book with Two Authors

George, D., & Trimbur, J. (2001). *Reading culture: Contexts for critical reading and writing* (4th ed.). New York: Longman.

Book with Editors

Hawisher, G., & Selfe, C. L. (Eds.). (1999). *Passions, pedagogies, and 21st century technologies.* Logan: Utah State University Press.

Essay in an Anthology

Sullivan, D. L., Martin, M. S., & Anderson, E. R. (2003). Moving from the periphery: Conceptions of ethos, reputation, and identity for the technical communicator. In T. Kynell-Hunt & G. Savage (Eds.), *Issues of power, status and legitimacy in technical communication: Evaluating the social and historical process of professionalization* (pp. 115–136). Amityville, NY: Baywood.

- Capitalize only the first word of the essay title and subtitle (and all proper nouns).
- Use *pp.* with inclusive page numbers.

Corporate or Institutional Author

American Telephone and Telegraph. (2005). *2004 annual report.* New York: Author.

- When the author is also the publisher, write *Author* for the publisher.
- In the text, the first citation reads this way (American Telephone and Telegraph [AT&T], 2005). Subsequent citations read (AT&T, 2005).
- This entry could also read

2004 annual report. (2005). New York: American Telephone and Telegraph.

- Cite this entry as (*2004 annual*).

Work Without Date or Publisher

Radke, J. (n.d.). *Writing for electronic sources.* Atlanta: Center for Electronic Communication.

The APA Method

- Use *n.p.* for no publisher or no place.

Brochure or Pamphlet

Teaching English in the 21st century [Brochure]. (n.d.). Houghton: Michigan Technological University.

- Treat brochures like books.
- Place any identification number after the title.
- Place the word *brochure* or *pamphlet* in brackets.
- This entry could also read

Michigan Technological University. (n.d.). *Teaching English in the 21st century* [Brochure]. Houghton: Author.

- In the text, reference this entry as (Michigan).

Later Edition of a Book

American Psychological Association. (2001). *Publication manual* (5th ed.). Washington, DC: Author.

Encyclopedia/Handbook

Phone recorder. (1991). In R. Graf (Ed.), *Encyclopedia of physical science and technology* (Vol. 3, pp. 616–617). Blue Ridge Summit, PA: Tab.

Posner, E. C. (1992). Communications, deep space. In *Encyclopedia of physical science and technology* (2nd ed., Vol. 3, pp. 691–711). San Diego: Academic Press.

- In the text, refer to the first entry and all works with no author this way (note the use of quotation marks): ("Phone," 1991).

Article in a Journal with Continuous Pagination

Sullivan, D. L., & Martin, M. S. (2001). Habit formation and story telling: A theory for guiding ethical action. *Technical Communication Quarterly, 10,* 251–272.

Article in a Journal Without Continuous Pagination

Fehler, B. (2003). Re-defining God: The rhetoric of reconciliation. *Rhetoric Society Quarterly, 33*(1), 105–128.

- Put the issue number in parentheses after the volume.
- You could also give the month or season, if that helps identify the work: (2001, Summer; 2003, January).

Article in a Monthly or Weekly Magazine

Simon, R. (2002, September). One year. *U.S. News and World Report*, 4–14.

▸ If the article has discontinuous pages, a comma indicates a break in sequence (4, 6–14).

Newspaper Article

Kerasotis, P. (2003, February 2). Florida's space coast grieves for NASA accidents in its own special way. *Green Bay Press Gazette*, p. A15.

▸ *Note:* If the article has multiple pages, use *pp.* (pp. A1, A15).

Personal Interview

Note: The Publication Manual of the American Psychological Association suggests that person and telephone interviews and letters should appear only in the text and not in the References. However, because these entries might be critical in research reports, a suggested form for their use in the References is given here.

1. In the text, reference personal communication material this way:

    M. Anderson (telephone interview, December 7, 2005) suggests that . . .

2. In the References, enter it this way:

    Anderson, M. (2005, December 7). [Personal interview].

▸ Arrange the date so the year is first.
▸ If the person's title is pertinent, place it in brackets.

Anderson, M. (2005, December 7). [Personal interview. CEO, Technology Innovations, San Diego, CA].

Telephone Interview

Anderson, M. (2005, December 7). [Telephone interview].

Personal Letter

Anderson, M. (2005, December 7). [Personal letter. CEO, Technology Innovations, San Diego, CA].

Professional or Personal Website—Homepage

Essential for citing webpages is that you give the date of the retrieval on which you viewed the site and the URL. Give as much other information as possible.

Anderson, M. (2006, February 17). *Techinnovations*. Retrieved March 14, 2006, from http://www.techinnovations.com

- Cite this version as (Anderson).

Explanation: Web owner; if available. (Date of the last update, if available). Title of article or document. Title of website. Date that you viewed the site and the site's URL. *Note:* If the owner and the date are not available, the above entry would look like this:

> Techinnovations. Retrieved March 14, 2006, from http://www.techinnovations.com

Cite this version as ("Techinnovations").

Professional or Personal Website—Internal Page

For an internal page of a website, give the URL of the document, not the homepage.

> Anderson, M. (2006, February 19). Single-sourcing and localization. *Techinnovations.* Retrieved March 16, 2006, from http://www.techinnovations.com./singlesrclocal.html

Explanation: Web owner, if available. Date of the last updating, if available—note that internal page updates and homepage updates can be different; use the date of the page whose information you use.) Title that appears on the document page. *Title that appears on that homepage.* Date that you saw the information and the URL.

E-Mail and Listservs

APA recommends that you cite e-mail and listserv postings in the same way as personal communication. In your text, such a citation would look like this:

> M. Anderson (personal communication, December 7, 2005) suggests that ...

- Notice that the first name initial is presented first, unlike the order used in the reference list.
- APA recommends that personal communications not appear in the reference list, but if you are required to use them, follow this:

> Anderson, M. (2005, December 7). [E-mail]

Listserv Archives

Many listservs have archives where the original postings are stored more or less permanently, available to anyone who joins the listserv. If you use an archived version of a listserv message (and you should, because archived messages are more accessible), put the item in the reference list. Use this form:

> Anderson, M. (2005, December 7). A key to effective localization. Message posted to Global Answers electronic mailing list, archived at http://www.globalanswers.org/cgi-bin/enter7.12.05

▶ *Explanation:* Author: (Date of the original posting). Title from the subject line. Message posted to name of listserv, archived at the URL of the archive.

Article from an On-Line Service

Many libraries and companies use on-line services like EBSCOhost to find full-text articles. An entry in the References would look like this:

> Anderson, M. (2005, December 7). A key to effective localization. *Global Technical Communication, 25,* 23–28. Retrieved January 12, 2006, from http://search.epnet.com/comm-generic from EBSCOhost (Academic Search Elite)

▶ *Explanation:* Author. (Date of original publication). Article title. *Periodical title. Volume number of the periodical.* Date that you retrieved the article, the URL of the service, and name of the service (name of the database).

Note: Databases like EBSCOhost often present publisher information in a source line that does not give the complete page numbers of the article.

Source: *Global Technical Communication,* 7 December 2005, Vol. 25, Issue 3, p. 23, 5p.

If the source line is the only information available, use this form for the page numbers: p. 23, 5p. In the text you will not be able to cite pages; just use the author's name and date.

Article Available from an On-Line Periodical

Treat an article from an on-line periodical like a hard copy article. Note that you must add the date of retrieval and the URL:

> Anderson, M. (2005, December). A key to effective localization. *e Global, 25.* Retrieved January 12, 2006, from http://eglobal.com/dec/articles/anderson.html

▶ *Explanation:* Author. (Date of original publication). Article title. *Periodical Title. Volume number of the periodical.* Date you retrieved the article and the URL of the periodical.

The MLA Method MLA方式

The following section describes variations in MLA citation and explains entries in the MLA Works Cited section.

MLA Citations MLA引用

Once you understand the basic theory of the method—to use names and page numbers to refer to the Works Cited—you need to be aware of the possible variations of placing the name in the text. In this method, unlike APA, each time you refer to a quotation or paraphrase, you give the page number only; do not use *p.* or *pg.*

1. The author's name appears as part of the introduction to the quotation or paraphrase.

   Sharpe notes, "Customers don't usually ask The Home Depot to carry wood products from forests that are sustainably managed and harvested—and independently verified as such" (22).

2. Author is not named in introduction to quotation.

   What seems quite evident is that "customers don't usually ask The Home Depot to carry wood products from forests that are sustainably managed and harvested—and independently verified as such" (Sharpe 22).

3. Author has several sources in the Works Cited.

   Sharpe points out that "customers don't usually ask The Home Depot to carry wood products from forests that are sustainably managed and harvested—and independently verified as such" (*Nature* 22).

4. Paraphrases are usually handled like quotations. Give the author's last name and the appropriate page numbers.

   Sharpe notes that even though consumers don't ask for timber that is verified as sustainable, The Home Depot handles this type of wood (22).

5. In block quotations, place the period before the page parentheses. Do not place quotation marks before and after the block quotation. Indent the left margin 10 spaces and double-space. Do not indent the right margin.

   According to Sharpe (2003),
   >   Customers don't usually ask The Home Depot to carry wood products from forests that are sustainably managed and harvested—and independently verified as such. Despite the absence of significant consumer demand, The Home Depot recently threw its support behind a Nature Conservancy project that aims to create a supply of certified wood from Indonesia, where unlawfully harvested wood—including protected species and trees felled in national parks—account for two-thirds of the wood cut annually. "Part of our culture is doing the right thing," explains Jarvis. (22)

6. If no author is given for the work, treat the author as the title because the title is listed first in the Works Cited list.

   To learn the Internet, it is useful to know that "the two most important parts are search engines and Boolean/logical operators" ("Tips" 78).

   "Tips for the Infohighway." *Cyberreal* July 2004: 78.

7. If the title of the book is very long, you may shorten the title when you discuss it in the text. For instance, Hawisher and Selfe's book is titled *Passions, Pedagogies, and 21st Century Technology.* In the text, you may simply refer to the book as *Passions.*

MLA Works Cited List MLA引用作品列表

The Works Cited list contains the complete bibliographic information on each source you use. The list is arranged alphabetically by the last name of the author or, if no author is named, by the first important word of the title.

Follow these guidelines:

- Present information for all the entries in this order: Author's name. Title. Publication information (including date).
- Capitalize the first letter of every important word in the title.
- Enclose article titles in quotation marks.
- Double-space an entry if it has two or more lines.
- Indent the second and succeeding lines 5 spaces.
- If the author appears in the Works Cited list two or more times, type three hyphens and a period instead of repeating the name for the second and succeeding entries. Alphabetize the entries by the first word of the title.

Several common entries appear below. For more detailed instructions, use the *MLA Handbook,* 6th ed., by Joseph Gibaldi (New York: MLA, 2003).

Book with One Author

Selfe, Cynthia L. *Technology and Literacy in the Twenty-First Century: The Perils of Not Paying Attention.* Carbondale: Southern Illinois University Press, 1999.

Winsor, Dorothy A. *Writing Like an Engineer: A Rhetorical Education.* Mahwah: Lawrence Erlbaum, 1996.

- Only the name of the publishing company needs to appear: You may drop "Co." or "Inc."

Book with Two Authors

George, Diana, and John Trimbur. *Reading Culture: Contexts for Critical Reading and Writing.* 4th ed. New York: Longman, 2001.

A long title may be shortened in the text, in this case to *Reading Culture.*

Book with Editors

Hawisher, Gail, and Cynthia L. Selfe, eds. *Passions, Pedagogies, and 21st Century Technologies.* Logan: Utah State University Press, 1999.

Mirel, Barbara, and Rachel Spilka, eds. *Reshaping Technical Communication: New Directions and Challenges for the 21st Century.* Mahwah: Lawrence Erlbaum, 2001.

Essay in an Anthology

Sullivan, Dale L., Michael S. Martin, and Ember Anderson. "Moving from the Periphery: Conceptions of Ethos, Reputation, and Identity for the Technical Communicator." *Issues of Power, Status and Legitimacy in Technical Communication: Evaluating the Social and Historical Process of Professionalization.* Ed. Teresa Kynell-Hunt and Gerald Savage. Amityville, NY: Baywood, 2003. 115–36.

- In the text, both the article title and the book title may be shortened; for example the article title could be "Conceptions" and the book title could be "Issues."

Corporate or Institutional Author

American Telephone and Telegraph. *2004 Annual Report.* New York: Author, 2005.

- When the author is also the publisher; write *Author* for the publisher.
- In the text, the first citation reads this way (American Telephone and Telegraph [AT&T]). Subsequent citations read (AT&T).
- This entry could also read

2004 Annual Report. New York: American Telephone and Telegraph, 2005.

- Cite this entry as (*2004 Annual*).

Work Without Date or Publisher

Radke, Jean. *Writing for Electronic Sources.* Atlanta: Center for Electronic Communication, n.d.

- Use *n.p.* for no publisher or no place.
- If neither publisher nor place is given "N.p.: n.p., 2004."

Brochure or Pamphlet

Teaching English in the 21st Century. Houghton: Michigan Technological University, n.d.

- If the pamphlet has an identification number, place it after the title.

Later Edition of a Book

American Psychological Association. *Publication Manual*. 5th ed. Washington, DC: APA, 2001.

Encyclopedia/Handbook

"Phone Recorder." *Encyclopedia of Physical Science and Technology*. Ed. Rudolph F. Graf. Vol. 3. Blue Ridge Summit: Tab, 1991. 616–17.

Posner, Edward C. "Communications, Deep Space." *Encyclopedia of Physical Science and Technology*. 2nd ed. Vol. 3. San Diego: Academic, 1992.

- No page numbers appear in Posner because entries in the book are arranged alphabetically.

Article in a Journal with Continuous Pagination

Sullivan, Dale L., and Michael S. Martin. "Habit Formation and Story Telling: A Theory for Guiding Ethical Action." *Technical Communication Quarterly* 10 (2001): 251–72.

Article in a Journal Without Continuous Pagination

Fehler, Brian. "Re-defining God: The Rhetoric of Reconciliation." *Rhetoric Society Quarterly* 33.1 (2003): 105–28.

Article in a Monthly or Weekly Magazine

Simon, Roger. "One Year." *U.S. News and World Report* Sept. 2001: 4+.

- If the article has discontinuous pages, give the first page only, followed by a plus sign: 4+.

Newspaper Article

Kerasotis, Peter. "Florida's Space Coast Grieves for NASA Accidents in Its Own Special Way." *Green Bay Press Gazette* 2 Feb. 2003: A15.

- Identify the edition, section, and page number: A reader should be able to find the article on the page.
- Omit the definite article (*the*) in the title of the newspaper in the text of the article: If the newspaper is a city newspaper and the city is not given in the title, supply it in brackets after the title (e.g. *Globe and Mail* [Toronto]).

Personal Interview

- In the text, interviews are cited like any other source: (Schmidt).
- In the Works Cited list, enter it this way:

Anderson, Marlon. Personal interview. 7 Dec. 2005.

- If the person's title or workplace are important, add them after the name:

Anderson, Marlon, CEO, Technology Innovations. San Diego: 7 Dec. 2005.

- Use this rule for telephone interviews and letters, too.

Telephone Interview

Anderson, Marlon. Telephone interview. 7 Dec. 2005. [Add title and workplace if necessary.]

Personal Letter

Anderson, Marlon. Letter to author. 7 Dec. 2005. [Add title and workplace if necessary.]

Professional or Personal Website—Homepage

Essential for citing webpages is that you give the date of the retrieval on which you viewed the site and the URL. Give as much other information as possible.

Anderson, Marlon. *Techinnovations*. 17 Feb. 2006. 14 March 2006 <http://www.techinnovations.com>.

Explanation: Web owner, if available. *Title of the Website*. Date of last update. Date of retrieval and <URL of the site>.

Note: If the owner and the date are not available, the above entry would look like this:

Techinnovations. 14 March 2006 <http://www.techinnovations.com>.

Cite this site as ("Techinnovations").

Professional or Personal Website—Internal Page

For an internal page of a website, give the URL of the document, not the homepage.

Anderson, Marlon. "Single-sourcing and Localization." 19 February 2006. *Techinnovations* 16 March 2006 <http://www.techinnovations.com/tc.html>.

Explanation: Author, if available. "Title of Internal Page." Date of last updating, if available. *Title of the Entire Website* (from the homepage) date of retrieval and <URL of the internal page, if possible>.

E-Mail

Treat e-mail like personal communication. Use this form in the Works Cited section:

> Anderson, Marlon. "Ways to Localize Translations." E-mail to author. 7 Dec. 2005.

Explanation: Author. "Title (taken from the subject line)." Description of the message, including recipient. Date of the message.

In text the citation would read:

> (Anderson)

Listservs

Although listservs are basically collections of e-mails, the entry for a listserv posting requires more data. In the Works Cited section, use this form.

> Anderson, Marlon. "A Key to Effective Localization." On-line posting. 7 Dec. 2005. Globalanswers listserv. 12 Jan. 2006 <globalwork-l@global answers.org>.

Note: If you can use an archived version of the document (and you should do so, if you can), give the URL of the archive, e.g., http://globalanswers.org/cgi-bin/enter.

Explanation: Author. "Title" (use the subject line). The phrase "On-line posting." Date of the posting. Name of the listserv. Date of the retrieval. <The on-line address of the listserv's website, or if that address is not available, the email address of the list's moderators>.

Article Available from an On-Line Source

Many libraries and companies use on-line services like EBSCOhost to find full-text articles. In your text, cite the full-text articles by using the author's last name. Usually you cannot present a page number, because the full-text articles are seldom paginated; just skip the page information if it is not available. An entry in the Works Cited section would look like this:

> Anderson, Marlon. "A Key to Effective Localization." *Global Technical Communication.* 7 Dec. 2005: 23–28. *Academic Search Elite.* EBSCOhost. Michigan Technological University. 12 Jan. 2006 <http://search.epnet.com/comm-generic> Keyword used: localization

Explanation: Author. "Title of Article." *Title of the Hard-Copy Periodical* date of original publication: page numbers, if available. *Title of the database.* Title of service. Library you used to reach the on-line service. Date you retrieved the article <URL of the on-line service>. Keyword you used to find the article (optional).

Note: Databases like EBSCOhost often present the publishing information in a source line that does not give the complete page numbers of the article.

> Source: *Global Technical Communication*, 7 Dec. 2005, Vol. 25, Issue 12, p. 23, 5p.

If the source line is the only information available, use this form for the page numbers: p. 23, 5p. In the text you will not be able to cite pages; just use the author's name.

Article Available from an On-Line Periodical

Treat an article from an on-line periodical like a hard copy article. Note that you must add a date of retrieval and the URL.

Anderson, Marlon. "A Key to Effective Localization." *eGlobal* Dec. 2005. Jan. 12, 2006 <http://eGlobal.com/dec/articles/anderson.html>.

Explanation: Author. "Title of Article." *Title of On-Line Periodical* date of original publication. Date of retrieval and <URL of the article>.

Numbered References 参考文献排序

The numbered method uses an arabic numeral, rather than a name or date, as the internal citation. The numeral refers to an entry in the bibliography. *Use APA form for the bibliographic entries.* The bibliography may be organized one of two ways:

- Alphabetically
- In order of their appearance in the text, without regard to alphabetization (ACS suggests this method)

Numbered references are another method of citation. Many periodicals have adopted this method because it is cheaper to print one number than many names and dates. The difficulty with the method is that if a new source is inserted into the list, all the items in the list and all the references in the text need to be renumbered. This issue has become less of a concern with the advanced abilities of word processing programs.

The following sample shows the same paragraph and bibliography arranged in two different ways. Note that the author's name may or may not appear in the text.

Alphabetically 按字母顺序

The inclusion of phthlates in toys has caused a major controversy. According to researchers, phthlates cause kidney and liver damage in rats (2). As a result of pressure brought by Greenpeace (1), the European Union outlawed phthlates in toys, especially teething toys, like teeth rings (2). As a result of the action, two alternate plasticizers, adipate and epoxidized soy bean (EOS), will be used more. EOS seems very promising because it has FDA approval (3). Many authorities, however, feel that the ban could politicize science (4). Another authority says that the concern is ungrounded because many earlier toxicological conferences concluded that the threats from phthlates to humans are minuscule (1).

1. Fanu, J. (1999, November 22). Behind the great plastic duck panic. *New Statesman, 128,* 11.
2. Melton, M. (1999, December 20). Lingering troubles in toyland. *U.S. News and World Report, 127,* 71.
3. Moore, S. (1999, December 1). Phthlate ban could boost demand for alternatives. *Chemical Week, 161,* 17
4. Scott, A. (1999, October 27). EU warns on Sevesco directive. *Chemical Week 161,* 24.

By Position of the First Reference in the Text   按文中第一个参考文献的位置

The inclusion of phthlates in toys has caused a major controversy. According to researchers, phthlates cause kidney and liver damage in rats (1). As a result of pressure brought by Greenpeace (2), the European Union outlawed phthlates in toys, especially teething toys, like teeth rings (1). As a result of the action, two alternate plasticizers, adipate and epoxidized soy bean (EOS), will be used more. EOS seems very promising because it has FDA approval (3). Many authorities, however, feel that the ban could politicize science (4). Another authority says that the concern is ungrounded because many earlier toxicological conferences concluded that the threats from phthlates to humans are minuscule (2).

1. Melton, M. (1999, December 20). Lingering troubles in toyland. *U.S. News and World Report, 127,* 71.
2. Fanu, J. (1999, November 22). Behind the great plastic duck panic. *New Statesman, 128,* 11.
3. Moore, S. (1999, December 1). Phthlate ban could boost demand for alternatives. *Chemical Week, 161,* 17.
4. Scott, A. (1999, October 27). EU warns on Sevesco directive. *Chemical Week 161,* 24.

Examples

The following examples present three sample papers, one in each of the three formats. The first two (APA and Numbered) are excerpted from much longer papers. The MLA document briefly shows the use of the MLA format.

Example B.1

Excerpt in APA Format

MECHANICAL PROPERTIES

The mechanical properties of a film or coating describe how they will perform in the distribution environment. A thorough evaluation of edible films by a packaging engineer will include a look at their mechanical properties and a comparison of these attributes against other packaging materials. This section will describe two important mechanical properties: tensile strength and elongation.

Tensile Strength

Tensile strength can be described as the amount of force required to break a material. Knowing the package's tensile strength can help the packaging engineer decide if the material will remain intact as it flows through the packaging machinery. It will also help the engineer predict whether the material will break as it is stretched around a product. Table 4 summarizes the tensile strengths of various edible films. Banjeree and Chen (1995) found that whey protein films withstood 5.94 MPa of pressure before breaking. However, the addition of lipids to the whey film lowered the tensile strength to 3.15 MPa (p. 1681).

Table 4
Tensile Strength and Elongation

Film Material	Tensile Strength (MPa)	Elongation Thickness (%)	Source
Proteins			
Whey	5.94	22.74	Banerjee (1995)
Whey/Lipid	3.15	10.78	Banerjee (1995)
Milk	8.6	22.1	Maynes (1994)
Zein	38.3	—	Yamada (1995)
Rice	31.1	2.9	Shih (1996)
Soybean	7.2	0.75	Stuchell (1994)
Polysaccharides			
Cellulose	66.33	25.6	Park (1993)
Synthetics			
LDPE	13.1–27.6	100–965	Park (1993)
PVDC	48.4–138	20–40	Maynes (1994)

The tensile strengths of cellulose and grain-based edible films have also been measured and compared to synthetic plastics. Park, Weller, and Vergano (1993) found that cellulose films exhibited a tensile strength value of 66.33 MPa. In the same study, LDPE required from 13.1 to 27.6 MPa to break up (p. 1362). Yamada, Takahashi, and Noguchi (1995) discovered that zein protein films exhibit similar or higher tensile strengths than polyvinylide

(continued)

Example B.1 (continued)

chloride (PVDC) films. Shih (1996) found that rice protein films resisted breaking until 31.1 MPa of force was applied. Lastly, Brandenburg, Weller, and Testin (1993) and Stuchell and Krochta (1994) found that soy protein films took 7.2 MPa of force to break.

The thickness of the film can have a bearing on its tensile strength. Park et al. (1993) found that the tensile strength of cellulose did not improve as the thickness increased. However, no direct comparison of thicknesses between cellulose films and LDPE films was made. Therefore, it is difficult to make a true comparison. Yamada et al. (1995) discovered that in order to achieve tensile strengths similar to PVDC, zein protein films 7 times thicker than the PVDC had to be used. Most researchers do not list the thickness of the product when testing for tensile strength. This lack of completeness in reporting their results will cause some confusion on the part of packaging professionals.

Elongation

Elongation refers to the amount that a material will stretch before it breaks. Table 4 lists the percent of elongation of various edible films. Park et al. (1993) found that the cellulose elongation percentages varied widely among different molecular weights of films. Chen (1995) along with Maynes and Krochta (1994) found that milk protein films had significantly lower percentages of elongations than traditional plastic films. They found that the milk proteins elongated anywhere from 1 to 75 percent of their original length, whereas LPDE elongated to 5 times its original length before breaking. It is widely believed that the structure of proteins and the way that they crystallize negatively affects the film's elongation properties (McHugh & Krochta, 1994).

Polysaccharides have better elongation characteristics than proteins. Park et al. (1993) discovered that cellulose films can elongate from 10% to 200% of their original length. They compared these figures to LDPE, which was found to elongate 1 to 10 times its original length before breaking. As with tensile strength, a certain amount of elongation is dependent on the thickness of the material. The amount of elongation should be reported on the basis of the thickness of the sample tested.

References

Banerjee, R., & Chen, H. (1995). Functional properties of edible films using whey protein concentrate. *Journal of Dairy Science, 78,* 1673–1683.

Brandenburg, A. H., Weller, C. L., & Testin, R. F. (1993). Edible films and coatings from soy protein. *Journal of Food Science, 58,* 1086–1089.

Chen, H. (1995). Functional properties and applications of edible films made of milk proteins. *Journal of Dairy Science, 78,* 2563–2583.

Maynes, J., & Krochta, J. (1994). Properties of edible films from total milk protein. *Journal of Food Science, 59,* 909–911.

McHugh, T. and Krochta, J. (1994) Milk-protein-based edible films and coatings. *Food Technology, 48,* 97–103.

Park, H. J., Weller, C. L., & Vergano, P. J. (1993). Permeability and mechanical properties of cellulose-based edible films. *Journal of Food Science, 58,* 1361–1364, 1370.

Shih, F. (1996). Edible films from rice protein concentrate and pullulan. *Cereal Chemistry, 73,* 406–409.

Stuchell, Y., & Krochta, J. (1994). Enzymatic treatments and thermal effects on edible soy protein films. *Journal of Food Science, 59,* 1332–1337.

Yamada, K., Takahashi, H., & Noguchi, A. (1995). Improved water resistance in zein films and composites for biodegradable food packaging. *International Journal of Food Science and Technology, 30,* 599–608.

Example B.2

Excerpt with Numbered References

BRIEF HISTORY OF HTML

A Need for HTML

In 1989 Tim Berners-Lee, a CERN (Conseil Européen pour la Recherche Nucléaire) (1) employee, wrote a proposal for the creation of a system that would easily allow scientists to locate and browse one another's research documents, as well as post their own (2). CERN had employees all over the world and having such a system would have benefited the center's research greatly (3). This project was later dubbed "The World-Wide Web" or "WWW" for short. This should not be confused with the Internet, which is simply a large network that supports many things, of which the WWW is one.

The WWW proposal set forth certain requirements that the system was to meet. Embedded in these requirements and throughout the proposal was the call for a formatting language for the hypertext documents that would be shared on the WWW, as well as a transfer protocol for transmitting them over a network (3). The formatting language was named HTML, and the network protocol was called the HyperText Transfer Protocol, or HTTP for short (4). The proposal also called for a method of locating documents within the new system and was implemented via the Uniform Resource Locator, or URL (5). Of course, by having all these documents shared, one would need a way to locate a document. Therefore, a program was written to accomplish this and was referred to as the "search engine."

The Creation of HTML

By 1990 the WWW project was well underway. The first known code written by Berners-Lee to process a hypertext file was dated September 25, 1990, and

(continued)

Example B.2 (continued)

the first known HTML document on the Web was dated November 13, 1990 (6). By December of 1990 a simple text browser, as well as some simple hypertext documents, were available for viewing within the CERN community (7).

With initial work on both a hypertext language and browser behind him, Berners-Lee realized that no current hypertext system was adequate to his needs and officially proposed that a new language be developed to support the WWW system (4). The new language was to be called HTML and was to be a subset extracted from the broader SGML (4). In the summer of 1991 the specification of HTML and the first simple browser were put on the Internet for public download and use, and CERN launched the World Wide Web (3). Once the specification for HTML was released, other organizations were able to create websites and write their own browsers such as Cello, Viola, and MidasWWW (8). The number of documents available on the WWW quickly increased as more and more organizations were able to compose and post documents on any subject they wished.

REFERENCES

1. Wilson, B. (1997). Glossary of terms. Retrieved March 20, 2003, from http://jeffcovey.net/web/html/reference/html/misc/glossary.htm
2. Koly, W. Quick HTML history. Retrieved March 20, 2003, from http://www.highlatitude.com/comdex99/sld005.htm
3. Wilson, B. (1997). HTML overview. Retrieved March 20, 2003, from http://jeffcovey.net/web/html/reference/html/history/html.htm
4. The history of HTML, p. 2. Retrieved March 20, 2003, from http://howdyyall.com/HTML/HISTORY/HTMLhist2.htm
5. The history of HTML, p. 3. Retrieved March 20, 2003, from http://howdyyall.com/HTML/HISTORY/HTMLhist3.htm
6. Palmer, S. B. The early history of HTML. Retrieved March 20, 2003, from http://infomesh.net/html/history/early/
7. The history of HTML, p. 1. Retrieved March 20, 2003, from http://howdyyall.com/HTML/HISTORY/HTMLhist.htm
8. Some early ideas for HTML. (January 1, 2003). Retrieved March 20, 2003, from http://www.w3.org/MarkUp/historical

Example B.3

Excerpt in MLA Format

HTML 2.0 AND BEYOND

By late 1993, HTML had become a collage of standard tags and a wide range of unique tags created for individual browsers. In April 1994, Dan Connolly, a professional in on-line documentation and on-line formatting systems, proposed bringing HTML back to its roots in SGML and wrote a draft of what would become HTML 2.0. This draft was revised and rewritten, which caused it to lose much of its SGML tone, by Karen Muldrow in July 1994 and shortly thereafter was presented to the IETF (Internet Engineering Task Force) for approval (Wilson, "Glossary").

Unfortunately, the goal of the draft became muddled, and its main accomplishment was to support all of the browser tags in existence at the time, rather than a shift towards SGML. In September 1995, a finalized official version of HTML 2.0 was released, and most of its tags were supported by the majority of browsers (Wilson, "HTML"; Koly).

In 1994, while HTML 2.0 was being developed by a myriad of groups and individuals, Tim Berners-Lee and others formed what is now known as the W3C or the World Wide Web Consortium. The W3C was involved in the finalization of HTML 2.0 and is to date the primary organization involved in all work on the HTML standard. It was created in order to keep HTML standardization on the right track, but it took some time before they became effective (Shannon).

While under the W3C, HTML continued to evolve from 2.0 to 3.0. In fact, by the time version 2.0 was approved, a draft for 3.0 had already been written! HTML 3.0 was released as a draft in September 1995. It was a very unpopular version because it made huge changes in what tags should be used and what they should be used for. Version 3.2, which implemented fewer changes, quickly appeared in May 1996 and was much more widely accepted (Koly).

Most of the major changes from version 3.0 were reserved for 4.0, except for the creation of CSS (Cascading Style Sheets). After this point in time all HTML modifications were to be modular in nature, allowing the changes to take place slowly. At this point in time, Netscape was the dominant browser. Its implementation of numerous proprietary tags that were not in the specification caused a major setback for the standardization of HTML (Shannon).

HTML 4.0 was finalized by the W3C in 1997. Shortly thereafter, it was revised again into version 4.01. This version is the current official standard, but work is ongoing at the W3C to further improve HTML. These further improvements incorporate the idea of storing formatting information away from the HTML itself (Shannon).

Works Cited

Koly, William. "Quick HTML History." 1999. 20 Mar. 2003 <http://www.highlatitude.com/comdex99/sld005.htm>.

Shannon, Ross. "HTML Source: The History of HTML." 1999. 20 Mar. 2003. <http://www.yourhtmlsource.com/comdex99/sld005.htm>.

Wilson, Brian. "HTML 2.0." 1997. 20 Mar. 2003 <http://jeffcovey.net/web/html/reference/html/history/html20.htm>.

———. "Glossary." 1997. 20 Mar. 2003 <http://jeffcovey.net/web/html/reference/html/misc/glossary.htm>.

Exercises 练 习

1. Edit the following sentences to place an APA citation correctly and/or to place a MLA citation correctly.

   a. On page 29 of his 2002 article on the *ethos* of technical communicators, Mr. George Carlson notes that "Technical communicators often find it difficult to establish their *ethos* in the corporate environment."

   b. In 2003, Dr. Ellen Keenan said on page 46 that computer software has been both a bane and blessing for workers because of the updating of software versions and the lack of corresponding hardware updates.

   c. Dr. Tim Rongstad noted (p. 21, 2001) that "Generally speaking, it is significant that research demonstrates that good writing skills are learned as early as preschool."

   d. "The importance of oral communication when connected to written and visual communication should not be underestimated," according to Dr. Pamela Poole, a noted communication scholar, on p.112 in 2001.

2. Pick a paragraph from one of the three examples in this appendix and rewrite it in one of the other two citation styles (e.g., change APA to numbered or MLA).

3. Turn these sets of data into the APA References list and an MLA Works Cited list.

   Brett Peruzzi/Building bridges between marketing and technical publications teams/Retrieved 11 Aug. 2003/EServer TCLibrary/2001/TECHWR-L/ <http://tc.eserver.org/14499.html>.

   Dànielle DeVoss, Julia Jasken, Dawn Hayden/January 2002/pages 69–94/ the journal is *Journal of Business and Technical Communication*/ Volume 16(1)/the title is Teaching intra and intercultural communication: A critique and suggested method.

Writing Assignment 写作任务

Find three articles on a similar topic and write a memo in which you give the gist of all three to your supervisor. Do not just summarize them each in turn; blend them so they support a main point that you want to call to the supervisor's attention. Use any of the three methods of documenting.

Works Cited 引用的作品

Dodd, Janet S., ed. *The ACS Style Guide: A Manual for Authors and Editors.* 2nd ed. Washington, DC: American Chemical Society, 1997.

Gibaldi, Joseph. *MLA Handbook for Writers of Research Papers.* 6th ed. New York: MLA, 2003.

Publication Manual of the American Psychological Association. 5th ed. Washington, DC: APA, 2001.